WORLD WAR II

WORLD WAR II

An Encyclopedia of Quotations

Compiled and Edited by Howard J. Langer

Greenwood Press
Westport, Connecticut

Library of Congress Cataloging-in-Publication Data

World War II : an encyclopedia of quotations / compiled and edited by
Howard J. Langer.
p. cm.
Includes bibliographical references and index.
ISBN 0–313–30018–6 (alk. paper)
1. World War, 1939–1945—Quotations, maxims, etc.—Encyclopedias.
I. Langer, Howard.
D744.W67 1999
940.53'03—dc21 98–26436

British Library Cataloguing in Publication Data is available.

Library of Congress Catalog Card Number: 98–26436
ISBN: 0–313–30018–6

First published in 1999

Greenwood Press, 88 Post Road West, Westport, CT 06881
An imprint of Greenwood Publishing Group, Inc.

Printed in the United States of America

The paper used in this book complies with the Permanent Paper Standard issued by the National Information Standards Organization (Z39.48–1984).

10 9 8 7 6 5 4 3 2 1

Copyright Acknowledgments

The author and publisher gratefully acknowledge permission for use of the following material:

"Abortions" and "The Revisionists" appear courtesy of Joseph Broder. "Abortions" previously appeared in *The Beach Bell Echo*, the publication of the 446th Bomb Group Association.

Material from a personal interview with Hy Haas, August 29, 1996, appears courtesy Hy Haas.

All photos are from the National Archives.

For Fran and Arnie,
Bob and Sari,
Art and Cathy

Contents

Acknowledgments

To begin with, I would like to acknowledge the loving assistance of my wife, Florence. It is a cliché to use the phrase, "without whose help this book would not have been possible . . ." However, it is certainly justified here.

I wish to thank the staff of the New City (Rockland County, New York) Public Library for their gracious assistance, as well as the staff of the Finkelstein Memorial Library, Spring Valley, New York, the West Point Library, and the libraries that are part of the regional interlibrary loan program.

In addition, I would like to thank Bob Hagelstein, Jim Sabin, and Cynthia Harris of Greenwood Press; also Hirofumi Murabayashi of the Japanese consulate in New York City for providing statements by the Japanese government on the "Comfort Women" of World War II.

All the sources in the bibliography were helpful in the preparation of this volume. Several, however, were of special importance.

To begin, William L. Shirer's *The Rise and Fall of the Third Reich* was indispensable for dealing with the war in Europe. Shirer was extremely gracious in granting me an interview with him, allowing fresh insights into the character of both individuals and national groups. Brief excerpts from that interview appear in this volume. The reader is encouraged to read the full text in *Social Education* magazine.

Also indispensable was Winston Churchill's multivolume series *The Second World War*. Obviously written from the prime minister's point of view, the volumes offer massive material not only on the European and Pacific wars but on aspects of the war often given short shrift by American historians.

John Toland's *The Rising Sun* was especially valuable for Japanese viewpoints of the war in the Pacific. Louis L. Snyder's *Historical Guide to World War II* was most useful for checking specific names, dates, and places. Documents presented at the Nuremberg trials, published by the Office of United States Chief of Counsel for Prosecution of Axis Criminality in *Nazi Conspiracy and Aggression*, were invaluable in providing hitherto secret plans and discussions of the Axis leaders.

The Broken Seal, by Ladislas Farago, was a key source for the cracking of the Japanese code prior to Pearl Harbor—and the messages that reached American intelligence well before December 7, 1941.

The most readable book on the European war is undoubtedly *A Soldier's Story* by Omar N. Bradley. Not only is it well written; it is filled with insights and anecdotes about the clashing egos and agendas of men at war. A frank, honest, no-holds-barred account, it truly brings history to life.

The Fall of the Philippines, by Louis Morton, gives a vivid, authoritative account of a desperate effort to buy time for a wounded America in the months after Pearl Harbor. It is one of a series developed by the Office of the Chief of Military History, Department of the Army.

Veterans of the war were always extremely outspoken in discussing with me the decision to use the atomic bomb on Japan. They felt, very simply, that their lives might have been spared. Armed forces in Europe as well as the Far East concurred. The appendixes in *Code-Name Downfall: The Secret Plan to Invade Japan—and Why Truman Dropped the Bomb*, by Thomas B. Allen and Norman Polmar, spell out—army by army and division by division—exactly when and where each unit was scheduled to participate in the invasion of the Japanese home islands. The appendixes are a bonus to truly eye-opening disclosures on official thinking in both Washington and Tokyo.

A child during the war, I was filled with all the stereotypes of the enemy conveyed by the media. I found Terry Charman's *The German Home Front: 1939–45* to give an extraordinary view of German civilian life. Heavily illustrated, it is a remarkable collection of anecdotes and quotations. It is a balanced presentation of the human and the inhuman. The account of what happened when Frau Goebbels gave up her cook, who was sent to work in an armaments factory, is an example of humor in wartime. But the book ends with the discovery of the concentration camps—a solemn reminder of Nazi brutality.

Lawyer-author Lawrence Taylor summarizes the legal cases against the Japanese generals who were executed for war crimes following the end of the war. Although his point of view is obvious, his presentation of the relevant documents is powerful and persuasive in *A Trial of Generals: Homma, Yamashita, MacArthur*.

Andre Brissaud's sources provide a stunning view of the German intelligence operation in *Canaris*.

I laughed out loud at *See Here, Private Hargrove* many decades after his book was published on life in a citizen army. Although I have quoted Marion Hargrove's advice to new inductees, I was most taken by his description of an army buddy named John Bushemi, the camp photographer who ingratiated himself into Hargrove's own hometown and among his friends. I would have used sections from that piece except for one thing: Later in the war, Bushemi became a combat photographer and was killed in action. It did not seem appropriate somehow to use a humorous piece about Bushemi. If you want to see Bushemi's work, get a copy of *The Best from Yank.* There are several dramatic shots of GIs in battle. One photo in particular shows them wading through a river on a Pacific island. As they go through the jungle, on the lookout for Japanese snipers, you will find yourself holding your breath.

One of the most difficult tasks I faced was to get appropriate segments from the work of John Hersey. He was such a master craftsman that virtually every word he wrote was critical to the sentence, and every sentence was critical to the paragraph. I hope the quotations from *all* sources in this volume will encourage the reader to go back to the original. That especially applies to Hersey's work. While we are on Hersey, I must point out that in his *Into the Valley* I selected brief material about a near-panic after a Japanese trap was sprung. I included this piece to show that panic is possible, under certain circumstances, in any military force—even the toughest fighting outfit in the world, the U.S. Marines.

From Ralph Ingersoll's *Top Secret* I chose a remarkable segment describing Hitler's master plan for the Ardennes offensive (the Battle of the Bulge). This is the only source I have come upon that details the Fuehrer's quest for a second Dunkirk. The book is filled with judgments about specific British and American generals that should not be missed.

William Stevenson's *A Man Called Intrepid* offers a truly breathtaking account of the exploits of British spymaster William Stephenson and the secret armies he directed in Nazi-occupied Europe.

I need to say a few words about some of the items in the back of the book. There is a small item in Chapter 18, "Miscellaneous Quotations," called "Nazi Saboteurs." It is about the case of eight Germans who were brought to America by U-boats to carry out acts of sabotage. The item in this volume gives the barest facts of this extraordinary incident in American history. The complete story in Eugene Rachlis's *They Came to Kill* is highly recommended, particularly for the legal insights.

For Chapter 15, "War Movies," several sources were used, including *Projections of War: Hollywood, American Culture, and World War II*, by Thomas Doherty, *Winners: The Blue Ribbon Encyclopedia of Awards*, by Claire Walter, and *The Blockbuster Guide to Movies and Videos*, edited by Ron Casten. I used the last book not only to check out titles, cast names, and dates but to find movies whose names I had long since forgotten—but small details of which I remembered. For example, I remembered something about a musical in which Fred MacMurray found a magic lamp that took him back into American history. I hadn't the foggiest idea what the title was, but the Casten book has wonderful indexes. In the actors' index, under "MacMurray," I found a movie called *Where Do We Go from Here?* Sure enough, that was the movie. That also happened with a movie about Nazis being pursued in Canada prior to Pearl Harbor. I recalled the final scene of that movie—when Raymond Massey and his Nazi captor come across the American border in a freight car. When the U.S. border guard sends the freight car back into Canada, Massey grins, straightens his cap, and gets ready to take on the Nazi. That was all I remembered. I found the movie—*49th Parallel*—under the Massey listing in the index.

There were nine separate reports, inquiries, and investigations concerning Pearl Harbor in the literature. That is material enough not merely for an entire book but for a set of encyclopedias. I chose to include in Chapter 13, "Institutional Quotations," material from the Roberts Commission, which issued the first such report in January 1942. For material on other investigations, see *President Roosevelt and the Coming of the War 1941*, by Charles A. Beard. This is a thoroughly documented work by the noted historian. The book deals with President Roosevelt's antiwar statements versus his pro-war actions. The records of Nazi aggression and Japanese militarism do not appear to be relevant to the noted historian.

In addition to those to whom this volume is dedicated, I wish to thank the following individuals for books, articles, and personal reminiscences: Herb Giller, Harold Klein, Lenny Kohl, Al Libuser, Arnold Mayer, Carl Radin, Marilyn Roberts, Bob Rosenthal, Carl Sifakis, and Hank Wexler. I appreciated the help of Joan Pomeranz and Debbie Rosenthal when my computer developed a mind of its own.

A special word about the newspaper of record, *The New York Times*. In addition to being a historical source, it was also a provider for the names of people I had never heard of before. They showed up as entry possibilities in news and feature stories, as well as in obituaries.

As a general rule, I have tried to indicate the original source of a quotation whenever possible. There are still some gaps in the book, particularly in biographical references, such as dates of birth and death. Additions and corrections would be welcomed for future editions.

In final acknowledgment, my personal heroes of the war—in alphabetical order—were Jimmy Doolittle, Howard Gilmore, Bill Mauldin, Ernie Pyle, and Bert Wyman.

Introduction

There was no period like it in all of American history. The years from Pearl Harbor to V-J Day were a time of the greatest American unity ever. Historians tell us that in the American Revolution no more than a third of the colonists favored American independence; another third were loyal to the king. The rest were on the fence. There was strong opposition to the War of 1812 as well as the Mexican War. The Civil War literally tore the country in two. American participation in World War I, the Korean War, the Vietnam War, and Desert Storm all had their opponents.

But once we were in it, World War II was America's own Great Patriotic War. Some historians would later call it the "Good War." Soldiers, sailors, marines, airmen, and men of the Coast Guard and Merchant Marine took part in global battle against the common enemy. Women played a crucial role as well—in uniformed services, as nurses, and in defense plants.

On the home front, everyone was in it one way or another. If you were a child, you collected old pots and pans for the scrap metal drive. If you were a housewife, you carefully saved up your ration coupons for the big holiday dinner. You sang the songs, cheered the war movies, bought the war bonds, and booed Hitler in the newsreels. You also scanned the casualty lists in the newspapers—and dreaded the sight of a Western Union messenger boy.

World War II was an unprecedented shared American experience. It was the school assembly listening to the president asking for a declaration of war. It was a common prayer on D-Day. It was the commander in chief on the radio inviting you to look at a map in the newspaper as he explained the strategy of defeating Hitler first.

We remember the pictures in *Life* and the Bill Mauldin cartoons. Because it was a radio age, we remember the spoken word: "a date which will live in infamy," "peace in our time," "the hand that held the dagger," "give us the tools and we will finish the job," "four essential human freedoms," and "our sons will triumph."

These are some of the most memorable quotes. They are all here, but there is a lot more. There are quotations from our Allies—the British, the Russians, the French, and the Chinese. Here also are the words of our enemies—the Germans, the Japanese, and the Italians. In addition, quotations from other countries such as Spain, Ethiopia, and Poland are included.

Much of this book consists of material that did not become known until long after the war. There are the memoirs of individuals such as Churchill and Eisenhower and Marshall, as well as the great historical works by William L. Shirer, Robert E. Sherwood, and scores of others. Equally important are documents that had been secret throughout the war—documents that came out at the war crimes trials and documents revealed by the breaking of the Japanese and German secret codes. Such material is included here—plus reminiscences from men and women who were largely unknown during the war but whose exploits can now be told. There are stories of bravery and savagery, deliverance and despair, defiance and betrayal.

One aspect of the war is touched on only briefly: the Holocaust. The Nazi war against the Jews of Europe was a war that was compartmentalized not only by the Nazis but by the Allies as well. Hitler never allowed the European war to interfere with the Holocaust. Except for warning about postwar justice, the Allies virtually ignored it. I have dealt with the Holocaust in historical perspective in *The History of the Holocaust: A Chronology of Quotations*.

Also touched on briefly in this work are such prewar events as the Italo-Ethiopian War, the dismemberment of Czechoslovakia, and the Sino-Japanese War. Each served as a prelude to the world war that would follow.

As the twenty-first century unfolds, those who remember the last Good War will be passing on, but their words will survive for the benefit of those yet unborn. When freedom is challenged once again, there is much that can be learned from those who fought on behalf of freedom, from those who cringed in the face of tyranny, and from those who tried to destroy the very essence of humanity and civilization.

The words of that era will give us much to think about. To remember the words is to remember the sacrifices of blood and treasure during those glorious and terrible days.

Scope of This Book

The major portion of this work consists of quotations from more than 300 individuals on some aspect of World War II. Represented are major war leaders and their military staffs as well as diplomats, historians, warriors, civilians, journalists, intelligence officials, chaplains, scientists, government officials, and others.

Each group appears in its own chapter. Thus, in Chapter 2, "Military Officers," will appear not just Eisenhower, Patton, and Halsey but also Montgomery, Rommel, Zhukov, and Yamamoto. In Chapter 4, diplomats include Hull as well as Ribbentrop, and Molotov as well as Kennedy.

In addition, there are chapters entitled "Anonymous Quotations" and "Institutional Quotations" plus "War Movies," "War Songs," and "War Lexicon," a chapter on slang words, code names, and nicknames.

Chapter 18, "Miscellaneous Quotations," identifies quotations that relate to specific events of the war, from the Bataan Death March and the *Indianapolis* Disaster to the Dunkirk Evacuation and the Battle of Stalingrad. Other items in this true miscellany include the America First Committee, Slave Labor, Magic, Ultra, and *Mein Kampf*.

There is an extensive bibliography plus two indexes: one on individuals and the other on subject matter. Because they are already in alphabetical sequence, the "War Movies," "War Songs," and "War Lexicon" listings are not duplicated in the subject index. Every item, however, has been numbered. This will enable the reader to find selected references chosen by the editor. Such references would not be located easily in a simple alphabetical listing.

One final point: The "q.v." reference will refer the reader to a specific cross entry for an individual, battle, policy statement, place, and so on. Because they are so well known and cited frequently, no "q.v." will appear after the names of Franklin Roosevelt, Winston Churchill, Adolf Hitler, Joseph Stalin, Dwight D. Eisenhower, Douglas MacArthur, or George C. Marshall.

WORLD WAR II

1

The War Leaders

WINSTON CHURCHILL

(1874–1965)

Winston Churchill was British prime minister during most of World War II—from the fall of France until just before the Japanese surrender. First Lord of the Admiralty during World War I, he was blamed for the failure of the Dardanelles campaign and was forced to resign. In the years between the wars, he warned against Hitler and fought attempts to appease him. In 1940, Churchill became prime minister amidst catastrophic defeats in northern France. He forged an alliance with President Roosevelt before Pearl Harbor, and his brilliant oratory kept British morale high during the worst days of the London Blitz. After the war in Europe ended, a Labor Party victory removed Churchill as prime minister.

1. Dictators ride to and fro upon tigers which they dare not dismount. And the tigers are getting hungry. (1936; from *While England Slept*, by Winston S. Churchill.)

2. The German dictator, instead of snatching the victuals from the table, has been content to have them served to him course by course. (Speech to House of Commons, October 5, 1938.)

[Following the Munich Agreement (q.v.) with Hitler.]

3. I find unendurable the sense of our country falling into the power, into the orbit and influence of Nazi Germany, and of our existence becoming dependent upon their good will or pleasure. (Debate in the House of Commons following the Munich conference, October 1938.)

4. We have passed an awful milestone in our history, when the whole equilibrium of Europe has been deranged, and that the terrible words have for the time being been pronounced against the Western Democracies: "Thou art weighed in the balance and found wanting." And do not suppose that this is the end. This is only the beginning of the reckoning. This is only the first sip, the first foretaste of a bitter cup which will be proffered to us year by year unless, by a supreme recovery of moral health and martial vigor, we arise again and take our stand for freedom as in the olden time. (Ibid.)

5. Disaster of the first magnitude has befallen Britain and France. We have sustained total and unmitigated defeat. . . . Czechoslovakia, left to herself, would have been able to get better terms than we have given her. . . . We have sustained a defeat without war. (Speech to the House of Commons, October 1938.)

[During a debate on Prime Minister Neville Chamberlain's (q.v.) appeasement policy, which turned over the Sudetenland to Hitler. The House of Commons approved the policy by a vote of 366 to 144.]

6. I cannot forecast to you the action of Russia. It is a riddle wrapped in a mystery inside an enigma. (Radio speech, October 1, 1939.)

[Following the carving up of Poland by Hitler and Stalin.]

7. I would say to the House, as I said to those who have joined this Government: I have nothing to offer but blood, toil, tears and sweat. (Address to Parliament upon becoming prime minister, May 13, 1940.)

8. You ask, what is our policy? I will say: It is to wage war, by sea, land, and air, with all our might and with all the strength that God can give us; to wage war against a monstrous tyranny, never surpassed in the dark, lamentable catalogue of human crime. (Ibid.)

9. You ask, what is our aim? I can answer in one word: It is victory, victory at all costs, victory in spite of all terror, victory, however long and hard the road may be, for without victory there is no survival. (Ibid.)

10. Behind this armored and mechanized onslaught came a number of German divisions in lorries, and behind them again there plodded comparatively slowly the dull brute mass of the German army and German people, always so ready to be led to the trampling down in other lands of liberties and comforts which they have never known in their own land. (Speech to the House of Commons, June 4, 1940.)

[Reporting on the Dunkirk Evacuation (q.v.) of May 27–June 4, 1940. Some 338,000 British, French, and Belgian troops were evacuated from the French beaches by nearly

"I have nothing to offer but blood, toil, tears and sweat."
—WINSTON CHURCHILL

Smoke swirls around the dome of St. Paul's Cathedral during the London Blitz.

900 naval vessels, from warships to fishing trawlers and yachts. This was the culmination of a catastrophic defeat suffered by the Allies in northern France.]

11. When, a week ago today, I asked the House to fix this afternoon as the occasion for a statement, I feared it would be my hard lot to announce the greatest military disaster in our long history. I thought—and some good judges agreed with me—that perhaps 20,000 or 30,000 men might be re-embarked. But it certainly seemed that the whole of the French First Army and the whole of the British Expeditionary Force north of the Amiens-Abbeville gap would be broken up in the open field or else would have to capitulate for lack of food and ammunition. These were the hard and heavy tidings for which I called upon the House and nation to prepare themselves a week ago. The whole root and core and brain of the British Army, on which and around which we were to build, and are to build, the great British Armies in the later years of the war, seemed about to perish upon the field or to be led into an ignominious and starving captivity. (Ibid.)

12. [Our evacuation forces] had to operate upon the difficult coast, often in adverse weather, under an almost ceaseless hail of bombs and an increasing concentration of fire. Nor were the seas . . . themselves free from mines and torpedoes. (Ibid.)

13. Suddenly the scene has cleared, the crash and thunder has for the moment—but only for the moment—died away. A miracle of deliverance achieved by valor, by perseverance, by perfect discipline, by faultless service, by resource, by skill, by unconquerable fidelity, is manifest to us all. The enemy was hurled back by the retreating British and French troops. He was so roughly handled that he did not hurry their departure seriously. (Ibid.)

14. We must be very careful not to assign to this deliverance the attributes of a victory. Wars are not won by evacuations. (Ibid.)

15. I have . . . full confidence that if all do their duty, if nothing is neglected, and if the best arrangements are made, as they are being made, we shall prove ourselves once again able to defend our Island home, to ride out the storm for years, if necessary alone. (Ibid.)

16. Even though large tracts of Europe and many old and famous States have fallen or may fall into the grip of the Gestapo and all the odious apparatus of Nazi rule, we shall not flag or fail. (Ibid.)

17. We shall go on to the end, we shall fight in France, we shall fight on the seas and oceans, we shall fight with growing confidence and growing strength in the air, we shall defend our Island, whatever the cost may be, we shall fight on the beaches, we shall fight on the landing grounds, we shall fight in the fields and in the streets, we shall fight in the hills, we shall never surrender, and even if, which I do not for a moment believe, this Island or a large part of it were subjugated and starving, then our Empire beyond the seas, armed and guarded by the British Fleet, would carry on the struggle, until, in God's good time, the New World, with all its power and might, steps forth to the rescue and the liberation of the old. (Ibid.)

18. I urged the French Government to defend Paris. I emphasized the enormous absorbing power of the house-to-house defense of a great city upon an invading army.

I recalled to Marshal Petain [q.v.] [events of World War I] . . . and how he, as I put it, not mentioning Marshal Foch, had restored the situation. I also reminded him how Clemenceau had said, "I will fight in front of Paris, in Paris, and behind Paris."

The Marshal replied very quietly and with dignity that in those days he had a mass of manpower of upwards of sixty divisions; now there was none. He mentioned that there were then sixty British divisions in the line. Making Paris into a ruin would not affect the final event. (Recalling events of June 11, 1940; from *The Second World War: Their Finest Hour*, by Winston S. Churchill.)

19. L'homme du destin. (Addressing General Charles de Gaulle [q.v.] following a meeting in which French officials indicated they were considering peace with Hitler, June 13, 1940; Ibid.)

20. Let us therefore brace ourselves to our duties, and to bear ourselves that, if the British Empire and its Commonwealth last for a thousand years, men will say: "This was their finest hour." (Speech to the House of Commons, June 18, 1940.)

[After France had asked for an armistice.]

21. The gratitude of every home in our Island, in our Empire, and indeed throughout the world, except in the abodes of the guilty, goes out to the British airmen, who, undaunted by odds, unwearied in their constant challenge and mortal danger, are turning the tide of world war by their prowess and by their devotion. (Tribute to the Royal Air Force, address to Parliament, August 10, 1940.)

22. Never in the field of human conflict was so much owed by so many to so few. (Ibid.)

23. All hearts go out to the fighter pilots, whose brilliant actions we see with our own eyes day after day, but we must never forget that all the time, night after night, month after month, our bomber squadrons travel far into Germany, find their targets in the darkness . . . and their attacks, often under the heaviest fire, often with serious loss . . . and inflict shattering blows upon the whole of the technical and war-making structure of the Nazi power. (Ibid.)

24. The need of American destroyers is more urgent than ever in view of the losses and the need of coping with the invasion threat as well as keeping the Atlantic approaches open and dealing with Italy. There is nothing that America can do at this moment that would be of greater help than to send 50 destroyers except sending 100. (Message to American officials, August 1940; cited in *From the Morgenthau Diaries*, by John Morton Blum.)

25. Our supreme effort must be to gain overwhelming mastery in the air. The fighters are our salvation, but the bombers alone provide the means to victory. (September 1940.)

26. We are waiting for the long-promised invasion. So are the fishes. (Radio speech, October 21, 1940.)

27. It seems now to be certain that the Government and people of the United States intend to supply us with all that is necessary for victory. In the last war the United States sent two million men across the Atlantic. But this is not a war of vast armies, firing immense masses of shells at one another. We do not need the gallant armies which are forming throughout the American Union. We do not need them this year, nor next year, nor any year that I can foresee. (Radio broadcast, February 9, 1941.)

28. I regard these developments [about appointment of Admiral Darlan (q.v.) as successor to Marshal Petain (q.v.)] with misgiving and distrust. We have received nothing but ill-treatment from Vichy. It would have been better to have had Laval [q.v.], from our point of view, than Darlan, who is a dangerous, bitter, ambitious man, without the odium which attaches to Laval. . . . In the meantime an end should be put to the cold-shouldering of General De Gaulle [q.v.] and the Free French movement, who are the only people who have done anything for us, and to whom we have made very solemn engagements. The emphasis should be somewhat shifted. (Note to Foreign Office, February 27, 1941; from *The Second World War: The Grand Alliance*, by Winston S. Churchill.)

29. This man [Rudolf Hess (q.v.)], like other Nazi leaders, is potentially a war criminal, and he and his confederates may well be declared outlaws at the close of the war. (Memo to Foreign Secretary, May 13, 1941.)

[Following the flight of Rudolf Hess to Scotland. Hess, chief deputy to Adolf Hitler, attempted to make peace with England prior to the Nazi invasion of the Soviet Union.]

30. No one has been a more consistent opponent of Communism than I have for the last 25 years. I will unsay no word that I have spoken about it. But all this fades away before the spectacle which is now unfolding. (Radio address on the Nazi invasion of Russia, June 22, 1941.)

31. This bloodthirsty guttersnipe [Hitler] must launch his mechanized armies upon new fields of slaughter, pillage and devastation. Poor as are the Russian peasants, workmen and soldiers, he must steal from them their daily bread; he must devour their harvests; he must rob them of the oil which drives their ploughs, and thus produce a famine without example in human history. And even the carnage and ruin which his victory, should he gain it—he has not gained it yet—will bring upon the Russian people, will itself be only a stepping stone. (Ibid.)

32. It is not too much to say here this summer evening that the lives and happiness of a thousand million additional people are now menaced with brutal Nazi violence. (Ibid.)

33. We have to contemplate the descent from the air of perhaps a quarter million parachutists, glider-borne or crash-landed aeroplane troops. Everyone in uniform, and anyone else who likes, must fall upon these wherever they find them and attack them with the utmost alacrity—

> "Let every one
> Kill a Hun."

(Memo to Secretary of State for War, June 29, 1941; from *The Second World War: The Grand Alliance*, by Winston S. Churchill.)

34. We will have no truce or parley with you [Hitler], or the grisly gang who work your wicked will. You do your worst—and we will do our best. (Speech, London, July 14, 1941.)

35. You will, perhaps, have noticed that the President of the United States and the British representative, in what is aptly called the Atlantic Charter [q.v.], have jointly pledged their countries to the final destruction of the Nazi tyranny. That is a solemn and grave undertaking. It must be made good. It will be made good. And, of course, many practical arrangements to fulfill that purpose have been and are being organized and set in motion. (Radio broadcast, August 24, 1941.)

[Following the meeting with Roosevelt that produced the Atlantic Charter.]

36. If Hitler occupies Hell I will ask the House of Commons for aid for the Devil. (Following the invasion of the Soviet Union, ca. summer 1941; quoted in *Stalin*, by Edvard Radzinsky.)

37. I do not think it would be any use for me to make a personal appeal to Roosevelt at this juncture to enter the war. At the Atlantic meeting I told his circle that I would rather have an American declaration of war now and no supplies for six months than double the supplies and no declaration. When this was repeated to him he thought it a hard saying. We must not underrate his constitutional difficulties. . . . He went so far as to say to me, "I may never declare war; I may make war. If I were to ask Congress to declare war they might argue about it for three months." (Letter to General Jan C. Smuts, November 9, 1941; from *The Second World War: The Grand Alliance*, by Winston S. Churchill.)

38. As I turned over and twisted in bed the full horror of the news sank in upon me. There were no British or American capital ships in the Indian Ocean or the Pacific except the American survivors of Pearl Harbor, who were hastening back to California. Over all this vast expanse of waters Japan was supreme, and everywhere we were weak and naked. (On receiving news of the sinking of the H.M.S. *Repulse* and *Prince of Wales* by the Japanese, December 10, 1941; Ibid.)

39. Last night President [Roosevelt] urged upon me appointment of a single officer to command Army, Navy, and Air Force of Britain, America, and Dutch [in the Southwest Pacific], and this morning General [George C.] Marshall visited me at my request and pleaded case with great conviction. American Navy authorities take opposite view, but it is certain that a new far-reaching arrangement will have to be made. The man the President has in mind is [British] General [Archibald] Wavell. . . . So far I have been critical of plan, and while admitting broadmindedness of offer have expressed anxiety about effects on American opinion. (Cable to cabinet in London, December 28, 1941.)

[Churchill agreed to the plan and the appointment. The principle of unity of command was thus established.]

40. When I warned [the leaders of the French government] that Britain would fight on alone whatever they did, their generals told their prime minister and his divided cabinet, "In three weeks England will have her neck wrung like a chicken." Some chicken! Some neck! (Speech, Ottawa, Canada, December 30, 1941.)

41. 1. Your prime and main duty will be to take or destroy at the earliest opportunity the German-Italian army commanded by Field Marshal Rommel [q.v.], together with all its supplies and establishments in Egypt and Libya.

2. You will discharge, or cause to be discharged, such other duties as pertain to your Command without prejudice to the task described in paragraph one, which must be considered paramount in His Majesty's interests. (Orders to General Harold Alexander [q.v.], August 15, 1942.)

[Two months later, the British launched an offensive at El Alamein (q.v.), and drove Rommel's forces back across North Africa. The battle for Africa would end in Tunisia, with Axis forces defeated.]

42. If I could meet [Admiral Jean] Darlan [q.v.], much as I hate him, I would cheerfully crawl on my hands and knees for a mile if by doing so I could get him to bring that fleet of his into the circle of Allied Forces. (Spoken to Eisenhower, mid-October 1942; quoted in *Crusade in Europe*, by Dwight D. Eisenhower.)

[The Allies were readying an invasion of French North Africa. Darlan had signaled an interest in cooperating with, rather than resisting, the Allied invasion forces.]

43. This is not the end, nor is it the beginning of the end. It is, perhaps, the end of the beginning. (Speech, London, November 10, 1942.)

[Following the Allied invasion of North Africa.]

44. I have not become the King's First Minister in order to preside over the liquidation of the British Empire. (Ibid.)

45. Mr. President, I believe you are trying to do away with the British Empire. Every idea you entertain about the structure of the postwar world demonstrates it. But in spite of that—in spite of that—we know that you constitute our only hope. And you know that *we* know it. *You* know that *we* know that without America, the Empire won't stand. (Spoken to President Roosevelt, Casablanca, North Africa, January 1943; quoted in *As He Saw It*, by Elliott Roosevelt.)

46. We are . . . possessed of very powerful and growing forces, with great masses of munitions coming along. The problem is to bring these forces into action. The United States has vast oceans to cross in order to close with her enemies. We also have seas or oceans to cross . . . and then for both of us there is the daring and complicated enterprise of landing on defended coasts and also the building-up of all the supplies and communications necessary for vigorous campaigning . . . once a landing has been made. (Report to Parliament, February 11, 1943.)

47. It is because of this that the U-boat warfare takes the first place in our thoughts. There is no need to exaggerate the danger of the U-boats or to worry our merchant seamen by harping upon it unduly, because the British and American Governments have . . . given the task of overcoming them the first priority. (Ibid.)

48. The losses we suffer at sea are very heavy, and they hamper us and delay our operations. They prevent us from coming into action with our full strength, and thus they prolong the war, with its certain waste and loss and all its unknowable hazards.

Progress is being made in the war against the U-boats. . . . The losses in the last two months are the lowest sustained for over a year. The number of U-boats is increasing, but so are their losses, and so are the means of attacking them and protecting the convoys. (Ibid.)

49. Let the enemy, if he will, nurse his vain hopes of averting his doom by U-boat warfare. He cannot avert it, but he may delay it, and it is for us to shorten that delay by every conceivable effort we can make. (Report to Parliament on the Casablanca Conference [q.v.], February 11, 1943.)

50. It was only after full and cold, sober and mature consideration of all the facts, on which our lives and liberties certainly depend, that the President, with my full concurrence as agent of the War Cabinet, decided that the note of the Casablanca Conference should be the unconditional surrender of all our foes. But our inflexible insistence upon unconditional surrender does not mean that we shall stain our victorious arms by any cruel treatment of whole populations. But justice must be done upon the wicked and the guilty, and, within her proper bounds, justice must be stern and implacable. No vestige of the Nazi or Fascist power, no vestige of the Japanese war plotting machine, will be left by us when the work is done, and done it certainly will be. (Ibid.)

51. The collapse of Italy would cause a chill of loneliness over the German people, and might be the beginning of their doom. (Washington, D.C., May 15, 1943.)

[During an Anglo-American conference on future military activity. The Americans pressed for an early cross-channel invasion. Churchill wanted to knock Italy out of the war and temporarily delay the invasion of France.]

52. In our conferences in January 1942, between the President and myself . . . it was evident that while the defeat of Japan would not mean the defeat of Germany, the defeat of Germany would inevitably mean the ruin of Japan. (Address to the U.S. Congress, May 19, 1943.)

53. Lots of people can make good plans for winning the war if they have not got to carry them out. I dare say if I had not been in a responsible position, I should have made a lot of excellent plans, and very likely I should have brought them in one way or another to the notice of the executive authorities. But it is not possible to have full, open arguments about these matters. That is an additional hardship to those in charge—that such questions cannot be argued out and debated in public, except with enormous reticence and even then there is great danger that the watching and listening enemy may derive some profit from what they hear. (Ibid.)

54. I do not intend to be responsible for any suggestion that the war is won or will soon be over. That it will be won by us I am sure. But how or when cannot be foreseen, still less foretold. I was driving the other day not far from the field of Gettysburg. . . . No one after Gettysburg doubted which way the dread balance of war would incline. Yet far more blood was shed after the Union victory at Gettysburg than in all the fighting which went before. (Ibid.)

55. Twice in my lifetime the long arm of destiny has reached across the ocean and involved the entire life and manhood of the United States in a deadly struggle. There was no use saying, "We don't want it. We won't have it. Our forebears left Europe to avoid these quarrels. We have founded a new world which has no contact with the old." There was no use in that. The long arm reaches out remorselessly and everyone's existence, environment and outlook undergo a swift and irresistible change.

What is the explanation . . . and what are the deep laws to which they respond? . . .

The price of greatness is responsibility. (Speech, Harvard University, September 6, 1943.)

56. We are sending our aeroplanes to land in your territory, after delivering supplies to Warsaw. If you do not treat them properly all convoys will be stopped from this moment by us. (Message he wanted to send to Stalin—but didn't, September 4, 1944; from *The Second World War: Triumph and Tragedy*, by Winston S. Churchill.)

[Following Soviet refusal to allow British or American planes to use Russian airfields. This was during the Warsaw uprising when the Polish underground army appealed for arms.]

57. The United States troops have done almost all the fighting and have suffered almost all the losses [in the Battle of the Bulge (q.v.)]. They have suffered losses almost equal to those of both sides at the Battle of Gettysburg. The Americans have engaged 30 or 40 men for every one we have engaged and have lost 60 to 80 men to every one of ours. . . .

Care must be taken in telling our proud tale not to claim for the British armies undue share of what is undoubtedly the greatest American battle of the war. (Speech, House of Commons, January 18, 1945.)

58. I have every intention of working to the utmost for a Poland free to manage its own affairs and to which Polish soldiers in our service will be glad to return. If this fails we must provide for the Poles in arms inside the British Empire, which can easily accommodate such brave and serviceable men. . . .

There may always be a certain number of individual Poles who will not wish to go back to Poland because of their inveterate hostility to Russia. For these . . . the alternative of British citizenship must be open. (Memo to the Foreign Secretary, March 5, 1945; from *The Second World War: Triumph and Tragedy*, by Winston S. Churchill.)

59. German soldiers, who are fighting bravely to defend your native land, do you realize what will be the consequences of the war being carried on throughout the whole of Germany during the present spring and summer? You are told you are defending your homes and families and the German people. But though you may delay, you cannot stop our overrunning your whole country both from the east and west in the next few months. We feel it our duty to give you this warning, that if by your tenacity you destroy the means of production in your country and prevent or neglect the spring sowings, you will condemn Germany to a winter famine the like of which has never been seen in Europe.

It will be quite impossible for us, with our duties to our own peoples and the liberated countries, to accept any responsibility for feeding Germany in the winter of 1945–46. We may do what we can, but the available transport, and the available food which we could supply would be utterly insufficient to handle or bear so heavy a burden. If therefore you force us to carry the war on through the homelands of Germany, so that these are devastated by war, you will not protect your wives and families from suffering, but on the contrary you will condemn a very large proportion of the German people to death by starvation when winter comes. Your leaders at the top will not run short as long as you continue fighting; but the population of Germany will assuredly undergo a frightful reduction by famine unless the crops of this year are sown in time and gathered fully in peace.

The decision is yours, and we can only tell you that if you continue to fight, as we can well understand good soldiers would wish to do, you will not save your nation but doom it to horrors far beyond any you have endured so far and far beyond our power to give you help. (Proposed proclamation to the German army to be signed by Roosevelt, Churchill, and Stalin; submitted to Roosevelt for his comments, March 18, 1945; cited in *Churchill & Roosevelt: The Complete Correspondence*, edited by Warren F. Kimball.)

[Roosevelt rejected the idea, saying that this sort of thing should be left to the propaganda people. The appeal was never made.]

60. I say quite frankly that Berlin remains of high strategic importance. Nothing will exert psychological effect or despair upon all German forces of resistance equal to that of the fall of Berlin. It will be the supreme signal of defeat to the German people. On the other hand, if left to itself to maintain a siege by the

Russians among its ruins and as long as the German flag flies there, it will animate the resistance of all Germans under arms.

There is moreover another aspect which it is proper for you and me to consider. The Russian armies will no doubt overrun all Austria and enter Vienna. If they also take Berlin, will not their impression that they have been the overwhelming contributor to our common victory be unduly imprinted in their minds, and may this not lead them into a mood which will raise grave and formidable difficulties in the future? I therefore consider that from a political standpoint we should march as far east into Germany as possible and that should Berlin be in our grasp we should certainly take it. This also appears sound military grounds. (Message to President Roosevelt, April 1, 1945, from the National Archives; cited in *On to Berlin*, by James M. Gavin.)

61. One day the world, and history, will know what it owes to your President. (Spoken to Edward R. Murrow [q.v.] on the death of Franklin Roosevelt, April 13, 1945.)

62. Let me tell you what General Eisenhower has meant to us. In him we have had a man who set the unity of the Allied Armies above all nationalistic thoughts. In his headquarters unity and strategy were the only reigning spirits. . . . At no time has the principle of alliance between noble races been carried and maintained at so high a pitch. In the name of the British Empire and Commonwealth I express to you our admiration of the firm, far-sighted, and illuminating character and qualities of General of the Army Eisenhower. (Message to President Harry Truman [q.v.], May 9, 1945.)

63. There was one final danger from which the collapse of Germany has saved us. In London and the southeastern counties we have suffered for a year from various forms of flying bombs . . . and rockets, and our Air Force and our ack-ack batteries have done wonders against them. . . . But it was only when our armies cleaned up the coast and overran all the points of discharge, and when the Americans captured vast stores of rockets of all kinds near Leipzig . . . that we knew how grave had been the peril, not only from rockets and flying bombs, but from multiple long-range artillery which was being prepared against London. Only just in time did the Allied armies blast the viper in his nest. (Broadcast, May 13, 1945.)

[Delivered several days after the German surrender.]

64. For the same period the Germans had prepared a new U-boat fleet and novel tactics which, though we should have eventually destroyed them, might well have carried anti-U-boat warfare back to the high peak days of 1942. Therefore we must rejoice and give thanks, not only for our preservation when we were all alone, but for our timely deliverance from new suffering, new perils not easily to be measured. (Ibid.)

65. On the continent of Europe we have yet to make sure that the simple and honorable purposes for which we entered the war are not brushed aside or overlooked in the months following our success, and that the words "freedom," "democracy," and "liberation" are not distorted from their true meaning as we have understood them. There would be little use in punishing the Hitlerites for their crimes if law and justice did not rule, and if totalitarianism or police Governments were to take the place of the German invaders. (Ibid.)

66. Forward, unflinching, unswerving, indomitable, till the whole task is done and the whole world is safe and clean. (Ibid.)

67. I have had to bear many crosses during this war, but the heaviest was the Cross of Lorraine. (Attributed, ca. 1945.)

[Referring to the Free French symbol of Charles de Gaulle (q.v.).]

68. If you will not fight for the right when you can easily win without bloodshed; if you will not fight when your victory will be sure and not too costly; you may come to the moment when you will have to fight with all the odds against you and only a precarious chance of survival. There may even be a worse case. You may have to fight when there is no hope of victory, because it is better to perish than live as slaves. (1948; from *The Second World War: The Gathering Storm*, by Winston S. Churchill.)

[Commenting on appeasement and its ultimate consequences.]

69. The moral principles of modern civilization seem to prescribe that the leaders of a nation defeated in war shall be put to death by the victors. This will certainly stir them to fight to the bitter end in any future war, and no matter how many lives are needlessly sacrificed, it costs them no more. It is the masses of the people who have so little to say about the starting or ending of wars who pay the additional cost. Julius Caesar followed the opposite principle, and his conquests were due almost as much to his clemency as to his prowess. (1953; from *The Second World War: Triumph and Tragedy*, by Winston S. Churchill.)

70. Battles are won by slaughter and maneuver. The greater the general, the more he contributes in maneuver, the less he demands in slaughter. There are many kinds of maneuvers in war, some only of which take place upon the battlefield. There are maneuvers far to the flank or rear. There are maneuvers in time, in diplomacy, in mechanics, in psychology, all of which are removed from the battlefield, but react often decisively upon it, and the object of all is to find easier ways, other than sheer slaughter, of achieving the main purpose. (1962; from *Great Destiny*, by Winston S. Churchill.)

ADOLF HITLER
(1889–1945)

Dictator of Nazi Germany from 1933 to 1945. Born in Austria, Hitler fought in the German army in World War I, where he was gassed. After the war, he joined a small group of malcontents that would become the National Socialist Party [see *Mein Kampf* (q.v.)]. A Violent anti-Semite, Hitler rode into power in Germany on the heels of a devastating inflation that destroyed the middle class and an economic depression with massive unemployment. He bluffed England and France into appeasing him and signed a nonaggression pact with the Soviet Union to protect his Eastern Front. In 1939, Germany invaded Poland. This brought France and England into the war. After the fall of France, Hitler tried to bomb England into submission, but it did not work. Hitler invaded the Soviet Union but was stopped by a devastating Russian winter. Committed by treaty to back Japan in a war with the United States, Hitler declared war on America after Pearl Harbor. It was a move that sealed the fate of Nazi Germany. His war against the Jews of Europe resulted in 6 million Jewish dead. In April 1945, with armies from east and west closing in on Berlin, Hitler committed suicide.

71. The blood shed on the European continent in the course of the last three hundred years bears no proportion to the national result of the events. In the end France has remained France, Germany Germany, Poland Poland, and Italy Italy. What dynastic egotism, political passion and patriotic blindness have attained in the way of apparently far-reaching political changes by shedding rivers of blood has, as regards national feeling, done no more than touched the skin of the nations. It has not substantially altered their fundamental characters. If these states had applied merely a fraction of their sacrifices to wiser purposes the success would certainly have been greater and more permanent. (Speech to Reichstag, May 21, 1935.)

72. Germany needs peace and desires peace! (Ibid.)

73. Germany has solemnly recognized and guaranteed France her frontiers as determined after the Saar plebiscite. . . . We thereby finally renounced all claims to Alsace-Loraine, a land for which we have fought two great wars. (Ibid.)

74. Without taking the past into account Germany has concluded a nonaggression pact with Poland. . . . We shall adhere to it unconditionally. . . . We recognize Poland as the home of a great and nationally conscious people. (Ibid.)

75. Germany neither intends nor wishes to interfere in the internal affairs of Austria, to annex Austria, or to conclude an Anschluss. (Ibid.)

76. The German government is ready to agree to any limitation which leads to abolition of the heaviest arms, especially suited for aggression, such [as] heaviest artillery and the heaviest tanks. . . . Germany declares herself ready to agree to any limitation whatsoever of the caliber of artillery, battleships, cruisers and torpedo boats. (Ibid.)

77. Whoever lights the torch of war in Europe can wish for nothing but chaos. We, however, live in the firm conviction that in our time will be fulfilled not the decline but the renaissance of the West. That Germany may make an imperishable contribution to this great work is our proud hope and our unshakable belief. (Ibid.)

78. In this historic hour, when, in the Reich's western provinces [the Rhineland], German troops are at this minute marching into their future peacetime garrisons, we all unite in two sacred vows:

First, we swear to yield to no force whatever in restoration of the honor of our people.

Secondly, we pledge that now, more than ever, we shall strive for an understanding between the European peoples, especially for one with our Western neighbor nations. (Speech to the Reichstag, March 7, 1936.)

79. We have no territorial demands to make in Europe. . . . Germany will never break the peace! (Ibid.)

80. The forty-eight hours after the march into the Rhineland were the most nerve-racking in my life. If the French had then marched into the Rhineland, we would have had to withdraw with our tails between our legs, for the military resources at our disposal would have been wholly inadequate for even a moderate resistance. (Cited later in *Hitler's Interpreter*, by Paul Schmidt.)

[Quotations by Hitler for November 5, 1937, appear in Chapter 18, "Miscellaneous Quotations," under "Hossbach Memorandum."]

81. I have only to give an order, and in one single night all your ridiculous defense mechanisms will be blown to bits. You don't seriously believe that you can stop me for half an hour, do you? I would very much like to save Austria from such a fate, because such an action would mean blood. (Statement to Austrian Chancellor Kurt von Schuschnigg at Berchtesgaden, February 12, 1938.)

[A month later, following a Nazi invasion, Austria was proclaimed a province of the German Reich.]

82. Don't think for one moment that anybody on earth is going to thwart my decisions. Italy? I see eye to eye with Mussolini [q.v.]. England? England will not move one finger for Austria. And France? [After failing to move against Germany in the Rhineland] now it is too late for France. (Ibid.)

83. It is my unshakable will that Czechoslovakia shall be wiped off the map! (Statement to German military leaders, May 28, 1938.)

84. I will decide to take action against Czechoslovakia only if I am firmly convinced that France will not march and that therefore England will not intervene. (Directive to military, June 18, 1938.)

85. Would Britain agree to a secession of the Sudeten region, or would she not? A secession on the basis of the right of self-determination? (Question addressed to British Prime Minister Neville Chamberlain [q.v.] at Berchtesgaden meeting, September 15, 1938.)

[Both German and English sources agree that Chamberlain responded that he had to talk to his cabinet and to the French about the matter. The German source—supposedly based on notes taken at the meeting—said that Chamberlain added that he, himself, personally favored the principle of the Sudetenland being detached from Czechoslovakia.]

86. I assured him [British Prime Minister Chamberlain (q.v.)], moreover, and I repeat it here, that when this problem is solved there will be no more territorial problems for Germany in Europe. (Speech during the Czech crisis, September 26, 1938.)

87. This is the last territorial claim which I have to make in Europe. . . . I shall not be interested in the Czech State any more, and I can guarantee it. We don't want any Czechs any more. (To Prime Minister Neville Chamberlain [q.v.], Munich conference, ca. September 29, 1938.)

87a. We must inevitably count on a war with the Western democracies in the course of a few years, perhaps three or four. (Quoted by Joachim von Ribbentrop [q.v.]; cited in *Ciano's Hidden Diary*, by Galeazzo Ciano.)

[At a meeting on October 28, 1938, among German Foreign Minister Ribbentrop, Mussolini (q.v.) and Italian Foreign Minister Ciano (q.v.)]

88. If the international Jewish financiers in and outside Europe should succeed in plunging the nations once more into a world war, then the result will not be the Bolshevization of the earth and the victory of Jewry, but the end of the Jewish race in Europe! (Speech, January 30, 1939.)

89. For a thousand years, the provinces of Bohemia and Moravia formed part of the *Lebensraum* of the German people. . . . Czechoslovakia showed its inherent inability to survive and has therefore now fallen a victim to actual dissolution. The German Reich cannot tolerate continuous disturbances in these areas. Therefore the German Reich, in keeping with the law of self-preservation, is now resolved to intervene decisively to rebuild the foundations of a reasonable order in Central Europe. (Proclamation, March 16, 1939.)

[Following his invasion of Czechoslovakia, Hitler proclaimed a "protectorate" over Bohemia and Moravia.]

"If the international Jewish financiers in and outside Europe should succeed in plunging the nations once more into a world war, then the result will not be the Bolshevization of the earth and the victory of Jewry, but the end of the Jewish race in Europe!"

—ADOLF HITLER

90. I'll cook them a stew they'll choke on. (Comment, March 31, 1939.)

[In response to a statement by British Prime Minister Neville Chamberlain (q.v.) that England would defend Poland if invaded.]

91. If they [Britain and France] expect the Germany of today to sit patiently by until the very last day while they create satellite States and set them against Germany, they are mistaking the Germany of today for the Germany of before the war. (Speech, April 1, 1939.)

92. He who declares himself ready to pull the chestnuts out of the fire for these powers must realize he burns his fingers. (Ibid.)

93. Our object [the forthcoming invasion of Poland] must be kept secret even from the Italians and the Japanese. (Remark to top German leaders, May 23, 1939.)

94. The Dutch and Belgian air bases must be occupied by armed force. Declarations of neutrality must be ignored. . . . Therefore, if England intends to intervene in the Polish war, we must occupy Holland with lightning speed. We must aim at securing a new defense line on Dutch soil up to the Zuider Zee. (Minutes of a secret conference of top German military and political leaders, May 23, 1939.)

95. The German friendship for the Yugoslav nation is not only a spontaneous one. It gained depth and durability in the midst of the tragic confusion of the world war [of 1914–1918]. The German soldier then learned to appreciate and respect his extremely brave opponent. I believe that this feeling was reciprocated. This mutual respect finds confirmation in common political, cultural and economic interests. We therefore look upon your Royal Highness's present visit as a living proof of the accuracy of our view, and at the same time on that account we derive from it the hope that German-Yugoslav friendship may continue further to develop in the future and to grow ever closer. . . .

I believe this all the more because a firmly established reliable relationship of Germany to Yugoslavia, now that, owing to historical events [the Anschluss with Austria], we have become neighbors with common boundaries fixed for all time, will not only guarantee lasting peace between our two peoples and countries, but can also represent an element of calm to our nerve-wracked continent. (On the occasion of a state dinner in honor of the Prince Regent of Yugoslavia, Berlin, June 1, 1939.)

96. The great drama is now approaching its climax. . . . The men I got to know at Munich are not the kind that start a new world war. (Conversation, August 1939.)

[As German and Russian political and military leaders negotiated the Nazi-Soviet Pact (q.v.), including a partition of Poland.]

97. I consider it of the utmost importance that we clarify as soon as possible the questions arising from our non-aggression pact. There is no time to be lost. The tension between Germany and Poland has become intolerable. I suggest that you receive my Minister of Foreign Affairs on Tuesday, 22 August or at the latest on Wednesday, 23 August. He will have full powers to complete and sign the agreement and the protocol. (Message to Stalin, August 20, 1939.)

98. No shrinking back from anything. Everyone must hold the view that we have been determined to fight the Western powers right from the start. A life-and-death struggle. (Military conference, August 22, 1939.)

99. In 1918 the [German] nation collapsed because the spiritual prerequisites were insufficient. Frederick the Great endured only because of his fortitude. (Ibid.)

100. Close your hearts to pity! Eighty million people must obtain what are their rights. . . . The stronger man is right. . . . Be harsh and remorseless! Be steeled against all signs of compassion! (Ibid.)

101. Destruction of Poland is the foreground. The aim is elimination of living forces, not the arrival at a certain line. Even if war should break out in the West, the destruction of Poland shall be the primary objective. (Speech to his commanders, Obersalzburg, August 22, 1939.)

102. I shall give a propagandistic cause for starting the war—never mind whether it is plausible or not. The victor shall not be asked later on whether we told the truth or not. In starting and making a war, not the Right is what matters but Victory. (Ibid.)

103. I am only afraid that at the last minute some *Schweinehund* will make a proposal for mediation. (Ibid.)

104. A beginning has been made for the destruction of England's hegemony. (Ibid.)

105. [INDIRECT DISCOURSE: In his message, Hitler requested of Italy three things:]

1. That we not divulge our decision to remain neutral so long as it was not necessary to do so.
2. That Italy make military preparations so as to fool the French and the English.
3. That Italian workers be sent to Germany to replace those Germans in the countryside and the factories who had been mobilized. (Message to Mussolini [q.v.], August 27, 1939, following Italy's decision to stay neutral in the impending war; cited in *My Truth*, by Edda Mussolini Ciano.)

106. MOST SECRET ORDER: Now that all the political possibilities of disposing by peaceful means of a situation of the Eastern Frontier which is intolerable for Germany are exhausted, I have determined on a solution by force.

The attack on Poland is to be carried out in accordance with the preparations made for "Fall Weiss" [code name for the invasion]. . . .

Date of attack—1 September 1939

Time of attack—04:15 [inserted in red pencil]

("Directive No 1 for the conduct of the war" to the armed forces, August 31, 1939.)

107. The Polish Government, unwilling to establish good neighborly relations as aimed at by me, wants to force the issue by way of arms.

The Germans in Poland are being persecuted with bloody terror and driven from their homes. Several acts of frontier violation which cannot be tolerated by a great power show that Poland is no longer prepared to respect the Reich's frontiers. To put an end to these mad acts I can see no other way but from now onwards to meet force with force.

The German Armed Forces will with firm determination take up the struggle for the honor and the vital rights of the German people.

I expect every soldier to be conscious of the high tradition of the eternal German soldierly qualities and to do its duty to the last.

Remember always and in any circumstances that you are the representatives of National Socialist Greater Germany.

Long live our people and the Reich. (Proclamation to his armed forces, September 1, 1939.)

108. I first want to thank you for your last attempt at mediation. [On the third day of the German invasion of Poland—and the day that England and France had declared war on Germany—Mussolini had proposed an armistice, to be followed by a conference with the belligerents.] I would have been ready to accept, but only under condition, that there would be a possibility to give me certain guarantees that the conference would be successful. . . .

I believe that a way could have been found, if England would not have been determined to wage war under all circumstances. I have not given in to the English, because, Duce, I do not believe that peace could have been maintained for more than one-half year or one year. Under these circumstances, I thought that, in spite of everything, the present moment was better for resistance. (Letter to Mussolini [q.v.], ca. early September 1939.)

109. Recently you have given me the kind assurance that you think you will be able to help me in a few fields. I acknowledge this in advance with sincere thanks. But I believe also—even if we march now over different roads—that fate will finally join us. (Ibid.)

110. I have no war aims against Great Britain and France. My sympathies are with the French *poilu* [soldier]. What he is fighting for he does not know. (Speech, Danzig, September 19, 1939.)

111. Germany has no further claims against France. . . . I have always expressed to France my desire to bury forever our ancient enmity and bring together these two nations. . . . I have devoted no less effort to the achievement of Anglo-German understanding . . . more than that of an Anglo-German friendship. (Speech to the Reichstag, Berlin, October 6, 1939.)

112. Preparations should be made for offensive action on the northern flank of the Western Front crossing the area of Luxembourg, Belgium and Holland. The attack must be carried out as soon and as forcefully as possible. . . . The object of this attack is to acquire as great an area of Holland, Belgium and northern France as possible. (Secret orders to army chief Wilhelm Keitel [q.v.], navy head Erich Raeder [q.v.], and air force commander Hermann Goering [q.v.], October 9, 1939.)

113. Since England, in spite of her hopeless military situation, shows no signs of being ready to come to an understanding, I have decided to begin to prepare for, and if necessary to carry out, an invasion of England. . . . The aim of this operation will be to eliminate the English homeland as a base for the prosecution of the war against Germany, and, if necessary, to occupy it completely. (Directive No. 16, July 16, 1940.)

114. From Britain I now hear only a single cry—not of the people but of the politicians—that the war must go on! I do not know whether these politicians already have a correct idea of what the continuation of this struggle will be like. They do, it is true, declare that they will carry on with the war and that, even if Great Britain should perish, they would carry on from Canada. I can hardly believe that they mean by this that the people of Britain are to go to Canada. Presumably only those gentlemen interested in the continuation of their war will go there. (Speech to the Reichstag, July 19, 1940.)

115. In this hour I feel it to be my duty before my own conscience to appeal once more to reason and common sense in Great Britain as much as elsewhere. I consider myself in a position to make this appeal since I am not the vanquished begging favors, but the victor speaking in the name of reason. I can see no reason why this war must go on. (Ibid.)

116. The massing of [German] troops in Roumania serves a threefold purpose

a. An operation against Greece.
b. Protection of Bulgaria against Russia and Turkey.
c. Safeguarding the guarantee to Roumania.

Each of these tasks requires its own group of forces . . . whose deployment far from our base requires a long time.

Desirable that this deployment is complete without interference from the enemy. Therefore disclose the game as late as possible. The tendency will be to cross the Danube at the last possible moment and to line up for attack at the earliest possible moment. (Statement, January 20, 1941.)

[Statement following a meeting with Mussolini (q.v.) on Italian setbacks in Greece. Germany would come to the aid of its Axis partner.]

117. The war against Russia will be such that it cannot be conducted in a knightly fashion. This struggle is one of ideologies and racial differences and will have to be conducted with unprecedented, unmerciful and unrelenting harshness. (Talk to top military leaders, March 1941.)

118. The commissars are the bearers of ideologies directly opposed to National Socialism. Therefore the commissars will be liquidated. German soldiers guilty of breaking international law will be excused. Russia has not participated in the Hague Convention and therefore has no rights under it. (Ibid.)

119. From the beginning of the struggle it has been England's steadfast endeavor to make the Balkans a theater of war. British diplomacy did, in fact, using the model of the World War, succeed in first ensnaring Greece by a guarantee offered to her, and then finally in misusing her for Britain's purposes.

The documents published today [by Germany] afford a glimpse of a practice which, in accordance with very old British recipes, is a constant attempt to induce others to fight and bleed for British interests.

In the face of this I have always emphasized that:

(1) The German people have no antagonism to the Greek people but that

(2) We shall never, as in the World War, tolerate a power establishing itself on Greek territory with the object of at a given time of being able to advance thence from the southeast into German living space. We have swept the northern flank free of the English; we are resolved not to tolerate such a threat in the south. (Proclamation on the invasion of Greece and Yugoslavia, April 6, 1941.)

120. In the interests of a genuine consolidation of Europe it has been my endeavor since the day of my assumption of power above all to establish a friendly relationship with Yugoslavia. I have consciously put out of mind everything that once took place between Germany and Serbia. I have not only offered the Serbian people the hand of the German people, but in addition have made efforts as an honest broker to assist in bridging all difficulties which existed between the Yugoslav State and various Nations allied to Germany. (Ibid.)

121. He [Winston Churchill] is the most bloodthirsty or amateurish strategist in history. For over five years this man has been chasing around Europe like a madman in search of something that he could set on fire. (Speech to the Reichstag, May 4, 1941.)

122. As a soldier he [Churchill] is a bad politician and as a politician an equally bad soldier. (Ibid.)

123. Your armies will shatter the Russian colossus. It will be a hard fight—the Asiatics are cruel and cunning, but you will meet them with a determination as hard and cold as ice. Only one people will come out of this alive—our people. You must make your troops put aside all their notions of restraint and humanity. I expect to annihilate the bulk of the Red Army in the great battles on the frontier. . . . This will be the last campaign of this war, and it will ensure the security of the Reich for many generations. This is a struggle between two antithetical ideologies. We cannot refuse to give battle, and one day the world will thank us for having responded to the call of destiny. (Address to German High Command, late June 1941; cited in *Operation Valkyrie*, by Pierre Galante with Eugene Silianoff.)

[On the eve of the invasion of the Soviet Union.]

124. I am one of those men who in adversity simply becomes more determined. (Letter to Mussolini [q.v.], November 20, 1942; cited in *Inside Hitler's Headquarters*, by Walter Warlimont.)

125. In the year 1933, Germany obtained the political . . . and material prerequisites for carrying on a battle which today is deciding the fate of the world. Just as at that time there were only two possibilities in the interior: Either victory of the National Socialist revolution and, in consequence, a planned social reconstruction of the Reich, or the Bolshevik revolution and, in consequence, the destruction and enslavement of all; so today there are only these two alternatives: Either Germany, the German armed forces and along with us the allied countries, so that Europe will win, or the Central Asiatic Bolshevik tide will break in from the East over the oldest civilized continent, just as destructively and annihilatingly as it did in Russia itself. (Proclamation, on the tenth anniversary of his rise to power, January 30, 1943.)

126. Jodl [q.v.]! I demand to know! Yes or no? Is Paris burning now? (To Chief of Staff Alfred Jodl, August 25, 1944; cited in *Is Paris Burning?*, by Larry Collins and Dominique Lapierre.)

[This was Hitler's verbal follow-up to the German army's order of two days earlier: "Paris must not fall into the hands of the enemy, or, if it does, he must find there nothing but a field of ruins." General Dietrich von Choltitz never carried out the destruction order.]

127. The Hindu brigade is a practical joke. There are Hindus who won't kill a louse—they'd rather be eaten alive—so it's hardly likely that they'd kill an Englishman. That just seems ludicrous to me. Why would the Hindus fight more bravely to defend our country than they fought at home, even under the leadership of Chandra Bose, to free India from the English? Why would they be any braver back here? I suppose that if we used the Hindus to turn prayer wheels, or some similar occupation, there'd be no stopping them then. But the thought of using them in a real, bloody battle is ridiculous. Since we hardly have a surplus of materiel at our disposal, these hare-brained propaganda stunts are totally unacceptable. (Briefing, March 23, 1945; cited in *Operation Valkyrie*, by Pierre Galante with Eugene Silianoff.)

[Hitler was referring to a brigade of Hindu volunteers recruited by the Indian nationalist Chandra Bose. The Hindu brigade in Germany was a propaganda ploy, focusing attention on the issue of Indian independence from Britain. A similar volunteer group did fight for the Japanese against the British in Burma and India.]

128. Berlin will remain German and Vienna will become German again. (On the fall of Vienna, April 13, 1945.)

129. Now that fate has removed from the earth the greatest war criminal of all time, the turning point of this war will be decided. (Order of the Day, on the death of President Roosevelt, April 15, 1945.)

130. Anyone who proposes or even approves measures detrimental to our power or resistance is a traitor! He is to be shot or hanged immediately! This applies even if such measures have allegedly been ordered on the instructions of Reich Minister Dr. Goebbels [q.v.], the Gauleiter, or even in the name of the Fuehrer. (Proclamation to the People of Berlin, *Der Panzerbar*, April 23, 1945.)

131. I will fight before Berlin, in Berlin, or behind Berlin. (Attributed, ca. April 23, 1945; quoted in *The Memoirs of Field Marshal Keitel*, edited by W. Goerlitz and D. Irving.)

[Some historians question this quote. It parallels the statement of a French general speaking of Paris during World War I.]

132. I shall defend the city to the end. Either I survive this battle for the capital or I go down in Berlin with my men. (Ibid.)

133. My wife and I choose to die in order to escape the shame of overthrow or capitulation. It is our wish that our bodies be burnt immediately in the place where I have performed the greater part of my daily work during 12 years' service to my people. (Last will, April 29, 1945; cited in *The Last Days of Hitler*, by H. R. Trevor-Roper.)

134. It is untrue that I, or anybody else in Germany, wanted war in 1939. It was wanted and provoked exclusively by those international politicians who either came of Jewish stock, or worked for Jewish interests. After all my offers of disarmament, posterity cannot place the responsibility for this war on me. (Final testament, April 29, 1945; cited in ibid.)

135. After a six-years' war, which in spite of all setbacks will one day go down in history as the most glorious and heroic manifestation of a people's will to live, I cannot forsake the city which is the capital of this state. Since our forces are too small to withstand any longer the enemy's attack on this place, and since our own resistance will be gradually worn down by an army of blind automata, I wish to share the fate that millions of others have accepted and to remain here in the city. Further, I will not fall into the hands of an enemy who requires a new spectacle, exhibited by the Jews, to divert his hysterical masses. I have therefore decided to remain in Berlin, and there to choose death voluntarily at the moment when I believe that the residence of the Fuehrer and Chancellor can no longer be held. (Ibid.)

FRANKLIN D. ROOSEVELT

(1882–1945)

President Roosevelt took the oath of office five weeks after Adolf Hitler became German chancellor. The only American president to win election to the office four times, Roosevelt recognized the peril of Nazism and supported aid to the Allies long before Pearl Harbor. After the Japanese attack, Roosevelt led a united nation against Axis forces throughout the world. He gambled an unprecedented amount of money to develop the atomic bomb. He died several weeks before the German surrender and four months before the Japanese capitulation.

136. There is a mysterious cycle in human events. To some generations much is given. Of other generations much is expected. This generation of Americans has a rendezvous with destiny. (Acceptance speech, Democratic National Convention, Philadelphia, June 27, 1936.)

137. In this world of ours in other lands, there are some people, who, in times past, have lived and fought for freedom, and seem to have grown too weary to carry on the fight. They have sold their heritage of freedom for the illusion of living. They have yielded their democracy.

I believe in my heart that only our success can stir their ancient hope. They begin to know that here in America we are waging a great and successful war. It is not alone a war against want and destitution and economic demoralization.

It is more than that; it is a war for the survival of democracy. We are fighting to save a great and precious form of government for ourselves and for the world. (Ibid.)

138. It seems to be unfortunately true that the epidemic of world lawlessness is spreading.

When an epidemic of physical disease starts to spread, the community approves and joins in a quarantine of the patients in order to protect the health of the community against the spread of the disease. (Speech, October 9, 1937.)

[Civil war was raging in Spain, with Nazi Germany helping the forces of Franco (q.v.) and the Soviet Union helping the loyalists. Japan had moved into China.]

139. War is a contagion, whether it be declared or undeclared. It can engulf states and peoples remote from the original scene of hostilities. We are determined to keep out of war, yet we cannot insure ourselves against the disastrous effects of war and the dangers of involvement. We are adopting such measures, as will minimize our risk of involvement, but we cannot have complete protection in a world of disorder in which confidence and security have broken down. (Ibid.)

140. America hates war. America hopes for peace. Therefore, America actively engages in the search for peace. (Ibid.)

141. Without a declaration of war and without warning or justification of any kind, civilians, including vast numbers of women and children, are being ruthlessly murdered with bombs from the air. In times of so-called peace, ships are being attacked, and sunk by submarines without cause or notice. Nations are fomenting and taking sides in civil warfare in nations that have never done them any harm. Nations claiming freedom for themselves deny it to others. Innocent peoples, innocent nations, are being cruelly sacrificed to a greed of power and supremacy which is devoid of all sense of justice and humane consideration. (Ibid.)

142. If those things come to pass in other parts of the world, let no one imagine that America will escape, that America may expect mercy, that this Western Hemisphere will not be attacked, that it will continue tranquilly and peacefully to carry the ethics and the arts of civilization.

If those days come, "there will be no safety by arms, no help from authority, no answer in science. The storm will rage till every flower of culture is trampled and all human beings are leveled to a vast chaos."

If those days are not to come to pass—if we are to have a world in which we can breathe freely and live in amity without fear—the peace-loving nations must make a concerted effort to uphold laws and principles in which alone peace can rest secure. (Ibid.)

143. You must master at the outset a simple but unalterable fact in modern foreign relations between nations. When peace has been broken anywhere, the peace of all countries everywhere is in danger. . . . Passionately though we may desire detachment, we are forced to realize that every word that comes through the air, every ship that sails the sea, every battle that is fought, does affect the American future. (Fireside Chat, September 3, 1939.)

[On this date, England and France declared war on Germany.]

144. I should like to be able to offer the hope that the shadow over the world might swiftly pass. I cannot. The facts compel my stating, with candor, that darker periods may lie ahead. The disaster is not of our making; no act of ours engendered the forces which assault the foundations of civilization. Yet we find ourselves affected to the core, our currents of commerce are changing, our minds are filled with new problems, our position in world affairs has already been altered. (Message to Congress, September 21, 1939.)

[Message on repealing the embargo provisions of the Neutrality Law. At this time, Poland was crumbling under the Nazi invasion from the west and the Soviet invasion from the east.]

145. These are ominous days—days whose swift and shocking developments force every neutral nation to look to its defenses in the light of new factors. The brutal force of modern offensive war has been loosed in all its horror. New powers of destruction, incredibly swift and ready, have been developed; and those who wield them are ruthless and daring. (Address to Congress, calling for an increase in defense spending, May 16, 1940.)

146. No old defense is so strong that it requires no further strengthening, and no attack is so unlikely or impossible that it may be ignored. (Ibid.)

147. Surely the developments of the past few weeks have made it clear to all our citizens that the possibility of attack on vital American zones ought to make it essential that we have the physical, the ready ability, to meet those attacks and to prevent them from reaching their objectives. (Ibid.)

148. We have the lesson before us over and over again—nations that were not ready and were unable to get ready found themselves overrun by the enemy. (Ibid.)

149. So-called impregnable fortifications no longer exist. (Ibid.).

150. For more than three centuries we Americans have been building on this continent a free society, a society in which the promise of the human spirit may find fulfillment. Commingled here are the blood and genius of all the peoples of the world who have sought this promise.

We have built well. We are continuing our efforts to bring the blessings of a free society, of a free and productive economic system, to every family in the land. This is the promise of America.

It is this that we must continue to build—it is this that we must continue to defend.

It is the task of our generation, yours and mine. But we build and defend not for our generation alone. We defend the foundations laid down by our fathers. We build a life for generations yet unborn. We defend and we build a way of life, not for America alone, but for all mankind. (Address, as German armies smashed into France, trapping Allied forces at Dunkirk [q.v.], May 26, 1940.)

151. On this 10th day of June, 1940, the hand that held the dagger has struck it into the back of its neighbor. (Speech on the Italian invasion of France, now crushed by the Nazis, June 10, 1940.)

152. We will pursue two obvious and simultaneous goals: we will extend to the opponents of force the material resources of this nation and, at the same time, we will harness and speed up the use of those resources in order that we ourselves in the Americas may have equipment and training equal to the task of any emergency and every defense. . . . We will not slow down or detour. Signs and sights call for speed—full speed ahead. (Ibid.)

153. As I have already stated to you and to Mr. Churchill, this Government is doing everything in its power to make available to the Allied Governments the materials they so urgently require, and our efforts to do still more are being redoubled. This is so because of our faith in and our support of the ideals for which the Allies are fighting.

The magnificent resistance of the French and British Armies has profoundly impressed the American people.

I am, personally, particularly impressed by your declaration that France will continue to fight on behalf of Democracy, even if it means slow withdrawal, even to North Africa and the Atlantic. It is most important to remember that the French and British Fleets continue mastery of the Atlantic and other oceans; also to remember that vital materials from the outside world are necessary to maintain all armies.

I am also greatly heartened by what Prime Minister Churchill said a few days ago about the continued resistance of the British Empire, and that determination would seem to apply equally to the great French Empire all over the world. (Response to message from Premier Reynaud [q.v.] of France, calling on the United States to enter the war against Germany, ca. June 12, 1940.)

154. Should the French government . . . permit the French Fleet to be surrendered to Germany, the French government will permanently lose the friendship and goodwill of the government of the United States. (Note to the Petain [q.v.] government, as it sought an armistice with Nazi Germany, June 17, 1940.)

155. If you learn anything in Africa of special interest, send it to me. Don't bother going through State Department channels. (To Robert Murphy [q.v.], White House, September 1940; quoted in *Diplomat among Warriors*, by Robert Murphy.)

[This meeting established Murphy as a personal representative of the president. It set him off on the first of a number of secret wartime missions on behalf of Roosevelt.]

156. There are those in the Old World who persist in believing that here in this new hemisphere the Americas can be torn by the hatreds and fears which have drenched the battle grounds of Europe for so many centuries. Americans as individuals, American Republics as nations, remain on guard against those who seek to break up our unity by preaching ancient race hatreds, by working on old fears, or by holding out glittering promises which they know to be false.

"Divide and conquer!" That has been the battle cry of the totalitarian powers in their war against the democracies. It has succeeded on the continent of Europe for the moment. On our continents it will fail. (Speech, October 12, 1940.)

157. I have said this before, but I shall say it again and again and again: Your boys are not going to be sent into any foreign wars. (Campaign speech, Boston, October 30, 1940.)

[The 1940 Democratic Party platform also opposed getting involved in any "foreign wars" but added the words "unless we are attacked."]

158. The experience of the past two years has proven beyond doubt that no nation can appease the Nazis. No man can tame a tiger into a kitten by stroking it. There can be no appeasement with ruthlessness. There can be no reasoning with an incendiary bomb. We know now that a nation can have peace with the Nazis only at the price of total surrender. (Radio address, December 29, 1940.)

159. In the future days, which we seek to make secure, we look forward to a world founded upon four essential human freedoms.

The first is freedom of speech and expression—everywhere in the world.

The second is freedom of every person to worship God in his own way—everywhere in the world.

The third is freedom from want—which, translated into world terms, means economic understandings which will secure to every nation a healthy peace time life for its inhabitants—everywhere in the world.

The fourth is freedom from fear—which, translated into world terms, means a world-wide reduction of armaments to such a point and in such a thorough fashion that no nation will be in a position to commit an act of physical aggression against any neighbor—anywhere in the world.

That is no vision of a distant millennium. It is a definite basis for a kind of world attainable in our own time and generation. (State of the Union Address, January 6, 1941.)

160. When the dictators are ready to make war upon us they will not wait for an act of war on our part. They, not we, will choose the time and the place and the method of their attack. (Ibid.)

161. I cannot bring a divided nation into war. I learned that from the First World War. I felt the same urgency then that your people feel now. But [President Woodrow] Wilson taught me a lesson. I am going to be sure, very sure, that if the United States publicly enters the war, it will enter united. (Spoken to William Stephenson [q.v.] British intelligence official, January 1941; quoted in *A Man Called Intrepid*, by William Stevenson.)

162. Wendell Willkie [q.v.] will give you this—he is truly helping to keep politics out over here. I think that this verse applies to your people as it does to us:

> Sail on, O ship of state;
> Sail on, O Union strong and great;
> Humanity with all its fears,

With all the hopes of future years,
Is hanging breathless on thy fate!

(Letter to Winston Churchill, February 1941.)

[Willkie was Roosevelt's opponent in the 1940 presidential election. Churchill read this verse from Longfellow during a radio broadcast on February 9, 1941. He said, "Here is the answer which I will give to President Roosevelt: Give us the tools and we will finish the job!"]

163. The British people are braced for invasion whenever such attempt may come—tomorrow—next week—next month. In this historic crisis, Britain is blessed with a brilliant and great leader in Winston Churchill. But, knowing him, no one knows better than Mr. Churchill himself that it is not alone his stirring words and valiant deeds that give the British their superb morale. The essence of that morale is in the masses of plain people, who are completely clear in their minds about the one essential fact that they would rather die as free men than live as slaves. (Speech supporting Lend-Lease [q.v.] bill, March 15, 1941.)

164. The British people . . . need ships. From America, they will get ships.
They need planes. From America they will get planes.
They need food and from America, they will get food. (Ibid.)

165. Our country is going to be what our people have proclaimed it must be—the arsenal of democracy. (Ibid.)

166. I have said on many occasions that the United States is mustering its men and its resources only for purposes of defense—only to repel attack. I repeat that statement now. But we must be realistic when we use the word "attack"; we have to relate it to the lightning speed of modern warfare. (Speech, May 27, 1941.)

167. Some people seem to think that we are not attacked until bombs actually drop on New York or San Francisco or New Orleans or Chicago. But they are simply shutting their eyes to the lesson we must learn from the fate of every nation that the Nazis have conquered.

The attack on Czechoslovakia began with the conquest of Austria. The attack on Norway began with the occupation of Denmark. The attack on Greece began with the occupation of Albania and Bulgaria. The attack on the Suez Canal began with the invasion of the Balkans and North Africa. The attack on the United States began with the domination of any base which menaces our security—north or south. (Ibid.)

168. Nobody can foretell tonight just when the acts of the dictators will ripen into attack on this hemisphere and us. But we know enough by now to realize that it would be suicide to wait until they are in our front yard.

When your enemy comes at you in a tank or a bombing plane, if you hold your fire until you see the whites of his eyes, you will never know what hit you. Our Bunker Hill of tomorrow may be several thousand miles from Boston. (Ibid.)

169. Anyone with an atlas and a reasonable knowledge of the sudden striking force of modern war knows that it is stupid to wait until a probable enemy has gained a foothold from which to attack. Old-fashioned common sense calls for the use of a strategy which will prevent such an enemy from gaining a foothold in the first place.

We have, accordingly, extended our patrol in North and South Atlantic waters. We are steadily adding more and more ships and planes for that patrol. It is well known that the strength of the Atlantic fleet has been greatly increased during the past year, and is constantly being built up. (Ibid.)

170. An unlimited national emergency confronts this country. (Radio address, May 27, 1941.)

171. From the point of view of strict naval and military necessity, we shall give every possible assurance to Britain and to all who, with Britain, are resisting Hitlerism or its equivalent with force of arms. Our patrols are helping now to insure delivery of the needed supplies to Britain. All additional measures necessary to deliver the goods will be taken. Any and all further methods or combination of methods, which can or should be utilized, are being devised. (Ibid.)

172. There are some timid ones among us who say that we must preserve peace at any price—lest we lose our liberties forever. To them I say: never in the history of the world has a nation lost its democracy by a successful struggle to defend democracy. (Ibid.)

173. Today the whole world is divided between human slavery and human freedom—between pagan brutality and the Christian ideal. (Ibid.)

174. We will not accept a Hitler-dominated world. And we will not accept a world, like the post-war world of the 1920s, in which the seeds of Hitlerism can again be planted and allowed to grow. (Ibid.)

175. The total disregard shown for the most elementary principles of international law and of humanity brands the sinking of the *Robin Moor* as an act of an international outlaw. [It is] a first step in assertion of the supreme purpose of the German Reich to seize control of the high seas. (Message to Congress, June 20, 1941.)

[On May 21, the *Robin Moor*, an American freighter, had been sunk in the South Atlantic by a German submarine. The U-boat captain had ordered passengers and crew into lifeboats before the ship was torpedoed.]

176. To collect and analyze all information and data which bear upon national security; to correlate such information and data and to make it available to the President, and to such departments and officials of the Government as the President may determine. . . . [And to carry on] such supplementary activities as may facilitate the securing of information, important for national security. (Executive Order creating the Office of Coordinator of Information, July 11, 1941.)

[The coordinator was William J. Donovan (q.v.). In June 1942, the office's name would be changed to Office of Strategic Services. After the war, the OSS would evolve into the Central Intelligence Agency.]

177. Normal practices of diplomacy—note writing—are of no possible use in dealing with international outlaws who sink our ships and kill our citizens. . . . No matter what it takes, no matter what it costs, we will keep open the line of legitimate commerce in these defensive waters. (Fireside Chat, September 11, 1941.)

[After several American vessels had been sunk and an American destroyer was attacked with torpedoes.]

178. When you see a rattlesnake poised to strike, you do not wait until he has struck before you crush him. These Nazi submarines and raiders are the rattlesnakes of the Atlantic. They are a menace to the free pathways of the high seas. They are a challenge to our sovereignty. (Ibid.)

179. From now on, if German or Italian vessels of war enter the waters, the protection of which is necessary for American defense, they do so at their own peril. The orders which I have given as Commander-in-Chief of the United States Army and Navy are to carry out that policy—at once. (Ibid.)

[This would become known as the "shoot-on-sight" order.]

180. Hitler has attacked shipping in areas close to the Americas in the North and South Atlantic.

Many American-owned merchant ships have been sunk on the high seas. One American destroyer [the *Greer* (q.v.)] was attacked on September 4 [1941]. Another destroyer [the *Kearny*] was attacked and hit on October 7 [1941]. Eleven brave and loyal men of our Navy were killed by the Nazis.

We have wished to avoid shooting. But the shooting has started. And history has recorded who fired the first shot. In the long run, however, all that will matter is who fired the last shot. (Radio address, October 27, 1941.)

181. This means war. (Spoken to Harry Hopkins [q.v.], December 6, 1941.)

[After receiving a decoded copy of the Japanese message scheduled to be presented to Secretary of State Hull (q.v.) the following day. It broke off further diplomatic negotiations.]

182. We are all in the same boat now. (Telephone conversation with Winston Churchill, December 7, 1941.)

183. Yesterday, December 7, 1941—a date which will live in infamy—the United States of America was suddenly and deliberately attacked by naval and air forces of the Empire of Japan.

The United States was at peace with that Nation and, at the solicitation of

Japan, was still in conversation with its Government and its Emperor looking toward the maintenance of peace in the Pacific.

Indeed, one hour after Japanese air squadrons had commenced bombing in Oahu, the Japanese Ambassador to the United States and his colleague delivered to the Secretary of State a formal reply to a recent American message. While this reply stated that it seemed useless to continue the existing diplomatic negotiations, it contained no threat or hint of war or armed attack.

It will be recorded that the distance of Hawaii from Japan makes it obvious that the attack was deliberately planned many days or even weeks ago. During the intervening time the Japanese Government has deliberately sought to deceive the United States by false statements and expressions of hope for continued peace. (Address to Congress, December 8, 1941.)

184. Yesterday the Japanese Government also launched an attack against Malaya.

Last night Japanese forces attacked Hong Kong.

Last night Japanese forces attacked Guam.

Last night the Japanese attacked Wake Island.

This morning the Japanese attacked Midway Island.

Japan has, therefore, undertaken a surprise offensive extending throughout the Pacific area. The facts of yesterday speak for themselves. (Ibid.)

185. Always will we remember the character of the onslaught against us.

No matter how long it may take us to overcome this premeditated invasion, the American people in their righteous might will win through to absolute victory.

I believe I interpret the will of the Congress and of the people when I assert that we will not only defend ourselves to the uttermost but will make very certain that this form of treachery shall never endanger us again.

With confidence in our armed forces—with the unbounded determination of our people—we will gain the inevitable triumph—so help us God.

I ask that the Congress declare that since the unprovoked and dastardly attack by Japan on Sunday, December 7, a state of war has existed between the United States and the Japanese Empire. (Ibid.)

186. On the morning of December 11 [1941] the Government of Germany, pursuing its course of world conquest, declared war against the United States.

The long known and the long expected has thus taken place. The forces endeavoring to enslave the entire world now are moving toward this hemisphere.

Never before has there been a greater challenge to life, liberty, and civilization.

Delay invites greater danger. Rapid and united effort by all the peoples of the world who are determined to remain free will insure a world victory of the forces of justice and of righteousness over the forces of savagery and of barbarism.

Italy also has declared war against the United States.

I therefore request the Congress to recognize a state of war between the United

"December 7th, 1941—a date which will live in infamy . . ."

—FRANKLIN D. ROOSEVELT

Japanese view of Hawaii attack: Smoke rises from Hickam Field, above, and Pearl Harbor, below.

States and Germany and between the United States and Italy. (Message to Congress, December 11, 1941.)

187. TO THE PRESIDENT OF THE UNITED STATES IN 1956:

I am writing this letter as an act of faith in the destiny of our country. I desire to make a request which I make in full confidence that we shall achieve a glorious victory in the war we now are waging to preserve our democratic way of life.

My request is that you consider the merits of a young American youth of goodly heritage—Colin P. Kelly, III—for appointment as a Cadet in the United States Military Academy at West Point. I make this appeal in behalf of this youth as a token of the Nation's appreciating of the heroic services of his father who met death in the line of duty at the very outset of the struggle which was thrust upon us by the perfidy of a professed friend.

In the conviction that the service and example of Captain Colin P. Kelly, Jr. will be long remembered, I ask for this consideration in behalf of Colin P. Kelly, III. (Letter, December 17, 1941.)

[The letter would end up on the desk of President Dwight D. Eisenhower. Young Kelly decided to go through the regular process of applying for West Point and was admitted on his own.]

188. War costs money. So far we have hardly even begun to pay for it. We devoted only 15 percent of our national income to national defense. As will appear in my budget message tomorrow, our war program for the coming fiscal year will cost $56 billion, or in other words more than half of the estimated annual national income. (State of the Union Address, January 6, 1942.)

189. Our enemies are guided by military cynicism, by unholy contempt for the human race. We are inspired by a faith which goes back through the years to the first chapter of the Book of Genesis—"God created man in His own image."

We on our side are striving to be true to that divine heritage. We are fighting, as our fathers have fought, to uphold the doctrine that all men are equal in the sight of God. Those on the other side are striving to destroy this deep belief and to create a world in their own image, a world of tyranny and cruelty and serfdom. (Ibid.)

190. I should like to tell you . . . about the men we have in our armed forces.

There is, for example, Dr. Corydon M. Wassell. He was a missionary, well known for his good works in China. He is a simple, modest, retiring man, nearly 60 years old, but he entered the service of his country and was commissioned a lieutenant commander in the Navy.

Dr. Wassell was assigned to duty in Java caring for wounded officers and men of the cruisers *Houston* and *Marblehead* which had been in heavy action in the Java seas.

When the Japanese advanced across the island, it was decided to evacuate as many as possible of the wounded to Australia. But about twelve of the men were so badly wounded that they could not be moved. Dr. Wassell remained with them, knowing that he would be captured by the Japanese enemy. But he decided to make a last desperate attempt to get the men out of Java. He asked each of them if he wanted to take the chance, and every one agreed.

He first had to get the twelve men to the sea coast—50 miles away. To do that, he had to improvise stretchers for the hazardous journey. The men were suffering severely, but Dr. Wassell kept them alive by his skill, inspired them by his own courage.

And as the official report said, was "almost like a Christ-like shepherd devoted to his flock."

On the sea coast, he embarked the men on a little Dutch ship. They were bombed, they were machine-gunned by waves of Japanese planes. Dr. Wassell took virtual command of the ship, and by great skill avoided destruction, hiding in little bays and little inlets.

A few days later, Dr. Wassell and his little flock of wounded men reached Australia safely.

And today Dr. Wassell wears the Navy Cross. (Radio broadcast, April 28, 1942; cited in the *New York Times*, April 29, 1942.)

191. In every camp and on every naval vessel soldiers, sailors, and marines are inspired by the gallant struggle of their comrades in the Philippines. The workmen in our shipyards and munitions plants redouble their efforts because of your example. (Message to General Wainwright [q.v.], May 5, 1942.)

[The message was actually prepared by General Marshall. It was on the eve of the surrender at Corregidor. Marshall wanted to have Wainwright awarded the Congressional Medal of Honor. That move was blocked by MacArthur. After the war, President Truman (q.v.) presented the medal to Wainwright.]

192. INDIRECT DISCOURSE: [Roosevelt] said MacArthur's assurance to his men early in December [1941], after the attack, that ample reinforcements of men, planes, tanks, and materiel were on the way and would reach the Philippines very soon—in ample time to relieve shortage—was unjustifiable. MacArthur knew this was not true. [It is] justifiable to give incorrect information in some circumstances in time of war; but criminal to raise false hopes—hopes that MacArthur knew could not be fulfilled. (July 11, 1942; quoted in *Off the Record with F.D.R.*, by William D. Hassett.)

193. The United Nations are going to win this war. When victory has been achieved, it is the purpose of the Government of the United States, as I know it is the purpose of each of the United Nations, to make appropriate use of the information and evidence in respect to these barbaric crimes of the invaders, in Europe and in Asia. It seems only fair that they should have this warning that the time will come when they shall have to stand in courts of law in the very countries which they are now oppressing and answer for their acts. (Statement, August 21, 1942.)

194. You will at an early date contact personally and through your Psychological Warfare and other assistants those French nationals whom you consider reliable, and give them the following information:

Information having been received from a reliable source that the Germans and Italians are planning an intervention in French North Africa, the United States contemplates sending at an early date a sufficient number of American troops to land in that area with the purpose of preventing occupation by the Axis and of preserving French sovereignty in Algeria, and the French administrations in Morocco and Tunisia.

No change in the existing French Civil Administrations is contemplated by the United States.

Any resistance to an American landing will, of course, have to be put down by force of arms.

The American forces will hope for and will welcome French assistance. (Directive to Robert D. Murphy [q.v.] September 22, 1942; cited in *Our Vichy Gamble*, by William L. Langer.)

195. My friends, who suffer day and night under the crushing yoke of the Nazis, I speak to you as one who was with your army and navy in France in 1918. I have held all my life the deepest friendship for the French people—for the entire French people. I retain and cherish the friendship of hundreds of French people in France and outside France. I know your farms, your villages, and your cities. I know your soldiers, professors, and workmen. I know what a precious heritage of the French people are your homes, your culture, and the principles of democracy in France. I salute again and reiterate my faith in Liberty, Equality, and Fraternity. No two nations exist which are more united by historic and mutually friendly ties than the people in France and the United States.

Americans, with the assistance of the United Nations, are striving for their own safe future as well as the restoration of the ideals, the liberties, and the democracy of all those who have lived under the tricolor. (Broadcast to the French people, November 7, 1942.)

[The broadcast, in French, was made as American forces were invading French North Africa, then under the control of Vichy France. The idea was to keep French military resistance to a minimum.]

196. Day in and day out we shall heap tons upon tons of explosives on their war factories and utilities and seaports. Hitler and Mussolini [q.v.] will understand the enormity of their miscalculations—that the Nazis would always have the advantage of superior air power. That superiority has gone—forever.

Yes—the Nazis and the Fascists have asked for it—and they are going to get it. (Annual Message to Congress, January 7, 1943.)

197. Our forward progress in this war has depended upon our progress on the production front. There has been criticism of the management and conduct of our war production. Much of this self-criticism has had a healthy effect. It has spurred us on. It has reflected a normal American impatience to get on with the job. We are the kind of people who are never quite satisfied with anything short of miracles. . . .

[In 1942] we produced about 48,000 military planes—more than the airplane production of Germany, Italy and Japan put together. . . . I suspect Hitler and Tojo [q.v.] will find it difficult to explain to the German and Japanese people just why it is that a "decadent, inefficient democracy" can produce such phenomenal quantities of weapons and munitions—and fighting men. (Ibid.)

198. We have given the lie to certain misconceptions—especially the one which holds that the various blocs or groups within a free country cannot forego their political and economic differences in time of crisis and work together toward a common goal. (Ibid.)

199. While we have been achieving this miracle of production, during the past year, our Armed Forces have grown from a little over 2,000,000 to 7,000,000. In other words, we have withdrawn from the labor force and the farms some 5,000,000 of our younger workers. And in spite of this, our farmers have contributed their share to the common effort by producing the greatest quantity of food ever made available during a single year in all our history. (Ibid.)

200. Washington may be a madhouse—but only in the sense that it is the Capital City of a nation which is fighting mad. . . . And I think that Berlin and Rome and Tokyo, which had such contempt for the obsolete methods of democracy, would now gladly use all they could get of that same brand of madness. (Ibid.)

201. Victory in this war is the first and greatest goal before us. Victory in the peace is the next. That means striving toward the enlargement of the security of man here and throughout the world—and, finally, striving for the Fourth Freedom—Freedom from Fear. (Ibid.)

202. Undoubtedly a few Americans, even now, think that this Nation can end this war comfortably and then climb back into an American hole and pull the hole in after them.

But we have learned that we can never dig a hole so deep that it would be safe against predatory animals. We have also learned that if we do not pull the fangs of the predatory animals of this world, they will multiply and grow in strength—and they will be back at our throats once more in a short generation. (Ibid.)

203. In an attempt to ward off the inevitable disaster, the Axis propagandists are trying all of their old tricks in order to divide the United Nations. They seek to create the idea that if we win this war, Russia, England, China, and the United States are going to get into a cat-and-dog fight.

This is their final effort to turn one nation against another, in the vain hope that they may settle with one or two at a time—that any of us may be so gullible and so forgetful as to be duped into making "deals" at the expense of our Allies.

To these panicky attempts to escape the consequences of their crimes, we say—all the United Nations say—that the only terms on which we shall deal with an Axis government or any Axis factions are the terms proclaimed at Casablanca: "Unconditional Surrender." (Address following the Casablanca Conference [q.v.] February 12, 1943.)

204. Ask them [our servicemen] what they are fighting for, and every one of them will say: "I am fighting for my country." Ask them what they really mean by that and you will get what, on the surface, may seem to be a wide variety of answers. One will say he is fighting for the right to say what he pleases and to read and listen to what he likes.

Another will say he is fighting because he never wants to see the Nazi swastika flying over the First Baptist Church on Elm Street.

Another soldier will say he is fighting for the right to work and earn three square meals a day for himself and his folks.

Another will say he is fighting in this World War so that his children and grandchildren will not have to go back to Europe, or Africa or Asia to do this ugly job all over again.

But all these answers really add up to the same thing: every American fights for freedom. And today the personal freedom of every American and his family depends, and in the future will increasingly depend, upon the freedom of his neighbors in other lands. For today the whole world is one neighborhood. (Speech, White House Correspondents Association dinner, February 12, 1943.)

205. President Lincoln said in 1862, "Fellow Citizens, we cannot escape history. We of this Congress and this administration will be remembered in spite of ourselves. No personal significance or insignificance can spare one or another of us. The fiery trial through which we pass will light us . . . in honor or dishonor, to the latest generation."

Today, eighty years after Lincoln delivered that message, the fires of war are blazing across the whole horizon of mankind—from Kharkov to Kunming—from the Mediterranean to the Coral Sea—from Berlin to Tokyo.

Again—we cannot escape history. We have supreme confidence that with the help of God, honor will prevail. We have faith that future generations will know that here, in the middle of the Twentieth Century, there came the time when men of good will found a way to unite and produce and fight to destroy the forces of ignorance, intolerance, slavery, and war. (Ibid.)

206. From time to time since the present war began there have been reports that one or more of the Axis powers were seriously contemplating use of poisonous or noxious gases or other inhumane devices of warfare.

I have been loath to believe that any nation, even our present enemies, could or would be willing to loose upon mankind such terrible and inhumane weapons.

However, evidence that the Axis powers are making significant preparations indicative of such an intention is being reported with increasing frequency from a variety of sources.

Use of such weapons has been outlawed by the general opinion of civilized mankind. This country has not used them, and I hope that we never will be compelled to use them. I state categorically that we shall under no circumstances resort to the use of such weapons unless they are first used by our enemies. . . .

Any acts of this nature committed against any one of the United Nations will be regarded as having been committed against the United States itself and will be treated accordingly. (Statement, Washington, D.C., June 8, 1943.)

207. At this moment the combined armed forces of the United States and Great Britain . . . are carrying the war deep into the territory of your country. This is the direct consequence of the shameful leadership to which you have been subjected by Mussolini [q.v.] and his Fascist regime. (Joint statement with Prime Minister Churchill, addressed to the people of Italy after the invasion of Sicily, July 16, 1943.)

208. Mussolini [q.v.] carried you into this war as the satellite of a brutal destroyer of peoples and liberties.

Mussolini plunged you into this war, which he thought Hitler had already won. . . .

The time has now come for you, the Italian people, to consult your own self-respect and your own interest and your own desire for a restoration of national dignity, security and peace. The time has come for you to decide whether Italians shall die for Mussolini and Hitler—or live for Italy and for civilization. (Ibid.)

209. Among many other things, we are, today, laying plans for the return to civilian life of our gallant men and women in the armed services. They must not be demobilized into an environment of inflation and unemployment, to a place on a bread line or on a corner selling apples. We must, this time, have plans ready—instead of waiting to do a hasty, inefficient, and ill-considered job at the last moment.

I have assured our men in the armed forces that the American people would not let them down when the war is won. (Speech, laying the foundation for the "G.I. Bill of Rights," July 28, 1943.)

210. The least to which they are entitled [are] . . .

1. Mustering-out pay . . . to cover a reasonable period of time between his discharge and the finding of a job.

2. In case no job is found, . . . unemployment insurance. . . .

3. An opportunity for members of the armed services to get further education or trade training at the cost of their government.

4. Allowance of credit . . . under unemployment compensation and federal old-age and survivors insurance, for their period of service.

5. Improved and liberalized provisions for hospitalization, rehabilitation, and medical care for [the] disabled. . . .

6. Sufficient pensions for disabled. (Ibid.)

211. There are now rumors that Mussolini [q.v.] and members of his Fascist gang may attempt to take refuge in neutral territory. One day Hitler and his gang and Tojo [q.v.] and his gang will be trying to escape from their countries. I find it difficult to believe that any neutral country would give asylum to or extend protection to any of them. I can only say that the government of the United States would regard the action by a neutral government in affording asylum to Axis leaders or their tools as inconsistent with the principles for which the United Nations are fighting and that the United States Government hopes that no neutral government will permit its territory to be used as a place of refuge or otherwise assist such persons in any effort to escape their just deserts. (Statement after Mussolini was deposed by the king of Italy, July 30, 1943.)

212. Now is the time for every Italian to strike his blow. The liberating armies of the Western World are coming to your rescue. . . . The German terror in Italy will not last long. . . . Strike hard and strike home. . . . Have faith in your future. All will come well. March forward with your American and British friends in the great world movement toward freedom. (Statement to the Italian people, issued jointly with Winston Churchill, September 10, 1943.)

[Following the surrender of Italy and the Allied invasion of the Italian mainland.]

213. I hope, some day, everybody in America will realize what a debt he owes to George Marshall. There's just nobody like him. Nobody! (Spoken to Elliott Roosevelt [q.v.], Teheran, November 1943; quoted in *As He Saw It*, by Elliott Roosevelt.)

214. I learned more just talking to the Chiangs last night than I did from more than four hours of meeting with the Combined Chiefs. . . . More about the war that *isn't* being fought, and why. Chiang [Kai-shek's (q.v.)] troops aren't fighting at all—despite the reports that get printed in the papers. He claims his troops aren't trained, and have no equipment—and that's easy to believe. But it doesn't explain why he's been trying so hard to keep Stilwell [q.v.] from training Chinese troops. And it doesn't explain why he keeps thousands and thousands of his best men up in the northwest—up on the borders of Red China. (Spoken to Elliott Roosevelt [q.v.], Cairo, November 1943; Ibid.)

215. Buccaneer is off. (Message to Churchill, December 5, 1943.)

[Buccaneer was the code name of a planned amphibious operation off Burma. It would have been combined with a Chinese military offensive operation against the Japanese. Its cancellation indicated decreased confidence in Chiang Kai-shek's (q.v.) Chinese forces and increased emphasis on the forthcoming cross-Channel invasion of Europe.]

216. The commander selected to lead the continued attack from these other points [the invasion of Europe] is General Dwight D. Eisenhower. His performances in Africa, in Sicily and in Italy have been brilliant. He knows by practical and successful experience the way to coordinate air, sea and land power. All of these will be under his control. (Christmas Eve broadcast, December 24, 1943.)

217. The war is now reaching the stage where we shall all have to look forward to large casualty lists—dead, wounded and missing.

War entails just that. There is no easy road to victory. And the end is not yet in sight. (Ibid.)

218. Almighty God. Our sons, pride of our nation, this day have set upon a mighty endeavor, a struggle to preserve our republic, our religion, and our civilization, and to set free a suffering humanity. Lead them straight and true, give strength to their arms, stoutness to their hearts, steadfastness to their faith. (Radio broadcast, Prayer for the Normandy Invasion, D-Day [q.v.], June 6, 1944.)

219. The enemy is strong. He may hurl back our forces. But we shall return again and again, and we know that by Thy grace and by the righteousness of our cause, our sons will triumph. Some will never return. Embrace these, Father, and receive them, Thy heroic servants, into Thy Kingdom. (Ibid.)

220. With Thy blessing, we shall prevail. . . . Lead us to the saving of our country, and with our sister nations into a world unity that will spell a sure peace. (Ibid.)

221. [D-Day (q.v.) prayer for the armed forces] God of the Free, we pledge our hearts and lives today to the cause of all free mankind. Grant us victory over the tyrants who would enslave all free men and nations. Grant us faith and understanding to cherish all those who fight for freedom as if they were our brothers. Grant us brotherhood in hope and union, not only for the space of this bitter war but for the days to come which shall and must unite all the children of earth. (*Yank, the Army Weekly*, ca. June 7, 1944; quoted in *Yank: The Story of World War II Written by the Soldiers*.)

222. Our earth is but a small star in the great universe—yet of it we can make, if we choose, a planet unvexed by war, untroubled by hunger or fear, undivided by senseless distinctions of race, color, or theory. (Ibid.)

223. Grant us that courage and foreseeing to begin this task today, that our children and our children's children may be proud of the name of Man. The spirit of man has awakened and the soul of man has come forth. Grant us the wisdom and the vision to comprehend the greatness of man's spirit that suffers and endures so hugely for a goal beyond his own brief span. Grant us honor for our dead who died in the faith, honor for our living who work and strive for the faith, redemption and security for all captive lands and peoples. Grant us patience with the deluded and pity for the betrayed, and grant us the skill and valor that so cleansed the world of oppression and the old base doctrine that the strong must eat the weak because they are strong. (Ibid.)

224. Yet, most of all, grant us brotherhood, not only for this day but for all our years, a brotherhood not of words, but of acts and deeds. We are all of us children of earth—grant us that simple knowledge. If our brothers are oppressed, then we are oppressed. If they hunger, we hunger. If their freedom is taken away, our freedom is not secure. Grant us a common faith that man shall know bread and peace, that he shall know justice and righteousness, freedom and security, an equal opportunity and an equal chance to do his best, not only in our own lands but throughout the world, and in that faith let us march toward the clean world our hands can make.

Amen. (Ibid.)

225. Personally, I wished much in Honolulu [where a meeting on Pacific strategy had taken place] that you and I could swap places and personally, I have a hunch that you would make more of a go as President than I would as General in the retaking of the Philippines. (Letter to MacArthur, August 1944.)

226. These Republican leaders have not been content with attacks upon me, or my wife, or my sons—they now include my little dog, Fala. Unlike the members of my family, he resents this. Being a Scottie, as soon as he learned that the Republican fiction writers had concocted a story that I had left him behind on an Aleutian island and had sent a destroyer back to find him—at a cost to the taxpayers of two or three or twenty million dollars—his Scotch soul was furious. He has not been the same dog since. (Presidential campaign address, September 23, 1944.)

[The president, speaking to the International Teamsters Union, was responding to reports of an alleged misadventure during a wartime trip.]

227. It is all very well for us to make all kinds of preparations for the treatment of Germany, but there are some matters in regard to such treatment that lead me to believe that speed on these matters is not an essential at the present moment. It may be in a week, or it may be in a month, or it may be several months hence. I dislike making detailed plans for a country which we do not yet occupy. (Memo to Cordell Hull [q.v.], October 20, 1944; cited in *Diplomat among Warriors*, by Robert Murphy.)

228. We must emphasize the fact that the European Advisory Commission [a group of Americans, Britons, and Russians working on German occupation plans] is "advisory," and that you and I are not bound by this advice. This is something which is sometimes overlooked, and if they do not remember that word "advisory" they may go ahead and execute some of the advice which, when the time comes, we may not like at all. (Ibid.)

229. In view of the fact that we have not occupied Germany, I cannot agree at this moment as to what kind of a Germany we want in every detail. (Ibid.)

230. You know peace, like war, can succeed only when there is a will to enforce it, and where there is available power to enforce it. (Speech, October 21, 1944.)

231. I live in a small town and I always think in small town terms, but this goes for small towns as well as for big towns. A policeman would not be a very effective policeman, if when he saw a felon break into a house, he had to go to the town hall and call a town meeting to issue a warrant before the felon could be arrested.

So to my simple mind, it is clear that, if the world organization is to have any reality at all, our American representative must be endowed in advance by the people themselves, by constitutional means through their representatives in Congress, with authority to act. (Ibid.)

232. If we do not catch the international felon when we have our hands on him, if we let him get away with his loot, because the town council has not passed an ordinance authorizing his arrest, then we are not doing our share to prevent another world war. (Ibid.)

233. We seek peace—enduring peace. More than an end to war, we want an end to the beginnings of all wars—yes, an end to this brutal, inhuman and thoroughly impractical method of settling the differences between governments. (Jefferson-Jackson Day speech, scheduled for delivery on April 13, 1945.)

[Roosevelt died the day before.]

234. The once powerful, malignant Nazi state is crumbling, the Japanese war lords are receiving, in their own homeland, the retribution for which they asked when they attacked Pearl Harbor.

But the mere conquest of our enemies is not enough. We must go on to do all in our power to conquer the doubts and the fears, the ignorance and the greed, which made this horror possible. (Ibid.)

235. Today we are faced with the pre-eminent fact that, if civilization is to survive, we must cultivate the science of human relationships—the ability of all peoples, of all kinds, to live together and work together in the same world, at peace. (Ibid.)

236. Today as we move against the terrible scourge of war—as we go forward toward the greatest contribution that any generation of human beings can make in this world—the contribution of lasting peace, I ask you to keep up your faith. . . . And to you, and to all Americans who dedicate themselves with us to the making of an abiding peace, I say:

The only limit to our realization of tomorrow will be our doubts of today. Let us move forward with strong and active faith. (Ibid.)

JOSEPH STALIN

(1879–1953)

Stalin was dictator of the Soviet Union during World War II. A Communist revolutionary as a youth, he was twice sent to Siberia for his activities. After the Communist Revolution, he rose to power quickly. After the death of Lenin, he took charge. In August 1939, he concluded a nonaggression pact with Nazi Germany in which the two agreed to split up Poland. When the Nazis invaded the Soviet Union in June 1941, Stalin rallied his forces to defend Mother Russia. For three years, he pushed the Allies for a second front in Europe. He agreed to come into the war against Japan three months after victory in Europe. The declaration of war came just ninety days after V-E Day. For Russia, it was the shortest, cheapest war in its history, lasting less than a week.

237. I hope that the German-Soviet nonaggression pact will bring about a decided turn for the better in the political relations between our countries. (Telegram to Hitler, August 21, 1939.)

238. The assent of the German Government to the conclusion of a nonaggression pact provides the foundation for eliminating the political tension and for the establishment of peace and collaboration between our countries.

The Soviet Government have instructed me to inform you that they agree to Herr von Ribbentrop's [q.v.] arriving in Moscow on August 23. (Ibid.)

239. We had formed the impression that the British and French Governments were not resolved to go to war if Poland were attacked, but that they hoped the diplomatic lineup of Britain, France, and Russia would deter Hitler. We were sure it would not. (Recalling events of summer 1939 prior to the signing of the Nazi-Soviet Nonaggression Pact [q.v.], related to Winston Churchill, August 1942; quoted in *The Second World War: The Gathering Storm*, by Winston Churchill.)

240. INDIRECT DISCOURSE: Stalin was sure that the Germans [who invaded on June 22, 1941] would be defeated, but by the most sacrificial means; the Red Army would retreat and destroy everything as it went, and "our forces are numberless." In short, a war of attrition. Britain and America, Stalin noted in passing, had said that they would send aid, but his message to the Soviet people was that their sacrifices alone would overwhelm the Germans. (Radio broadcast, July 3, 1941; from *Stalin: Man and Ruler*, by Robert H. McNeal.)

"The assent of the German Government to the conclusion of a nonaggression pact provides the foundation for eliminating the political tension and for the establishment of peace and collaboration between our countries."
—JOSEPH STALIN, TELEGRAM TO HITLER

Two days later, Soviet Foreign Minister Molotov signs the Nazi-Soviet Pact while German Foreign Minister Ribbentrop and Stalin look on.

241. We secured peace for our country for one and a half years, as well as an opportunity of preparing our forces for defense if fascist Germany risked attacking our country in defiance of the pact. (Radio broadcast, July 3, 1941.)

[Referring to the Nazi-Soviet Nonaggression Pact of 1939.]

242. Not a step backward! (Order of the Day, July 28, 1942.)

243. The situation at Stalingrad has deteriorated further. The enemy stands two miles from the city. Stalingrad may fall today or tomorrow if the northern group of forces does not give immediate assistance. See to it that the commanders of forces north and northwest of Stalingrad strike the enemy at once. . . . No delay can be tolerated. To delay now is tantamount to a crime. (Message to Marshal Zhukov [q.v.], September 3, 1942; cited in *Enemy at the Gates*, by William Craig.)

244. In view of the absence of a second front in Europe, the Red Army alone is bearing the whole weight of the war.

Nevertheless the Red Army has not only stood firm against the onslaught of the German Fascist hordes, but has also in the course of the war become a menace to the Fascist army. (Order of the Day on the 25th anniversary of the Red Army, February 22, 1943.)

245. The struggle against the German invaders is not yet ended. . . . It would be stupid to suppose the Germans will give up even one kilometer of our land without a struggle.

The Red Army has before it a severe struggle against the cunning, cruel and as yet strong enemy. . . .

Long live our great motherland! Long live our glorious Red Army, our valiant Red Navy, our intrepid men and women guerrillas! . . .

Death to the German invaders! (Ibid.)

246. The babble about peace in the fascist camp only indicates that they are going through a grave crisis.

But of what kind of peace can one talk with the imperialist bandits from the German-fascist camp who have flooded Europe with blood and studded it with gallows? Is it not clear that only the utter routing of the Hitlerite armies and the unconditional surrender of Hitlerite Germany can bring peace to Europe? Is it not because the German fascists sense the coming catastrophe that they babble about peace? (Order of the Day, May 1, 1943.)

247. The Great Patriotic War of the Soviet Union. (Designation first used by Stalin, July 1943.)

248. The Pope? How many divisions does *he* have? (Attributed, ca. end 1943.)

249. There has been no instance yet in the history of wars of the enemy jumping into the abyss by himself. To win a war one must lead the enemy to the abyss and push him in to it. (Order of the Day, February 23, 1944.)

250. The history of war never witnessed such a grandiose operation [as the cross-Channel invasion]. Napoleon himself never attempted it. Hitler envisaged it but was a fool for never having attempted it. (Conversation with Averell Harriman, June 10, 1944.)

251. INDIRECT DISCOURSE: There was dissatisfaction, he [Stalin] continued, because the Polish Government was not elected. It would naturally be better to have a Government based on free elections, but the war had so far prevented that. But the day was near when elections could be held. Until then we must deal with the Provisional Government, as we had dealt, for instance, with General De Gaulle's [q.v.] Government in France, which also was not elected. (Statement at Yalta Conference [q.v.], February 8, 1945; cited in *The Second World War: Triumph and Tragedy*, by Winston Churchill.)

[Following the German invasion of 1939, the Polish government had fled to London to set up a government-in-exile. When the Soviet Union drove the Germans out of Poland, it created what it called a provisional government for Poland. Stalin supported the provisional government as the legitimate one, while the United States and Great Britain backed the one in exile. The issue of a democratic Polish government was discussed at length at Yalta.]

252. INDIRECT DISCOURSE: He [Stalin] did not know whether Bierut [of the Moscow-supported Polish provisional government] or General De Gaulle [q.v.] enjoyed greater authority, but it had been possible to make a treaty with General De Gaulle, so why could we not do the same with an enlarged Polish Government, which would be no less democratic? It was not reasonable to demand more from Poland than from France. . . . If we approached the matter without prejudice we should be able to find common ground. The situation was not as tragic as I [Churchill] thought, and the question could be settled if too much importance was not attached to secondary matters and if we concentrated on essentials. (Ibid.)

[Stalin promised Roosevelt and Churchill that the provisional government of Poland would be expanded and that free elections would be held. Neither promise was kept.]

253. On behalf of the Soviet government and myself, personally, I express our profound condolence to the government of the United States of America on the occasion of the premature death of President Roosevelt. . . .

The government of the Soviet Union expresses sincere sympathy to the American people in their great loss and their conviction that the policy of friendship between the great powers who are shouldering the main burden of war against the common enemy will continue in the future. (Message on the death of Roosevelt, April 13, 1945.)

[Another message is attributed to Stalin: that he asked his ambassador in Washington to find out if an autopsy had been performed on Roosevelt's body. Stalin apparently suspected that the president might have been poisoned.]

254. The Fatherland and the Party will never forget the role played by the commanders of the Soviet armies in our national defensive struggle. The names of all these generals who gained the victories and saved the Fatherland will stand forever carved on the tablets of honor which history will erect on the battlefields. Of these battlefields, one is of very special significance, that is the field on which the battle of Moscow, the capital of our Soviet Union, was fought. And the name of Comrade [Georgi] Zhukov [q.v.] remains indissolubly connected with this battlefield as the symbol of victory. (Banquet speech, Moscow, May 25, 1945.)

2

Military Officers

HAROLD ALEXANDER
(1891–1969)

A field marshal in the British army, Alexander took part in many crucial battles of the war, including Dunkirk, El Alamein (q.v.), Tunisia, Sicily, and Italy. Some military historians believe that the victory at El Alamein, credited to Bernard Montgomery (q.v.), really belonged to Alexander, who laid out the plan that Montgomery carried out. It is no secret that Eisenhower asked for Alexander instead of Montgomery to head British forces in the invasion of Western Europe.

255. The knowledge not only of the enemy's precise strength and disposition but also how, when and where he intends to carry out his operations has brought a new dimension into the prosecution of the war. (Tunisia, ca. March 1943; cited in *The Ultra Secret*, by F. W. Winterbotham).

SEIZO ARISUE

(n.d.)

Seizo Arisue was a lieutenant general on the Imperial Japanese Army general staff. He and Lieutenant General Torashiro Kawabe were the sources for the evaluation below.

256. INDIRECT DISCOURSE:The strategists at Imperial General Headquarters [Arisue and Kawabe] believed that, if they could succeed in inflicting unacceptable losses on the United States in the Kyushu operation, convince the American people of the huge sacrifices involved in an amphibious invasion of Japan, and make them aware of the determined fighting of the Japanese army and civilian population, they might be able to postpone, if not escape altogether, a crucial battle in the Kanto [Tokyo] area. In this way, they hoped to gain time and grasp an opportunity which would lead to the termination of hostility on more favorable terms than those which unconditional surrender offered. (Intelligence report to General MacArthur, based on interviews after the war, ca. late 1945; cited in *Code-Name Downfall: The Secret Plan to Invade Japan—and Why Truman Dropped the Bomb*, by Thomas B. Allen and Norman Polmar.)

HENRY H. ARNOLD

(1886–1950)

The Deputy Chief of Staff for Air before Pearl Harbor, Arnold would later become commanding general of the U.S. Army Air Forces.

257. Issue following instructions to all units under your command. The present critical situation demands that all precautions be taken at once against subversive activities. Take steps to protect your personnel against subversive propaganda, protect all activities against espionage, and protect against sabotage of your equipment, property, and establishments. This does not authorize any illegal measures. Avoid unnecessary alarm and publicity. Protective measures should be confined to those essential to security. On or before December 5, this year, reports be submitted to Chief of Army Air Forces of all steps initiated by you to comply with these instructions. (Cable to General MacArthur, November 28, 1941; cited in *The Brereton Diaries*, by Lewis H. Brereton.)

258. How in the hell could an experienced airman like you get caught with your planes on the ground? That's what we sent you there for, to avoid just what happened. (Telephone call to General Lewis H. Brereton [q.v.] in the Philippines, December 11, 1941; Ibid.)

[In his book, Brereton says that he told Arnold that he had tried to do everything he could to get authorization to attack Japanese air bases on Formosa on December 8 but had been relegated to a "strictly defensive attitude." Although he did not say it to Arnold at the time, Brereton adds in his book: "Weather, fatigue, badly needed repairs and widely dispersed aircraft seriously curtailed our operations."]

CLAUDE AUCHINLECK
(1884–1981)

This British field marshal led forces in Norway, India, North Africa, and Burma. He was replaced in North Africa by Field Marshal Harold Alexander (q.v.).

259. There exists a real danger that our friend Rommel [q.v.] is becoming a kind of magician or bogey-man to our troops, who are talking far too much about him. He is by no means a superman, although he is undoubtedly very energetic and able. Even if he were a superman it would still be highly undesirable that our men should credit him with supernatural powers. I wish you to dispel by all possible means the idea that Rommel represents something more than an ordinary German general. The important thing now is to see that we do not always talk of Rommel when we mean the enemy in Libya. We must refer to "the Germans" or "the Axis powers" or "the enemy" and not always keep harping on Rommel. Please ensure that this order is put into immediate effect, and impress upon all Commanders that, from a psychological point of view, it is a matter of the highest importance. (Letter to all commanders and chiefs of staff, North Africa, 1942; quoted in *Rommel: The Desert Fox*, by Desmond Young.)

PATRICK BELLINGER

(1886–1962)

Patrick Bellinger was an American admiral in charge of the Pacific fleet's air corps at Pearl Harbor.

260. Air raid Pearl Harbor. This is no drill! (First report of the attack, December 7, 1941.)

WERNER VON BLOMBERG

(1878–1946)

Blomberg was the Reich Minister for War and commander in chief of the German Armed Forces before the war began. Later, Hitler would personally assume that role.

261. The intention to unleash a European war is held just as little by Germany. Nevertheless, the politically fluid world situation, which does not preclude surprising incidents, demands a continuous preparedness for war of the German Armed Forces.

To counter attacks at any time, and to enable the military exploitation of politically favorable opportunities should they occur.

The further working on mobilization without public announcement in order to put the Armed Forces in a position to begin a war suddenly and by surprise both as regards strength and time. (Directive for the United Preparation for War of the Armed Forces, to come into force on August 1, 1937; issued June 24, 1937 [Top Secret]; cited in *Nazi Conspiracy and Aggression*, by the Office of United States Chief of Counsel for Prosecution of Axis Criminality.)

262. Special preparations are to be made for the following eventualities: Armed intervention against Austria, warlike entanglement with Red Spain [then in a civil war]. . . .

[German actions against Austria and Czechoslovakia might involve] England, Poland, Lithuania [who might] take part in a war against us. (Ibid.)

263. Probable warlike eventualities. . . .

War on two fronts with focal point in the West.

Suppositions. In the West, France is the opponent. Belgium may side with France, either at once or later or not at all. It is also possible that France may violate Belgium's neutrality if the latter is neutral. She will certainly violate that of Luxembourg. (Ibid.)

264. The military-political starting point used as a basis for concentration plans . . . can be aggravated if either England, Poland or Lithuania join on the side of our opponents. Thereupon our military position would be worsened to an unbearable, even hopeless, extent. The political leaders will therefore do everything to keep these countries neutral, above all England and Poland. (Ibid.)

GUENTHER BLUMENTRITT

(n.d.)

Blumentritt was a German general who became Chief of Staff to General von Rundstedt (q.v.). He was involved in the German assault on France in 1940 and on the Soviet Union in 1941.

265. Hitler . . . gave us his opinion that the war would be finished in six weeks. After that he wanted to conclude a reasonable peace with France, and then the way would be free for an agreement with Britain. (Rundstedt headquarters, Charleville, France, events of May 24, 1940, the day after Hitler ordered a puzzling halt to German forces about to cut off British forces from Dunkirk; from *The German Generals Talk*, by B. H. Liddell Hart.)

266. He [Hitler] then astonished us by speaking with admiration of the British Empire, of the necessity for its existence, and of the civilization that Britain had brought into the world. . . . He said that all he wanted from Britain was that she should acknowledge Germany's position on the Continent. . . . He concluded by saying that his aim was to make peace with Britain on a basis that she would regard as compatible with her honor to accept. (Ibid.)

267. INDIRECT DISCOURSE: He [Blumentritt] felt that the "halt" [at Dunkirk] had been called for more than military reasons, and that it was part of a political scheme to make peace easier to reach. If the British Army had been captured at Dunkirk, the British people might have felt that their honor had suffered a stain which they must wipe out. By letting it escape Hitler hoped to conciliate them. (Ibid.)

268. Then the weather suddenly broke and almost overnight the full fury of the Russian winter was upon us. The thermometer suddenly dropped to thirty degrees of frost. This was accompanied by heavy falls of snow. Within a few days the countryside presented the traditional picture of a Russian winter. (Winter, 1941; from *The Fatal Decisions*, edited by Seymour Freiden and William Richardson.)

269. The battle of Moscow was the first major German defeat on land during the Second World War. It marked the end of the Blitzkrieg technique which had won Hitler and his Wehrmacht such spectacular victories. . . . It was in Russia that the first fatal decisions were taken. From the political point of view, perhaps the most fatal of all had been the decision to attack that country in the first place. . . . Many of our leaders had grossly underestimated the new enemy. This was partly due to ignorance. . . . Several of our responsible senior officers had never campaigned in the East, having spent the whole of the First World War on the Western Front, and had no idea of the difficulties presented by the terrain nor of the toughness of the Russian fighting man. They chose to ignore the warnings of the experts. (October 1941; Ibid.)

270. When Moscow was . . . almost in sight, the mood both of commanders and troops changed. With amazement and disappointment we discovered in late October and early November [1941] that the beaten Russians seemed quite unaware that as a military force they had almost ceased to exist. During these weeks enemy resistance stiffened. . . . Marshal Zhukov [q.v.] had now assumed command. . . . For weeks his men had been constructing a defensive position in depth. . . . Skillfully camouflaged strong points, wire entanglements and thick minefields now filled the forests which covered the western approaches to Moscow. (Ibid.)

271. Within the next few days Marshal Zhukov [q.v.] was to launch the great Russian counteroffensive which began on December 6th [1941]. . . . The turning point in the East had been reached: our hopes of knocking Russia out of the war in 1941 had been dashed. (Ibid.)

272. Every soldier outside Moscow knew that this was a battle for life or death. . . . In 1941 the choice for the Germans was only to hold fast or to be annihilated. (Ibid.)

TADEUSZ BOR-KOMOROWSKI

(1895–1966)

Bor-Komorowski led the underground uprising against the Germans in Warsaw in August 1944. The battle began as the Russian army approached the gates of the city.

273. At exactly five o'clock [on August 1, 1944] thousands of windows flashed as they were flung open. From all sides a hail of bullets struck passing Germans, riddling their buildings and their marching formations. In the twinkling of an eye the remaining civilians disappeared from the streets. From the entrances of houses our men streamed out and rushed to the attack. In 15 minutes an entire city of a million inhabitants was engulfed in the fight. Every kind of traffic ceased. As a big communications center where roads from north, south, east, and west converged, in the immediate rear of the German front, Warsaw ceased to exist. The battle for the city was on. (Events of August 1, 1944; quoted in *The Second World War: Triumph and Tragedy*, by Winston Churchill.)

[The Red Army not only stopped its advance on Warsaw but actually pulled back several miles. The Soviet leaders not only refused to aid the uprising but vetoed allowing British or American supply planes from landing on Soviet airfields after long-range flights from Italian bases to Warsaw. After two months, the uprising was crushed by the Germans. Churchill would later call the affair "the martyrdom of Warsaw."]

OMAR N. BRADLEY
(1893–1981)

One of the top American commanders in the European theater, General Bradley led armies in North Africa, Sicily, France, Belgium, and Germany. His armies landed at Normandy, broke out at St. Lo, liberated Paris, were bloodied at the Battle of the Bulge (q.v.), crossed the Rhine, and linked up with Russian forces on the Elbe River.

274. Patton [q.v.] snapped at the assignment to Tunisia when Ike offered it to him. In the words of Eisenhower, Patton was to rejuvenate the jaded II Corps and bring it to a "fighting pitch." By the third day after his arrival, the II Corps staff was fighting mad—but at Patton, not the Germans.

For George had set out deliberately to shock II Corps into a realization that the easygoing days were ended. Rather than wait for the effect of this change in command to filter down to the divisions, Patton sought a device that would instantly bring it home to every GI in the corps. He found what he was looking for in uniform regulations. [Patton set up a system of fines for soldiers who violated dress regulations.] (Events of March 1943, Tunisia; from *A Soldier's Story*, by Oman N. Bradley.)

275. In a radio message from Rome [Premier Badoglio (q.v.)] begged Ike to delay the [Italian] surrender until after the Allied landing [at Salerno].

Eisenhower minced no words. . . . "I intend to broadcast the existence of the armistice at the hour originally planned. . . ."

At the same time, however, he reluctantly ordered [General Matthew] Ridgway to cancel the drop of his 82d Division on Rome. Badoglio had indicated that the Italian government could not guarantee a safe landing. Eisenhower also called for the immediate return to Carthage of Brigadier General Maxwell D. Taylor, then underground in Rome. . . . Taylor was to have arranged for safe delivery of the airdromes in the vicinity of Rome. This hasty switch on the eve of [General Mark] Clark's [q.v.] invasion was to shelve the 82d Division at a time when it was most desperately needed. For there was insufficient time left to shift the 82d back to its original objective at Capua in support of the Salerno landing. (Recalling events of September 1943; Ibid.)

276. Because England had been counted upon to quit with the fall of France, the enemy had failed to provide the craft he would require for a cross-Channel invasion. That failure perhaps more than any other doomed Germany to defeat. (ca. June 1945; Ibid.)

277. Among the Western Allies three . . . giants towered above all others during the last World War—Roosevelt, Churchill, and Marshall. Together they probably influenced the lives of more men than any other triumvirate in the history of mankind. (Ibid.)

278. Montgomery's luster was dimmed not by timidity as his critics allege, but by his apparent reluctance to squeeze the utmost advantage out of every gain or success. For Monty insisted upon a "tidy" front even when tidiness forced him to slow down an advance. (Ibid.)

279. Patton . . . had one enemy he could not vanquish and that was his own quick tongue. (Ibid.)

280. [In the spring of 1944] we could still not free our minds from the fear that Stalin might make a deal and leave us to face the Axis alone. If we were to fail on the Overlord invasion, we might never get a second chance. (Ibid.)

281. [T]he battle belonged that morning [D-Day (q.v.)] to the thin, wet line of khaki that dragged itself ashore on the Channel coast of France. (Ibid.)

282. You must know after what has happened I cannot serve under Montgomery [q.v.]. If he is to be put in command of all ground forces, you must send me home, for if Montgomery goes in over me, I will have lost the confidence of my command. (Statement to Eisenhower, January 1945; Ibid.)

[Following rumors of a Montgomery promotion.]

WALTHER VON BRAUCHITSCH
(1881–1948)

Brauchitsch was commander in chief of the German army from 1938 to 1941. Initial victories in Poland, the Low Countries, and France were overshadowed by defeats in the Soviet Union. Following his resignation, Brauchitsch was succeeded by Hitler himself.

283. You ought not to have shown this to me. It is a matter of high treason. We cannot under any pretext contemplate that sort of thing. We are at war. It may be permissible to discuss whether we can make contact with a foreign power in time of peace, but in wartime nothing of this kind can be done. Moreover it is less a question of parties now; this is an ideological struggle. The elimination of Hitler would serve no purpose. (Spoken to General Franz Halder [q.v.], February 1940; cited in *Canaris*, by Andre Brissaud.)

[Brauchitsch was referring to a document shown to him by Halder. Report X, as it was called, had come about through secret discussions of anti-Nazi Germans, the Vatican, and Allied diplomatic figures. The document cited the possible conditions under which peace could be concluded with the Allies. It included the elimination of Hitler and the Nazis from power in Germany. The Sudeten territory of Czechoslovakia would remain with Germany, and plebiscite votes would be held in the disputed area of the Polish Corridor as well as Austria.]

284. A frontal attack against a defense line, on too narrow a front, with no good prospects of surprise, and with insufficient forces reinforced only in driblets. (Analysis of Operation Sea Lion, Hitler's plan to invade England, September 1940; cited in *Operation Sea Lion*, by Peter Fleming.)

LEWIS H. BRERETON
(1890–1967)

A U.S. Army general, Brereton was in charge of the Far East Air Force in the Philippines at the time of Pearl Harbor. On the first day of the war—December 8 in the Philippines—Brereton was ready to launch a bombing raid on Japanese air bases on the island of Formosa. His superiors, however, had put the air force in a defensive posture, and a Japanese air attack on Clark Field destroyed a large part of Brereton's force. Brereton was reassigned to Java in the Dutch East Indies. Later, he would serve in Australia, the Middle East, and Europe. He helped plan the Ploesti Raid (q.v.) of 1943. In the summer of 1944, he headed the 1st Allied Airborne Army in operation Market-Garden (q.v.), an unsuccessful thrust into Holland.

285. Two messages from the War Department alerted us to the possibility of an attack by Japan at any hour. (Diary excerpt, Manila, November 30, 1941; from *The Brereton Diaries*, by Lewis H. Brereton.)

286. I grabbed the phone and talked to General [Richard] Sutherland, who informed me that the Japs had bombed Pearl Harbor . . . and that a state of war existed. It came as a surprise to no one. (Diary excerpt, Manila, December 8, 1941; Ibid.)

287. The force of 164 bombers roared at tree-top level [over the Ploesti oil fields] through a curtain of ground fire and, in some cases, concentrated attacks by enemy fighters. Explosions of boilers and gas-storage tanks spread flame and smoke. . . .

Liberators flew so low that they dipped their wings through tree tops. One plane actually brought back pieces of corn stalks in its bomb bay. . . . One boiler house exploded so violently that it destroyed a Liberator flying over the target. Many of the men said that it became almost unbearably hot in their planes as they flew through the wall of flames, licking 300 feet and higher. (Diary excerpt, Benghazi, North Africa, August 1, 1943; Ibid.)

288. The German progress with jet aircraft places them way ahead of us in this field. If they can make them in sufficient strength they may become a serious threat to our deep heavy-bomber penetration. (Diary excerpt, Normandy, France, July 30, 1944; Ibid.)

289. Despite the failure of the 2nd Army to get through to Arnhem and establish a permanent bridgehead over the Lower Rhine, Operation Market was a brilliant success. The 101st Division took all its objectives as planned; the 82nd Division dominated the southern end of the bridge at Nijmegen until noon of D-plus-l, by which time it had been planned for the Guards Armored to be there; the 1st British Division similarly dominated the Arnhem bridge from its northern end until noon of D-plus-3, 24 hours later than the time set for the arrival of the 2nd Army. Hence the airborne troops accomplished what was expected of them. It was the breakdown of the 2nd Army's timetable on the first day—their failure to reach Endhoven in 6 to 8 hours as planned—that caused the delay in the taking of the Nijmegen bridge and the failure at Arnhem. (Report to General George Marshall and General Henry Arnold [q.v.], October 3, 1944; Ibid.)

[This was from Brereton's report to his superiors on Market-Garden (q.v.). Market was the airborne operation. Garden was the ground operation, which failed to reach its objectives.]

MARK W. CLARK

(1896–1984)

Clark was an American general who led U.S. forces in the invasion of French North Africa and Italy. Prior to the African operation, he landed by submarine to negotiate as bloodless an invasion as possible. He was in charge of American landings at Salerno and Anzio, Italy. His most controversial command was the assault across the Rapido River.

290. YBSOB [for "yellow-bellied son of a bitch"]. (Algiers, North Africa, November 1942; cited in *Diplomat among Warriors*, by Robert Murphy.)

[Used, in reports to Eisenhower, to describe French officials in North Africa who were slow in responding to Allied requests.]

291. I maintain that it is essential that I make that attack [across the Rapido River], fully expecting heavy losses, in order to hold all the German troops on my front and draw more to it, thereby clearing the way for "Shingle" [code name for the Anzio landing]. (Diary excerpt, January 20, 1944; from *Calculated Risk*, by Mark Clark.)

292. The men had to cross a low, muddy area, heavily mined, to reach the steep river-bank. Heavy enemy fire not only caused casualties, but destroyed the white tape that had been used to mark lanes previously cleared through the minefields. Visibility was poor, considerable confusion developed, and it was nine o'clock in the evening by the time elements of A and B Companies of the 1st Battalion had forced a way across the Rapido. . . .

Under the most intense and steady resistance by hostile artillery, mortars, and *Nebelwerfer* [rocket launchers], as well as machine-gun and rifle fire, the 1st Battalion put up a tremendous fight to secure its position. Engineers struggled with footbridges, most of which were destroyed by mines or artillery as they were being erected. From remnants of four damaged and destroyed bridges one was finally installed to permit the rest of Companies A and B to get across the river. The Company C attack put only a few men across, despite the efforts of the other two companies to silence the enemy fire along the west bank. Men were swept down the icy river. Mines on the banks and in the water took a heavy toll. Rubber boats were sunk by small-arms fire. Assault boats were knocked out by mortar fire. On the hostile bank the men who had crossed successfully encountered barbed wire, mines, machine-gun fire, and steady artillery barrage. (Description of events of January 20–21, 1944; Ibid.)

[The excerpt deals with a handful of the units involved in the Rapido River assault. Clark mentions several others, who fought as bravely and met similar fates.]

292a. The Anzio convoys are at sea. We have no indications, as yet, that the enemy has discovered them. (Diary excerpt, January 21, 1944; Ibid.)

BELTON COOPER

(n.d.)

Cooper was a captain in the U.S. Third Armored Division. It entered Nordhausen, Germany, in April 1945. It was near the location of a German V-2 rocket factory. The captain came upon some of the slave laborers.

293. A strange apparition emerged from the side of the building. A tall frail-looking creature with striped pants and naked from the waist up. . . . I could not tell whether it was male or female. There was no face, merely a gaunt human skull staring out. The teeth were exposed in a broad grin and in place of eyes were merely dark sockets. . . .

We passed three large stacks of what appeared to be waste paper and garbage piled in rows six feet high and 400 feet long. The stench was overwhelming and as I looked I noticed that parts of the stack were moving. To my absolute horror, it dawned on me that these stacks contained the bodies of naked human beings. A few were still alive and they were writhing in the excrement and human waste. (Recalling events of April 11, 1945, memoir, Eisenhower Center, University of New Orleans; cited in *Citizen Soldiers*, by Stephen E. Ambrose.)

ANDREW B. CUNNINGHAM
(1883–1963)

A British admiral serving in the Mediterranean, Cunningham protected the British lifeline from Gibraltar to Suez. He led naval forces in the invasions of North Africa, Sicily, Italy, and southern France. In 1943 he became First Sea Lord.

294. Be pleased to inform their Lordships that the Italian Battle Fleet now lies at anchor under the guns of the fortress at Malta. (Message to London, September 10, 1943.)

[Reporting the safe arrival of the Italian fleet, following the surrender of Italy.]

W. SCOTT CUNNINGHAM
(n.d.)

Defended by 400 U.S. Marines, Wake Island held out against the Japanese invaders for two weeks before surrendering the Pacific outpost. Here, Navy Commander Cunningham tells the story behind an oft-quoted quotation.

295. We had heard with pride that President Roosevelt himself had hailed Wake's resistance effort, and we had tried to discount as propaganda for enemy consumption the gloomy reports that relief for Wake would not be expected. But now we heard something that set our teeth on edge.

When Pearl Harbor asked the defenders of Wake if there was anything that could be done for them, the story went, an answer came back:

"Yes. Send us more Japs."

If there was anything we didn't need at Wake it was more Japs. I had sent no such message, and since the release of dispatches was at all times under my direct control, I dismissed the story as a reporter's dream, as did most of the others on the atoll who heard it. Not until years later, in fact, did I learn through Bucky Henshaw, one of the decoding officers, how the story began. . . .

Part of the decoders' job is to "pad" messages with nonsense at the beginning and end as a device to throw off enemy code-breakers. Such padding was either entirely meaningless or, on occasion, something involving a private joke. . . . It was not expected that the padding would be filed with the text of the message.

On the morning we turned back the invasion fleet . . . [the decoder] had done the padding on my message. He had begun it:

SEND US STOP NOW IS THE TIME FOR ALL GOOD MEN TO COME TO THE AID OF THEIR PARTY STOP CUNNINGHAM MORE JAPS. . . .

What the world took as a gesture of defiant heroism from Wake Island was actually nothing of the kind and was never intended to be. (From *Wake Island Command*, by W. Scott Cunningham, with Lydel Sims.)

CHARLES de GAULLE
(1890–1970)

De Gaulle was a French general who decided to carry on the war against Nazi Germany even after the French government had signed an armistice in June 1940. De Gaulle became head of the Free French National Committee, which was based in London. Tens of thousands of French colonial troops were mobilized to fight the Nazis. Later in the war, de Gaulle competed for leadership with Admiral Jean Darlan (q.v.) and General Henri Giraud. After the former was assassinated and the latter dropped from the scene, de Gaulle became undisputed leader of Free France. He insisted on taking part in the liberation of Paris in 1944. After the war, he became the most powerful French political leader.

296. Certain circles [in France] saw the enemy in Stalin rather than in Hitler. They busied themselves with finding means of striking Russia, either by aiding Finland or bombarding Baku or landing at Istanbul, much more than in coming to grips with Germany. (Recalling events of March 1940; from *Memoires de Guerre*, Vol. 1, by Charles de Gaulle.)

297. The leaders who, for many years past, have been at the head of the French armed forces, have set up a government.

Alleging the defeat of our armies, this government has entered into negotiations with the enemy with the view to bringing about a cessation of hostilities. It is quite true that we were, and still are, overwhelmed by enemy mechanized forces, both on the ground and in the air. It was the tanks, the planes, and the tactics of the Germans, far more than their numbers, that forced our armies to retreat. It was the German tanks, planes and tactics that took our leaders by surprise and brought them to their present plight.

But has the last word been said? Must we abandon all hope? Is our defeat final? No! (Radio broadcast, London, June 18, 1940; cited in *Churchill and de Gaulle*, by François Kersaudy.)

298. Speaking in full knowledge of the facts, I ask you to believe me when I say that the cause of France is not lost. The very factors that brought about our defeat may one day lead us to victory.

For France is not alone! She is not alone! She is not alone! Behind her is a vast empire, and she can make common cause with the British Empire, which commands the seas and is continuing the struggle. Like England, she can draw unreservedly on the immense industrial resources of the United States. (Ibid.)

299. This war is not limited to our unfortunate country. The outcome of the struggle has not been decided by the Battle of France. This is a world war. Mistakes have been made. There have been delays and untold suffering, but the fact remains that there still exists in the world everything we need to crush our enemies some day. Today we are crushed by the sheer weight of mechanized force hurled against us, but we can still look to a future in which even greater mechanized force will bring us victory. Therein lies the destiny of the world. (Ibid.)

300. I, General de Gaulle, now in London, call on all French officers and men who are at present on British soil, or may be in the future, with or without their arms; I call on all engineers and skilled workmen from the armament factories who are at present on British soil, or may be in the future, to get in touch with me. Whatever happens, the flame of French resistance must not and shall not die. (Ibid.)

301. The battle is about to begin and I will speak on the wireless. That is all right. But as regards discussing the question of administration [of liberated French territory], it is clear that the President [Roosevelt] has never wanted to see me, and yet now suddenly I am being told, I must go and talk to the President, etc. . . . Why do you seem to think that I need to submit my candidacy for the authority in France to Roosevelt? The French government exists. I have nothing to ask, in this respect, of the United States of America nor of Great Britain. (Statement to Winston Churchill just outside General Eisenhower's headquarters in southern England, June 4, 1944; Ibid.)

[With D-Day (q.v.) less than forty-eight hours away, de Gaulle complains about the forthcoming administration of French territory.]

302. This being said, it is important for all the Allies that the relations between the French administration and the military command should be organized. Nine months ago we proposed as much. Since the armies are about to land in France, I understand your haste to see the question settled. We ourselves are ready to do so. But where is the American representative? Without him, as you well know, we can decide nothing in this respect. Furthermore, I notice that the Washington and London governments have made arrangements to do without an agreement with us. I have just learned, for example, that despite our warnings, the troops and services about to land are provided with so-called French currency, issued by foreign powers, which the government of the republic refuses to recognize and which, according to orders of the inter-Allied command, will have compulsory circulation on French territory. I expect that tomorrow General Eisenhower, acting on the instructions of the President of the United States and in agreement with you, will proclaim that he is taking France under his authority. How do you expect us to come to terms on this basis? (Ibid.)

303. The decisive battle has begun. . . . Of course, it is the battle of France, and it is France's battle! . . . For the sons of France, whoever they may be, wherever they may be, the simple and sacred duty is to fight the enemy with all available means. . . . The directives issued by the French government and by the French leaders who have been delegated to issue them must be followed to the letter. . . . Behind the heavy clouds of our blood and our tears, the sunshine of our greatness is presently reappearing! (Broadcast to the people of France, June 6, 1944; Ibid.)

KARL DITTMAR

(n.d.)

General Dittmar commented on German military affairs over Berlin radio. His analyses were regarded as unusually frank.

304. I always felt that I was walking a tightrope with a noose around my neck. (Quoted in *The German Generals Talk*, by B. H. Liddell Hart.)

KARL DOENITZ

(1891–1980)

Commander in chief of the German navy, Doenitz was personally chosen by Hitler to take over the German government on the Fuehrer's death. A week after Hitler's suicide, Doenitz authorized the unconditional surrender of the Reich. Early in the war, Doenitz was in charge of the U-boat operation. It was he who conceived the idea of a "wolf-pack" approach to destroy Allied shipping. Immensely successful in the early years of the war, the U-boat was doomed by new detection techniques. Convicted of crimes against peace at Nuremberg, Doenitz served ten years in prison.

305. The enemy knows all our secrets and we know none of his. (Ca. January 1945; cited in *Historical Guide to World War II*, by Louis L. Snyder.)

306. I assume command of all services of the armed forces with the firm intention of continuing the fight against the Bolsheviks until our troops and the hundreds of thousands of German families in our eastern provinces have been saved from slavery or destruction. Against the English and the Americans I must continue to fight for as long as they persist in hindering the accomplishment of my primary mission. (Order of the Day, May 1, 1945.)

[After taking over as head of the German government, following Hitler's suicide.]

307. In view of the present situation, I have decided to dispense with your further assistance as Reich Minister of the Interior and member of the Reich Government, as Commander-in-Chief of the Replacement Army, and as Chief of the Police. I now regard all your offices as abolished. I thank you for the service which you have given to the Reich. (Letter to Heinrich Himmler [q.v.], May 5, 1945; cited in *The Last Days of Hitler*, by H. R. Trevor-Roper.)

[According to Trevor-Roper, similar letters were addressed to other top Nazi officials. It signaled the end of the Nazi regime.]

ERNEST DUPUY

(n.d.)

Dupuy was General Eisenhower's press aide.

308. Under the command of General Eisenhower, Allied naval forces, supported by strong air forces, began landing Allied armies this morning on the northern coast of France. (Press statement, June 6, 1944.)

DWIGHT D. EISENHOWER

(1890–1969)

Eisenhower was Supreme Commander of Allied forces in Western Europe during World War II. He was handpicked by General George C. Marshall to work in the War Plans Division of the U.S. Army. Later, he was sent to Europe to head American forces assembling in Britain. Eisenhower headed the North African campaign, the invasion of Italy, and—finally—the invasion of France and the defeat of Nazi Germany. After the war, he was tapped for the presidency and served two terms.

309. Of more immediate importance to me was the decision [at the Casablanca Conference (q.v.)] that the British Eighth Army and the Desert Air Force, coming up through Tripoli and lower Tunisia, would be assigned to the Allied forces under my command when once they had entered the latter province. During the day I spent at Casablanca, I was informed of this general plan, but not until General [George C.] Marshall later came to Algiers did I learn that it had been definitely approved. General [Harold] Alexander [q.v.] was to become the deputy commander of the Allied forces. . . .

This development was extraordinarily pleasing to me because it meant, first and foremost, complete unity of action in the central Mediterranean and it provided needed machinery for effective tactical and strategical co-ordination. I informed the President and the Chief of Staff that I would be delighted to serve under Alexander if it should be decided to give him the supreme authority. I made this suggestion because the ground strength of the Allied Force, after amalgamation with the desert units, would be even more predominantly British. All announced ourselves as satisfied and thus there began what was, for me, an exceptionally gratifying experience in the unification of thought and action in an allied command. (Recalling events of January 1943; from *Crusade in Europe*, by Dwight D. Eisenhower.)

310. Anglo-Canadian armed forces have today launched an offensive against Sicily. It is the first stage in the liberation of the European Continent. There will be others. (Statement to the people of France, July 10, 1943.)

311. I call on the French people to remain calm, not to allow themselves to be deceived by the false rumors which the enemy might circulate. . . . When the hour of action strikes, we will let you know. (Ibid.)

312. Following upon the conclusion of hostilities, there must be no room for doubt as to who won the war. Germany must be occupied. More than this, the German people must not be allowed to escape a sense of guilt, of complicity in the tragedy that has engulfed the world. Prominent Nazis, along with certain industrialists, must be tried and punished. Membership in the Gestapo and in the SS should be taken as *prima facie* evidence of guilt. The General Staff must be broken up, all its archives confiscated, and members suspected of complicity in starting the war or in any war crime should be tried. The German nation should be responsible for reparations to such countries as Belgium, Holland, France, Luxembourg, Norway, and Russia. The war-making power of the country should be eliminated. Possibly this could be done by strict controls on industries using heavy fabricating machinery or by the mere expedient of preventing any manufacture of airplanes. The Germans should be permitted and required to make their own living, and should not be supported by America. Therefore choking off natural resources would be folly. (Conversation with U.S. Secretary of the Treasury Henry L. Morgenthau, Jr. [q.v.], 1944; from *Crusade in Europe*, by Dwight D. Eisenhower.)

[Morgenthau had conceived a plan to turn postwar Germany from an industrial to an agricultural society.]

313. If you had called him a bastard, that would be one thing. But you called him a *British* bastard. For that, I'm sending you home. (Addressed to an American officer, Supreme Allied Headquarters, London, attributed, ca. spring 1944.)

314. From February 1 to June 1 [1944], I visited 26 divisions, 24 airfields, five ships of war, and numerous depots, shops, hospitals, and other important installations. . . . Soldiers like to see the men who are directing operations; they properly resent any indication of neglect or indifference to them on the part of their commanders and invariably interpret a visit, even a brief one, as evidence of the commander's concern for them. . . . It pays big dividends in terms of morale, and morale, given rough equality in other things, is supreme on the battlefield. (Recalling events of 1944 prior to the Normandy Invasion, June 1, 1944; from *Crusade in Europe*, by Dwight D. Eisenhower.)

315. Our landings in the Cherbourg-Havre area have failed to gain a satisfactory foothold and I have withdrawn the troops. My decision to attack at this time and place was based upon the best information available. The troops, the air, and the Navy did all that bravery and devotion to duty could do. If any blame or fault attaches to the attempt it is mine alone. (Communiqué never released, prepared ca. June 5, 1944; cited in *My Three Years with Eisenhower*, by Harry C. Butcher.)

[If the Normandy landings had failed, Eisenhower was fully prepared to take the blame for it. He shared the draft of the proposed communiqué with Butcher on July 11, 1944, telling him that similar communiqués had been prepared in advance for every previous amphibious landing under his command.]

316. Because this opportunity may be grasped only through the utmost in zeal, determination and speedy action, I make my present appeal to you more urgent than ever before.

I request every airman to make it his direct responsibility that the enemy is blasted unceasingly by day and by night, and is denied safety either in fight or in flight.

I request every sailor to make sure that no part of the hostile forces can either escape or be reinforced by sea, and that our comrades on the land want for nothing that guns and ships and ships' companies can bring to them.

I request every soldier to go forward to his assigned objective with the determination that the enemy can survive only through surrender: let no foot of ground once gained be relinquished nor a single German escape through a line once established. (Order of the Day, August 13, 1944.)

[In August 1944, a major Allied breakout in France was being challenged by a severe German counterattack. Eisenhower would later compare it with the Ardennes offensive four months later. The German attack in August, fought in good weather and with intensive Allied air support, would be quickly repulsed.]

317. It was literally possible to walk for hundreds of yards at a time stepping on nothing but dead and decaying flesh. (Events of August 1944; quoted in *Rommel: The Desert Fox*, by Desmond Young.)

[Describing the site of a vast area filled with German soldiers and French farm animals killed during the battle of the Falaise gap. It marked the breakout from Normandy; the Second Battle of France was now well under way.]

318. There would be some reason to hope Germany would call it a day. But I think as early as August [1944] it became evident all along the front the German was fighting in many instances because the Gestapo made him. The Gestapo's control is as firm as ever as far as we can see, so the German is going to battle it out to the end. I feel that Hitler's leading gang of brigands has nothing to lose, and as long as he has this powerful weapon in his hands to make others fight, he

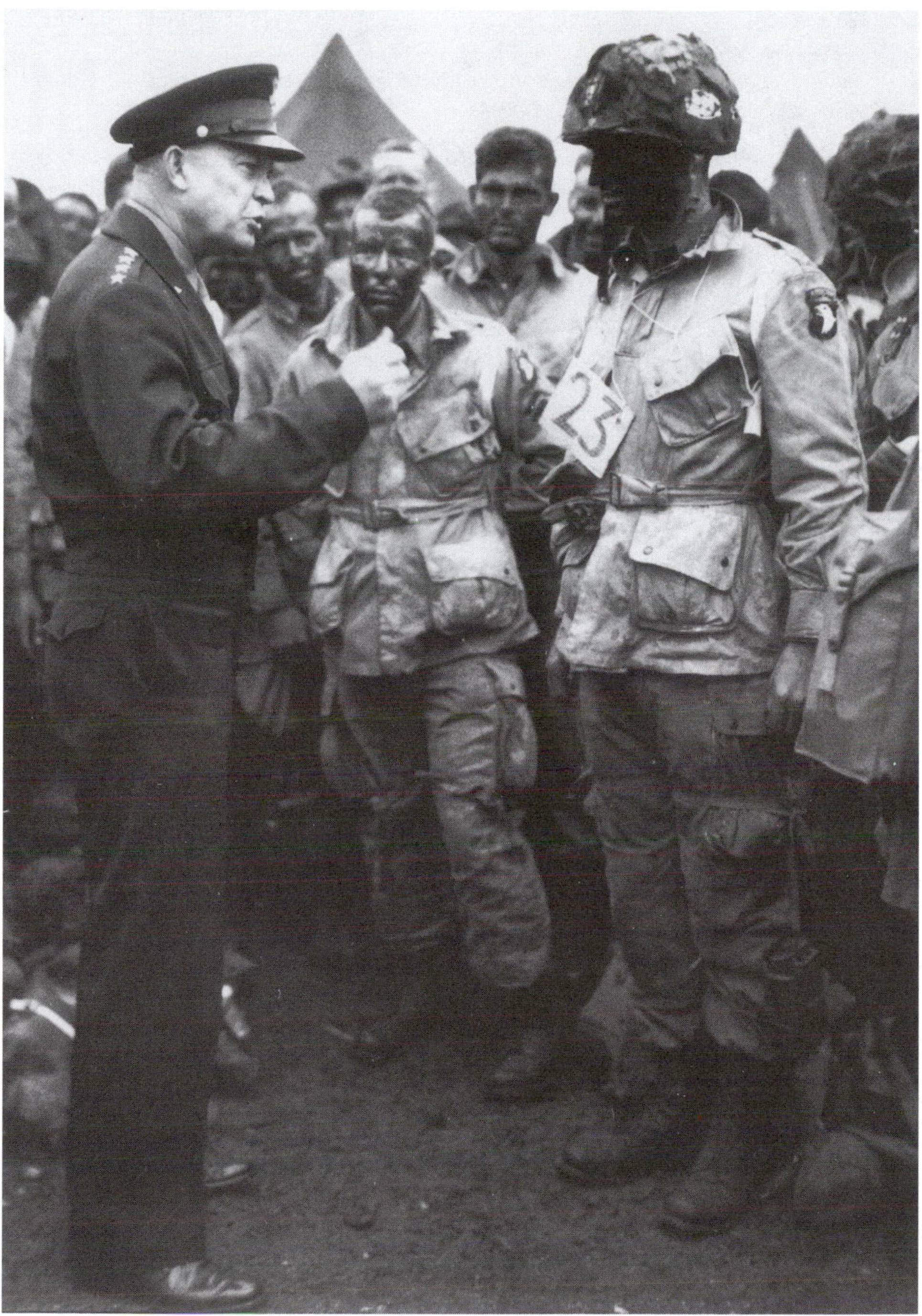

"Soldiers like to see the men who are directing operations. . . . [They] interpret a visit, even a brief one, as evidence of the commander's concern for them. . . . It pays big dividends in terms of morale, and morale, given rough equality in other things, is supreme on the battlefield."

—DWIGHT D. EISENHOWER

Calling on American paratroops as D-Day approached.

and his gang don't care. They are ready to fight it out to destruction. (Press conference, Paris, November 21, 1944.)

319. So far as the troops are concerned, I have not yet had reported to me a single instance where a V-2 [German rocket] killed a soldier. . . . The Germans are shooting principally at our supply centers and at London. (Ibid.)

320. We cannot be content with his mere repulse. By rushing out from his fixed defenses the enemy may give us the chance to turn his great gamble into his worst defeat. . . . let everyone hold before him a single thought—to destroy the enemy on the ground, in the air, everywhere—destroy him! (Order of the Day during the Battle of the Bulge [q.v.], December 21, 1944.)

321. The enemy is making his supreme effort to break out of the desperate plight into which you forced him by your brilliant victories of the summer and fall. He is fighting savagely to take back all that you have won and is using every treacherous trick to deceive and kill you. He is gambling everything, but already, in this battle, your unparalleled gallantry has done much to foil his plans. In the face of your proven bravery and fortitude, he will completely fail. . . . United in this determination and with unshakable faith in the cause for which we fight, we will, with God's help, go forward to our greatest victory. (Order of the Day to all Allied forces during the Battle of the Bulge [q.v.], December 23, 1944.)

322. Field Marshal Montgomery [q.v.], like General Patton [q.v.], conformed to no type. He [Montgomery] deliberately pursued certain eccentricities of behavior, one of which was to separate himself habitually from his staff. He lived in a trailer, surrounded by a few aides. This created difficulties in the staff work that must be performed in timely and effective fashion if any battle is to result in victory. He consistently refused to deal with a staff officer from any headquarters other than his own, and, in an argument, was persistent up to the point of decision. (1944; from *Crusade in Europe*, by Dwight D. Eisenhower.)

323. I would say the German as a military force on the Western Front . . . is a whipped enemy. (Press conference, Paris, March 28, 1945.)

324. This is my honest opinion—there will be no negotiated unconditional surrender. It will be an imposed unconditional surrender. I believe that the Allied Armies and the Russians from the East have to take over everything, and that will be unconditional surrender. (Ibid.)

325. This is a military conference today, not political. But I should say this: our experience to date leads to the view that you have got to take each locality, go in and establish an order over it that can prevail until finally that time comes when our governments can decide what must be done. The first thing is to establish order, and we are going to have to do that with force of arms. (Ibid.)

[In answer to a question regarding what German personalities might be involved in a surrender.]

326. Well, I think mileage alone ought to make them [the Russians] do it [i.e., reach Berlin first]. After all, they are 33 miles [away] and we are 250. I wouldn't want to make any prediction. They have a shorter race to run, although they are faced by the bulk of the German forces. (Ibid.)

327. Such trouble as I have ever had in press relations in this war . . . with very, very minor exceptions . . . usually come from the headline writers at home. (Ibid.)

328. Personal Message to Marshal Stalin:

My immediate operations are designed to encircle and destroy the enemy forces defending the Ruhr, and to isolate that area from the rest of Germany. This will be accomplished by developing offensives around the north of the Ruhr and from Frankfurt through Kassel, until the ring is closed. The enemy enclosed in this ring will then be mopped up. (March 28, 1945, from the National Archives; cited in *On to Berlin*, by James M. Gavin.)

[This quotation—and those immediately following—constitute what is arguably Eisenhower's most controversial communication of the war. Many top British political and military figures were outraged by two things: First, that Eisenhower had communicated directly with Stalin; second, that his message indicated that he did not seem to regard Berlin as a major military objective at this point in the war.]

329. I estimate that this phase of operations will terminate in late April or even earlier, and my next task will be to divide the enemy's remaining forces by joining hands with your forces. (Ibid.)

330. For my forces the best axis on which to effect this juncture would be Erfurt-Leipzig-Dresden; moreover, I believe, this is the area to which the main German governmental departments are being moved. It is along this axis that I propose to place my main effort. In addition, as soon as the situation allows, a secondary advance will be made to effect a junction with your forces in the Regensburg-line area, thereby preventing the consolidation of German resistance in a redoubt in southern Germany. (Ibid.)

331. Before deciding firmly on my future plans, I think it most important that they should be coordinated as closely as possible with yours both as to directions and timing. Could you, therefore, tell me your intentions, and let me know how the proposed operations outlined in this message conform to your probable action? (Ibid.)

332. If we are to complete the destruction of the German armies without delay, I regard it as essential that we coordinate our action and make every effort to perfect the liaison between our advancing forces. I am prepared to send officers to you for this purpose. (Ibid.)

[Stalin would respond that the plan was a good one, that Berlin was not really a military objective anymore. The Soviet leader then secretly set his top generals to work to plan the Berlin attack.]

333. I visited every nook and cranny of the camp [near Gotha] because I felt it my duty to be in a position from then on to testify at first hand about these things in case there ever grew up at home the belief or assumption that "the stories of Nazi brutality were just propaganda." (Events of April 1945; from *Crusade in Europe*, by Dwight D. Eisenhower.)

334. The mission of this Allied force was fulfilled at 0241 local time, May 7, 1945. (Message to the Combined Chiefs of Staff following the German surrender, May 7, 1945.)

335. You will, officially and personally, be held responsible if the terms of this surrender are violated, including its provisions for German commanders to appear in Berlin at the moment set by the Russian high command to accomplish formal surrender to that government. That is all. (To General Jodl [q.v.] after the surrender documents were signed, Reims, France, May 7, 1945.)

336. The route you have traveled through hundreds of miles is marked by the graves of former comrades. Each of the fallen died as a member of the team to which you belong, bound together by a common love of liberty and a refusal to submit to enslavement. Our common problems of the immediate and distant future can be best solved in the same conceptions of cooperation and devotion to the cause of human freedom as have made this Expeditionary Force such a mighty engine of righteous destruction.

Let us have no part in the profitless quarrels in which other men will inevitably engage as to what country, what service, won the European war. Every man, every woman, of every nation here represented has served according to his or her ability, and the efforts of each have contributed to the outcome. This we shall remember—and in doing so we shall be revering each honored grave, and be sending comfort to the loved ones of comrades who could not live to see this day. (Victory Order of the Day, ca. May 9, 1945.)

337. This war was a holy war. More than any other in history this war has been an array of the forces of evil against those of righteousness. (Speech, Frankfurt, Germany, June 10, 1945.)

338. Americans assess the cost of war in terms of human lives, the Russians in the over-all drain on the nation. The Russians clearly understood the value of morale, but for its development and maintenance they apparently depended upon over-all success and upon patriotism, possibly fanaticism.

As far as I could see, [Marshal Georgi] Zhukov [q.v.] had given little concern to methods that we considered vitally important to the maintenance of morale among American troops: systematic rotation of units, facilities for recreation, short leaves and furloughs, and, above all, the development of techniques to avoid exposure of men to unnecessary battlefield risks, all of which, although common practices in our Army, seemed to be largely unknown in his. (1948; from *Crusade in Europe*, by Dwight D. Eisenhower.)

339. As a matter of fact I approved that one [an execution order for desertion during World War II]. It was for a repeated case of desertion. The man [Eddie Slovik (q.v.)]—he was one of those guardhouse lawyers—he refused to believe that he would ever be executed. At the very last moment I sent my Judge Advocate General to see him. He was on the gibbet. And I said, "If you will go back and serve in your company honorably until this war is over, you'll get an honorary discharge and not the death sentence." He said, "Baloney," or words to that effect. And so he was executed. (Recalling events of January 1945; interview with historian Bruce Catton, February 1963; cited in *The Execution of Private Slovik*, by William Bradford Huie.)

[Huie's reaction to the above: "Those statements are as puzzling to me as they are to the Army's Office of the Judge Advocate General."]

JOHN EISENHOWER

(1922–)

John Eisenhower was a lieutenant in the U.S. Army when he visited the Soviet Union with his father, the Supreme Commander in Europe.

340. I have been in Russia several days and have listened to many toasts. I have heard the virtues of every Allied ruler, every prominent marshal, general, admiral, and commander toasted. I have yet to hear a toast to the most important Russian in World War II. Gentlemen, will you please drink with me to the common soldier of the great Red Army. (Leningrad, 1945; quoted in *Crusade in Europe*, by Dwight D. Eisenhower.)

THOMAS F. FARRELL

(1891–1968)

Farrell was the number-two man of the Manhattan Project to develop the atomic bomb. He served directly under Leslie Groves (q.v.). Farrell was a brigadier general in the U.S. Army.

341. The faith of those who had been responsible for the initiation and the carrying-on of this Herculean project had been justified. I personally thought of Blondin crossing Niagara Falls on his tightrope, only to me this tightrope had lasted for almost three years. (On the test explosion of the A-bomb Alamogordo, New Mexico, July 16, 1945; quoted in Groves's memo to Henry Stimson [q.v.] of July 18, 1945.)

ERICH FELLGIEBER

(n.d.)

Fellgieber was one of the German generals involved in the plot to kill Hitler on July 20, 1944.

342. The bomb has exploded. Hitler is dead. (Telephone call to conspirators in Berlin, July 20, 1944; cited in *Operation Valkyrie*, by Pierre Galante with Eugene Silianoff.)

[Half right. The bomb *had* exploded—but Hitler had survived.]

MAURICE GAMELIN
(1872–1958)

Gamelin was one of the top French Army commanders prior to and during Hitler's invasion of France in 1940. Two years after the French surrender, he was arrested by the Vichy government. He spent the rest of the war years in German prisons, until freed by the Allies.

343. If the Belgians only call on us at the moment when they are attacked by the Germans, there is no doubt that they lack the means of defending themselves until they are reinforced. And we would have to run the risk of a battle of confrontation with the difficulty of supporting their retreating armies. This would be an arduous task. (Letter to Premier Daladier, September 1, 1939; from *Servir*, Vol. III, by Maurice Gamelin.)

[On the problem of how to respect Belgian neutrality while preparing for an invasion through that country.]

HERMANN GOERING
(1893–1946)

Head of the German Luftwaffe, Goering was chosen by Hitler to be his successor in the event of the Fuehrer's death. At the close of the war, when Hitler announced that he would stay in Berlin and fight to the death, Goering tried to take over German leadership. He was promptly denounced by Hitler as a traitor. Captured by the Allies after the war, Goering was put on trial at Nuremberg, convicted, and sentenced to be hanged. He cheated the hangman by taking poison.

344. The worst is over; things will improve for we possess the territories with the most fertile soil. We shall send our best agriculturists to follow the fighting troops; they will provide our troops and the homeland with the produce of the land. . . . We have taken the best provinces from the Russians. I have seen how the people live in Holland, Belgium, France, Norway and Poland. And I have formed a great resolve: foremost in the feeding of the hungry come the German people. . . . If there is any hunger, it will not be in Germany. (Speech, Harvest Festival, October 4, 1942.)

345. My Fuehrer!

In view of your decision to remain in the fortress of Berlin, do you agree that I take over at once the total leadership of the Reich, with full freedom of action at home and abroad as your deputy, in accordance with your decree of June 29, 1941? If no reply is received by 10 o'clock tonight, I shall take it for granted that you have lost your freedom of action, and shall consider the conditions of your decree as fulfilled, and shall act for the best interests of our country and our people. You know what I feel for you in this gravest hour of my life. Words fail me to express myself. May God protect you, and speed you quickly here in spite of all. (Message to Hitler, April 23, 1945.)

[Goering really believed that this was Hitler's wish. He had checked out his feelings with key Nazi leaders, who told him that the leadership was his to assume. When Hitler received the message, he denounced Goering as a traitor.]

LESLIE R. GROVES
(1896–1970)

An American army general, Groves was selected to run the supersecret Manhattan Project to develop and build the atomic bomb. Before the project was finished, Groves had put together a workforce of more than 100,000, from scientists to construction workers. The price tag came to an unprecedented $2 billion.

346. Operated on this morning. Diagnosis not yet complete but results seem satisfactory and already exceed expectations. (Message to President Truman [q.v.] at Potsdam Conference [q.v.], Germany, July 16, 1945.)

[Translation: The atomic device exploded successfully.]

347. At 0530, 16 July 1945, in a remote section of the Alamogordo Air Base, New Mexico, the first full-scale test was made of the implosion type atomic fission bomb. For the first time in history there was a nuclear explosion. And what an explosion! . . . I estimate the energy generated to be in excess of the equivalent of 15,000 to 20,000 tons of TNT, and this is a conservative estimate. (Memo to Secretary of War Henry L. Stimson [q.v.], July 18, 1945; cited in *Now It Can Be Told*, by Leslie R. Groves.)

348. There are tremendous blast effects. For a brief period there was a lighting effect within a radius of 20 miles equal to several suns in midday; a huge ball of fire was formed which lasted for several seconds. This ball mushroomed and rose to a height of over 10,000 feet before it dimmed. The light from the explosion was seen clearly at Albuquerque, Santa Fe, Silver City, El Paso and other points generally to about 180 miles away. The sound was heard to the same distance in a few instances, but generally about 100 miles. Only a few windows were broken, although one was some 125 miles away. A massive cloud was formed which surged and billowed upward with tremendous power, reaching the substratosphere at an elevation of 41,000 feet, 36,000 feet above the ground, in about 5 minutes. (Ibid.)

349. We still have no reason to anticipate the loss of our plane in an actual operation, although we cannot guarantee safety. (Ibid.)

350. A blind woman saw the light [of the test explosion of the atomic bomb]. (Ibid.)

HEINZ GUDERIAN
(1888–1954)

Guderian was the German general who developed armored warfare tactics. These resulted in major German victories first in Poland and later in France. These "blitzkrieg" tactics worked initially in the invasion of the Soviet Union, but the harsh Russian winter and muddy spring bogged down the Nazi advances. When Guderian tried to pull back at the beginning of the Russian winter, Hitler fired him. Later in the war, he would hold other less important military posts.

351. Hitler [visiting Guderian's headquarters in Poland in 1939] asked about casualties. I gave him the latest figures that I had received, some 150 dead and 700 wounded for all the four divisions under my command during the Battle of the [Polish] Corridor. He was amazed at the smallness of these figures, and contrasted them with the casualties of his own regiment, the List Regiment, during the First World War. On the first day of battle that one regiment alone had lost more than 2,000 dead and wounded.

I was able to show him that the smallness of our casualties in this battle against a tough and courageous enemy was primarily due to the decisiveness of our tanks. Tanks are a life-saving weapon. (From *Panzer Leader*, by Heinz Guderian.)

352. Hitler wanted to know what had proved particularly satisfactory about our tanks and what was still in need of improvement. . . . For their further development their present speed was sufficient, but they needed to be more heavily armored, particularly in front; the range and power of penetration of their guns also needed to be increased, which would mean longer barrels and a shell with a heavier charge. This applied equally to our anti-tank guns. (Ibid.)

FRANZ HALDER
(1884–1972)

Halder was the German general who organized the Polish campaign. He later fell out of favor with Hitler over the Soviet invasion and was dismissed from his post. Arrested after the plot to kill Hitler in July 1944, he was imprisoned at Dachau until the war ended.

353. Our left wing consisting of armor and motorized forces, which has no enemy before it, will thus be stopped dead in its tracks upon direct orders of the Fuehrer! Finishing off the encircled enemy is to be left to Air Force! (Diary entry, May 24, 1940.)

[After receiving orders to stop the assault on the English and French trapped at Dunkirk.]

354. These orders from the top just make no sense. The tanks are stopped as if they were paralyzed. (May 26, 1940; Ibid.)

[On May 27, Hitler ordered the attack to resume—but it was too late.]

355. The pocket [at Dunkirk] would have been closed at the coast if only our armor had not been held back. Now we must stand by and watch countless thousands of the enemy get away to England under our noses. (May 30, 1940; Ibid.)

356. The success against Poland [in September 1939] was only possible by our almost completely baring our Western border. If the French . . . had used the opportunity presented by the engagement of nearly all our forces in Poland they would have been able to cross the Rhine without our being able to prevent it and would have threatened the Ruhr, which was decisive for the German conduct of the war. (Testimony at Nuremberg war crimes trial, ca. 1946.)

"Launch planes. To Col. Doolittle and gallant command good luck and God bless you."
—ADMIRAL WILLIAM F. HALSEY, JR., MESSAGE TO CARRIER *HORNET*

Col. James Doolittle and army fliers take off from the *Hornet* to bomb Tokyo and other Japanese cities.

WILLIAM F. HALSEY, JR.

(1882–1959)

A U.S. naval officer, Admiral Halsey was involved in numerous battles with the Japanese in the South Pacific. He led the small naval force that accompanied the carrier *Hornet*, which carried the Doolittle (q.v.) bombers to their rendezvous off Japan. Halsey also took part in battles off the Santa Cruz islands, the Marshalls, the Gilberts, and the Solomons. His most controversial engagement took place in October 1944. Ordered to guard the San Bernardino Strait during the invasion of Leyte in the Philippines, Halsey was drawn away by a decoy Japanese force. The move could have been disastrous to the American landing force. However, the main Japanese fleet withdrew before taking advantage of the situation.

357. Launch planes. To Col. Doolittle [q.v.] and gallant command good luck and God bless you. (Message to carrier *Hornet*, April 18, 1942.)

[Halsey's small naval force was escorting the *Hornet* to a point from which it would launch the Doolittle raiders. Believing that enemy ships had spotted them, Halsey ordered the raiders to take off immediately.]

358. We are drowning and burning the bestial apes all over the Pacific, and it is just as much pleasure to burn them as to drown them. (Newsreel interview, ca. March 1944; cited in *Memoirs of a Revolutionist*, by Dwight Macdonald.)

359. I hate Japs. I'm telling you men that if I met a pregnant Japanese woman, I'd kick her in the belly. (Dinner with newspapermen, Washington, D.C., ca. March 1944; Ibid.)

360. The back of the Jap navy has been broken in the course of supporting our landings in Leyte. (Broadcast message, October 25, 1944; cited in *Master of Sea Power: A Biography of Fleet Admiral Ernest J. King*, by Thomas B. Buell.) [Following the battle of Leyte Gulf.]

361. The pursuit phase of the Battle of the Western Pacific is now in progress. . . . And those that escape the surface and air forces are committed to the tender mercies of the implacable submarines. (October 26, 1944; Ibid.)

362. We had two fleets in Philippine waters under separate commands [in the Leyte invasion]; my Third Fleet was under command of Admiral Nimitz [q.v.]; Kinkaid's [q.v.] Seventh Fleet was under command of General MacArthur. If we had been under the same command, with a single system of operational control and intelligence, the Battle for Leyte Gulf might have been fought differently to a different result. It is folly to cry over spilled milk, but it is wisdom to observe the cause, for future avoidance. When blood has been spilled, the obligation becomes vital. (ca. October 26, 1944; from *Admiral Halsey's Story*, by William F. Halsey, Jr., and J. Bryan III.)

363. We have chosen our antagonist [a Japanese carrier force coming from the north]. It remained only to choose the best way to meet him. . . .

1. I could guard San Bernardino with my whole fleet and wait for the Northern Force to strike me. Rejected. It yielded to the enemy the double initiative of his carriers and his fields on Luzon and would allow him to use them unmolested.

2. I could guard San Bernardino with TF 34 while I struck the Northern Force with my carriers. Rejected. The enemy's potential surface and air strength forbade half-measures. If his shore-based planes joined his carrier planes, together they might inflict far more damage on my half-fleets separately than they could inflict on the fleet intact.

3. I could leave San Bernardino unguarded and strike the Northern Force with my whole fleet. Accepted. It preserved my fleet's integrity, it left the initiative with me, and it promised the greatest possibility of surprise. Even if the Central [Japanese] Force meanwhile penetrated San Bernardino and headed for Leyte Gulf, it could hope only to harry the landing operation. It could not consolidate any advantage because no transports accompanied it and no supply ships. It could merely hit and run. (Ibid.)

GOTTHARD HEINRICI

(1889–1931)

Heinrici, a German general, led armies on the Russian front. He specialized in defensive tactics in front of Moscow in 1942 and at the Oder River in 1945.

364. [Expecting an imminent enemy attack, he would withdraw his forces under cover of darkness to a secondary defense position a few miles back.] It was like hitting an empty bag. The Russian attack would lose its speed because my men, unharmed, would be ready. Then my troops on sectors that had not been attacked would close in and reoccupy the original front lines. (Quoted in *The Last Battle*, by Cornelius Ryan.)

365. The German defeat in the East was, in my opinion, due to one main reason—that our troops were compelled to cover immense spaces without the flexibility, in the command, that would have enabled them to concentrate on holding decisive points. Thus they lost the initiative permanently. (Quoted in *The German Generals Talk*, by B. H. Liddell Hart.)

366. Hitler always tried to make us fight for every yard, threatening to court-martial anyone who didn't. No withdrawal was officially permitted without his approval—even a small-scale withdrawal. This principle was so hammered into the army that it was a common saying that battalion commanders were afraid "to move a sentry from the window to the door." (Ibid.)

367. When the Russians were found to be concentrating for an attack [late in the war, as they pushed toward Berlin], I withdrew my troops from the first line under cover of night to the second line—usually about 2 kilometers behind. The result was that the Russian blow hit the air, and its further attack did not have the same impetus. (Ibid.)

ADOLF HEUSINGER

(1897–1982)

A lieutenant in World War I, Heusinger would become a lieutenant general in World War II, serving the German High Command as chief of the Operations Section. He was suspected in the 1944 plot to kill Hitler. Though never tried, Heusinger had reason to believe that the SS (Schutzstaffel) would try to kill him. At the end of the war, Heusinger surrendered to American authorities. He was questioned by U.S. Army Intelligence about many aspects of the war. His candid opinions offer remarkable insights into the German military mind at key points in the war. His military career was capped with his work for the North Atlantic Treaty Organization.

368. In 1939 Hitler assured Brauchitsch [q.v.] that England and France would not declare war when Germany moved against Poland. The general staff expected a war of two or three months' duration. After France and England declared war, the opinion was that it would last a long time, but no definite time was predicted. Both Brauchitsch and the chief of the general staff had grave doubts as to Germany's ability to conduct a prolonged struggle.

In the general planning it was estimated that we would require a four months' reserve of armaments and munitions to carry through the period of conversion to war production. At the outbreak of the war, however, we had only a two months' reserve. This gap was bridged during the inactive period of the war between the Polish and western campaigns. (Interview, Military Intelligence Center, Oberursel, Germany, September 12, 1945; obtained through the National Archives; cited in *Operation Valkyrie*, by Pierre Galante with Eugene Silianoff.)

369. The general staff was of the opinion that a French attack in the west [during the Sudeten crisis of 1938] would have broken through, as our fortifications were not complete, nor were they in 1939, when the French could have broken through, although at heavier cost. The West Wall was completed only from Trier south to the Rhine in 1939. Northward it was incomplete and without any depth. After 1940 construction ceased. To a certain extent the West Wall was a bluff, like the Atlantic Wall. With regard to the latter it was impossible to fortify the entire coast and every military man must have concluded that a landing and a penetration of five kilometers would end all difficulties as far as fortifications were concerned. (Ibid.)

370. In professional circles [prior to 1939] the following were the most highly regarded [in the German army]: Beck, Halder [q.v.], Manstein, Heinrich Stulpnagel, Fritzsche [q.v.], and Brauchitsch [q.v.]. Also Rundstedt [q.v.], although he was not as active in the War Ministry. General Beck was undoubtedly the greatest spirit in the general staff. However, he was always of the opinion that war would be a catastrophe and in this opinion he found a great friend in General Gamelin [q.v.]. In the general staff we always said that General Halder and General Manstein had received "the necessary two drops of the wisdom of Solomon." In the top level of the general staff, Manstein was regarded as the ablest and most original planner. That is also my opinion. However, there was no Schlieffen. (Ibid.)

371. The first plan for an offensive campaign [in the West] was formulated in November 1939. In substance it was a repetition of the 1914 Schlieffen plan. As the start of the campaign was delayed, doubts arose as to the achievement of any surprise with this plan. The basic idea of the new plan—the breakthrough in the Ardennes, crossing of the Meuse, and the trapping of British, French and Belgian forces in the north by pushing the tank forces through to the Channel—came to several minds at once. And in justice it should be said that one of these was Hitler's. However, General Manstein, then chief of staff to Marshal Rundstedt [q.v.], deserves the greater credit. He worked out the plan and proposed its adoption. The order was given to the Operations Division in February 1940 to replan the campaign along the proposed lines. From February 1940 to May 1940 the plan was subject to the sharpest criticism. Among the critics was General Guderian [q.v.], who described the plan as a "crime against Panzers." General Halder [q.v.] deserves the credit for defending the plan against all critics and insisting upon its execution. General Bock was also opposed to it and appealed to the chief of the general staff. Halder said once that he would stick to the plan if the chances of succeeding were only ten percent. (Ibid.)

372. [The German general staff was] very well informed [of British defenses after Dunkirk]. All equipment of the expeditionary force was lost, and we knew that there were few reserves of men and materiel in the homeland. Never in modern times had Britain been in a more critical situation. Only a man like Winston Churchill could have brought the country through such a crisis. We had no plans for an invasion and no equipment and specially trained forces with which to undertake the invasion. Hence the delay, the hesitation, and finally Hitler's decision not to risk it. Whether we should have risked it is of course now only a matter of historical interest. Admiral Wagner, with whom I have discussed this question recently and who was then chief of Naval Operations, is of the opinion that it would have failed. I think it could have been done. Militarily, this was for us one of the lost opportunities of the war.

With regard to the air attack in August and September [1940]—the Battle of Britain—I can speak only from the standpoint of the army. It was not thought possible to conquer Britain from the air. The objective was to destroy British air power and gain control of the air. This failed. English aircraft were greater in number than estimated or Britain's production was higher than estimated. By the middle of September it was obvious that the attack against London would not be decisive. Our losses in aircraft from improved flank and other defense measures became too high in proportion to results achieved. The air attacks were then switched to new objectives—the production and armament plants became targets with a view of knocking out or delaying British rearmament. But in my opinion these were only substitute objectives fixed after the failure to achieve the first main objective—to destroy the British air power and gain control of the air over London and the south coast. (Ibid.)

373. [The original timetable for the Russian invasion] called for the launching of the campaign in May [1941], with the objectives to be reached in five months—that is, in October. But the campaign did not begin until late June, bringing the terminal date into November. Originally, Hitler, the C[ommander] in C[hief], and the chief of the general staff agreed that wherever they stood in November, they would close down operations. However, they gambled with the weather, which in the late autumn was favorable, just as it was to Napoleon in 1812, and kept saying, "We can risk it." Then came the bitter weather, and the German armies started to retreat.

As far as winter preparations were concerned, measures had been taken by the supply services, but they were inadequate. Clothing was prepared for a hard German winter, but it was inadequate for a severe Russian winter. The transport failed because German locomotives were not equipped for extremely low temperatures. Moreover the Russians in their retreat destroyed all the water tanks and this created enormous difficulties in train operations. The campaign should have been halted earlier and necessary measures taken to hold the positions already taken.

When the German armies began to retreat, Hitler dismissed Brauchitsch [q.v.] and personally took command. He always maintained thereafter that he personally saved the German army from the fate that had overtaken Napoleon's forces in the retreat from Moscow. (Ibid.)

COURTNEY HODGES

(1887–1966)

Hodges was an American general who commanded the First Army in Europe.

373a. Brad, we've gotten a bridge. (Telephone call to Bradley [q.v.], March 7, 1945; quoted in *A Soldier's Story*, by Omar N. Bradley.)

[First news that American troops had seized a Rhine bridge intact at Remagen.]

MASAHARU HOMMA

(1888–1946)

Homma was a Japanese general who successfully invaded Luzon Island in the Philippines in December 1941. After the war, he was charged with being responsible for the Bataan Death March (q.v.). Homma pleaded that he knew nothing of the atrocities committed by the Japanese army but was found guilty and executed.

374. Things don't look very good. I was amazed to hear the details of Japanese atrocities. Even Major [John] Skeen [his defense counsel] says that although he is doing his best for me, the case is quite hopeless. (Manila, the Philippines, January 1946; quoted in *A Trial of Generals: Homma, Yamashita, MacArthur*, by Lawrence Taylor.)

[Spoken to his wife during a recess in his war crimes trial.]

375. INDIRECT DISCOURSE: He [Homma] said that the military force is a thing which should be used to defend the Motherland, and work in harmony and try to preserve the world peace, and should never be used to invade the other countries. He also said, constantly, that if a country ever engaged in a war of invasion, that country will inevitably lose. . . . Because he studied about the United States, and England, because he was always interested in the world trends and kept his eyes open on it, and also because he understood Japan thoroughly, he realized that the spread of war was not only a misfortune for Japan but to all mankind. This view was not welcomed and was not popular among the people. People used to call him pro-American, a pro-American element. At that time that name was an insult. (Testimony of Mrs. Fujiko Homma on her husband's feelings about the Japanese military; Ibid.)

HASTINGS ISMAY

(1887–1965)

Ismay was the chief military adviser to Winston Churchill during the war.

376. He [Admiral Ernest J. King (q.v.)] was as tough as nails and carried himself as stiffly as a poker. He was blunt and stand-offish, almost to the point of rudeness. At the start, he was intolerant and suspicious of all things British, especially the Royal Navy; but he was almost equally intolerant and suspicious of the American Army. War against Japan was the problem to which he had devoted the study of a lifetime, and he resented the idea of American resources being used for any other purpose than to destroy Japanese. He mistrusted Churchill's powers of advocacy, and was apprehensive that he would wheedle President Roosevelt into neglecting the war in the Pacific. (Ca. January 1943; from *The Memoirs of General Lord Ismay*, by Hastings Ismay.)

ALFRED JODL

(1890–1946)

Jodl, a German general, along with Admiral Hans von Friedeburg, signed the unconditional surrender of Germany on May 7, 1945. An active participant in Hitler's crimes, Jodl was tried at Nuremberg, found guilty, and hanged.

377. Alarming news from Holland, cancelling of furloughs, evacuations, roadblocks, other mobilization measures; according to reports of the intelligence service the British have asked for permission to march in, but the Dutch have refused. (Diary excerpt, May 8, 1940.)

[Two days later, the Nazis attacked. The Dutch had refused British army units prior to the attack in order to maintain their neutrality, as spelled out by international treaty.]

378. The planned attack on Greece from the North [by Nazi Germany in April 1941] was not executed merely as an operation in aid of an ally. [Italy had invaded Greece in the autumn of 1940—and was being trounced.] Its real purpose was to prevent the British from gaining a foothold in Greece and from menacing our Rumanian oil area from that country. (Lecture, November 7, 1943.)

378a. General Eisenhower insists that we sign today. If not, the Allied fronts will be closed to persons seeking to surrender individually [to the Western Allies rather than to the Russians]. I see no alternative; chaos or signature. I ask you to confirm to me immediately by wireless that I have full powers to sign capitulation. (Message to Admiral Karl Doenitz [q.v.], the German chief of state, May 7, 1945.)

379. We, the undersigned, acting by authority of the German High Command, hereby surrender unconditionally to the Supreme Commander, Allied

Expeditionary Force, and simultaneously to the Soviet High Command, all forces of land, sea, and the air who are at this date under German control. (Instrument of Surrender, Reims, France, May 7, 1945.)

380. With this signature the German people and the German Armed Forces are, for better or worse, delivered into the hands of the victors. In this war, which has lasted more than five years, both have achieved and suffered more than perhaps any other people in the world. In this hour I can only express the hope that the victor will treat them with generosity. (Statement after signing document of unconditional surrender, Reims, France, May 7, 1945.)

381. If we did not collapse in 1939, that was due to the fact that during the Polish campaign [in 1939] the approximately 110 French and British divisions in the West were held completely inactive against the 23 German divisions. (Testimony at Nuremberg war crimes trial, ca. 1946.)

WILHELM KEITEL

(1883–1946)

An early military adviser to Hitler, Keitel rose to become a field marshal of the German army during the war. Although he opposed the attack on the Soviet Union, he carried out Hitler's orders, including the execution of hostages and destruction of entire villages, such as Lidice. He was hanged at Nuremberg.

382. No document must be lost, since otherwise enemy propaganda will make use of it. Matters communicated orally cannot be proven; they can be denied. (Statement to aides, May 22, 1933.)

[Keitel was secretly building up the German army, contrary to the provisions of the Treaty of Versailles.]

HUSBAND E. KIMMEL

(1882–1968)

Commander of the U.S. Pacific Fleet at the time of Pearl Harbor, Kimmel was accused of dereliction of duty and was relieved of his command. He was never court-martialed and was permitted to retire from the navy. Kimmel insisted to the end that if he had been made aware of the intercepted Japanese coded messages about ship movements at Pearl Harbor, he would have been prepared to resist the Japanese attack.

383. I cannot excuse those in authority in Washington for what they did. And I do not believe that thousands of mothers and fathers whose sons perished on that tragic 7th day of December 1941 will excuse them. They will be judged at the bar of history. In my book they must answer on the Day of Judgment like any other criminal. (From *Admiral Kimmel's Story*, by Husband E. Kimmel.)

EDWARD P. KING, JR.

(1884–1958)

King was major general in charge of the Bataan defense on Luzon Island, the Philippines. In April 1942, he surrendered Bataan to the Japanese.

384. INDIRECT DISCOURSE: At the outset he [King] made it clear that he had not called the meeting to ask for the advice or opinion of his assistants. The "ignominious decision" [to surrender Bataan], he explained, was entirely his and he did not wish anyone else to be "saddled with any part of the responsibility." "I have not communicated with General [Jonathan] Wainwright [q.v.]," he declared, "because I do not want him to be compelled to assume any part of the responsibility." Further resistance, he felt, would only be an unnecessary and useless waste of life. "Already our hospital, which is filled to capacity and directly in the line of hostile approach, is within range of enemy light artillery. We have no further means of organized resistance." (Meeting with officers on Bataan shortly after midnight, April 9, 1942; from *The Fall of the Philippines*, by Louis Morton.)

385. Tell General Wainwright [q.v.] that I have decided to surrender Bataan. This decision is solely my own, no member of my staff nor of my command has helped me to arrive at this decision. In my opinion, if I do not surrender to the Japanese, Bataan will be known as the greatest slaughter in history. (Telephone call from Bataan to Brig. Gen. Lewis C. Beebe on Corregidor, April 9, 1942; Ibid.)

386. INDIRECT DISCOURSE: After this telephone conversation King told his staff . . . that if he survived he expected to be court-martialed, and he was certain that history would not deal kindly with a commander who would be remembered for having surrendered the largest force the United States had ever lost. (April 9, 1942; Ibid.)

ERNEST J. KING

(1878–1956)

Commander in chief of America's Atlantic fleet prior to Pearl Harbor, King was put in charge of the Pacific fleet as well, following the surprise attack. Several months later, he also became chief of Naval Operations. He emphasized the role of carriers in the Pacific war.

387. I have been concerned for many years over the increasing tendency—now grown almost to "standard practice"—of flag officers and other group commanders to issue orders and instructions in which their subordinates are told "how" as well as "what" to do to such an extent and in such detail that the "Custom of the service" has virtually become the antithesis of that essential element of command—"initiative of the subordinate." (Memo, Cinclant Serial 053, January 21, 1941; cited in *Master of Sea Power: A Biography of Fleet Admiral Ernest J. King*, by Thomas B. Buell.)

388. We are preparing for—and are now close to—those active operations (commonly called war) which require the exercise and the utilization of the full powers and capabilities of every officer in command status. There will be neither time nor opportunity to do more than prescribe the several tasks of the several subordinates (to say "what," perhaps "when" and "where," and usually, for their intelligent cooperation, "why"); leaving to them—expecting and requiring of them—the capacity to perform the assigned tasks (to do the "how"). (Ibid.)

389. If they [subordinates] are not habituated to think, to judge, to decide and to act for themselves in their several echelons of command—we shall be in sorry case when the time of "active operations" arrives. (Ibid.)

390. Reference: My confidential memorandum, serial 053, dated 21 January 1941. . . . Much progress has been made in improving the exercise of command through the regular echelons of command—from forces through groups and units to ships. It has, however, become increasingly evident that correct methods for the exercise of initiative are not yet thoroughly understood. . . .

When told "what" to do—make sure that "how" you do it is effective not only in itself but as an intelligent, essential and correlated part of a comprehensive and connected whole. (Memo, Cinclant Serial 0328, April 22, 1941; Ibid.)

391. You have expressed the view—concurred in by all of your chief military advisers—that we should determine on a *very few* lines of military endeavor [in the Pacific] and concentrate our efforts on these lines. . . .

[The memo deals first with a broad look at military operations by our allies in other parts of the world. King then offers his "very few" recommendations.]

Australia—and New Zealand—are "white man's countries" which it is essential that we shall not allow to be overrun by Japanese because of the repercussions among the non-white races of the world. . . .

Our primary concern in the Pacific is to hold Hawaii and its approaches (via Midway) from the westward and to maintain its communications with the West Coast. . . .

When "strong points" are made reasonably secure, we shall not only be able to cover the line of communications—to Australia (and New Zealand) but—given the naval forces, air units, and amphibious troops—we can drive northwest from the New Hebrides into the Solomons and the Bismarck Archipelago after the same fashion of step-by-step advances that the Japanese used in the South China Sea. (Memo for President Roosevelt, March 5, 1942; Ibid.)

392. When the going gets rough, they call out the sons of bitches. (Ca. 1942; cited in *George C. Marshall: Organizer of Victory, 1943–1945*, by Forrest C. Pogue.)

393. One of the rules of General Jackson was "mislead, mystify and confuse the enemy." If that's their [the Japanese] strategy, why that's what they may have been doing. (Press conference, October 1944, during the battle of Leyte Gulf; cited in *Master of Sea Power: A Biography of Fleet Admiral Ernest J. King*, by Thomas B. Buell.)

[A reporter had asked why the attacking Japanese fleet had divided their forces into three separate parts.]

394. If one can only hold on for a little time longer, things will be eased up and in due time the trouble will iron out. That has been my own belief, not to say creed, but it works out for me.

No fighter ever won by covering up—by merely fending off the other fellow's blows. The winner hits and keeps on hitting even though he has to take some stiff blows in order to be able to keep on hitting. (Undated; Ibid.)

WILLIAM D. LEAHY
(1875–1959)

The U.S. chief of Naval Operations before the outbreak of World War II, Leahy became ambassador to the Vichy government after the fall of France. Later, he became Chief of Staff to Presidents Roosevelt and Truman (q.v.).

395. He [Marshal Henri Petain (q.v.)] has told me that when the German demands appear to him to be outside the Armistice Agreement, and when he objects on that ground, the Germans claim the right to take the final interpretation, and when he disagrees, they carry out their intention without regard to his attitude in the matter. (Memorandum of conversation, ca. March 1941; cited in *Our Vichy Gamble*, by William L. Langer.)

396. [Shortly before the Allied invasion of French North Africa, Admiral Jean Darlan (q.v.) arrives in Algiers to be with his polio-stricken son. Leahy informs the president.] The first thing that impressed Roosevelt was the nature of the boy's illness. Roosevelt remembered his own illness and proposed that we send a letter to Darlan. I replied I thought it would be a very nice thing to do. Later Roosevelt sent Darlan's son to Warm Springs [a Georgia treatment center for polio] and kept him there for a considerable time. Darlan was most grateful, and it is my belief that this thoughtfulness on the part of the president helped us in the critical situation that was developing. (From the Leahy Memoirs; cited in *Diplomat among Warriors*, by Robert Murphy.)

[The "critical situation" was a series of negotiations to allow the landing of U.S. troops in French North Africa with a minimum of resistance. Finally, a deal was struck with Darlan.]

397. I had then [during the time he was U.S. ambassador to Vichy France], as I have now, the conviction that your principal concern was the welfare and protection of the helpless people of France. It was impossible for me to believe that you had any other concern. However, I must, in all honesty, repeat my opinion as expressed to you at the time that positive refusal to make any concessions to Axis demand, while it might have brought immediately increased hardship to your people, would in the long view, have been advantageous to France. (Letter to Henri Petain [q.v.]; quoted in the *New York Times*, August 2, 1945.)

[Petain, facing trial for treason in France, had requested a letter from Leahy regarding Petain's actions as head of the Vichy government.]

RAYMOND E. LEE

(1896–1958)

Lee was a U.S. Army general who was a military observer in London.

398. I . . . believe the British can resist invasion. It will be hard, bloody business, but what has occurred so far in Crete [invasion by the Germans from the air] does not alter my opinion. By some error of judgment or lack of imagination, the R.A.F. withdrew all its planes [from Crete]. Even a few fighters would have wrought havoc amongst the German troop carriers at the outset and would have been well expended. There is likely to be serious criticism of this decision and technical reasons will not serve to quell it. (Analysis, London, May 27, 1941; cited in *Roosevelt and Hopkins*, by Robert E. Sherwood.)

399. At the same time I have never believed and cannot see how the British Empire can defeat Germany without the help of God or Uncle Sam. Perhaps it will take both. God has undoubtedly been on the side of the big battalions so far, but may change sides. (Ibid.)

DOUGLAS MacARTHUR

(1880–1964)

MacArthur was commander of Allied forces in the Pacific. A veteran of World War I, MacArthur served in the Philippines, building up local defense forces. Upon the Japanese invasion of the Philippines, MacArthur was ordered to leave Bataan for Australia to take command of the Allied forces. He led campaigns in New Guinea, the Philippines, and other islands on the way to Japan. Upon the Japanese surrender, he was appointed Supreme Commander of Allied forces. After the war, he served brilliantly as United Nations commander in the Korean War. He was replaced by President Truman (q.v.) after policy disagreements.

400. Since I have no air or sea protection you must be prepared at any time to figure on the complete destruction of this command. You must determine whether the mission of delay would be better furthered by the temporizing plan of Quezon or by my continued battle effort. (Message to President Roosevelt, February 8, 1942.)

[MacArthur was referring to an enclosed message from President Manuel Quezon asking that the United States declare immediate independence for the Philippines. The United States and Japan would be asked to withdraw all military forces from the islands, thus neutralizing them. The Quezon message came after many requests for reinforcements and supplies—which could come only by submarine. Roosevelt's response to Quezon was that the United States had to carry on the fight against Japanese militarism, that any Japanese promise could not be trusted, and that the United States would live up to its commitment to grant independence to the Philippines in 1946.]

401. The temper of the Filipinos is one of almost violent resentment against the United States. Every one of them expected help and when it has not been forthcoming they believe they have been betrayed in favor of others. (Ibid.)

402. So far as the military angle [in the Philippines] is concerned, the problem presents itself as to whether the plan of President Quezon might offer the best possible solution of what is about to be a disastrous debacle. (Ibid.)

403. The President of the United States ordered me to break through the Japanese lines and proceed from Corregidor to Australia for the purpose, as I understand it, of organizing the American offensive against Japan, a primary object of which is the relief of the Philippines. (On arrival in Australia, March 17, 1942.)

404. I came through and I shall return. (Ibid.)

405. "Tokyo Rose" had announced gleefully that, if captured, I would be publicly hanged on the Imperial Plaza in Tokyo, where the Imperial towers overlooked the traditional parade ground of the Emperor's Guard divisions. Little did I dream that bleak night [when he was leaving the Philippines by PT (patrol torpedo) boat to take command in Australia] that five years later, at the first parade review of Occupation troops, I would take the salute as supreme commander for the Allied Powers on the precise spot so dramatically predicted for my execution. (Recalling March 1942; from *Reminiscences*, by Douglas MacArthur.)

406. [I am] utterly opposed, under any circumstances or conditions, to the ultimate capitulation of this command [on Bataan]. . . . If it is to be destroyed it should be upon the actual field of battle taking full toll from the enemy. (Message to General George Marshall, April 1, 1942, cited in *The Fall of the Philippines*, by Louis Morton.)

407. INDIRECT DISCOURSE: In this message MacArthur had explained that he had "long ago" prepared a "comprehensive plan," and that he had not told [General Jonathan] Wainwright [q.v.] about it "as I feared it might tend to shake his morale and determination." He offered also to attempt to return to the

"I came through and I shall return."

—DOUGLAS MacARTHUR

Two and a half years after pledging he would return to the Philippines, MacArthur wades ashore at Leyte Island.

Philippines "to rejoin this command temporarily and take charge of this movement." (Ibid.)

408. The Bataan Force went out as it would have wished, fighting to the end its flickering, forlorn hope. No army has done so much with so little, and nothing became it more than its last hour of trial and agony. To the weeping mothers of its dead, I can only say that the sacrifice and halo of Jesus of Nazareth has descended upon their sons, and that God will take them unto Himself. (Statement on the fall of Bataan, April 1942.)

409. The fall of Corregidor and the collapse of resistance in the Philippines, with the defeat of Burma, brings about a new situation. At least two enemy divisions and all the air force in the Philippines will be released for other missions. Japanese troops in Malaya and the Netherlands East Indies are susceptible of being regrouped for an offensive effort elsewhere since large garrisons will not be required because of the complacency of native population. The Japanese Navy is as yet unchallenged and is disposed for further offensive effort. A preliminary move is now underway probably initially against New Guinea and the line of communications between the United States and Australia. The series of events releases an enormously dangerous enemy potential in the Western Pacific. That the situation will remain static is most improbable. (Memo to President Roosevelt, May 8, 1942.)

410. I am of the opinion that the Japanese will not undertake large operations against India at this time. That area is undoubtedly within the scope of their military ambitions, but it would be strategically advisable for them to defer it until a later date. On the other hand, the enemy advance toward the south has been supported by the establishment of a series of bases while his left is covered from the Mandated Islands. He is thus prepared to continue in that direction. Moreover, operations in these waters will permit the regrouping of his naval and air forces from the East. Such is not the case in movement towards India. He must thrust into the Indian Ocean without adequate supporting bases, relinquishing the possibilities of concentrating his naval strength in either ocean. The military requirements for a decisive Indian campaign are so heavy that it can not be undertaken under those conditions. On the other hand, a continuation of the southern movement at this time will give added safety for his eventual move to the west. (Ibid.)

[MacArthur had been asked to comment on Churchill's belief that the Japanese would invade India next.]

411. In view of this situation I deem it of the utmost importance to provide adequate security for Australia and the Pacific area, thus maintaining a constant frontal defense against a flank threat against further movement to the southward. This should be followed at the earliest possible moment by offensive action. (Ibid.)

412. Corregidor needs no comment from me. It has sounded its own story at the mouth of its guns. It has scrolled its own epitaph on enemy tablets. But through the bloody haze of its last reverberating shot, I shall always seem to see a vision of grim, gaunt, ghastly men, still unafraid. (Statement on the fall of Corregidor, ca. May 8, 1942.)

413. Orders emanating from General [Jonathan] Wainwright [q.v.] have no validity. If possible separate your force into small units and initiate guerrilla operations. You, of course, have full authority to make any decision that immediate emergency may demand. (Message to General William Sharp, in the southern Philippines, from Melbourne, Australia, May 9, 1942.)

[Before the surrender of Corregidor, Sharp had been informed by Wainwright that Sharp should take command of his area in the southern Philippines. At the same time, Sharp was instructed to take his orders directly from MacArthur. Shortly afterward, Sharp had received new orders from Wainwright to surrender, so he had asked MacArthur what he should do.]

414. I believe Wainwright [q.v.] has temporarily become unbalanced, and his condition renders him susceptible of enemy use. (Message to General George Marshall, in Washington, from Melbourne, Australia, May 9, 1942.)

[Following a radio broadcast by Wainwright from Manila, calling on all American forces in the Philippines to surrender. Wainwright had attempted to surrender Corregidor only, but the Japanese had demanded total surrender of the Philippines. With the Corregidor garrison now completely disarmed, Wainwright feared a slaughter of his men if he did not give in to Japanese demands.]

415. It was not until several months later [after the fall of Corregidor], when three Americans who escaped prison with the help of the guerrillas and were later brought to Brisbane by submarine told me the story, that I received the agonizing details of the Death March and the atrocities of the prison camps in which its survivors were confined.

I directed the issuance of the story to the press, but that very day Washington forbade the release of any of the details of the prisoner-of-war atrocities. Perhaps the Administration, which was committed to a Europe-first effort, feared American public opinion would demand a greater reaction against Japan, but whatever the cause, here was the sinister beginning of the "managed news" concept by those in power. (Recalling events of summer 1942 [ca. August]; from *Reminiscences*, by Douglas MacArthur.)

416. People of the Philippines: I have returned. By the grace of Almighty God, our forces stand again on Philippine soil—soil consecrated in the blood of our two peoples. We have come, dedicated and committed to the task of destroying every vestige of enemy control over your daily lives, and of restoring upon a foundation of indestructible strength, the liberties of your people. (Broadcast, upon landing in the Philippines, October 1944.)

417. There were no survivors from the Japanese 16th Division, the unit which had conducted the infamous "Death March." (Recalling the reconquest of the Philippines, including enemy casualties, ca. December 1944; from *Reminiscences*, by Douglas MacArthur.)

418. I see that the old flag pole still stands. Have your troops hoist the colors to its peak, and let no enemy ever haul them down. (To Colonel George Jones after retaking Corregidor, February 1945.)

419. It is my earnest hope—indeed the hope of all mankind—that from this solemn occasion a better world shall emerge out of the blood and carnage of the past, a world founded upon faith and understanding, a world dedicated to the dignity of man and the fulfillment of his most cherished wish for freedom, tolerance and justice. (Surrender ceremonies aboard the USS *Missouri*, Tokyo Bay, September 2, 1945.)

420. Today the guns are silent. A great tragedy has ended. A great victory has been won. The skies no longer rain death—the seas bear only commerce—men everywhere walk upright in the sunlight. The entire world is quietly at peace. The holy mission has been completed. (Radio broadcast following the surrender proceedings, September 2, 1945.)

421. Military alliances, balances of power, leagues of nations, all in turn failed, leaving the only path to be by way of the crucible of war. . . . The utter destructiveness of war now blots out this alternative. We have had our last chance. If we do not devise some greater and more equitable system, Armageddon will be at our door. (Ibid.)

422. It is not easy for me to pass penal judgment upon a defeated adversary in a major military campaign. I have reviewed the proceedings [of the war crimes trial of Tomoyuki Yamashita (q.v.)] in vain search for some mitigating circumstances on his behalf. I can find none. Rarely has so cruel and wanton a record been spread to public gaze. . . .

The traditions of fighting men are long and honorable. They are based upon the noblest of human traits—sacrifice. This officer, of proven field merit, entrusted with high command involving authority adequate to responsibility, has failed his irrevocable standard; has failed his duty to his troops, to his country, to his enemy, to mankind; has failed utterly his soldier faith. . . . I approve the findings and sentence of the Commission and direct the Commanding General, Army Forces in the Western Pacific, to execute the judgment upon the defendant, stripped of uniform, decorations and other appurtenances signifying membership in the military profession. (Statement upholding the death sentence for Yamashita, February 1946; cited in *A Trial of Generals: Homma, Yamashita, MacArthur*, by Lawrence Taylor.)

423. Of all the faulty decisions of war perhaps the most unexplainable one was the failure to unify the command in the Pacific. The principle involved is the most fundamental one in the doctrine and tradition of command. In this instance it did not involve choosing one individual out of a number of Allied officers, although it was an accepted and entirely successful practice in the other great theaters. The failure to do so in the Pacific cannot be defended in logic, in theory or in common sense. Other motives must be ascribed. It resulted in divided effort, the waste, diffusion, and duplication of force, and the consequent extension of the war, with added casualties and cost. (From *Reminiscences*, by Douglas MacArthur.)

HASSO VON MANTEUFFEL

(1897–1978)

Manteuffel was one of Germany's younger generals. He fought first on the Russian front and then led a Panzer unit in the second Ardennes offensive—the Battle of the Bulge (q.v.).

424. Hitler had read a lot of military literature. . . . In this way, coupled with his personal experience of the last war as an ordinary soldier, he had gained a very good knowledge of the lower level of warfare—the properties of the different weapons; the effect of ground and weather; the mentality and morale of troops. He was particularly good in gauging how the troops felt. . . .

On the other hand he had no idea of the higher strategical and tactical combinations. He had a good grasp of how a single division moved and fought, but he did not understand how armies operated. . . .

He had a real flair for strategy and tactics, especially for surprise moves, but he lacked a sufficient foundation of technical knowledge to apply it properly. Moreover, he had a tendency to intoxicate himself with figures and quantities. When one was discussing a problem with him, he would repeatedly pick up the telephone, ask to be put through to some departmental chief, and ask him, "How many so and so have we got?" Then he would turn to the man who was arguing with him, quote the number, and say: "There you are," as if that settled the problem. (Quoted in *The German Generals Talk*, by B. H. Liddell Hart.)

GEORGE C. MARSHALL

(1880–1959)

Marshal was Chief of Staff of the U.S. Army. He took the army from a peacetime 200,000 to more than 8 million. President Roosevelt's chief strategist, he pushed for a Second Front in northern France as the quickest way to defeat Nazi Germany. Instead of leading the Allied armies into Europe, Marshall stayed behind in Washington to run the entire war. He selected Eisenhower to head the invasion of Europe. After the war, he won the Nobel Peace Prize for his work on the Marshall Plan.

425. Immediately alert complete defensive organization to deal with possible trans-Pacific raid to greatest extent possible without creating public hysteria or provoking undue curiosity of newspapers or alien agents. Suggest maneuver basis. Maintain alert until further notice. Instructions for secret communication direct with Chief of Staff will be furnished you shortly. Acknowledge. (Message to General Herron, commander of the Hawaiian Department, June 17, 1940; cited in *George C. Marshall: Ordeal and Hope*, by Forrest C. Pogue.)

426. Yesterday we had time but no money and . . . today we have money but no time. (Comment, summer 1940; Ibid.)

427. We must treat them [draftees] as soldiers, we cannot have a political club and call it an Army. I regard these disturbing activities from outside the Army, gentlemen, as sabotage of a very dangerous character. (Statement to the House Committee on Military Affairs, July 24, 1941.)

[The committee was considering the extension of the Selective Service Act, scheduled to expire in October 1941. Senator Burton K. Wheeler (q.v.) had sent out a million franked postcards calling for the defeat of the draft extension. Some of those cards had been received by draftees in uniform, who were circulating petitions to their representatives to kill draft extension. The extension would be approved by a single vote.]

428. Without discipline an Army is not only impotent but it is a menace to the state. (Ibid.)

429. The Japanese are presenting 1 P.M. Eastern Standard Time today what amounts to an ultimatum. Also they are under orders to destroy their code machine immediately. Just what significance the hour set may have we do not know, but be on alert accordingly. Inform the Navy. (Message to army commanders in the Philippines, Hawaii, the Canal Zone, and the Presidio in San Francisco, December 7, 1941.)

[Because of atmospheric conditions that affected official communications, the message to Hawaii was sent by Western Union and arrived after the attack.]

430. Prepare for and carry on military operations in the European Theater against the Axis Forces and their Allies. (Instructions to Eisenhower, commanding general, U.S. Army Forces in the British Isles, June 8, 1942.)

431. In the past two days [the invasion of North Africa], we have had a most impressive example of the practicable application of unity of command, an American Expeditionary Force . . . supported by the British fleet, by British fliers, and by a British Army, all commanded by an American commander-in-chief, General Eisenhower. . . . The instructions of the British Cabinet to guide their Army commander serving under General Eisenhower furnish a model of readiness of a great nation to cooperate in every practicable manner. I go into detail because this should not be a secret. It will be a most depressing news to our enemies. It is the declaration of their doom. (Speech, New York City, November 10, 1942.)

432. As I recall, [President Roosevelt] asked me after a great deal of beating about the bush just what I wanted to do [i.e., stay in Washington as Chief of Staff or go on to London to head the Allied invasion of Europe]. Evidently it was left up to me. . . . I just repeated again in as convincing language as I could that I wanted him to feel free to act in whatever way he felt was in the best interest of the country and to his satisfaction and not in any way to consider my feelings. I would cheerfully go whatever way he wanted me to go and I didn't express any desire one way or the other. . . . Then he evidently assumed that concluded the affair and that I would not command in Europe. Because he said, "Well I didn't feel I could sleep at ease if you were out of Washington." (Recollection of events of ca. December 5, 1943, Cairo; cited in *George C. Marshall: Organizer of Victory*, by Forrest C. Pogue.)

433. [I assure you] that neither the Secretary of War nor the president has any indication whatsoever that such a letter has been addressed to you or that the preparation or sending of such a communication was being considered. . . . I am trying my best to make plain to you that this letter is being addressed to you solely on my own initiative. Admiral [Ernest J.] King [q.v.] having been consulted only after the letter was drafted, and I am persisting in the matter because the military hazards involved are so serious that I feel some action is necessary to protect the interests of our armed forces. (Letter to Governor Thomas E. Dewey, September 27, 1944.)

[General Marshall had learned that Governor Dewey, Republican candidate for president, had gotten word that the United States had broken the Japanese code. Dewey was preparing a speech to charge that—because of the broken code—President Roosevelt, his campaign rival, had known in advance about Pearl Harbor.]

434. You will understand the utterly tragic consequences if the present political debates regarding Pearl Harbor disclose to the enemy, German or Jap, any suspicion of the vital sources of information we now possess. . . . I am presenting this matter to you . . . in the hope that you will see your way clear to avoid the tragic results with which we are now threatened in the present political campaign. (Ibid.)

[Dewey did not mention the code issue during the campaign.]

435. The beaches of Normandy were chosen for the assault after long study of the strength of German coastal defenses and the disposition of German divisions. The absence of large ports in the area was a serious obstacle, but it was offset in some measure by the relative weakness of the German defenses and elaborate construction in Britain of two artificial harbors [called "Mulberries"] to be emplaced on the beaches. (*Biennial Report* to the Secretary of War, July 1, 1943, to June 30, 1945.)

436. The selection of target dates and hours for the assault required an accurate forecast of the optimum combination of favorable weather, tide, and light conditions. Moonlight was desirable for the airborne operations. D-Day [q.v.] was scheduled for 5 June; this date was changed to 6 June because of unfavorable but clearing weather. Hundreds of craft, enroute from distant ports on the west coast of England, were already approaching the invasion area; they had to backtrack or seek shelter in the overcrowded harbors on the south coast. The final forecast for the attack day predicted high winds; the sea was still rough, but rather than accept a delay of several weeks until tide and moon provided another favorable moment, General Eisenhower made the fateful decision to go ahead. (Ibid.)

437. Remember that the investigation was intended to crucify Roosevelt, not to get me. There was no feeling in the War Department that we had anything to hide. (Commenting on congressional hearings on Pearl Harbor conducted between November 1945 and May 1946, interview, November 14, 1956; cited in *George C. Marshall: Ordeal and Hope*, by Forrest C. Pogue.)

LESLEY McNAIR

(1883–1944)

McNair was head of the American "Phantom Army," supposedly set to invade northern France across the Pas de Calais. It tied up the German 15th Army for several weeks, preventing the Germans from reinforcing the Normandy beaches. General McNair was subsequently killed in battle by "friendly fire" during an American bombing attack. Before the United States entered the war, McNair had critiqued army maneuvers. The lessons learned would later stand the U.S. Army in good stead on the battlefields of Europe.

438. The essential effectiveness of supply was an outstanding feature of the [Louisiana] maneuvers. The magnitude of the problem alone was sufficient to warrant apprehension as to whether the troops would be supplied adequately. Combat commanders and the services alike deserve the highest praise for the results achieved. (Critique of Louisiana Maneuvers, September 1941, from *Second Army vs. First Army, Critiques*, by Lesley McNair.)

439. There is no question that many of the weaknesses developed in these maneuvers are repeated again and again for lack of discipline. Our troops are capable of the best of discipline. If they lack it, leadership is faulty. A commander who cannot develop proper discipline must be replaced. (Ibid.)

F. W. VON MELLENTHIN

(n.d.)

Mellenthin was a major general in the German army. He was a key military figure in the battle of Kursk. That battle, which took place in the summer of 1943, is regarded by some historians as being equal in importance to the Battle of Stalingrad (q.v.).

440. At the very beginning of the offensive [against Kursk], the piercing of the forward Russian lines, deeply and heavily mined as they were, had proved much more difficult than we anticipated. The terrific Russian counterattacks, with masses of men and material ruthlessly thrown in, were also an unpleasant surprise. German casualties had not been light, while our tank losses were staggering. The Panthers [tanks] did not come up to expectations; they were easily set ablaze, the oil and gasoline feeding systems were inadequately protected, and the crews were insufficiently trained. Of the 80 Panthers available when battle was joined only a few were left on 14 July. (Recalling events of July 1943; from *Panzer Battles: A Study of the Employment of Armor in the Second World War*, by F. W. von Mellenthin.)

WALTHER MODEL
(1891–1945)

Model was a German army officer who led campaigns in the Soviet Union, France, Holland, and the Battle of the Bulge (q.v.). Facing Allied capture in April 1945, he killed himself.

441. I have asked the president of the Reich Tribunal to open a criminal procedure for breach of discipline against General der Infanterie Dietrich von Choltitz and his accomplices.

General von Choltitz failed to live up to what was expected of him as the general assigned to defend Paris. (Message to the German General Staff Command Personnel, August 28, 1944; cited in *Is Paris Burning?* by Larry Collins and Dominique Lapierre.)

[This was for failing to destroy Paris before allowing it to fall into Allied hands.]

BERNARD MONTGOMERY
(1887–1976)

Montgomery, a British army officer, participated in the battle of France early in the war, including the Dunkirk Evacuation (q.v.). He led the British 8th Army to victory in Egypt against Rommel's (q.v.) Afrika Korps and subsequent triumphs in Sicily and Italy. Promoted to field marshal in 1944, he played a major role in the invasion and conquest of Nazi-held Europe.

442. It is now clear that his [Rommel's (q.v.)] intention is to defeat us on the beaches. (May 1944; quoted in *Rommel: The Desert Fox*, by Desmond Young.)

443. He [Rommel (q.v.)] is an energetic and determined commander; he has made a world of difference since he took over [preparing for the impending Allied invasion]. He is best at the spoiling attack; his forte is disruption; he is too impulsive for a set-piece battle. He will do his level best to "Dunkirk" us—not to fight the armored battle on ground of his choosing but to avoid it altogether and prevent our tanks landing by using his own tanks well forward. On D-Day [q.v.] he will try (a) to force us from the beaches; (b) to secure Caen, Bayeux, Catentan. Thereafter he will continue his counterattacks. (Ibid.)

444. We must blast our way on shore [on D-Day (q.v.)] and get a good lodgment before he [Rommel (q.v.)] can bring up sufficient reserves to turn us out. [Our] [a]rmored columns must penetrate deep inland and quickly. We must gain space rapidly and peg our claims well inland. While we are engaged in doing this, the air must hold the ring and must make very difficult the movement of enemy reserves by train or road towards the lodgment areas. The land battle will be a terrible party and we shall require the support of the air all the time—and laid on quickly. (Ibid.)

445. In the annals of the British Army there are many glorious deeds. In our army we have always drawn great strength and inspiration from past traditions, and endeavored to live up to the high standards of those who have gone before.

But there can be few episodes more glorious than the epic of Arnhem, and those that follow after will find it hard to live up to the standards that you have set.

So long as we have in the armies of the British Empire officers and men who will do as you have done, then we can indeed look forward with complete confidence to the future.

In years to come it will be a great thing for a man to be able to say: "I fought at Arnhem." (Letter to General Robert E. Urquhart, who led the First Airborne Division at Arnhem during Market-Garden [q.v.], September 1944.)

446. The enemy is at present fighting a defensive campaign on all fronts, his situation is such that he cannot stage major offensive operations. Furthermore, at all costs he has to prevent the war from entering on a mobile phase; he has not the transport or the petrol that would be necessary for mobile operations, nor could his tanks compete with ours in the mobile battle. (Published at 21st Army Group, December 16, 1944, the eve of the German Ardennes offensive; cited in *A Soldier's Story*, by Omar N. Bradley.)

[Estimate of German offensive capacity.]

447. The enemy is in a bad way; he has had a tremendous battering and has lost heavily in men and equipment. On no account can we relax, or have a "stand still," in the winter months; it is vital that we keep going, so as not to allow him time to recover and so as to wear down his strength still further. There will be difficulties caused by mud, cold, lack of air support during periods of bad weather, and so on. But we must continue to fight the enemy hard during the winter months. (Ibid.)

448. Von Rundstedt [q.v.] attacked [the Ardennes] on December 16 [1944]. He obtained tactical surprise. He drove a deep wedge into the center of First U.S. Army and split the American forces in two. The situation looked as if it might become awkward; the Germans had broken right through a weak spot and were heading for the Meuse.

As soon as I saw what was happening, I took certain steps myself to ensure that *if* the Germans got to the Meuse they would certainly not get over that river. And I carried out certain movements so as to provide balanced dispositions to meet the threatened danger; these were, at the time, merely precautions, i.e. I was thinking ahead.

Then the situation began to deteriorate. But the whole allied team rallied to meet the danger; national considerations were thrown overboard; General Eisenhower placed me in command of the whole Northern front.

I employed the whole available power of the British Group of Armies; this power was brought into play very gradually and in such a way that it would not interfere with the American lines of communication. Finally it was put into battle with a bang, and today British divisions are fighting hard on the right flank of First U.S. Army.

You thus have the picture of British troops fighting on both sides of American forces who have suffered a hard blow. This is a fine allied picture.

The battle has been most interesting; I think possibly one of the most interesting and tricky battles I have ever handled, with great issues at stake. (Press conference, January 7, 1945.)

449. I would like . . . to say what a privilege and an honor it has been to serve under you. I owe much to your wise guidance and kindly forbearance. I know my own faults very well and I do not suppose I am an easy subordinate; I like to go my own way. But you have kept me on the rails in difficult and stormy times, and have taught me much. (Letter to General Eisenhower, June 7, 1945; cited in *Crusade in Europe*, by Dwight D. Eisenhower.)

CHESTER W. NIMITZ

(1885–1966)

Shortly after Pearl Harbor, Nimitz was named commander in chief of the Pacific fleet. He went about rebuilding the Pacific fleet almost from scratch. He represented the U.S. Navy at the Japanese surrender aboard the USS *Missouri* in September 1945.

450. The whole world wants to know where is Task Force 34. (Message to Admiral William F. Halsey [q.v.] during the battle of Leyte Gulf, October 1944.)

[Halsey had left the San Bernardino strait unguarded to pursue a Japanese decoy force. Upon receiving the message, Halsey is said to have snapped to a subordinate, "Send him our latitude and longitude."]

EDMUND NORTH
(1911–1990)

North was a captain in the U.S. Army Signal Corps Photographic Center. He was involved in the *Fighting Men* training film series.

451. There has been no attempt made in this series to be inspirational. War has not been painted as a delightful or glorious experience, but simply and straightforwardly as the cold, grim, scientific business that it is. (From *The Secondary or Psychological Phase of Training Films*, 1942; cited in *Projections of War*, by Thomas Doherty.)

GEORGE S. PATTON, JR.
(1885–1945)

Patton, a U.S. Army general, took part first in the invasion of French North Africa and led American troops in Tunisia. Later, he commanded U.S. forces in the invasion of Sicily. He caused an uproar when it was learned that he had slapped a shell-shocked soldier in an army hospital. Temporarily sidetracked, Patton would come back to lead the Third Army in France, Belgium, and Germany. Troops under his leadership went through the snow in the dead of winter to relieve the surrounded garrison at Bastogne during the Battle of the Bulge (q.v.). Several months after the war ended, Patton died of injuries he received in an automobile accident. He is buried at a military cemetery in Luxembourg, with his men.

452. In spite of my unfortunate proficiency in profanity, I have at bottom a strongly religious nature. It is my considered opinion that the success of the operation [the invasion of North Africa] was largely dependent on what people generally call "luck," but what I believe to be Divine help. (Letter to General Marshall, November 15, 1942; cited in *George C. Marshall: Ordeal and Hope*, by Forrest C. Pogue.)

[Patton was referring to unusually good weather, enabling the landings to take place in extremely calm waters.]

453. The idea of these [service] clubs could not be better because undoubtedly it is our destiny to rule the world. (Speech at the dedication of a service club in England, spring 1944.)

454. All real Americans love the sting of clash of battle. America loves a winner. America will not tolerate a loser. . . . America never will lose a war, for the very thought of losing is hateful to an American. (Address to his troops, France, July 1944; cited in *Memoirs of a Revolutionist*, by Dwight Macdonald.)

455. You are not all going to die. . . . Death must not be feared. Every man is frightened at first in battle. If any man says he isn't, he's a god-damned liar. But a real man will never let the fear of death overpower his honor, his sense of duty to his country and to his manhood. (Ibid.)

456. You've bitched about what you call "this chicken-shit drilling." That drilling was for a purpose: instant obedience to orders and to create alertness. If not, some son-of-a-bitch of a German will sneak up behind him and beat him to death with a sock full of shit. (Ibid.)

457. An army is a team. It lives, sleeps, eats and fights as a team. This individual hero stuff is a lot of crap. The bilious bastards who wrote that kind of stuff for the *Saturday Evening Post* don't know any more about real fighting under fire than they know about f——g. (Ibid.)

458. We want to get the hell over there and clean the god-damn thing up. And then we'll have to take a little jaunt against the purple pissing Japs and clean them out before the Marines get all the credit. (Ibid.)

459. Thirty years from now, when you are sitting at the fire with your grandson on your knee and he asks you what you did in the Great World War II, you won't have to say: "I shoveled shit in Louisiana." (Ibid.)

460. Hell, let's have the guts to let the sons of bitches go all the way to Paris. Then we'll really cut 'em off and chew 'em up. (Comment at a staff meeting to discuss how to handle the German breakout in the Ardennes, December 19, 1944.)

461. To hell with Montgomery [q.v.]. We'll take the whole f——g German Army and jam it up his ass! (On learning that Montgomery had put the First Army on the defensive during the Ardennes campaign—the Battle of the Bulge [q.v.], December 1944.)

462. Brad, this time the Kraut's stuck his head in a meatgrinder. And this time I've got hold of the handle. (Comment to Bradley [q.v.] during the Battle of the Bulge [q.v.], December 1944; quoted in *A Soldier's Story*, by Omar N. Bradley.)

463. I've waited a long time to do that. I didn't even piss this morning when I got up so I would have a really full load. Yes, sir, the pause that refreshes. (After urinating in the Rhine River, March 23, 1945; from *War as I Knew It*, by George S. Patton.)

464. You'll never believe how bastardly these Krauts can be until you've seen this pesthole yourself. (Statement to Bradley [q.v.], April 1945; quoted in *A Soldier's Story*, by Omar N. Bradley.)

[Upon discovery of the Nazi concentration camp at Ohrdruf.]

465. Well, I'll tell you. This Nazi thing. It's just like a Democratic-Republican election fight. The outs are always coming around saying that the ins are Nazis. . . . More than half the German people were Nazis and you'd be in a hell of a fix if you tried to remember all the Party members. (Press statement, fall 1945.)

[Defending the use of former Nazi Party members in posts in the occupation government.]

FRIEDRICH VON PAULUS

(1890–1957)

Paulus was a German general who led the German Sixth Army at Stalingrad (*see* Battle of Stalingrad [q.v.]). When Hitler refused permission for the Sixth Army to withdraw temporarily to re-form its lines, Paulus became trapped by the Russians. He surrendered on February 1, 1943. Toward the end of the war, he was making broadcasts aimed at German troops urging them to surrender. After the war, he settled in what was then Soviet-dominated East Germany.

466. Ammunition and fuel are running short. . . . A timely and adequate replenishment is not possible. . . . I must forthwith withdraw all the divisions from Stalingrad itself and further considerable forces from the northern perimeter.

In view of the situation, I request you to grant me complete freedom of action.

Heil mein Fuehrer! (Message to Hitler, November 23, 1942.)

[Hitler flatly refused the request.]

WILLIAM N. PORTER

(1886–1973)

Porter was a major general who was chief of the U.S. Army's chemical warfare service.

467. The initiative in gas warfare is of the greatest importance. We have an overwhelming advantage in the use of gas. Properly used gas could shorten the war in the Pacific and prevent loss of many American lives. (Memo to Major General Joseph McNarney, December 17, 1943, following the invasion of Tarawa; cited in *Code-Name Downfall: The Secret Plan to Invade Japan—and Why Truman Dropped the Bomb*, by Thomas B. Allen and Norman Polmar.)

ERICH RAEDER

(1876–1960)

The chief naval adviser to Hitler early in the Nazi regime, Raeder would rise to commander of the German navy. He retired from the post early in 1943. He was convicted at Nuremberg of helping to plan aggressive war and was sentenced to life imprisonment. Released from prison in 1955 for ill health, he died five years later.

468. Fuehrer's instructions: No mention must be made of a displacement of 25–26,000 tons, but only of improved 10,000-ton ships. . . . The Fuehrer demands complete secrecy on the construction of the U-boats. (Memo, June 1934.) [Germany's naval plans were in violation of the Treaty of Versailles.]

GENERAL ROHRICHT

(n.d.)

General Rohricht was in charge of the Training Department of the German General Staff.

469. Morale and discipline were better in the later part of this war than in the later part of the first [world] war. Between 1916 and 1918 the soldiers' morale was gradually undermined by the infiltration of Socialistic ideas, and the suggestion that they were fighting the Emperor's war, whereas this time they had and kept such extraordinary confidence in Hitler that they remained confident of victory in face of all the facts. (Quoted in *The German Generals Talk*, by B. H. Liddell Hart.)

ERWIN ROMMEL

(1891–1944)

Rommel was a German general who led troops in Hitler's 1940 invasion of France, in North Africa, and in Normandy defending against an Allied invasion. His reputation was well known not only in Germany but among the Allies as well. His Afrika Korps fought brilliantly in North Africa until it was squeezed between the British Eighth Army on the east and newly landed Allied troops on the west. He was thwarted in his plan to hold the Allies on the beaches and drive them into the sea on D-Day (q.v.). Shortly after the aborted July 20, 1944, plot to kill Hitler, he was given the choice of going on trial for treason or committing suicide. By choosing the latter, he assured the safety of his family. Historians differ on his implication in the plot to kill Hitler, although many believe he was seen as a likely successor to negotiate peace with the Allies.

470. The war will be won or lost on the beaches. We'll have only one chance to stop the enemy and that's while he's in the water struggling to get ashore. Reserves will never get up to the point of attack and it's foolish even to consider them. The . . . [main line of resistance] will be here [on the beaches]. . . . Every-

"The war will be won or lost on the beaches. We'll have only one chance to stop the enemy and that's while he's in the water struggling to get ashore. . . . The first 24 hours of the invasion will be decisive. . . . For the Allies, as well as Germany, it will be the longest day."

—ERWIN ROMMEL

Rommel was in charge of defending the coast of northern France from an Allied invasion. D-Day would come on June 6, 1944.

thing we have must be on the coast. (Statement to his aide, Captain Helmuth Lang, on a beach of northern France, ca. March 1944; cited in *The Longest Day: June 6, 1944*, by Cornelius Ryan [q.v.].)

471. Believe me, Lang, the first 24 hours of the invasion will be decisive. . . . For the Allies, as well as Germany, it will be the longest day. (Ibid.)

ELLIOTT ROOSEVELT

(1910–1990)

Roosevelt was one of the president's sons who accompanied his father to the major Big Three conferences. In his book *As He Saw It*, Elliott recounted extraordinary father-son conversations about what was going on.

472. "British still raising objections, are they?" [Elliott is asking about the cross-Channel Second Front.]

"Well," [the president responds] "now Winston is talking about two operations at once. I guess he knows there's no use trying to argue against the western invasion anymore. . . ."

"What does Churchill mean, Pop, two invasions at once?"

"One in the west, and one up through guess where."

"The Balkans?"

"Of course. . . . Whenever the P.M. [prime minister] argued for our invasion through the Balkans, it was quite obvious to everyone in the room what he really meant. That he was above all else anxious to knife up into central Europe, in order to keep the Red Army out of Austria and Rumania, even Hungary, if possible. . . . Everybody knew it. . . ."

[Elliott wonders if Churchill might not be right about a two-pronged invasion, and his father responds.]

"Elliott, our chiefs of staff are convinced of one thing. The way to kill the most Germans, with the least loss of American soldiers, is to mount one great big invasion and then slam 'em with everything we've got." (Teheran, November 1943; from *As He Saw It*, by Elliott Roosevelt.)

GERD VON RUNDSTEDT
(1875–1953)

Rundstedt, a German general, was continually either in or out of favor with Hitler. He commanded the German armies that won spectacular victories in the Low Countries and France in 1940. A year later, he led the invasion of the Soviet Union. He was put in charge of the Atlantic Wall, to keep Allied invaders out of northern Europe. He failed in this attempt, as he did in the Ardennes offensive of December 1944, also known as the Battle of the Bulge (q.v.).

473. INDIRECT DISCOURSE: The French army was "loyal and aided our troops," and . . . the French police were equally helpful. (Based on a diary excerpt, November 11, 1942; cited in *Klaus Barbie: The Butcher of Lyons*, by Tom Bower.)

[Referring to the occupation of Vichy France by Germany after the Allied invasion of French North Africa.]

474. End the war! What else can you do? (Response to Keitel [q.v.], following the Allied breakout from the beachhead, July 1944; quoted in *The German Generals Speak*, by B. H. Liddell Hart.)

[Keitel had asked Rundstedt what should be done. Shortly after Rundstedt's reply was received in Berlin, he was relieved of his command.]

475. A pitiless destiny has snatched him [Rommel (q.v.)] from us. (Funeral oration, October 18, 1944.)

[The language is ironic. Suspected of taking part in the plot to kill Hitler, Rommel was given the choice of committing suicide and saving his family or going on trial to meet certain execution. He chose suicide. The official cause of death was complications caused by wounds, and he was given a hero's funeral.]

476. Soldiers of the Western front! Your great hour has struck! Everything is at stake! (Order of the Day, prior to the Ardennes offensive, December 16, 1944.)

477. We gamble everything now—we cannot fail. (Order of the Day, on the eve of the Ardennes offensive, December 1944.)

FRANK A. SCHOFIELD

(n.d.)

Schofield was commander in chief of the U.S. Pacific Fleet until his retirement in the early 1930s.

478. An acute situation exists in the Pacific. War is imminent but not declared. The enemy will strike where the fleet is concentrated. The enemy will use carriers as the basis of his striking force. The enemy may make raids on Hawaiian Islands or the West Coast prior to declaration of war. Consider any Black [enemy] forces east of 180th meridian as possible. (Fleet Problem XIV, 1932; cited in *The Broken Seal*, by Ladislas Farago.)

[The problem was carried out as a war game by U.S. naval forces in February 1933. The "enemy" force was successful.]

GORDON S. SEAGRAVE

(1897–1965)

Seagrave was descended from a long line of evangelical missionaries in the Far East. He became a medical missionary in Burma. Several months after the war broke out, he and his Burmese nurses joined the retreat from Burma led by General Joseph W. Stilwell (q.v.). Seagrave kept a diary of that trek and published a book about his life as a Burma surgeon. He was commissioned in the U.S. Army medical corps, rising to the rank of lieutenant colonel. He served in the China-Burma-India theater.

479. The general [Stilwell (q.v.)] got us all together around him and made us a speech. All the different groups were to turn in their food supplies into a pool, then abandon everything they had except what they felt they would be able to carry themselves. I got the [Burmese] nurses together . . . and told them the Chin Hills and Naga Hills which our trail would cross were famous for their steepness and therefore they certainly could not carry so much stuff as to make them lag on the march. . . . Each girl must take a little first-aid kit, with the drugs for malaria, dysentery, headaches, etc. . . .

I find my feet don't hurt much if the ground is fairly smooth and can set my feet down squarely. It is this ghastly heat! I noticed the girls were carrying water in sulfathiazole bottles. About fifteen thousand tablets of the only sulfathiazole in India must be all over the ground back there! (May 6, 1942; from *Burma Surgeon*, by Gordon S. Seagrave.)

480. I have never seen jungles so full of monkeys! The minute they spot us they start whooping and hollering. Nurses claim they are yelling, "daddy, daddy, daddy!" They can get a laugh out of anything! . . . Thorns were everywhere, and the girls kept picking them out of their bare feet. But the ants were positively vicious! (May 8, 1942; Ibid.)

481. The general had secured three large rafts and one small one, and we are to float down the Uru [River] to the Chindwin. Each of the rafts consists of three sections fastened together with rattan. . . .

The current is now much stronger. Time after time it was almost impossible to keep the raft from breaking up. All hands had to plunge overboard and pull the entire length of the 80-foot raft with every ounce of strength, the sand washing away from under our feet as we struggled. (May 10, 1942; Ibid.)

WALTER BEDELL SMITH
(1895–1961)

Chief of Staff for SHAEF (Supreme Headquarters of the Allied Expeditionary Forces), "Beetle" Smith led the Allied delegation that accepted Nazi Germany's unconditional surrender.

482. Ike thinks it may be a good idea to turn over to Monty [Bernard Montgomery (q.v.)] your two Armies on the north and let him run that side of the Bulge from 21st Group. It may save us a great deal of trouble, especially if your communications with [Courtney] Hodges [q.v.] and [William] Simpson go out. (Telephone call to Bradley [q.v.], December 19, 1944; quoted in *A Soldier's Story*, by Omar N. Bradley.)

[This was one of the most controversial command decisions of the war. The two American armies put under Montgomery's temporary command did not take offensive action in the Battle of the Bulge (q.v.) for twelve days while Montgomery was "tidying" up his lines.]

483. During that phase of the operation [the drive to the Elbe River], it became increasingly apparent to us, from our various sources of intelligence, that Berlin, the second heart of Germany, had ceased to have much military significance. We were aware from various reports through neutral countries and otherwise that much of the German government had moved from Berlin. It had a psychological value, but nothing like the center of German communications and the center of German government. That factor weighed very heavily with General Eisenhower in planning his future operations. (Press conference, Paris, April 21, 1945.)

484. The so-called "thrust on Berlin," from a purely military standpoint, has ceased to be of any great importance to us. Berlin is going to fall, anyway. We don't care who fights their way into Berlin. (Ibid.)

485. Of the [German generals] . . . left, if he were allowed full complete authority . . . Kesselring is pretty good. . . . Kesselring is a damn good man professionally. He's got a very good chief of staff. His chief of staff on the West Wall was formerly his chief of staff, then Rundstedt's [q.v.] chief of staff, and now Kesselring's. He's a very good man and a thoroughly trained professional soldier. (Ibid.)

[In answer to a question about which of the German generals left he considered the best.]

486. Some of our generals are making [German] civilians come in and look [at the liberated concentration camps], and they all cover up their faces and won't look. Sometimes their hands have to be removed by force and pulled down and made to look. (Ibid.)

BREHON B. SOMERVELL

(1892–1955)

Somervell was in charge of all U.S. Army supply services during the war.

487. It is directed that Colonel L. R. Groves [q.v.] be relieved from his present assignment in the Office of Engineers for special duty in connection with the DSM project [the early code name for the Manhattan Project]. (Memorandum for the Chief of Engineers, September 17, 1942.)

[From official U.S. Army memo assigning Leslie R. Groves to head the atomic bomb project.]

HAROLD R. STARK

(1880–1972)

Stark was U.S. chief of Naval Operations until several months after Pearl Harbor. He was replaced by Admiral Ernest J. King (q.v.).

488. This dispatch is to be considered a war warning. (Dispatch to Admiral Kimmel [q.v.] at Pearl Harbor, November 27, 1941.)

[The dispatch talked about possible Japanese action against Thailand, Borneo, the Philippines, and other areas. Neither Pearl Harbor nor Hawaii were mentioned as possible targets.]

CLAUS VON STAUFFENBERG

(1907–1944)

A colonel in the German army, Stauffenberg had been badly wounded in Tunisia, losing an arm and an eye. Despising Hitler, he conspired with other army officers and civilians to dispose of the Fuehrer. On July 20, 1944, he planted a bomb at Hitler's military headquarters. Although the bomb killed several German officers, Hitler escaped with his life. A bloodbath followed.

489. Long live our holy eternal Germany! (Before a firing squad, Berlin, July 20, 1944; cited in *Operation Valkyrie*, by Pierre Galante with Eugene Silianoff.)

JOSEPH W. STILWELL

(1883–1946)

Commanding general of all U.S. forces in the China-Burma-India theater of operations, Stilwell earned a reputation for straight-talking honesty. Early in the war he had to walk through 140 miles of Burmese jungle to escape from the advancing Japanese army. Later, he would return to win victory over Japanese forces. He was assigned to work with Chiang Kai-shek and to build up the Chinese army. After years of fighting, there was danger of China being overrun by the Japanese. Stilwell was frustrated by Chiang's government, which was more concerned with the Chinese Communists than with fighting the Japanese enemy.

490. I claim we got a hell of a beating. We got run out of Burma and it is humiliating as hell. I think we ought to find out what caused it, go back and retake it. (Press conference, New Delhi, India, May 24, 1942.)

491. My belief in the decisive strategic importance of China is so strong that I feel certain a serious mistake is being made in not sending American combat units into this theater. (Message to War Department, May 25, 1942.)

492. INDIRECT DISCOURSE: Stilwell's [solution] for China's sake, the war's sake, and his own, was reform of the army. He saw the 300 [Chinese] divisions "sprawled all over China," on the average 40 percent understrength, with commanders drawing pay for full strength and "officers getting rich, men dying of malnutrition, malaria, dysentery, cholera, the sick simply turned loose. Ammo and weapons being sold. Open traffic with the enemy on all 'fronts.' Transport being used for smuggling. None to move troops." . . . Chiang Kai-shek . . . and his constant talk about trucks, planes and guns "only reveals his complete ignorance of the necessity for training, replacements, leadership, medical care." (From *Stilwell and the American Experience in China: 1911–45*, by Barbara W. Tuchman; material in quotes from *Stilwell's Mission to China*, by Charles Romanus and Riley Sunderland.)

493. You will hear a lot of talk about how this or that generation messed things up and got us into war. What nonsense. All living generations are responsible for what we do and all dead ones as well. (Letter to West Point graduating class, ca. May 1945.)

494. Illegitimati non carborundum. [Don't let the bastards grind you down.] (Motto, 1946.)

CHARLES TENCH

(n.d.)

Tench was a U.S. Army colonel who was a member of General MacArthur's staff. He was the first American to occupy Japan at the end of the war.

495. No hostile action encountered. (Message to General MacArthur, August 28, 1945.)

[Upon landing at Atsugi airfield with an initial force of 150 men.]

MATOI UGAKI

(n.d.)

Matoi Ugaki was a rear admiral in the Japanese navy and Yamamoto's (q.v.) chief of staff.

496. A gigantic fleet . . . has massed at Pearl Harbor. This fleet will be utterly crushed with one blow at the very beginning of hostilities. . . . The success of our surprise attack on Pearl Harbor will prove to be the Waterloo of the war to follow. (Statement to flag officers, November 11, 1941; cited in *The Broken Seal*, by Ladislas Farago.)

JONATHAN WAINWRIGHT

(1883–1953)

Wainwright, a U.S. Army officer, took over command in the Philippines after General MacArthur was ordered to Australia. After Bataan fell in April 1942, Wainwright fought on from the fortified island of Corregidor in Manila Bay. He was forced to surrender on May 6, 1942. A prisoner of the Japanese for more than three years, Wainwright suffered the same privations as his men. He was flown to Tokyo Bay to witness the surrender of Japan on board the USS *Missouri*. He would be awarded the Congressional Medal of Honor.

497. With broken heart and head bowed in sadness but not in shame I report to your excellency that today I must arrange terms for the surrender of the fortified islands of Manila Bay. (Last message from Corregidor, addressed to President Roosevelt, May 6, 1942.)

[At about this point in the message, transmission was interrupted. The full text did not become known until after the war. The remainder of the text follows.]

498. There is a limit of human endurance and that limit has long since been passed. Without prospect of relief I feel it is my duty to my country and to my gallant troops to end this useless effusion of blood and human sacrifice. (Ibid.)

499. If you agree, Mr. President, please say to the nation that my troops and I have accomplished all that is humanly possible and that we have upheld the best traditions of the United States Army. (Ibid.)

500. May God bless and preserve you and guide you and the nation in the effort to ultimate victory. (Ibid.)

501. With profound regret and with continued pride in my gallant troops I go to meet the Japanese commander. Goodbye, Mr. President. (Ibid.)

WALTER WARLIMONT

(n.d.)

Warlimont was a general attached to German army headquarters.

502. As early as January 1944 Admiral [Wilhelm] Canaris [q.v.] had discovered the text of a radio message to be transmitted from England shortly before the date of the [D-Day (q.v.)] invasion as a standby signal to the French Resistance. The message consisted of two completely innocent sounding lines of poetry from Verlaine's *Chanson d'Automne*; the first, "*Les sanglots longs des violons de l'automne*," formed the warning order to be given on the first or 15th of the invasion month; the second, "*Blessent mon coeur d'une longueur monotone*," the more immediate warning to be given 48 hours before the start of the invasion. On the afternoon of 5 June [1944] the Intelligence Service informed [General Alfred] Jodl [q.v.] that during the night of 4 June the second of these two sentences had been heard by the Security Service of 15th Army. But no action was taken. (From *Inside Hitler's Headquarters*, by Walter Warlimont.)

503. Hitler himself was now quite obviously a sick man. His actual injuries on 20 July [1944 in the unsuccessful assassination attempt] had been minor but it seemed as if the shock had brought into the open all the evil of his nature, both physical and psychological. He came into the map room bent and shuffling. His glassy eyes gave a sign of recognition only to those who stood closest to him. His chair would be pushed forward for him and he would slump down into it, bent almost double with his head sunk between his shoulders. As he pointed to something on the map his hand would tremble. On the slightest occasion he would demand shrilly that "the guilty" be hunted down. (Ibid.)

PAUL M. WENNEKER

(n.d.)

Wenneker, a rear admiral, was the German naval attaché in Tokyo.

504. Japan will not attack Russia. . . . The next steps planned are occupation of Dutch oil fields simultaneously with an attack on Manila, and the blockading of Singapore by cutting off all access routes. (Teletype to German Admiralty in Berlin, August 22, 1941; cited in *The Broken Seal*, by Ladislas Farago.)

MAXIME WEYGAND

(1867–1965)

Weygand, a French general, led army forces at the time of the 1940 surrender of France. He served briefly in the Vichy government. Because of his opposition to some policies that favored Germany, he was arrested and imprisoned by the Nazis. After the war, a French court cleared him of collaboration charges.

505. The Battle of France has begun. . . . The fate of our country, the safeguarding of her liberties, the future of our children, depends on your tenacity. (Order of the Day, June 5, 1940.)

506. The position of foreign nationals who have sought asylum in France will form the subject of a later agreement on the basis of honor and humanity. (June 22, 1940; cited in *The Collapse of the Third Republic*, by William L. Shirer [q.v.].)

[Proposed change in one clause of the armistice terms presented to France. The clause dealt with Germans who had fled to France for asylum. The original armistice clause required France to turn over those refugees to German authorities. The Germans rejected Weygand's proposal. The original clause would stand—and the Vichy government would carry out this term of the armistice faithfully.]

507. No. 43/DN. Order is given to the French delegation . . . to sign the armistice convention with Germany. (Order telephoned to General Charles Huntziger, June 22, 1940; Ibid.)

[Huntziger had insisted that he not be given *permission* to sign the armistice terms but be *ordered* to do so.]

508. Dunkirk was certainly not a victory but merely the least unfortunate liquidation of what could have been a catastrophe. (From *Rappele au Service*, by Maxime Weygand.)

I. E. YAKIR

(n.d.)

Yakir was a Soviet general in command of the Ukrainian and Kiev military districts in the 1930s. He was one of thousands of Soviet military officers who were executed for treason in the Red Army purges of 1937–1938. He is included in this book as one of the military leaders who was not around in June 1941, when Hitler moved against the Soviet Union.

509. I am an honest soldier, dedicated to the Party, the state and the people, as I have been for many years. All my conscious life has been spent in selfless and honest work before the Party and its leaders. . . . I shall die with words of love for you, the Party and the country, and with a boundless faith in the victory of Communism. (Letter to Stalin, spring 1937; cited in *Zhukov*, by Otto Preston Chaney, Jr.)

[Stalin wrote on the letter: "Scoundrel and prostitute." Yakir was shot.]

ISORUKU YAMAMOTO

(1884–1943)

Yamamoto was the Japanese admiral who planned the attack on Pearl Harbor. Yamamoto had real misgivings about getting Japan into war with the United States, but he carried out his duty as he saw it. He was killed when the plane in which he was flying was shot down by U.S. Navy planes while he was on an inspection trip. The navy pilots had known of his flight plans—and were on a deliberate mission to take him down.

510. What is strange position I find myself in now—having to make a decision diametrically opposed to my own personal opinion, with no choice but to push full speed in pursuance of that decision. (Letter to Teikichi Hori, November 11, 1941; cited in "Admiral Yamamoto," by James A. Field, Jr.)

511. Climb Mount Niitaka. (December 7, 1941.)

[Signal to Japanese strike force to carry out attack on Pearl Harbor.]

512. I shall not be content merely to capture Guam and the Philippines and to occupy Hawaii and San Francisco. I am looking forward to dictating peace in the United States in the White House in Washington. (Attributed, ca. 1942.)

TOMOYUKI YAMASHITA

(1885–1946)

Yamashita, a Japanese general, conquered Malaya and forced the surrender of Singapore in 1942. Earlier in his career he had served as a military attaché in several European capitals, including Berlin. As head of the Japanese army occupying the Philippines, he was to be charged with atrocities carried out by Japanese soldiers. After the war, he was tried and executed.

513. All I want to hear from you is yes or no. I expect to put the same question to MacArthur. (Ultimatum to General Arthur Percival, Singapore, February 15, 1942.)

514. The facts are that I was constantly under attack by large American forces, and I had been under pressure day and night. Under those circumstances, I had to plan, study, and carry out plans of how to combat superior American forces, and it took all my time and effort. (Testimony under cross-examination at his war crimes trial, Manila, the Philippines, October 1945; cited in *A Trial of Generals: Homma, Yamashita, MacArthur*, by Lawrence Taylor.)

[This was in response to the question, How come you didn't know about the atrocities committed by Japanese troops during the American liberation of the Philippines?]

515. At the time of my arrival, I was unfamiliar with the Philippine situation. . . . I was confronted with a superior American force. Another thing was that I was not able to make a personal inspection and to coordinate the units under my command. As a result of the inefficiency of the . . . Japanese army system, it was impossible to unify my command, and my duties were extremely complicated.

Another matter was that troops were scattered about a great deal, and the communications would, of necessity, have to be good, but the Japanese communications were very poor. . . .

Reorganization of the military force takes quite a while, and these various troops which were not under my command, such as the air force and the Third Marine Command, and the navy, were gradually entering the command one at a time, and it created a very complicated situation. . . . Under these circumstances, I was forced to confront the superior United States forces with subordinates whom I did not know and with whose character and ability I was unfamiliar. . . .

I tried to dispatch staff officers and various people to the outlying units, but the situation was such that they would be attacked by guerrillas en route and would be cut off. Consequently, it became very difficult to know the situation in these separated groups. And under conditions like this and with both the communication equipment and personnel of low efficiency and old type, we managed to maintain some liaison, but it was gradually cut off, and I found myself completely out of touch with the situation.

I believe that under the foregoing conditions I did the best possible job I could have done. However, due to the above circumstances, my plans and my strength were not sufficient to the situation, and if these things happened, they were absolutely unavoidable. They were beyond anything that I would have expected. If I could have foreseen these things, I would have concentrated all my efforts toward preventing it. (Ibid.)

HARRY E. YARNELL
(1875–1959)

Yarnell was an American admiral.

516. The following are considered the fundamentals of adequate national defense:

a. A navy and an air force equal to that of any nation or coalition that threatens our security.

b. An army adequate to garrison outlying bases and to provide a highly mobile, fully equipped force of about 600,000 men, thoroughly trained in modern warfare. We should never send an army of millions abroad in any future war.

The navy and air force must be adequate to carry on offensive war in enemy waters. The frontier must be the enemy's coast. (Memorandum, January 9, 1941.)

GEORGI K. ZHUKOV
(1896–1974)

Zhukov was a field marshal of the Red Army. He played a vital role in the defense of the Soviet Union and the final drive into Nazi Germany. A survivor of the 1937–1938 purge of Red Army officers, Zhukov won the confidence and support of Stalin. He was directly involved in many campaigns of the war, including the defense of Leningrad, the battle of Kursk, and the assault on Berlin.

517. Evidently the enemy, collecting a maximum of his forces, including up to 13–15 tank divisions, supported by a large amount of aviation, will deliver a strike by his Orel-Kromy groupings to envelop Kursk from the southeast. . . . One must expect that this year the enemy will count on tank divisions and aviation for the offensive, since his infantry is considerably weaker for carrying out offensive actions than last year. (Report to Stalin, April 8, 1943; cited in *Zhukov*, by Otto Preston Chaney, Jr.)

518. [Instead of launching an offensive], it would be better if we wore the enemy down on our defenses, knocked out his tanks, and then, introducing fresh reserves, by going over to the general offensive finally finish off his main forces. (Ibid.)

[After some hesitation, Stalin went along with Zhukov's recommendation. The battle of Kursk, which took place in the summer of 1943, was one of the outstanding Russian victories of the war.]

519. Soon I'll have that slimy beast Hitler locked up in a cage. And when I send him back to Moscow, I'll ship him by way of Kiev so you can have a look at him. (Telephone call to Nikita Khrushchev [q.v.], ca. March 1945; quoted in *Khrushchev Remembers*, by Nikita S. Khrushchev.)

520. I won't be able to keep my promise after all. That snake Hitler is dead. He shot himself, and they burned his corpse. We found his charred carcass. (Telephone call to Nikita Khrushchev [q.v.], May 1945; Ibid.)

521. There are two kinds of mines; one is the personnel mine and the other is the vehicular mine. When we come to a mine field our infantry attacks exactly as if it were not there. The losses we get from personnel mines we consider only equal to those we would have gotten from machine guns and artillery if the Germans had chosen to defend that particular area with strong bodies of troops instead of with mine fields. The attacking infantry does not set off the vehicular mines, so after they have penetrated to the far side of the field they form a bridgehead, after which the engineers come up and dig out channels through which our vehicles can go. (ca. June 1945; quoted in *Crusade in Europe*, by Dwight D. Eisenhower.)

3

Government Officials

PIETRO BADOGLIO
(1871–1956)

Badoglio was Italian chief of staff and a political leader. Following the overthrow of Mussolini (q.v.), Badoglio negotiated the surrender to the Allies. When Germany occupied Italy and attacked Italian forces, Badoglio announced a state of war with Nazi Germany.

522. Italians! There will not be peace in Italy as long as a single German remains upon our soil. Shoulder to shoulder, we must march forward with our friends of the United States, of Great Britain, of Russia, and of all the other United Nations. Wherever Italian troops may be, in the Balkans, Yugoslavia, Albania, and in Greece, they have witnessed similar acts of aggression and cruelty [such as those perpetrated in Italy] and they must fight against the Germans to the last man. . . .

Italians! I inform you that His Majesty the King has given me the task of announcing today, the 13th day of October, the Declaration of war against Germany. (Proclamation to the people of Italy, following German occupation and acts of violence and destruction after Italy's surrender, October 13, 1943.)

KLAUS BARBIE

(1913–1991)

German SS (Schutzstaffel) officer Barbie rounded up Jews in Holland and France during the war. In Lyons, France, he was head of the Gestapo, dealing with the French Resistance, Jewish affairs, and acts of sabotage against the occupation. His brutal treatment of members of the French Resistance and Jews was so well known that he was called "the Butcher of Lyons." Shortly after the war, his intelligence archives and contacts made him useful to American intelligence. Nearly four decades later, he was extradited from Bolivia to be put on trial in France for war crimes. On July 3, 1987, Barbie was convicted of crimes against humanity and sentenced to life imprisonment.

523. At the beginning [of the German occupation of France] it was very hard for us. We had very few contacts. Everything was new. I had to build an effective team, carefully hand picking each recruit. We were showered with denunciations of the Resistance by the French and I usually tried to find long-term collaborators from amongst the denunciators. (Cited in *Klaus Barbie: The Butcher of Lyons*, by Tom Bower.)

WILLIAM BEAVERBROOK

(1879–1964)

British financier and newspaper publisher Beaverbrook had originally favored appeasing Hitler. Once war came, he took an active part in the British government. He held several cabinet posts at different times, including Minister of Aircraft Production, Minister of Supply, and Lord Privy Seal. He was also one of Churchill's chief troubleshooters.

524. We loyally hushed up the betrayal of U.S. Embassy communications. But [U.S. Ambassador Joseph P.] Kennedy [q.v.] was soon back at it. He wanted an unconditional guarantee that we send the whole British fleet to American ports in the likely event of our surrender. To the very last, he was worried about money. The British should be made to pay cash for arms. British-owned securities in the United States should be taken over and sold to raise the money. He feared Roosevelt was holding private conversations with you, so nothing would get on record about the President's blank-check arrangements for unsecured British credit. When Churchill said we shall defend our island whatever the cost may be, Kennedy warned Washington: "Remember all speeches are being made in beautiful sunshiny weather." Even Russian Ambassador Ivan Maisky was astonished at Kennedy's state of panic, and is commenting acidly about "Capitalist Kennedy seeking personal concessions on imports of Haig & Haig whisky and Gordon's Gin, for which he holds exclusive distribution rights in the United States, in exchange for his help in obtaining American supplies, a crude form of blackmail." The London *Spectator* thinks there seem to be plenty of eminent persons in the United States to give isolationist advice without the Ambassador, knowing our ordeal, joining their number. (Message sent to William Stephenson [q.v.], a top British intelligence official meeting in Washington, fall 1940; cited in *A Man Called Intrepid*, by William Stevenson.)

[Beaverbrook was summarizing Kennedy's last weeks in Britain as U.S. ambassador.]

ALEXANDER CADOGAN
(1884–1968)

Cadogan was a member of the British cabinet during the war.

525. Cabinet 6.30. We endured the usual passionate anti–De Gaulle [q.v.] harangue from PM [Prime Minister Churchill]. On subject, we get away from politics and diplomacy and even common sense. It's a girls' school. Roosevelt, PM, and—it must be admitted De Gaulle—all behave like girls approaching the age of puberty. (Cabinet meeting notes, London, June 5, 1944; from *The Diaries of Sir Alexander Cadogan, O.M., 1938–1945*, edited by David Dilks.)

[It was the eve of D-Day. At the time of the British cabinet meeting, it was believed that de Gaulle would refuse to broadcast a message to France to back the forthcoming invasion. De Gaulle would relent and make the broadcast.]

NEVILLE CHAMBERLAIN
(1869–1940)

Prime minister of Great Britain from 1937 to 1940, Chamberlain pursued a policy of appeasing Hitler. This allowed the Nazi government to achieve a number of bloodless victories in Europe. In 1939, following the Nazi invasion of Poland, he declared war on Germany. He resigned the post in May 1940, to be succeeded by Winston Churchill.

526. We are resolved that the method of consultation shall be the method adopted to deal with any other questions that may concern our two countries, and we are determined to continue our efforts to remove possible sources of difference, and thus to contribute to assure the peace of Europe. (Statement drawn up by Chamberlain and signed by him and Hitler, September 30, 1938.)

527. I believe it is peace in our time. (On returning from the Munich conference, London, September 30, 1938.)

528. In the event of any action which clearly threatened Polish independence, and which the Polish government accordingly considered it vital to resist with their national forces, His Majesty's Government would feel themselves bound at once to lend the Polish government all support in their power. They have given the Polish government all assurance to this effect.

I may add that the French government have authorized me to make it plain that they stand in the same position in this matter as do His Majesty's Government. (Address to the House of Commons, March 31, 1939.)

[During Polish discussions with Nazi Germany regarding territorial demands.]

529. I am accordingly to inform your Excellency that unless the German Government are prepared to give His Majesty's Government satisfactory assurance that the German Government have suspended all aggressive action against Poland and are prepared promptly to withdraw their forces from Polish territory, His Majesty's Government in the United Kingdom will without hesitation fulfill their obligations to Poland. (Message to Hitler, September 1, 1939.)

530. Although this communication [above] was made more than 24 hours ago, no reply has been received but German attacks upon Poland have been continued and intensified. I have accordingly the honor to inform you that, unless not later than 11 o'clock, British Summer Time, today, 3d September, satisfactory assurances to the above effect have been given by the German Government, and have reached His Majesty's Government in London, a state of war will exist between the two countries as from that hour. (Message to Foreign Minister Ribbentrop [q.v.], September 3, 1939.)

531. This is a sad day for all of us, and to none is it sadder than to me. Everything that I have worked for, everything that I have believed in during my public life, has crashed into ruins. There is only one thing left for me to do: that is, to devote what strength and powers I have to forwarding the victory of the cause for which we have to sacrifice so much. I trust I may live to see the day when Hitlerism has been destroyed and a liberated Europe has been re-established. (Speech in the House of Commons, September 3, 1939.)

[After announcing that England was at war with Nazi Germany.]

CHIANG KAI-SHEK

(1887–1975)

Political and military leader of Nationalist China, Chiang planned the defense of China from the time of the Japanese invasion of 1937. After Pearl Harbor, the United States sent General Joseph W. Stilwell (q.v.) to help build up the Chinese army and to provide lend-lease armaments and equipment. Friction between Stilwell and Chiang led to Stilwell's recall to the United States. After the war, the Chinese Communists forced Chiang to abandon the mainland and set up his government on the island of Taiwan.

532. General [Joseph W.] Stilwell [q.v.] has more power in China than I have. (Comment to U.S. envoy Patrick Hurley, September 12, 1944.)

[Hurley had been sent to China to smooth out relations between Stilwell and Chiang.]

533. We Chinese share with our whole hearts the inexpressible satisfaction which this German surrender gives the civilized world. The whole stupendous weight of humanity now comes down on Japan. (Broadcast, May 8, 1945, following the German surrender.)

JEAN DARLAN

(1881–1942)

Admiral Darlan commanded all French naval forces during the war. Under the Vichy government, he became High Commissioner of Algeria, a post he held when Americans invaded French North Africa in November 1942. He negotiated a cease-fire with the Americans and was given a major political post in the newly formed government. On Christmas Eve 1942, he was assassinated in Algiers.

534. There is no question of doing so [surrendering the French fleet to the Nazis]; it would be contrary to our naval traditions and honor. (Briare, France, June 12, 1940.)

[Direct answer to Churchill, who raised the question as France teetered on the brink of asking for an armistice.]

535. The Chancellor [Hitler] did not ask me to hand over the fleet to him. Every one knows—the British better than anyone—that I will never hand it over.

The Chancellor did not ask me for any colonial territory. He did not ask me to declare war on England.

Why has he acted so?

Germany began the war alone and judges herself able to end it alone against no matter what coalition.

At no moment in the conversations was there any question of France abandoning in any way her sovereignty.

France is freely choosing the road she is taking. On her depends her present and her future. She will have the peace which she makes for herself. She will have the place in the organization of Europe which she will have made for herself. (Radio address, May 23, 1941, following a meeting with Hitler; cited in *Our Vichy Gamble*, by William L. Langer.)

[Several days later, Darlan signed an agreement that would have given the Germans such things as an air base at Aleppo, use of the Tunisian port of Bizerte, provision for the sale of guns and trucks, the use of French ships to transport German supplies, and the use of Dakar in French West Africa for use by German submarines, ships, and planes. The Vichy government, however, would not go along with Darlan's plan. It was scrapped.]

536. Would you mind suggesting to Major General [Mark] Clark [q.v.] that I am a five-star admiral? He should stop talking to me like a lieutenant junior grade. (Spoken to Robert Murphy [q.v.], Algiers, North Africa, ca. November 15, 1942; quoted in *Diplomat among Warriors*, by Robert Murphy.)

537. You know there are four plots in existence to assassinate me. Suppose one of these plots is successful. What will you Americans do then? (Asked of Robert Murphy [q.v.], Algiers, North Africa, December 23, 1942 [the day before his assassination]; Ibid.)

[Murphy later wrote that Darlan drew up a list of possible successors. It included the name of Charles de Gaulle (q.v.) but excluded Henri Giraud (q.v.). Darlan felt the latter "was only a good divisional commander."]

ELMER DAVIS
(1871–1958)

American newsman and radio commentator, Davis was appointed head of the Office of War Information (OWI) in 1942, a position he held until 1945. The OWI was set up to provide information about the war to the American public. It did this mainly through news stories and articles provided to the media.

537a. Your side of the case is propaganda, my side of the case is the simple objective truth. So feels the average man, even if he happens to be a prime minister or a dictator. (Reviewing *Mobilizing for Chaos*, by O. W. Riegel, the first study of modern propaganda techniques, *New York Times*, 1934.)

538. This Office [of War Information] recognizes the right of the Navy High Command and the Army High Command to revise our proposed publications in the interest of security as well as of factual accuracy, and I think you will acknowledge that the Navy's wishes on these points have been scrupulously respected.

We do not, however, recognize any right on your part to make revisions merely altering the language or presentation of a news story or its content, except insofar as security and factual accuracy are concerned. Writing a news story is a matter which requires some experience and technical skill. If those who lack this experience and skill undertake it, the result is apt to be very much as if I should make suggestions on naval strategy. (Letter to Ernest J. King [q.v.], March 1943; cited in *Master of Sea Power: A Biography of Fleet Admiral Ernest J. King*, by Thomas B. Buell.)

539. The version [of the article] which you approved has been stripped of virtually all material which could make it of interest to the public. With certain excisions it might be suitable for publication in a government manual, but it is the opinion of our editorial staff that very few newspapers would be interested in it. Besides, it contains certain eulogistic phrases, such as "the best military brains in the country," which, while undoubtedly true, represent editorial opinion such as is not ordinarily introduced into a news story and such as this Office could not issue without indicating the source. Accordingly, we feel it best to drop the whole matter of any endeavor to present the work of the Joint Chiefs of Staff to the public—an endeavor which, you will recall, was undertaken upon your suggestion. (Ibid.)

[The Office of War Information (OWI), at the request of the Joint Chiefs of Staff (JCS), had prepared an article on the JCS for release to the press. The proposed article was returned to the OWI, with revisions.]

FRANCISCO FRANCO
(1892–1975)

Following the Spanish Civil War of 1936–1939, Franco became dictator of Spain. During that war, he had the military support of Fascist Italy and Nazi Germany, while the Republicans (Spanish Loyalists) were supported by the Soviet Union. Thus, the Spanish Civil War became a prelude to World War II. When Hitler attacked Russia, Spain provided the Germans with the Blue Division—all "volunteers"—to fight on the Eastern Front. For a time during the war, Spain also provided supplies for German U-boats. But try as he might, Hitler could not get Franco to join the Tripartite Pact [q.v.], seize Gibraltar, or give him a base in the Canary Islands, despite offers of French territory in North Africa.

540. INDIRECT DISCOURSE: There were now two wars and . . . Spain could participate in a crusade against Russia without going to war with the western Allies. (ca. late June 1941; cited in *Franco: A Biography*, by Paul Preston.)

[Response to a British diplomat who questioned Spain's decision to provide a division to fight on the Russian front.]

541. [Franco spoke of] these moments when the German armies lead the battle for which Europe and Christianity have for so many years longed, and in which the blood of our youth is to mingle with that of our comrades of the Axis as a living expression of our solidarity. (Speech, July 17, 1941; Ibid.)

[Speech was delivered several weeks after Germany invaded the Soviet Union.]

HANS FRANK

(1900–1946)

Following the invasion of Poland by Nazi Germany, Frank was appointed governor general of the occupied territory by Hitler. His murderous crimes against the population led to his indictment as a war criminal. He was hanged at Nuremberg.

542. A thousand years will pass and the guilt of Germany will not be erased. (Nuremberg, Germany, October 1946.)

HANS FRITZSCHE

(n.d.)

Fritzsche headed the German press department in the Propaganda Ministry. Tried at Nuremberg after the war, he was acquitted of any war crimes.

543. Militarily this war has already been decided. All that remains to be done is of predominantly political character both at home and abroad. The German armies in the East will come to a halt at some point, and we shall draw up a frontier there which will act as a bulwark against the East for Europe and for the European power bloc under German leadership. It is possible that military tensions and perhaps even small-scale military conflicts may continue for eight or ten years, but such a situation—and this is the will of the German leadership—will not prevent the reconstruction and organization of the European continent along the lines laid down by Germany. Certainly this will be a "Europe behind barbed wire," but this Europe will be entirely self-sufficient economically, industrially and agriculturally, and it will be basically unassailable militarily. The German state leadership has no intention of pursuing Britain and America into the wilderness in order to engage them in battle. This would be of no profit to Europe, and the expenditure in men and material would be out of proportion to the advantage to be derived. (Address, Berlin Foreign Press Association, October 13, 1941; cited in *The Secret Conferences of Dr. Goebbels*, edited by Willi A. Boelcke.)

WALTHER FUNK

(1890–1960)

Funk was Reichsbank president and Minister of Economics in the Nazi government. He was tried at Nuremberg, convicted of war crimes, and sentenced to life imprisonment.

544. The information given to me by Field Marshal Goering [q.v.], that you, my Fuehrer, yesterday evening approved in principle the measures prepared by me for financing the war and for shaping the relationship between wages and prices and for carrying through emergency sacrifices, made me deeply happy. (Letter to Hitler, August 25, 1939.)

545. I hereby report to you with all respect that I have succeeded by means of precautions taken during the last few months, in making the Reichsbank internally so strong and externally so unassailable, that even the most serious shocks in the international money and credit market cannot affect us in the least. (Ibid.)

546. In the meantime I have quite inconspicuously changed into gold all the assets of the Reichsbank and of the whole of German economy abroad which it was possible to lay hands on. (Ibid.)

547. Under the proposals I have prepared for a ruthless elimination of all consumption which is not of vital importance and of all public expenditure and public works which are not of importance for the war effort, we will be in a position to cope with all demands on finance and economy, without any serious shocks. (Ibid.)

GEORGE VI

(1895–1952)

King George VI of England took the throne upon the abdication of his brother, Edward VIII.

548. England, my country . . . is part of Europe. . . . We stand on the threshold of we know not what. Misery & suffering in War we know. But what of the future? The British mind is made up. I leave it at that. (Letter to U.S. Ambassador Joseph P. Kennedy [q.v.], September 12, 1939; cited in *A Man Called Intrepid*, by William Stevenson.)

[This was in response to a conversation with Kennedy three days earlier. At that time, the ambassador had warned that Britain would bankrupt itself in a new war and should get out while it still could.]

JOSEPH GOEBBELS
(1897–1945)

Goebbels was Minister of Popular Enlightenment and Propaganda during the Third Reich. Fiercely loyal to his Fuehrer, he stayed with Hitler in his Berlin bunker as the Russians closed in on the city. After Hitler committed suicide, Goebbels had his six children poisoned. Then he and his wife also committed suicide.

549. The Fuehrer has decided that the war cannot be brought to an end without an invasion of Britain. Operations planned in the East have therefore been cancelled. [I] cannot give any detailed dates, but one thing is certain: The invasion of Britain will start in three, or perhaps five weeks. (Propaganda Ministry conference, Berlin, June 5, 1941; quoted in *The Secret Conferences of Dr. Goebbels*, edited by Willi A. Boelcke.)

[A bit of disinformation. Goebbels was trying to counter the swirl of rumors in Germany that an invasion of the Soviet Union was imminent.]

550. The Japanese are yellow Aryans. (Attributed, ca. 1942.)

551. [Goebbels discussed various slogans used by the Germans during the war.]

First year of the war: We have won.
Second year of the war: We shall win.
Third year of the war: We must win.
Fourth year of the war: We cannot be defeated.

Such a development is disastrous and must on no account be repeated. Instead, the German public must be made to realize that we not only want to win and must win, but more particularly that we are also *able* to win. (Propaganda Ministry conference, Berlin, January 6, 1943; quoted in *The Secret Conferences of Dr. Goebbels*, edited by Willi A. Boelcke).

552. In English newspapers these days can be read that the German leaders, in their present difficulties, are citing the power of resistance of the English people, themselves, after the Dunkirk catastrophe, so as to encourage the German people. I declare to this, categorically: No German statesman and no German newspaper has submitted to this degradation. I know no reason, either, why the German people had to refer precisely to the English people, so as to cope with the difficulties of this second winter war in the East. (Broadcast, Berlin, January 30, 1943.)

553. A people whose history records a Frederick the Great does not need to look for models in English history. (Ibid.)

554. A nation which is led by Adolf Hitler does not need to take a drunkard like Churchill for a model. (Ibid.)

555. Now is not the time to ask how it [the disaster at Stalingrad (q.v.)] all happened. That must be left for a later accounting, which will be made with complete candor and will show the German people and the people of the world that the misfortune that has come to us in the last few weeks is possessed of a deep and fateful significance. The great heroic sacrifice made by our soldiers at Stalingrad has been of decisive historical significance for the whole Eastern front. It was not in vain! Why? That, the future will show. (Radio broadcast, February 18, 1943.)

556. Even if a marathon runner breaks down, unconscious, after having broken the tape, the wreath of laurel will yet adorn his brow. The same goes for a nation which has entered the struggle for its existence. Everything that it had to forsake for victory it will be able to regain through that victory. Everything, however, which that nation tried to keep back during the struggle for victory it will lose as a result of defeat. (Broadcast, October 3, 1943.)

557. If I had received these powers [as Reich Trustee of Total War in charge of total mobilization] when I wanted them so badly, victory would be in our pockets today, and the war would probably be over. But it takes a bomb under Hitler's arse to make Hitler see reason. (ca. July 30, 1944; cited in *The German Home Front 1939–45*, by Terry Charman.)

[Following the unsuccessful attempt on Hitler's life.]

558. The enemy has no intention of allowing any government to take office in Germany. In short the Reich will be dealt with like a Negro colony in Africa. (Diary excerpt, March 11, 1945; from *Final Entries 1945: The Diaries of Joseph Goebbels*, edited by H. R. Trevor-Roper [q.v.].)

559. There is no doubt . . . that shortly after the end of the war Churchill will be despatched to the wilderness. It is, after all, long-established British practice to tolerate men who amass an exaggerated plentitude of power in wartime but in peacetime to cast them off at once. . . . He is, after all, basically the old obdurate stubborn Tory who understands nothing whatsoever of social problems and so is about as well suited to our century as a dinosaur. (Diary excerpt, March 19, 1945; Ibid.)

560. The fact that they are finding the European continent in such a miserable state is causing the British some worry. Labor Party observers in particular lament that, instead of a blooming continent, a corpse is falling into their hands. The British public is now slowly beginning to realize that, even if the Anglo-Americans do win a victory over us, it will be a Pyrrhic victory. (Diary excerpt, March 25, 1945; Ibid.)

561. The Japanese in Berlin, even including those in the Embassy, have become very defeatist. Nevertheless they are urging us to continued resistance, following the old rule that any enemy whom we kill will not have to be killed by the Japanese. (Diary excerpt, March 29, 1945; Ibid.)

562. The reports from the Reich Propaganda Offices and the letters that I receive are naturally couched in most despairing terms. Their general trend is that people are now convinced that the war is lost. (Diary excerpt, March 31, 1945; Ibid.)

563. The Fuehrer has ordered me to leave Berlin, should the defence of the capital collapse, and act as a leading member of a government nominated by him.

For the first time in my life I must categorically refuse to comply with an order from the Fuehrer. My wife and children are at one with me in this refusal. Quite apart from the fact that emotionally and for reasons of personal loyalty we could never bring ourselves to desert the Fuehrer in this his direst moment, were I to do otherwise, for the rest of my life I should consider myself an infamous renegade and common blackguard. . . .

In the frenzy of betrayal in which the Fuehrer is enveloped during these critical days of the war there must be at least some to stand by him unconditionally and unto death even if this entails contravening a formal order. . . .

[I] hereby declare my irrevocable decision not to leave the Reich capital, even should it fall; we prefer to bring to an end at the side of the Fuehrer a life which for me personally has no further value unless I can use it in the service of the Fuehrer and at his side. (Appendix to Hitler's Will and Testament, April 29, 1945.)

HAILE SELASSIE

(1891–1976)

Haile Selassie assumed the throne as emperor of Ethiopia in 1928. In 1935, Haile Selassie led his people against an Italian invasion. Thoroughly overwhelmed by Mussolini's (q.v.) modern weaponry,

Haile Selassie pleaded for support from the League of Nations. The League rejected his request for a loan to buy weapons for the Ethiopians. The African nation was conquered. Haile Selassie lived in exile in England until Britain liberated his country in 1941. Many historians regard the Italo-Ethiopian War as the beginning of the end for the League of Nations and an early prelude to World War II.

564. On December 23 [1935], in the region of the River Takkaze, they [the Italian invaders] attacked our troops with various poison gases. This violation by Italy of an international agreement must be added to the long list of those she has previously contravened. (Message to the League of Nations, December 30, 1935; cited in *The Ethiopian War, 1935–1941*, by Angelo Del Boca.)

565. I, Haile Selassie I, Emperor of Ethiopia, am here today to claim that justice which is due to my people and the assistance promised to it eight months ago when 50 nations asserted that an aggression had been committed. None other than the emperor can address the appeal of the Ethiopian people to 50 nations. . . . Given that I am setting a precedent, that I am the first head of a state to address the Assembly, it is surely without precedent that a people, the victim of an iniquitous war, now stands in danger of being abandoned to the aggressor. . . .

I assert that the problem submitted to the Assembly today is a much wider one than the removal of sanctions. It is not merely a settlement of Italian aggression. It is collective. It is the very existence of the League of Nations. . . . In a word, it is international morality that is at stake. . . .

Representatives of the world, I have come to Geneva to discharge in your minds the most painful of the duties of a head of state. What reply shall I take back to my people? (Address, League of Nations, Geneva, Switzerland, June 30, 1936; Ibid.)

[As Haile Selassie rose to deliver his address, Italian journalists booed, hissed, and shouted insults at him. They were removed from the Assembly Hall, and the emperor made his appeal, in vain.]

PAUL HENNICKE

(n.d.)

Hennicke was a squad commander in the German SS (Schutzstaffel), the Nazi elite guard. Following the fall of France, Hennicke submitted a proposal for taking over and exploiting certain African colonies.

566. The copper and tin mines [of French and Belgian colonies in Africa], the building of roads and dams, the diamond, gold, and silver mines for the jewelry industry will offer a fabulous labor opportunity for the concentration camp inmates, who are to be found so profusely in Europe. This will keep the settlement space in Greater Germany clean. Government plantations will provide work for the colored peoples. (Letter to SS Obergruppenfuehrer Karl Wolf, July 2, 1940; cited in *Infiltration*, by Albert Speer.)

RUDOLF HESS

(1894–1987)

Hess was deputy to Adolf Hitler. On May 10, 1941, Hess parachuted into Scotland to try to negotiate peace with Britain. It was six weeks before the German invasion of the Soviet Union, and scholars still disagree over whether the flight was Hess's own idea or whether he went with Hitler's approval. In any case, the peace proposal was rejected, and Hess was taken as a prisoner of war. He was tried at Nuremberg as a war criminal, sentenced to life in prison, and—after several unsuccessful tries over the years—committed suicide in 1987. He had been imprisoned for forty-six years.

567. All National Socialists know, the highest law in war, as in peace, is as follows: preservation of the Race. Every custom, law and opinion has to give way and to adapt itself to this highest law. Such an unmarried mother may have a hard path. But she knows that when we are at war, it is better to have a child under the most difficult conditions than not to have one at all. It is taken for granted today that a woman and mother who is widowed or divorced may marry again. It must also be taken for granted that a woman who has a "war child" may enter into marriage with a man who is not the father of that child and who sees in the woman's motherhood the foundation of marriage and companionship. The family is the basis of the country: but a race, especially during war, cannot afford to neglect to keep and continue its national heritage. . . . The highest service which a woman may perform for the community as a contribution to the continuation of the nation is to bear racially healthy children. Be happy, good woman, that you have been permitted to perform this highest duty for Germany. Be happy that the man whom you love lives in your child. Heil Hitler. (Address to an unmarried mother, *Berliner Morgenpost*, December 24, 1939; cited in *The German Home Front, 1939–45*, by Terry Charman.)

568. I am on a mission of humanity. The Fuehrer does not want to defeat England and wants to stop fighting. (Statement to the Duke of Hamilton, the day after Hess parachuted into Scotland, May 11, 1941.)

REINHARD HEYDRICH

(1904–1942)

A key figure in Reich security matters before the war, Heydrich was personally chosen by Hitler to carry out the extermination of European Jewry. This program would later be called the Holocaust (q.v.). Heydrich was assassinated outside Prague, and the Nazis took terrible vengeance on the Czech people. The Holocaust, however, continued until Germany surrendered.

569. Photocopies of these documents will be sold to the Russians at a high price, and we will make it appear that they have been stolen from the files of the SD [Sicherheitsdienst]. We will also create the impression that we are investigating the German side of the conspiracy, but without mentioning names, as the Fuehrer is opposed to that. Stalin will break [Marshal Mikhail] Tuchachevsky, because he will receive this dossier through his own Secret Service and will be convinced that it is authentic. (Meeting with aides, Berlin, December 1936; cited in *Canaris*, by Andre Brissaud.)

[Referring to the preparation of forged documents aimed at framing Red Army Marshal Tuchachevsky. This was a convoluted conspiracy. Stalin feared the popularity of his marshal and wanted to get rid of him. At the same time, Nazi Germany wanted to see the marshal eliminated because he favored a preventive war against Hitler. The Nazis were delighted to ensure that Stalin find the "evidence" he was looking for. The Germans forged documents that were designed to portray the marshal as plotting to overthrow Stalin. The frame-up would be successful beyond the wildest Nazi dreams, resulting not only in the execution of Tuchachevsky but in the purge of thousands of Red Army officers. It would seriously cripple Soviet military forces in the early days of the Nazi invasion.]

570. In the course of the final solution, the Jews should be brought under appropriate direction in a suitable manner to the East for labor utilization. Separated by sex, the Jews capable of work will be led into these areas in large labor columns to build roads, whereby doubtless a large part will fall away through natural reduction.

The inevitable final remainder which doubtless constitutes the toughest element will have to be dealt with appropriately, since it represents a natural selection which upon liberation is to be regarded as a germ cell of a new Jewish development . . .

In the course of the practical implementation of the final solution, Europe will be combed from West to East. (Statement, Wannsee Conference, January 20, 1942.)

["Final Solution" was the Nazi euphemism for the extermination of European Jewry.]

HEINRICH HIMMLER
(1900–1945)

Head of the Gestapo (the German Security State Police) and the SS (Schutzstaffel—the Nazi elite guard), Himmler was Hitler's official assassin. He was responsible for arranging and ordering the deaths of millions of innocents. He began his career as a killer by carrying out the blood purge of 1934, in which scores of the Nazi faithful were murdered, by order of the Fuehrer. Himmler's trail of blood continued during the war when he carried out the genocide of European Jewry. In 1945, he tried to negotiate peace with the Western Allies through a Swedish intermediary and was denounced as a traitor by Hitler. Captured by the British at the close of the war, he committed suicide.

571. Gentlemen, it is easy to speak the sentence "The Jews must be exterminated" with its few words. But for the man who must carry out what it demands, it is the very highest and most difficult thing in the world. We were confronted with the question: What about the women and children? I made up my mind to find a very clear solution here, too. For I did not feel I had the right to exterminate the men—that is, kill or have them killed—and allow the vengeance seekers in the form of children and grandchildren to grow up. . . . The Jewish question in the countries occupied by us will be settled by the end of this year. There will only be remnants left, individual Jews who have slipped underground. (Speech to Reichsleiters and Gauleiters, Posen, October 6, 1943; cited in *Infiltration*, by Albert Speer.)

572. Let no one come and tell us that what you are doing [the killing of all relatives of those who conspired to kill Hitler] is bolshevism. No, that is not bolshevism but a very ancient Germanic custom. . . . When a man was outlawed, it was said: this man is a traitor, his blood is bad, it contains treason, it will be exterminated. . . . And . . . the entire family, including its remotest connections, was exterminated. We will do away with the Stauffenbergs including their remotest connections. (Address to Nazi Gauleiters, Posen, August 3, 1944; cited in *Berlin Diaries, 1940–1945*, by Marie Vassiltchikova.)

[Count Claus von Stauffenberg (q.v.) planted the bomb that failed to kill Hitler.]

HIROHITO
(1901–1989)

Emperor of Japan since 1926, Hirohito reigned from long before the war began until long after it had ended. Although historians disagree over what role he might have played in Japan's aggressive war policies, there is virtual unanimity in the belief that he personally broke the deadlock among Japanese officials and called for surrender to avoid further bloodshed. This was done in spite of attempts by key military figures who wanted to carry on the war even after Hiroshima, Nagasaki, and the Soviet Union's entry into the war. Hirohito alluded to this "fraternal contention" in his radio address to the Japanese people.

573. To our good and loyal subjects:
After considering deeply the general trends of the world and the actual conditions obtaining in Our Empire today, We have decided to effect a settlement of the present situation by resorting to an extraordinary measure.

We have ordered Our Government to communicate to the Governments of the United States, Great Britain, China and the Soviet Union that Our Empire accepts the provisions of their Joint Declaration [which called for unconditional surrender]. (Radio broadcast, August 15, 1945.)

574. We declared war on America and Britain out of Our sincere desire to ensure Japan's self-preservation and the stabilization of East Asia, it being far from Our thought either to infringe upon the sovereignty of other nations or to embark upon territorial aggrandizement. (Ibid.)

575. But now the war has lasted for nearly four years. Despite the best that has been done by everyone—the gallant fighting of military and naval forces, the diligence and assiduity of Our servants of the State and the devoted service of Our one hundred million people—the war situation has developed not necessarily to Japan's advantage. (Ibid.)

576. Moreover, the enemy has begun to employ a new and most cruel bomb, the power of which to do damage is indeed incalculable, taking the toll of many innocent lives. Should We continue to fight, it would not only result in an ultimate collapse and obliteration of the Japanese nation, but also it would lead to the total extinction of human civilization. (Ibid.)

577. Such being the case, how are We to save the millions of Our subjects, or to atone Ourselves before the hallowed spirits of Our Imperial Ancestors? This is the reason why We have ordered the acceptance of the provisions of the Joint Declaration of the Powers. (Ibid.)

578. The hardships and sufferings to which Our nation is to be subjected hereafter will certainly be great. We are keenly aware of the inmost feelings of all ye, our subjects. However, it is according to the dictate of time and fate that We have resolved to pave the way for a grand peace for all the generations to come by enduring the unendurable and suffering what is insufferable. (Ibid.)

579. Beware most strictly of any outbursts of emotion which may engender needless complications, or any fraternal contention and strife which may create confusion, lead ye astray and cause ye to lose the confidence of the world. Let the entire nation continue as one family from generation to generation, ever firm in its faith of the imperishableness of its divine land, and mindful of its heavy burden of responsibilities, and the long road before it. (Ibid.)

HARRY L. HOPKINS
(1890–1946)

As President Roosevelt's personal adviser during the war, Hopkins acted as his eyes and ears in numerous trips overseas. As head of the Lend-Lease (q.v.) program, Hopkins conferred with Churchill and Stalin, getting them the armaments they needed to carry on the war.

580. The president is determined that we shall win the war together. Make no mistake about it.

He has sent me here to tell you that at all costs and by all means he will carry you through, no matter what happens to him—there is nothing that he will not do so far as he has human power. (Addressed to Winston Churchill at their first meeting in London, ca. January 12, 1941.)

581. I suppose you could say that I've come here to try to find a way to be a catalytic agent between two prima donnas. (Statement to Edward R. Murrow [q.v.], London, January 1941; cited in *Roosevelt and Hopkins*, by Robert E. Sherwood.)

[Hopkins had arrived in London as the special representative of President Roosevelt to Prime Minister Churchill.]

582. Surely, Mr. President, here is the point we have got to settle. Are we going to face it or not? (Attributed to Hopkins by Winston Churchill, who dubbed him "Lord Root of the Matter," ca. 1944.)

JOHN HOUSEMAN

(n.d.)

John Houseman, a theatrical producer, served in the Office of War Information's overseas section, the Voice of America.

583. One of our best writers [at the Office of War Information] was fired because he'd been with the Abraham Lincoln Brigade [American volunteers who fought Franco (q.v.) during the Spanish Civil War]. Among the investigators were many who had worked for Henry Ford as union busters. They invented the term "premature anti-fascists," PAF. It was used in adverse reports that we received on people. (From *The Good War*, by Studs Terkel.)

ROBERT H. JACKSON

(1892–1954)

A member of the U.S. Supreme Court, Jackson was chosen to be chief prosecutor of the top Nazis at the Nuremberg war crimes trial of 1945–1946.

584. The wrongs which we seek to condemn and punish have been so calculated, so malignant and so devastating, that civilization cannot tolerate their being ignored because it cannot survive their being repeated. (Address to the court opening the American case under Count One of the indictment dealing with conspiracy, International Military Tribunal, Nuremberg, Germany, November 21, 1945.)

585. That four great nations [the United States, United Kingdom, Soviet Union, and France], flushed with victory and stung with injury, stay the hand of vengeance and voluntarily submit their captive enemies to the judgment of the law is one of the most significant tributes that Power ever has paid to Reason. (Ibid.)

586. This tribunal, while it is novel and experimental, is not the product of abstract speculations nor is it created to vindicate legalistic theories. This inquest represents the practical effort of four of the most mighty of nations, with the support of 17 more, to utilize International Law to meet the greatest menace of our times—aggressive war. The common sense of mankind demands that law shall not stop with the punishment of petty crimes by little people. It must also reach men who possess themselves of great power and make deliberate and concerted use of it to set in motion evils which leave no home in the world untouched. (Ibid.)

587. In the prisoners' dock sit 20-odd broken men. . . . It is hard now to perceive in these miserable men as captives the power by which as Nazi leaders they once dominated much of the world and terrified most of it. Merely as individuals, their fate is of little consequence to the world.

What makes this inquest significant is that those prisoners represent sinister influence that will lurk in the world long after their bodies have returned to dust. They are living symbols of racial hatreds, of terrorism and violence, and of the arrogance and cruelty of power. They are symbols of fierce nationalisms and militarism, of intrigue and war-making which have embroiled Europe generation after generation, crushing its manhood, destroying its homes, and impoverishing its life. They have so identified themselves with the philosophies they conceived and with the forces they directed that any tenderness to them is a victory and an encouragement to all the evils which are attached to their names. (Ibid.)

588. What these men stand for we will patiently and temperately disclose. We will give you undeniable proofs of incredible events. The catalogue of crimes will omit nothing that could be conceived by a pathological pride, cruelty, and lust for power. These men created in Germany, under the *Fuehrerprinzip*, a National Socialist despotism equated only by the dynasties of the ancient East. They took from the German people all those dignities and freedoms that we hold natural and inalienable rights in every human being. The people were compensated by inflaming and gratifying hatreds toward those who were marked as "scapegoats." Against their opponents, including Jews, Catholics, and free labor, the Nazis directed such a campaign of arrogance, brutality, and annihilation as the world has not witnessed since the pre-Christian ages. They executed the German ambition to be a "master race," which of course implies serfdom for

"The wrongs which we seek to condemn and punish have been so calculated, so malignant and so devastating, that civilization cannot tolerate their being ignored because it cannot survive their being repeated."

—ROBERT H. JACKSON

In Nuremberg, the top Nazis stand trial for war crimes and crimes against humanity.

others. They led their people on a mad gamble for domination. They diverted social energies and resources to the creation of what they thought to be an invincible war machine. They overran their neighbors. To sustain the "master race" in its war making, they enslaved millions of human beings and brought them into Germany, where these hapless creatures now wander as "displaced persons." (Ibid.)

589. Never before in legal history has an effort been made to bring within the scope of a single litigation the developments of a decade, covering a whole Continent, and involving a score of nations, countless individuals, and innumerable events. Despite the magnitude of the task, the world has demanded immediate action. This demand has had to be met, though perhaps at the cost of finished craftsmanship. In my country, established courts, following familiar procedures, applying well-thumbed precedents, and dealing with the legal consequences of local and limited events seldom commence a trial within a year of the event in litigation. Yet less than eight months ago today the courtroom in which you sit was an enemy fortress in the hands of German SS [Schutzstaffel] troops. Less than eight months ago nearly all our witnesses and documents were in enemy hands. The law had not been codified, and no procedures had been established, no Tribunal was in existence, no usable courthouse stood here, none of the hundreds of tons of official German documents had been examined, no prosecuting staff had been assembled, nearly all the present defendants were at large, and the four prosecuting powers had not yet joined in common cause to try them. I should be the last to deny that the case may well suffer from incomplete researches and quite likely will not be the example of professional work which any of the prosecuting nations would normally wish to sponsor. It is, however, a completely adequate case to the judgment we shall ask you to render, and its full development we shall be obliged to leave to historians. (Ibid.)

590. Unfortunately, the nature of these crimes is such that both prosecution and judgment must be by victor nations over vanquished foes. The worldwide scope of the aggressions carried out by these men has left but few real neutrals. Either the victors must judge the vanquished or we must leave the defeated to judge themselves. (Ibid.)

591. We must summon such detachment and intellectual integrity to our task that this trial will commend itself to posterity as fulfilling humanity's aspirations to do justice. (Ibid.)

592. We will not ask you to convict these men on the testimony of their foes. There is no count of the indictment that cannot be proved by books and records. The Germans were always meticulous record keepers, and these defendants had their share of the Teutonic passion for thoroughness in putting things on paper. Nor were they without vanity. They arranged frequently to be photographed in action. We will show you their own films. You will see their own conduct and hear their own voices as these defendants reenact for you, from the screen, some of the events in the course of the conspiracy. (Ibid.)

593. We would also make clear that we have no purpose to incriminate the whole German people. We know that the Nazi Party was not put in power by a majority of the German vote. We know it came to power by an evil alliance between the most extreme of the Nazi revolutionists, the most unrestrained of the German reactionaries, and the most aggressive of the German militarists. If the German populace had willingly accepted the Nazi program, no Stormtroopers would have been needed . . . and there would have been no need for concentration camps or the Gestapo. (Ibid.)

594. The fact of the war and the course of the war, which is the central theme of our case, is history. . . . That attack upon the peace of the world is the crime against international society. . . . This war did not just happen—it was planned and prepared for over a long period of time and with no small skill and cunning. (Ibid.)

595. Their seizure of the German state, their subjugation of the German people, their terrorism and extermination of dissident elements, their planning and waging of war, their calculated and planned ruthlessness in the conduct of warfare, their deliberate and planned criminality toward conquered peoples, all these are ends for which they acted in concert; and all these are phases of the conspiracy, a conspiracy which reached one goal, only to set out for another and more ambitious one. (Ibid.)

596. We shall also trace for you the intricate web of organizations which these men formed and utilized to accomplish these ends. We will show how the entire structure of offices and officials was dedicated to the criminal purposes and committed to use of the criminal methods planned by these defendants and their coconspirators, many of whom war and suicide have put beyond reach. (Ibid.)

597. These defendants were men of a station and rank which does not soil its hands with blood. They were men who knew how to use lesser folk as tools. We want to reach the planners and designers, the inciters and leaders without whose evil architecture the world would not have been for so long scourged with the violence and lawlessness, and wracked with the agonies and convulsions, of this terrible war. (Ibid.)

NIKITA S. KHRUSHCHEV

(1894–1971)

Khrushchev was a member of the Military Council in Kiev and Stalingrad and was a close confidante of Stalin and General Georgi Zhukov (q.v.). Following Stalin's death in 1953, Khrushchev watched a number of men assume leadership of the Soviet Union. He finally got his own chance to take control but was later ousted himself. Khrushchev is probably best known for a 1956 speech before the Communist Party Congress in which he denounced the excesses of Stalin.

598. After our great victory over the enemy which cost us so much, Stalin began to downgrade many of the commanders, who contributed so much to the victory over the enemy, because Stalin excluded every possibility that services rendered at the front should be credited to anyone but himself. . . . He asked me often for my opinion of [Georgi] Zhukov [q.v.]. I told him then, "I have known Zhukov for a long time; he is a good general and a good military leader."

After the war Stalin began to tell all kinds of nonsense about Zhukov, among others the following: "You have praised Zhukov, but he does not deserve it. It is said that before each operation at the front Zhukov used to behave as follows: he used to take a handful of earth, smell it and say, 'We can begin the attack' or the opposite, 'the planned operation cannot be carried out.' " I stated at that time, "Comrade Stalin, I do not know who invented this, but it is not true."

It is possible that Stalin himself invented these things for the purpose of minimizing the role and military talents of Marshal Zhukov. ("Secret Speech," 20th Communist Party Congress, Moscow, February 24–25, 1956.)

FRANK KNOX

(1874–1944)

Knox was U.S. Secretary of the Navy from mid-1940 until his death. Knox, a Republican, was chosen by Roosevelt to become Navy Secretary at the time of France's surrender to Hitler.

599. Too few of us realize, and still fewer acknowledge, the size of the disaster to American hemisphere safety if Germany, already the conqueror of France, should establish herself in Dakar, a French colonial possession. From there, with her surface ships, submarines and long-range bombers, a victorious Germany could substantially cut us off from all commerce with South America and make of the Atlantic Doctrine a scrap of paper. (Speech, New York City, April 24, 1941; cited in *Our Vichy Gamble*, by William L. Langer.)

600. This dispatch is to be considered a war warning. Negotiations with Japan looking toward stabilization of conditions in the Pacific have ceased and an aggressive move by Japan is expected within the next few days. . . . Execute appropriate defense deployment preparatory to carrying out the task assigned in WPL 46X. (Message to Admiral Husband Kimmel [q.v.], commander of the Pacific fleet at Pearl Harbor, November 27, 1941.)

[Under this WPL code, upon the outbreak of war with Japan, the Pacific fleet was to attack the Marshall Islands.]

PIERRE LAVAL

(1883–1945)

French official Pierre Laval held high posts in the government before the war. Following the fall of France, he became part of the Vichy government. He was an active collaborator with the Germans and tried to crush French resistance. After the war, he was put on trial for treason and executed by firing squad.

601. INDIRECT DISCOURSE: He [Laval] recounted a litany of incidents—financial, political, military—in which the British during his own career had thwarted France and him as Premier and Foreign Minister. During World War I, he declared, the British had let France bear the brunt of the bloodletting, so that France had lost 1,500,000 killed, from which loss the nation never had recovered. This time the British had tried the same trick again, he cried, but this time the British and not the French would pay for the war. (Spoken to Robert Murphy [q.v.], Vichy, France, ca. autumn 1940; quoted in *Diplomat among Warriors*, by Robert Murphy.)

LOUIS L. LUDLOW
(1873–1950)

Ludlow was a congressman from Indiana. In 1937, he proposed the following amendment to the U.S. Constitution.

602. Except in the event of an invasion of the United States or its Territorial possessions and attack upon its citizens residing therein, the authority of Congress to declare war shall not become effective until confirmed by a majority of all votes cast thereon in a Nation-wide referendum. Congress, when it deems a national crisis to exist, may by concurrent resolution refer the question of war or peace to the citizens of the States, the question to be voted on being, Shall the United States declare war on ———? (Joint Resolution, proposed February 5, 1937.)

[The proposed amendment came up for debate in December 1937. On January 10, 1938, it was shelved by a vote of 209 to 188.]

HENRY L. MORGENTHAU, JR.
(1891–1967)

Morgenthau, as U.S. Secretary of the Treasury, came up with a plan for postwar Germany.

603. I also gave him [Secretary of War Henry L. Stimson (q.v.)] my idea of the possibility of removing all industry from Germany and simply reducing them to an agricultural population of small land-owners. He said that the trouble with that was that Germany was that kind of a nation back in 1860, but then she had only 40 million people. He said that you might have to take a lot of people out of Germany. So I said, "Well, that is not nearly as bad as sending them to gas chambers." (Diary excerpt, August 23, 1944; cited in *Roosevelt and Morgenthau*, by John Morton Blum.)

[The so-called Morgenthau Plan was never implemented.]

FRANK MURPHY
(1890–1949)

Murphy was an associate justice of the U.S. Supreme Court at the time of the trial of Tomoyuki Yamashita (q.v.) for alleged war crimes. Chief Justice Harlan F. Stone (q.v.) delivered the majority opinion in the case, ruling that Yamashita had been lawfully tried. Murphy wrote a dissenting opinion, dealing with the issue of due process.

604. The grave issue raised by this case is whether a military commission so established and so authorized may disregard the procedural rights of an accused person as guaranteed by the Constitution, especially by the due process clause of the Fifth Amendment.

The answer is plain. The Fifth Amendment guarantee of due process of law applies to "any person" who is accused of a crime by the Federal Government or any of its agencies. No exception is made as to those who are accused of war crimes or as to those who possess the status of an enemy belligerent. (Dissenting opinion, February 4, 1946.)

605. No military necessity or other emergency demanded the suspension of the safeguards of due process. Yet [the defendant] was rushed to trial under an improper charge, given insufficient time to prepare an adequate defense, deprived of the benefits of some of the most elementary rules of evidence and summarily sentenced to be hanged. In all this needless and unseemly haste there was no serious attempt to charge or to prove that he committed a recognized violation of the laws of war. He was not charged with personally participating in the acts of atrocity or with ordering or condoning their commission. Not even knowledge of these crimes was attributed to him. (Ibid.)

606. The high feelings of the moment doubtless will be satisfied. But in the sober afterglow will come the realization of the boundless and dangerous implications of the procedure sanctioned today. No one in a position of command in an army, from sergeant to general, can escape those implications. Indeed, the fate of some future President of the United States and his chiefs of staff and military advisors may well have been sealed by this decision. (Ibid.)

BENITO MUSSOLINI
(1883–1945)

Mussolini was dictator of Fascist Italy. He came to power in 1922, warred on Ethiopia, backed Franco (q.v.) in the Spanish Civil War, and signed a pact with Nazi Germany. In 1940, he attacked France, which was then on the verge of surrender. After a series of military disasters, he was removed from office in 1943 and imprisoned. Following the surrender of Italy, a Nazi commando group rescued Mussolini, who attempted to set up a new government in northern Italy to continue the war. As the war came to a close in April 1945, he was seized by Italian partisans, who executed him.

607. He [Hitler] makes me think of Attila. Those men he has just killed are the same who helped him come to power. (To his wife, following the Blood Purge of June 1934; cited in *My Truth*, by Edda Mussolini Ciano.)

608. Italy sends the information, leaving, of course, every decision to the Fuehrer, that it still has a chance to call a conference with France, England and Poland on following basis: 1. Armistice which would leave the Army Corps where they are at present. 2. Calling the conference within two or three days. 3. Solution of the Polish-German controversy which would be certainly favorable for Germany as matters stand today.

This idea which originated with the Duce has its foremost exponent in France.

Danzig is already German and Germany is holding already securities which guarantee most of her demands. Besides, Germany has had already its "moral satisfaction." If it would accept the plan for a conference, it will achieve all her aims and at the same time prevent a war which already today has the aspect of being universal and of extremely long duration. (Message to Hitler, September 3, 1939.)

[Hitler turned down the offer.]

609. You are certainly aware of grave reasons of an historical and contingent character which have ranged our two countries in opposite camps. Without going back very far in time I remind you of the initiative taken in 1935 by your Government to organize at [the League of Nations in] Geneva sanctions against Italy, engaged in securing for herself a small space in the African sun [Ethiopia] without causing the slightest injury to your interests and territories or those of others. I remind you also of the real and actual state of servitude in which Italy finds herself in her own sea. If it was to honor your signature that your Government declared war on Germany, you will understand that the same sense of honor and respect for engagements assumed in the Italian-German Treaty guides Italian policy today and tomorrow in the face of any event whatsoever. (Response to a Churchill message in which the prime minister tried to keep Italy out of the war, May 1940.)

610. Fuehrer,

Now that the time has come to thrash England, I remind you of what I said to you at Munich [probably during the Sudeten crisis of September 1938] about the direct participation of Italy in the assault of the Isle. I am ready to take part in this with land and air forces, and you know how much I desire it. (Message to Hitler, June 1940.)

611. Faithful Black Shirts of all Italy! I again call you to work and to arms! The enemy's exultation over the surrender of Italy does not mean that they have total victory in their grasp, since the two great Empires, Germany and Japan, will never surrender.

Squadristi, re-form your battalions, which have performed heroic deeds.

Fascist Youth, enroll in the divisions which are to re-enact upon the soil of the Fatherland the glorious deeds of Bir-el-Gobi.

Airmen, return to the side of your German comrades, go back to your pilots' stations to make useless and difficult the enemy attacks upon our cities.

Fascist women, resume your work of moral and material aid, which is so necessary to the people. Peasants, workmen and employees, the State which will emerge from this mighty ordeal will be your State, and as such you will defend it against everyone who may dream of an impossible return to the past. Our will, our courage, our faith will restore to Italy her country, her future, her opportunity for life and her place in the world. More than a hope, this should be for all of you a supreme certainty.

Long live Italy! Long live the Republican Fascist Party! (Radio broadcast to the people of Italy, following his rescue by Hitler, September 18, 1943.)

HENRI PHILIPPE PETAIN

(1856–1951)

French military hero of World War I, Marshal Petain was vilified as a traitor after World War II. Following devastating French defeats in 1940, he took over from Premier Reynaud (q.v.) and made an armistice with Hitler. He headed the Vichy government for four years, collaborating with the Nazis. When the war ended, he was tried for treason, convicted, and sentenced to death. The sentence was later commuted to life imprisonment.

612. My country has been beaten and they are calling me back to make peace and to sign an armistice. . . . This is the work of 30 years of Marxism. They're calling me back to take charge of the nation. (Statement to Francisco Franco [q.v.], Madrid, Spain, ca. May 17, 1940; from *La Vie Exemplaire de Philippe Petain*, by Pierre Hering.)

[French Premier Reynaud had called Petain back to help raise morale during the German onslaught.]

613. INDIRECT DISCOURSE: So long as the British Army had been in Flanders the British had engaged their Air Force fully. But they had insisted that their Army should be taken off first (at Dunkirk) and that the French divisions should hold the lines fighting against the Germans while the British were embarked. Since all the British had been embarked the British had ceased to send their planes in anything like the number they had employed so long as the British Expeditionary Force was at Dunkirk.

Furthermore, at this moment when the French had almost no reserves and were facing the greatest attack in human history the British were pretending that they could send no reserves from England. Moreover, they had refused to send over the British aviation. (Message to President Roosevelt from U.S. Ambassador William C. Bullitt [q.v.], summarizing his conversation with Marshal Petain, following the Dunkirk Evacuation [q.v.], June 4, 1940; from *Foreign Relations of the United States, 1940*, Vol. 1.)

614. INDIRECT DISCOURSE: Under the circumstances he [Petain] was obliged to feel that the British intended to permit the French to fight without help until the last available drop of French blood . . . and that with quantities of troops on British soil and plenty of planes and dominant fleet the British after a very brief resistance, or even without resistance, would make a peace of compromise with Hitler, which might even evolve a British Government under a British fascist leader. (Ibid.)

615. INDIRECT DISCOURSE: The Marshal added that he felt unless the British Government should send to France, to engage in the battle which was imminent, both air force and reserve divisions, the French Government would do its utmost to come to terms immediately with Germany whatever might happen to England. (Ibid.)

616. INDIRECT DISCOURSE: He [Petain] said that continuance of the war [against Nazi Germany] would have been insanity, and that France would have been completely destroyed, since neither France nor Britain should have gone into a war for which they were wholly unprepared. With some emotion he declared that France could not afford again to have a million of its sons killed.

(Spoken to Robert Murphy [q.v.], Vichy, France, ca. autumn 1940; quoted in *Diplomat among Warriors*, by Robert Murphy.)

617. You invoke pretexts which nothing justifies. You attribute to your enemies intentions which have not ever been manifested in acts. I have always declared that we would defend our Empire if it were attacked; you should have known that we would defend against any aggressor, whoever he might be. You should have known that. (Message to President Roosevelt, November 8, 1942; cited in *Our Vichy Gamble*, by William L. Langer.)

[In response to Roosevelt's message that the United States was occupying French North Africa to prevent a takeover by the Axis Powers.]

618. Rebel commanders have chosen emigration and a return to the past. I have chosen France and her future. (Broadcast, April 4, 1943.)

619. The French people will not forget. They know that I defended them as I did at Verdun. (Statement at his treason trial, August 1945.)

NELSON POYNTER

(n.d.)

Poynter was the Hollywood chief of the government's Office of War Information. He was asked by *Communique*, the publication of the Hollywood Writers Mobilization, "Is it true that the Office of War Information does not want pictures which will promote hatred of the Japanese and Nazis?" This was his response:

620. No. Properly directed hatred is of vital importance to the war effort. The Office of War Information wishes only to insure that hatred will not be directed either at Hitler, Mussolini [q.v.], Tojo [q.v.] or a small group of Fascist leaders as personalized enemies on the one hand, or at the whole German, Japanese, or Italian people on the other hand. Hatred of the militaristic system which governs the Axis countries and of those responsible for its furtherance definitely should be promoted. (*Motion Picture Herald*, October 3, 1942; cited in *Projections of War*, by Thomas Doherty.)

PAUL REYNAUD
(1878–1966)

Premier of France in 1940, Reynaud saw French and British forces crumble under the German onslaught. Reynaud wanted to continue the war against Hitler by taking the French fleet to North Africa and continuing the fighting from there. His government fell, however, and the new government sued for peace. Following the French surrender, he was accused by the Vichy regime of having mishandled public funds. He was found guilty, sent to a German concentration camp, and remained imprisoned until after the war.

621. The Victor of Verdun [a World War I French triumph], Marshal Petain [q.v.], returned this morning from Madrid. He will now be at my side . . . putting all his wisdom and all his force in the service of the country. He will remain there until victory is won. (Radio address, May 18, 1940.)

622. Today the enemy is almost at the gates of Paris. We shall fight in front of Paris; we shall fight behind Paris; we shall close ourselves in one of our provinces to fight and if we should be driven out of it we shall establish ourselves in North Africa to continue the fight and if necessary in our American possessions.

A portion of the government has already left Paris. I am making ready to leave for the front. . . . It is my duty to ask you for new and even larger assistance. (Message to President Roosevelt, June 10, 1940.)

623. The French Government—the present one or another—might say: "We know you [England] will carry on. We would also, if we saw any hope of a victory. But we see no sufficient hopes of an early victory. We cannot count on American help. There is no light at the end of the tunnel. We cannot abandon our people to indefinite German domination. We must come to terms. We have no choice. . . .

"Will you acknowledge that France has given her best, her youth and lifeblood; that she can do no more; and that she is entitled, having nothing further to contribute to the common cause, to enter into a separate peace while maintaining the solidarity implicit in the solemn agreement entered into three months previously?" (Asked of Churchill as France stood on the brink of military collapse, ca. June 13, 1940; quoted in *The Second World War: Their Finest Hour*, by Winston Churchill.)

[Churchill's response to Reynaud was that England could not agree to the idea of a separate peace with Hitler. England would not reproach France if it did so, but England could not go along with the idea of making terms with Hitler.]

ROBERT R. REYNOLDS
(1884–1963)

Reynolds, a U.S. senator from North Carolina, was chairman of the Senate Military Affairs Committee.

624. Democracy is finished in Europe. Hitler and Mussolini [q.v.] have a date with destiny. It is foolish to oppose them. So why not play ball with them? (Cited in *Let's Go to Press*, by Ed Weiner.)

EDWARD V. RICKENBACKER
(1890–1973)

An air ace during World War I, Rickenbacker spent World War II as a consultant to Secretary of War Henry L. Stimson (q.v.). He went on inspection tours of military facilities around the world. It was on one of these missions that he crash-landed in the Pacific. He and the crew drifted in rafts, which were lashed together, for twenty-one days before being rescued. Rickenbacker's account of survival became a 1943 best-seller.

625. A good deal of what we went through was . . . hunger, thirst, heat, cold, and a slow rotting away. (From *Seven Came Through: Rickenbacker's Full Story*, by Edward V. Rickenbacker.)

626. My hands swelled and blistered; when the salt water got into the flesh, it burned and cracked and dried and burned again. . . . Our mouths became covered with ugly running sores. (Ibid.)

627. The eighth day . . . I was dozing with my hat pulled down over my eyes, [when] a gull . . . landed on my hat. I don't remember how it happened or how I knew he was there. But I knew it instantly, and I knew that if I missed this one, I'd never find another to sit on my hat. I reached up for him . . . gradually. The whole Pacific seemed to be shaking from the agitation in my body, but I could tell he was still there from the hungry, famished, almost insane eyes in the other rafts. Slowly and surely my hand got up there; I didn't clutch, but just closed my fingers, sensing his nearness, then closing my fingers hard.

I wrung his neck, defeathered him, carved up the body, divided the meat into equal shares, holding back only the intestines for bait. Even the bones were chewed and swallowed. No one hesitated because the meat was raw and stringy and fishy. It tasted fine. (Ibid.)

628. After Cherry had finished his piece, I baited a hook and passed it over to him. The hook, weighted with Whittaker's ring, had hardly got wet before a small mackerel bit it, and was jerked into the raft. I dropped the other line, with the same miraculous result. . . . All this food in the space of a few minutes bolstered us beyond words. . . . As that eighth night rose around us I was sure we could last forever. The ocean was full of fish, and we could catch them. (Ibid.)

SAMUEL I. ROSENMAN

(1896–1973)

Rosenman was an aide to President Roosevelt.

629. The president did something which affected us all very deeply. He asked a Secret Service man to wheel him slowly through all the wards that were occupied by veterans who had lost one or more arms and legs. He insisted on going past each individual bed. He wanted to display himself and his useless legs to those who would have to face the same bitterness. . . .

With a cheering smile to each of them, and a pleasant word at the bedside of a score or more, this man who had risen from a bed of helplessness ultimately to become President of the United States and leader of the free world was living proof of what the human spirit could do. (Oahu, Hawaii, July 1944; from *Working with Roosevelt*, by Samuel I. Rosenman.)

HANS RUMPF

(n.d.)

Hans Rumpf was inspector general of fire prevention in Germany. After the war, he wrote of the devastation visited upon Germany by Allied bombing.

630. According to British accounts the first attack on Berlin is said to have been carried out by three fast bombers. . . . [It] is said to have been . . . a practical joke on Goering [q.v.] who was due to address a great mass meeting, which is said to have been postponed for an hour in consequence. (From *The Bombing of Germany*, by Hans Rumpf.)

631. Allied statesmen and their Chiefs of Staff meeting in Casablanca in January 1943 expressly confirmed the decision of the British War Cabinet of 14th February, 1942, on "area bombing." In other words, it was decided that instead of confining bombing attacks to chosen military and industrial targets believed to be of importance for the prosecution of the war by Germany, the built-up residential areas of her towns were to be bombed—expressly without regard to the loss of civilian lives. (Ibid.)

632. The civilian population bore the burden placed on it because no one offered any alternative.

It was the Casablanca Directive which first turned the war into a people's war. The increasingly ruthless bombing that went on long after the war had been militarily decided was the factor which welded the people together and kept them together to the end. The suffering caused by the devastation of Germany's towns was the cement that not only held them together but held them to a State for which they no longer felt any enthusiasm. And the catastrophe which descended on Dresden aroused a last desperate effort amongst the exhausted masses, for now it seemed clear to them as never before that their enemies were intent on the physical destruction of the German people. The blind savagery of the last few months of the war could mean nothing but a systematic attempt to wipe them out altogether, both the enemy leadership and their own had condemned them to the same fate. (Ibid.)

ALBERT SPEER

(1905–1981)

An architect by training, Speer became Hitler's minister in charge of armaments and war production. He became deeply involved in organizing a huge slave labor (q.v.) force, which brought him into the dock at Nuremberg after the war. Imprisoned for twenty years, he emerged to write his memoirs.

633. [In July 1944, as Allied armies raced across France] Hitler had ordered far-reaching destruction of war industries [in Belgium, Holland, and France]. . . .

Army command West was responsible for carrying out these orders. . . . I informed the commanding generals that as far as I was concerned this destruction was senseless and that I, in my capacity of armaments Minister, did not consider [the destruction] necessary. . . . Thereupon no order to destroy these installations was given. By this, of course, I made myself responsible to Hitler for the fact that no destruction took place. (Testimony, Nuremberg war crimes trial, 1946.)

634. [I also prevented destruction] . . . in the industrial installations in the Government General [Poland], the ore mines in the Balkans, the nickel works in Finland, . . . industrial installations in northern Italy, . . . the oil fields in Hungary and industries in Czechoslovakia. (Ibid.)

635. He [Hitler] had no intention [of preserving German facilities when the Allies invaded the Reich]. On the contrary, he ordered the "scorched earth" policy with special application to Germany. (Ibid.)

636. This trial is necessary. There is a common responsibility for such horrible crimes in an authoritarian system. (Ibid.)

637. Hitler loved the film and had it shown over and over again; it became one of his favorite entertainments. (Interview, *Playboy* magazine, 1971.)

[Referring to the film of the hanging of the conspirators involved in the July 1944 plot to kill Hitler. Although there is no disagreement about films being made of the conspirators being hanged by wire on meathooks, there is considerable disagreement about whether Hitler viewed the films, either alone or with others. Asked by Gitta Sereny specifically about the quotation attributed to him, Speer denied it. He said, "I think a number of misquotes were probably due to linguistic misunderstandings, no doubt my fault—my English was not that good." According to William L. Shirer (q.v.), the film was shown once at a German military academy. The cadets ran screaming from the viewing room. After the war, the film vanished.]

638. I still recognize today that the grounds upon which I was convicted by the International Military Tribunal [q.v.] were correct. More than this, I still consider it essential today to take upon myself the responsibility, and thus the blame in general, for all crimes which were committed after I became a member of Hitler's government on February 8, 1942. It is not individual acts of commission, however grave, which weigh upon me, but my conduct as part of the leadership. This is why I accepted an overall responsibility in the Nuremberg trial and reaffirm this now. However, to this day, I still consider my main guilt to be my tacit acceptance of the persecution and the murder of millions of Jews. (From a letter to the South African Jewish Board of Deputies, 1977; from *Albert Speer: His Battle with Truth*, by Gitta Sereny.)

[The board wanted to prevent the publication of the Holocaust (q.v.) revisionist publication *The Hoax of the 20th Century*. The board asked Speer to state, under oath, his beliefs about the reality of the Holocaust. Sereny had translated the quotation above into English and had shown it to Speer. He felt that the German word translated as "tacit acceptance" really meant "looking away, not by knowledge of an order or its execution."

Sereny pressed Speer on why he admitted it finally, after so long denying. "For this purpose," he told her, "and with these people, I didn't wish to—I couldn't—hedge."]

HENRY L. STIMSON

(1867–1950)

Stimson was U.S. Secretary of War. A Republican, he was named by President Roosevelt to the cabinet post on the day France signed the armistice with Hitler. Stimson backed Lend-Lease (q.v.) for Britain before Pearl Harbor and supported an intense military effort once America was in the war. He also pushed the program to develop an atomic bomb.

639. Gentlemen do not read each other's mail. (After his appointment as Secretary of State in the Hoover administration, 1929.)

[He soon ended cryptanalysis funding.]

640. There was a basic agreement among us all. That in itself was very encouraging. All four agreed that this emergency could hardly be passed over without this country being drawn into the war eventually. (Diary entry, December 16, 1940; cited in *On Active Service*, by Henry L. Stimson and McGeorge Bundy.)

[The four included Stimson, Secretary of the Navy Frank Knox, General George Marshall, and Admiral Harold Stark.]

641. I am not one of those who think that the priceless freedom of our country can be saved without sacrifice. It can not. That has not been the way by which during millions of years humanity has slowly and painfully toiled upwards towards a better and more humane civilization. The men who suffered at Valley Forge and won at Yorktown gave more than money to the cause of freedom.

Today a small group of evil leaders have taught the young men of Germany that the freedom of other men and nations must be destroyed. Today those young men are ready to die for that perverted conviction. Unless we on our side are ready to sacrifice and, if need be, die for the conviction that the freedom of America must be saved, it will not be saved. Only by readiness for the same sacrifice can that freedom be preserved. (Radio address, May 6, 1941.)

642. 1. Germany will be thoroughly occupied in beating Russia for a minimum of one month and a possible maximum of three months.

2. During this period Germany must give up or slack up on

a. Any invasion of the British Isles.

b. Any attempt to attack herself or prevent us from occupying Iceland.

c. Her pressure on West Africa, Dakar and South America.

d. Any attempt to envelop the British right flank in Egypt by way of Iraq, Syria or Persia.

e. Probably her pressure in Libya and the Mediterranean. (Letter to President Roosevelt, June 23, 1941.)

[Immediately following Hitler's invasion of the Soviet Union, this was how America's top military leadership viewed the situation.]

643. Germany's action seems like an almost providential occurrence. By this final demonstration of Nazi ambition and perfidy, the door is opened wide for you [President Roosevelt] to lead directly towards the winning of the battle of the North Atlantic and the protection of our hemisphere in the South Atlantic. (Ibid.)

644. The trouble has come from the fact that we have [been] trying to train an army for war without any declaration of war by Congress and with the country not facing the danger before it. (Diary entry, September 15, 1941; cited in *On Active Service*, by Henry L. Stimson and McGeorge Bundy.)

645. At the [White House] meeting were [Secretary of State Cordell] Hull [q.v.], [Secretary of the Navy Frank] Knox [q.v.], [General George] Marshall, [Admiral Harold] Stark [q.v.], and myself. . . . He [the president] brought up the event that we were likely to be attacked perhaps next Monday, for the Japanese are notorious for making an attack without warning, and the question was what we should do. The question was how we should maneuver them into the position of firing the first shot without allowing too much danger to ourselves. (Diary excerpt, November 25, 1941; Ibid.)

646. Negotiations with Japan appear to be terminated to all practical purposes, with only the barest possibilities that the Japanese Government might come back and offer to continue. Japanese future action unpredictable, but hostile action possible at any moment. If hostilities cannot, repeat, cannot, be avoided, the United States desires that Japan commit the first overt act. This policy should not, repeat not, be construed as restricting you to a course of action that might jeopardize your defense. (Message to U.S. Pacific commanders, November 27, 1941.)

647. What do you think of the patriotism of a man or a newspaper which would take these confidential studies and make them public to the enemies of the country? (Press conference, December 5, 1941.)

[Attacking the *Chicago Tribune* for an article by Chesly Manly (q.v.). The writer had reported contingency plans of the War Department in the event of hostilities involving the United States.]

648. When the news first came that Japan had attacked us, my first feeling was of relief that the indecision was over and that a crisis had come in a way which would unite all our people. This continued to be my dominant feeling in spite of the news of catastrophes which quickly developed. For I feel that this country united has nothing to fear, while the apathy and divisions stirred up by unpatriotic men have been hitherto very discouraging. (Diary entry, December 7, 1941; cited in *On Active Service*, by Henry L. Stimson and McGeorge Bundy.)

649. Tonight I wish to speak to you about the subtle danger which, unless guarded against, may destroy our present bright hopes for a decisive victory. It arises out of a mental attitude which is quite prevalent among our people. . . . I think it can accurately be called the attitude of trying to win the war—the most fierce and dangerous war which has ever confronted the United States—in some easy manner and without too much trouble and sacrifice.

Abraham Lincoln met it in the Civil War even after that war had been going on for over a year and many bloody battles had been fought. He said to a caller at the White House, in September, 1862: "The fact is the people have not made up their minds that we are at war with the South. They have not buckled down to the determination to fight the war through; or they have got the idea into their heads that we are going to get out of this fix somehow by strategy. . . . They have no idea that this war is to be carried on and put through by hard, tough fighting; that it will hurt somebody, and no headway is going to be made while this delusion lasts."

Today this attitude, which Lincoln described, manifests itself when we say:

"The Russians have destroyed so many Germans that Germany will not be able to carry on any more offensives. . . . The German people are cracking. . . . The best way to win the war is to give our Allies plenty of weapons to fight for us. . . . If we make too big a military effort we shall so dislocate our economy that we shall never recover; we shall create a permanent dictatorship and lose our historic freedom."

Or when we say other things which at bottom represent merely wishful thinking or the dread of personal sacrifices and the desire to find a better way out. . . .

Even if, as Lincoln said in 1862, they [the American people] have not yet truly realized what it means to be at war, they will soon do so. And when they have done so, they will be ready to make any sacrifice for victory. (Radio address, Washington, D.C., March 9, 1943.)

650. We cannot now rationally hope to be able to cross the Channel and come to grips with our German enemy under a British commander. His Prime Minister and his Chief of the Imperial Staff are frankly at variance with such a proposal. The shadows of Passchendaele and Dunkirk still hang too heavily over the imagination of these leaders. (Memo to President Roosevelt prior to the Quebec conference, August 1943.)

651. I believe that the time has come when we must put our most commanding soldier in charge of this critical operation at this critical time. . . . General [George C.] Marshall already has a towering eminence of reputation as a tried soldier and as a broad-minded and skillful administrator. . . . I believe that he is the man who most surely can now by his character and skill furnish the military leadership which is necessary. (Ibid.)

[The conference agreed on an American commander for the Normandy assault. The issue of the supreme commander, however, was still to be settled. Late in 1943, Roosevelt decided that he could not spare Marshall away from Washington. Dwight D. Eisenhower was chosen instead.]

652. There is reason to believe that the operation for the occupation of Japan following the landing may be a very long, costly, and arduous struggle on our part. The terrain . . . [is] susceptible to a last ditch defense such as has been made on Iwo Jima and Okinawa. (Memorandum to President Truman [q.v.], July 2, 1945; cited in *On Active Service*, by Henry L. Stimson and McGeorge Bundy.)

653. If we once land on one of the main islands and begin a forceful occupation of Japan, we shall probably have cast the die of last ditch resistance. The Japanese are highly patriotic and certainly susceptible to calls for fanatical resistance to repel an invasion. Once started in actual invasion, we shall in my opinion have to go through with an even more bitter finish fight than in Germany. We shall incur the losses incident to such a war and we shall have to leave the Japanese even more thoroughly destroyed than was the case with Germany. (Ibid.)

654. Is there any alternative to such forceful occupation of Japan which will secure for us the equivalent of an unconditional surrender of her forces and a permanent destruction of her power again to strike an aggressive blow at the "peace of the Pacific"? I am inclined to think that there is enough such chance to make it well worth while our giving them a warning of what is to come and definite opportunity to capitulate. (Ibid.)

655. Japan has no allies.

Her navy is nearly destroyed and she is vulnerable to a surface and underwater blockade which can deprive her of sufficient food and supplies for her population.

She is terribly vulnerable to our concentrated air attack upon her crowded cities, industrial and food resources.

She has against her not only the Anglo-American forces but the rising forces of China and the continuous threat of Russia. (Ibid.)

656. I think the Japanese nation has the mental intelligence and versatile capacity in such a crisis to recognize the folly of a fight to the finish and to accept the proffer of what will amount to an unconditional surrender. . . .

It is therefore my conclusion that a carefully timed warning be given to Japan by the chief representatives of the United States, Great Britain, China, and, if then a belligerent, Russia, by calling upon Japan to surrender and permit the occupation of her country in order to insure its complete demilitarization for the sake of the future peace.

This warning should contain the following elements:

The varied and overwhelming character of the force we are about to bring to bear on the islands.

The inevitability and completeness of the destruction which the full application of this force will entail.

The determination of the Allies to destroy permanently all authority and influence of those who have deceived and misled the country into embarking on world conquest. . . .

A statement of our readiness, once her economy is purged of its militaristic influence, to permit the Japanese to maintain such industries, particularly of a light consumer character, as offer no threat of aggression against their neighbors. . . .

The withdrawal from her country as soon as the above objectives of the allies are accomplished, and as soon as there has been established a peacefully inclined government . . . of a character representative of the masses of the Japanese people. I personally think that if in saying this we should add that we do not exclude a constitutional monarchy under her present dynasty, it would substantially add to the chances of acceptance. (Ibid.)

657. Success of course will depend on the potency of the warning which we give her. She has an extremely sensitive pride, and, as we are now seeing every day, when actually locked with the enemy will fight to the very death. For that reason the warning must be tendered before the actual invasion has occurred and while the impending destruction, though clear beyond peradventure, has not yet reduced her to fanatical despair. If Russia is a part of the threat, the Russian attack, if actual, must not have progressed too far. Our own bombing should be confined to military objectives as far as possible. (Ibid.)

658. The outpost commander is like a sentinel on duty in the face of the enemy. His fundamental duties are clear and precise. . . . It is not the duty of the outpost commander to speculate or rely on the possibilities of the enemy attacking at some other outpost instead of his own. It is his duty to meet him at his post at any time and to make the best possible fight that can be made against him with the weapons with which he has been supplied. (Statement, Joint Committee of Congress investigating Pearl Harbor, March 21, 1946.)

659. As I look back over the five years of my service as Secretary of War, I see too many stern and heart-rending decisions to be willing to pretend that war is anything else than what it is. The face of war is the face of death; death is an inevitable part of every order that a wartime leader gives. (*Harper's*, February 1947.)

660. The decision to use the atomic bomb was a decision that brought death to over a hundred thousand Japanese. No explanation can change that fact and

I do not wish to gloss it over. But this deliberate, premeditated destruction was our least abhorrent choice. The destruction of Hiroshima and Nagasaki put an end to the Japanese war. It stopped the fire raids, and the strangling blockade; it ended the ghastly specter of a clash of great land armies. (Ibid.)

661. In this last great action of the Second World War we were given final proof that war is death. War in the 20th century has grown steadily more barbarous, more destructive, more debased in all its aspects. Now, with the release of atomic energy, man's ability to destroy himself is very nearly complete. The bombs dropped on Hiroshima and Nagasaki ended a war. They also made it wholly clear that we must never have another war. This is the lesson men and leaders everywhere must learn, and I believe that when they learn it they will find a way to lasting peace. There is no other choice. (Ibid.)

HARLAN F. STONE
(1872–1946)

Stone was Chief Justice of the United States at the time of the trial of Tomoyuki Yamashita (q.v.). The Japanese general, on trial for alleged war crimes, had been judged by a military commission, which had condemned him to death. Stone and five other justices ruled that Yamashita had been legally tried. A different opinion was offered by Associate Justice Frank Murphy (q.v.).

662. We are not concerned with . . . guilt or innocence. We considered here only the lawful power of the Commission to try [Yamashita] for the offense charged. (Supreme Court majority decision, February 4, 1946.)

663. If the military tribunals have lawful authority to hear, decide and condemn, their action is not subject to judicial review merely because they have made a wrong decision on disputed facts. Correction of their errors of decision is not for the courts but for the military authorities which are alone authorized to review their decisions. (Ibid.)

HANS-GEORG VON STUDNITZ

(n.d.)

Studnitz was in the press office of the German Foreign Ministry.

664. Their continued publication would be a farce anyway, seeing that there is hardly a stitch of clothing to be got anywhere. (1943; from *While Berlin Burns*, by Hans-Georg von Studnitz.)

[Commenting on the suspension of fashion magazine publications.]

HIDEKI TOJO

(1884–1948)

Tojo was Japanese premier from October 1941 to 1944. Regarded as a hard-liner, he backed military expansion and the attack on Pearl Harbor. When the war ended, he attempted suicide, was saved from death, and lived to hang as a war criminal.

665. Japan must go on and develop an ever-expanding program—there is no retreat. . . . If Japan's hundred millions merge and go forward, nothing can stop us. (Speech, October 26, 1941.)

666. Peace and order has been completely restored in Malay, Sumatra, Djawa, Borneo, and the Celebes. . . .

Peace and order have already been restored in Burma, and Burma is responding to the immutable policy of the Imperial Government . . . and is steadily progressing toward the establishment of Burma for the Burmese, thereby continuing to extend splendid efforts in the construction of Greater East Asia. . . .

To be able to make this [Burmese independence] clear in this Diet, is a great satisfaction to the Imperial Government, and this is beyond expression of congratulations for the sake of Burma, as well as for the sake of a new Greater East Asia.

However, Britain, with her attitude still unchanged, has arrested and interned the leaders of Indian independence creating further [hatred] among the fiery and indignant Indian masses. (Broadcast, Tokyo January 27, 1943.)

HARRY S TRUMAN

(1884–1972)

Harry Truman was president of the United States during the last four months of World War II. A U.S. senator from Missouri, Truman was credited with saving hundreds of millions of dollars as head of the committee investigating waste and corruption. In 1944, he was selected as Roosevelt's running mate in the presidential election. He became president on Roosevelt's death on April 12, 1945. It was Truman's decision to drop the atomic bomb on Japan in order to end the war quickly. Under his administration, the United States helped establish the United Nations, prevented a takeover of South Korea by the Communist North, launched the Marshall Plan, instituted an airlift to fly food and fuel into Berlin, and created the North Atlantic Treaty Organization.

667. If we see that Germany is winning the war we ought to help Russia, and if Russia is winning we ought to help Germany, and in that way let them kill as many as possible. (Attributed, 1941; cited in *Prime Time*, by Alexander Kendrick.)

668. This is a solemn but a glorious hour. I only wish that Franklin D. Roosevelt had lived to witness this day. General Eisenhower informs me that the forces of Germany have surrendered to the United Nations. The flags of freedom fly over all Europe. . . . Our victory is but half-won. The West is free, but the East is still in bondage to the treacherous tyranny of the Japanese. When the last Japanese division has surrendered unconditionally, then only will our fighting job be done. (Radio address on V-E Day, May 8, 1945.)

669. We must work to bind up the wounds of a suffering world—to build an abiding peace, a peace rooted in justice and in law. (Ibid.)

670. [Regarding a proposed directive for the occupation of Berlin, provision should be made for] free access for U.S. forces by air, road and rail to Berlin from Frankfurt and Bremen. (Message to Stalin, June 14, 1945; cited in *Diplomat among Warriors*, by Robert Murphy.)

671. The Charter of the United Nations which you have just signed is solid structure upon which we can build a better world. History will honor you for it. Between the victory in Europe and the final victory in Japan, in this most destructive of all wars, you have won a victory against war itself. (Statement to the

United Nations Conference on International Organization, San Francisco, June 26, 1945.)

672. Let us not fail to grasp this supreme chance to establish a world-wide rule of reason—to create an enduring peace under the guidance of God. (Ibid.)

673. Sixteen hours ago an American airplane dropped one bomb on Hiroshima, an important Japanese Army base. That bomb had more power than 20,000 tons of T.N.T. It had more than two thousand times the blast power of the British "Grand Slam" which is the largest bomb ever yet used in the history of warfare. (Statement, Washington, D.C., August 6, 1945.)

674. The Japanese began the war from the air at Pearl Harbor. They have been repaid many fold. And the end is not yet. With this bomb we have now added a new and revolutionary increase in destruction. . . . It is an atomic bomb. It is a harnessing of the basic power of the universe. The force from which the sun draws its power has been loosed against those who brought war to the Far East. (Ibid.)

675. Before 1939, it was the accepted belief of scientists that it was theoretically possible to release atomic energy. But no one knew a practical method of doing it. By 1942, however, we knew that the Germans were working feverishly to find a way to add atomic energy to the other energies of war with which they hoped to enslave the world. But they failed. We may be grateful to Providence that the Germans got the V-1's and the V-2's late and in limited quantities and even more grateful that they did not get the atomic bomb at all. (Ibid.)

676. We are now prepared to obliterate more rapidly and completely every productive enterprise the Japanese have above ground in any city. We shall destroy their docks, their factories, and their communications. Let there be no mistake; we shall completely destroy Japan's power to make war.

It was to spare the Japanese people from utter destruction that the ultimatum of July 20 was issued at Potsdam.

If they do not now accept our terms they may expect a rain of ruin from the air, the like of which has never been seen on this earth. (Ibid.)

677. I have just returned from Berlin, the city from which the Germans intended to rule the world. It is a ghost city. The buildings are in ruins, its economy and its people are in ruins. . . . The German people are beginning to atone for the crimes of the gangsters whom they placed in power and whom they wholeheartedly approved and obediently followed. (Radio broadcast, reporting on the Potsdam Conference [q.v.], August 9, 1945.)

678. What we are doing to Japan now—even with the new atomic bomb—is only a small fraction of what would happen to the world in a third World War. That is why the United Nations are determined that there shall be no next war. That is why the United Nations are determined to remain united and strong.

We can never permit any aggressor in the future to be clever enough to divide us or strong enough to defeat us. (Ibid.)

679. I have received this afternoon a message from the Japanese Government in reply to the message forwarded to that Government by the Secretary of State on August 11. I deem this reply full acceptance of the Potsdam Declaration which specifies the unconditional surrender of Japan. (News conference, Washington, D.C., August 14, 1945.)

ANDREI Y. VISHINSKY

(1883–1954)

A key figure in the Soviet purge trials of 1936–1938, Vishinsky rose in Communist Party ranks to become Deputy Foreign Minister during the war. Later he became the Soviet Union's permanent representative to the United Nations.

680. The Soviet Government cannot of course object to English or American aircraft dropping arms in the region of Warsaw, since this is an American and British affair. But they decidedly object to American or British aircraft, after dropping arms in the region of Warsaw, landing on Soviet territory, since the Soviet Government do not wish to associate themselves either directly or indirectly with the adventure. (Statement to U.S. ambassador, W. Averell Harriman, Moscow, August 16, 1944; cited in *The Second World War: Triumph and Tragedy*, by Winston Churchill.)

[The "adventure" was the Warsaw uprising against the German occupation. The Soviet Union would not help the Polish underground army and made it difficult for the Western Allies to do so.]

HENRY A. WALLACE

(1888–1965)

Wallace was vice president of the United States from 1941 to 1945. He was dropped from the Democratic ticket by Franklin Roosevelt in the 1944 election. Wallace was replaced by Harry Truman (q.v.), who became president on Roosevelt's death. In 1948, Wallace unsuccessfully opposed Truman by running on the Progressive Party ticket.

681. We seek a peace that is more than just a breathing space between the death of an old tyranny and the birth of a new one.

We will not be satisfied with a peace which will merely lead us from the concentration camps and mass-murder of Fascism—into an international jungle of gangster governments operated behind the scenes by power-crazed, money-mad imperialists. (Speech in Detroit, delivered a month after a race riot there killed thirty-four, July 25, 1943.)

682. Starvation has no Bill of Rights nor slavery a Magna Carta. Wherever the hopes of the human family are throttled, there we find the makings of revolt. . . .

Hunger and unemployment spawned the criminal free-booters of Fascism. Their only remedy for insecurity was war. Their only answer to poverty and denial of opportunity became the First Commandment of the Nazis: "Loot thy neighbor." (Ibid.)

683. Much of our propaganda after the first World War proclaimed the ingratitude of our Allies. We had given of our best blood and our separate fortunes only to be labelled the land of Uncle Shylock.

We changed it to Uncle Sap and said, "Never again."

How many of us after this second world-wide scourge of suffering and death will say, "Never again"?

Shall it be "Never again" to joining in seeking world peace? Shall it be "Never again" to living alone on an island of false security? Shall it be our second retreat from our responsibility in world co-operation? (Ibid.)

684. Ours must be a generation that will distill the stamina and provide the skills to create a war-proof world. We must not bequeath a second blood-bath to our children.

World leadership must be more concerned with welfare politics and less with power politics—more interested in opening channels of commerce than closing them by prohibitive tariffs—more mindful of the need for a stable currency among all countries than in high interest rates in loans. (Ibid.)

685. Many of our most patriotic and forward-looking citizens are asking, "Why not start now practicing these Four Freedoms in our own back yard?" . . .

We cannot fight to crush Nazi brutality abroad and condone race riots at home. Those who fan the fires of racial clashes for the purpose of making political capital here at home are taking the first step toward Nazism.

We cannot plead for equal opportunity for peoples everywhere and overlook the denial of the right to vote for millions of our own people. . . .

We cannot offer the blueprints and the skills to rebuild the bombed-out cities of other lands and stymie the rebuilding of our own cities. Slums have no place in America. (Ibid.)

686. Long before Pearl Harbor, many of us in government had done our best to build up a rubber stockpile, to encourage the growing of natural rubber in this hemisphere, and to get synthetic rubber production started. . . .

[I was interested in butyl rubber] because of the information I had obtained when Secretary of Agriculture from the co-inventor of butyl rubber who in 1940 was working for the United States Department of Agriculture. (Speech involving a cartel arrangement between I. G. Farben and the Standard Oil Company of New Jersey, September 11, 1943.)

687. What I didn't know and what 130,000,000 Americans did not know was that the private rulers of world industry had their own private approach to synthetic rubber. Synthetic rubber was the subject of a private treaty between a great American oil company and I. G. Farben, the German chemical colossus. These two great concerns made a deal. The Germans were given a world monopoly on synthetic rubber. The Americans were given a monopoly on synthetic gasoline. This monopoly was good over the entire world, with the exception of Germany. The Germans knew what they were after. They would not yield their own development in their own country to foreign interests.

This secret agreement between an American monopoly and a German cartel was submitted to no public authority in this country. It was far more important than most treaties but it was never acted upon by the United States Senate. The peoples and the governments of the world had unknowingly let the cartels and the monopolies form a super-government by means of which they could monopolize and divide whole fields of science and carve up the markets of the world at their own sweet pleasure. (Ibid.)

688. As a result of its deal, the American oil company had to choose between loyalty to the United States and its commercial obligation to its German partner. Because of its commitments to the German partner the oil company did three things:

1. It misled the government as to the restrictive character of the patent situation.

2. It assured government officials that every effort would be made to bring about a large production of synthetic rubber for tires and then offered licenses which were deliberately oppressive in order to prevent the production of tires from this rubber. It sued one company and threatened to sue a second for daring to produce buna rubber.

3. For five years the production of butyl rubber was held back although the American company had invented butyl and knew that it possessed greater possibilities than buna. Full information and regular reports about butyl were given to the German cartel partner but at the time the American company tried to

mislead the representative of the United States Navy who was sent specifically to learn about butyl. (Ibid.)

689. Food and jobs are two of the foundation stones of the century of the Common Man. (Speech in Cleveland, October 27, 1943.)

690. When I was leaving I said to the president, "Well, I am looking ahead with pleasure to the results of next week [the Democratic National Convention] no matter what the outcome." As I shook hands with him he drew me close and turned on his full smile and a very hearty handclasp, saying, "While I cannot put it just that way in public, I hope it will be the same old team." (Diary excerpt, June 1944; cited in *Love, Eleanor: Eleanor Roosevelt and Her Friends*, by Joseph P. Lash.)

[The issue was who would run with Roosevelt as his vice presidential candidate. Wallace was being dumped in favor of either Supreme Court Justice William O. Douglas or Senator Harry S Truman (q.v.). In the end, it would be the Missouri senator destined to become president ten months later.]

BURTON K. WHEELER
(1882–1975)

Wheeler, a Republican senator, was an avowed isolationist, against any American participation in the war prior to Pearl Harbor.

691. [The proposed Lend-Lease (q.v.) program is] the New Deal's triple-A foreign policy—it will plough under every fourth American boy. (Radio broadcast, *American Forum of the Air*, January 12, 1941.)

[At that time, statements given at presidential press conferences had to be in indirect discourse—unless the president specified otherwise. During this press conference two days later, Roosevelt called Wheeler's remark "the most untruthful, the most dastardly, unpatriotic thing that has ever been said. Quote me on that! That really is the rottenest thing that has been said in public life in my generation."]

ANDREI ZHDANOV

(1896–1948)

A member of the Politburo and close confidante to Stalin, Zhdanov directed the attack on Finland in 1939. Earlier that year, it was Zhdanov who gave the first hint that Stalin was about to make a deal with Hitler.

692. I permit myself to express a personal opinion although my friends do not share it. They still think that in beginning negotiations on a pact for mutual assistance with the USSR, the British and French governments had the serious intention of creating a powerful barrier against aggression in Europe. I believe that the British and French governments have no wish for an equal treaty with the USSR. . . . It seems to me that the British and French desire not a real treaty acceptable to the USSR but only talks about a treaty in order to play upon public opinion in their countries about the supposedly unyielding attitude of the USSR and thus to make it easier for themselves to make a deal with the aggressors. (Newspaper article, June 29, 1939; cited in *Khrushchev: A Career*, by Edward Crankshaw.)

4

Diplomats

WILLIAM C. BULLITT
(1891–1967)

Bullitt served as U.S. ambassador to the Soviet Union from 1933 to 1936 and as ambassador to France from 1936 to 1940, when France surrendered. Thereafter, he carried out special assignments for President Roosevelt in North Africa and the Middle East. He was strongly anti-Nazi and advised toughness with Hitler.

693. If the British now refuse this essential support [of planes requested by France], it will mean, I believe, that the British intend to conserve their fleet and air force and their army, and either before a German attack on England or shortly afterwards, to install eight Fascists trained under Oswald Mosley [leader of the British Fascist party] and accept vassalage to Hitler. (Message to President Roosevelt, June 5, 1940; from *Foreign Relations of the United States, 1940*, Vol. 1.)

[Message was sent following the British evacuation from Dunkirk.]

GALEAZZO CIANO

(1903–1944)

Italian Foreign Minister under Mussolini (q.v.), Count Ciano tried to keep Italy out of the war. However, in June 1940, with France prostrate, he could not prevent Mussolini from entering a war that appeared to be already won. Following the Allied invasion of Sicily in 1943, Mussolini was overthrown and Italy sued for peace. After he was rescued by the Germans, Mussolini revenged himself on those who had ousted him. One of those he condemned to death was Count Ciano, his own son-in-law. On January 11, 1944, the count was shot in the back by a Nazi firing squad—the traditional punishment for treason.

694. INDIRECT DISCOURSE: Count Ciano . . . expressed the great surprise on the Italian side over the completely unexpected seriousness of the position. [Hitler had told him that Germany was going to invade Poland and asked for Italian support.] Neither in the conversations in Milan nor in those which took place during his Berlin visit had there been any sign from the German side that the position with regard to Poland was so serious. On the contrary, Ribbentrop [q.v.] had said that in his opinion the Danzig question would be settled in the course of time. On these grounds, the Duce, in view of his conviction that a conflict with the Western Powers was unavoidable, had assumed that he should make his preparations for this event; he had made plans for a period of two or three years. If immediate conflict were unavoidable, the Duce, as he had told Ciano, would certainly stand on the German side, but for various reasons he would welcome the postponement of a general conflict until a later date. (Minutes of meeting with Hitler and Ribbentrop, Berlin, August 12–13, 1939.)

695. Italy believed that a conflict with Poland would not be limited to that country but would develop into a general European war. (Ibid.)

[Italy would not join in the war until the collapse of France in June 1940.]

696. Il Duce [Mussolini (q.v.)] is truly upset. His military instinct and his sense of honor prompted him to take part in the [forthcoming] combat, but reason has kept him from doing so. He is suffering terribly. On the military level, he has been badly served by his colleagues. Believing that peace would be eternal, they led him to foster grave illusions, and today he was forced to face up to harsh reality. It has been heartbreaking for Il Duce, but Italy has escaped a great catastrophe—which is lying in wait for the German people. (Journal entry, August 1939; cited in *My Truth*, by Edda Mussolini Ciano.)

[Following Germany's unsuccessful attempt to have Italy come into the imminent war, following the forthcoming invasion of Poland.]

697. I gave him [Mussolini (q.v.)] my frank opinion on people and events. I come home disgusted with Germany, with its leaders and their ways. They have deceived us and they have lied to us. Now they are about to drag us into an adventure that we do not relish and which may do harm to the regime and the country. They are traitors and we should have no scruples about abandoning them. (Diary excerpt, ca. August 15, 1939; Ibid.)

[Hitler was about to launch an attack on Poland and wanted Italy to join him.]

698. Prison for prison, I prefer to be here, an Italian among Italians, rather than in a German palace among Germans! (Attributed, upon entering Scalzi prison, ca. December 1943; Ibid.)

699. I feel the balls enter my back and pierce the nape of my neck while I sleep. What a horrible sensation! I shall not be able to endure being executed, but I shall not give those who wanted my death the pleasure of seeing me die a coward. (January 1944, prior to his execution; Ibid.)

JOSEPH E. DAVIES

(1876–1958)

An American observer in the Soviet Union, Davies was to become famous for his book *Mission to Moscow* and the film of the same name.

700. The resistance of the Russian Army has been more effective than was generally expected. In all probability the result will depend upon air power. If Hitler dominates the air, it is likely that the same thing will recur in White Russia and in the Ukraine that occurred in Flanders and France, namely, the inability of land forces, without air protection, to resist the combined attack by air, mechanized forces and infantry.

In such an event, Hitler will take White Russia, Moscow and the Ukraine which will provide him with 60% of the agricultural resources and 60% of the industrial production of Russia. (Memo to Harry Hopkins [q.v.], two weeks after the German invasion, July 8, 1941; cited in *Roosevelt and Hopkins*, by Robert E. Sherwood.)

701. If Hitler occupies White Russia and the Ukraine, as he may, and Stalin falls back into the interior, Hitler will be confronted with three major problems:

1. Guerrilla warfare and attacks.

2. Sabotage by the population who resent that "Holy Mother Russia" has been attacked.

3. The necessity of policing conquered territory and making it produce. (Ibid.)

702. There are two contingencies which might prevent such resistance. They are:

1. An internal revolution which would overthrow Stalin and by a coup d'etat put a Trotzkyite pro-German in power, who would make a Hitler peace. . . .

2. The possibility of Stalin himself making a Hitler peace. Stalin is oriental, coldly realistic and getting along in years. It is not impossible that he might again even "fall" for Hitler's peace as the lesser of two evils. He believes that Russia is surrounded by capitalistic enemies. In '38 and '39 he had no confidence in the good faith of either Britain or France or the capacity of the democracies to be effective against Hitler. He hated and feared Hitler then just as he does now. He was induced to make a pact of non-aggression with Hitler as the best hope he had for preserving peace for Russia, not so much on ideological grounds as on practical grounds to save his own government.

It is, therefore, of vital importance that Stalin be impressed with the fact that he is not "pulling the chestnuts out of the fire" for allies who have no use for him or who will be hostile to him after the war and who will be no less enemies, in the event of an allied peace, than the Germans in the event of their victory. (Ibid.)

JOSEPH C. GREW

(1880–1965)

A career diplomat, Grew served as U.S. ambassador to Japan from 1932 to 1941. He had entered the U.S. Foreign Service in 1904, serving at posts in Egypt, Mexico, Imperial Russia, Germany, Austria, Denmark, Switzerland, and Turkey. Several times he held administrative posts in the State Department, including Assistant Secretary of State, Under-Secretary, and once briefly as Secretary of State. After the war he served on the board of Radio Free Europe.

703. It is difficult for those who do not live in Japan to appraise the present temper of the country. An American Senator, according to reports, has recently recommended that we should accord parity to Japan in order to avoid future war.

Whatever the Senator's views may be concerning the general policy that we should follow in the Far East, he probably does not realize what harm that sort of public statement does in strengthening the Japanese stand and in reinforcing the aggressive ambitions of the expansionists. The Japanese press of course picks out such statements by prominent Americans and publishes them far and wide, thus confirming the general belief in Japan that the pacifist element in the United States is preponderantly strong and in the last analysis will control the policy and action of our Government. Under such circumstances there is a general tendency to characterize our diplomatic representations as bluff and to believe that they can safely be disregarded without fear of implementation. (Report to the State Department, December 27, 1934; cited in *Peace and War: United States Foreign Policy, 1931–1941*.)

704. It would be helpful if those who share the Senator's view could hear and read some of the things that are constantly being said and written in Japan, to the effect that Japan's destiny is to subjugate and rule the world and . . . realize the expansionist ambitions which lie not far from the surface in the minds of certain elements in the Army and Navy, the patriotic societies and the intense nationalists throughout the country. Their aim is to obtain trade control and eventually predominant political influence in China, the Philippines, the Straits Settlements, Siam and the Dutch East Indies, the Maritime Provinces and Vladivostok, one step at a time, as in Korea and Manchuria, pausing intermittently to consolidate and then continuing as soon as the intervening obstacles can be overcome by diplomacy or force. (Ibid.)

705. The United States and Great Britain are the leaders of a great group of English speaking nations around the world standing for a way of life which is being appallingly threatened today by a group of Germany, Italy, Soviet Russia and Japan whose avowed purpose is to impose by force of arms their will over conquered peoples. In attempting to deal with such powers the uses of diplomacy are in general bankrupt. Diplomacy may occasionally retard but cannot effectively stem the tide. Force or the display of force can alone prevent these powers from attaining their objectives. Japan today is one of the predatory powers; she has submerged all moral and ethical sense and has become frankly and unashamedly opportunist, seeking at every turn to profit by the weakness of others. Her policy of southward expansion is a definite threat to American interests in the Pacific and is a thrust at the British Empire in the East. (Memo to State Department, September 12, 1940; from *Turbulent Era*, by Joseph C. Grew.)

706. If we conceive it to be in our interest to support the British Empire in this hour of her travail, and I most emphatically do so conceive it, we must strive by every means to preserve the status quo in the Pacific at least until the European war has been won or lost. In my opinion this cannot be done nor can our interests be further adequately and properly protected by merely registering disapproval and keeping a careful record thereof. It is clear that Japan has been deterred from taking greater liberties with American interests only out of respect for our potential power; it is equally clear that she has trampled upon our rights to a degree in precise ratio to the strength of her conviction that the American people would not permit that power to be used. Once that conviction is shaken it is possible that the uses of diplomacy may again become accepted. (Ibid.)

707. There is a lot of talk around town to the effect that the Japanese, in case of a break with the United States, are planning to go all out in a surprise attack on Pearl Harbor. Of course I informed our government. (Diary excerpt, January 27, 1941; from *Ten Years in Japan*, by Joseph C. Grew.)

CORDELL HULL

(1871–1955)

Hull was Secretary of State from 1933 to 1944, longer than any other in American history. In addition to being a judge, Hull had been a member of the House of Representatives and the U.S. Senate before heading up the State Department. He was responsible for the "Good Neighbor Policy" with Latin American nations and stood firmly against the Axis Powers in the late 1930s. In 1945, he was awarded the Nobel Peace Prize.

708. I said that if [Marshal Henri] Petain [q.v.] should yield to pro-Hitler influences in his Government there might be left three courses for us and the British Government to pursue: 1) Either we or the British protest strongly; 2) We or the British take definite action with the use of force to establish ourselves at Dakar or Casablanca, to which he [Lord Halifax] added a supposition that neither of us was in a position to do that; 3) An attempt be made to get General [Maxime] Weygand [q.v.] to invite the British or some other force to come in and aid him against the German invasion. I remarked that General Weygand has softened considerably towards the British-American viewpoint and that Mr. [David] Eccles of the British Government and Mr. [Robert] Murphy [q.v.] for my Government have had full and more or less effective personal conferences with General Weygand on this question of Resistance against outside attack; that he has repeatedly said that he would fight Germany if she came in. (Memorandum on conversation with Lord Halifax, April 19, 1941; cited in *Our Vichy Gamble*, by William L. Langer.)

[There was concern that the Germans would invade French North Africa or West Africa. If so, pro-Nazi elements in the Vichy government might collaborate with the invaders.]

709. I have never seen a document that was more crowded with infamous falsehoods and distortions—infamous falsehoods and distortions on a scale so huge that I never imagined until today that any government on this planet was capable of uttering them. (Statement, December 7, 1941.)

[Directed to Japanese diplomats Nomura (q.v.) and Kurusu, who had just presented him with a Japanese statement explaining reasons for breaking off negotiations.]

710. Organized international cooperation can be successful only to the extent to which the nations of the world are willing to accept certain fundamental propositions.

First, each nation should maintain a stable government. Each nation should be free to decide for itself the forms and details of its governmental organization—so long as it conducts affairs in such a way as not to menace other nations.

Second, each nation should conduct its economic affairs in such a way as to promote the most effective utilization of its human and material resources and the greatest practicable measure of economic welfare and social security for all its citizens. Each nation should be free to decide for itself the forms of its internal economic and social organization—but it should conduct its affairs in such a way as to respect the rights of others and to play its necessary part in a system of sound international economic relations.

Third, each nation should be willing to submit differences . . . [with] other nations to processes of peaceful settlement. . . .

All of this calls for the creation of a system of international relations based on rules of morality, law, and justice as distinguished from the anarchy of unbridled and discordant nationalisms, economic and political. The outstanding characteristic of such a system is liberty under law for nations as well as individuals. (Broadcast, Washington, D.C., September 12, 1943.)

PAUL R. JOLLES

(n.d.)

Jolles worked in the Swiss embassy in Washington, starting in 1942. Later he would become a state secretary of Switzerland. In the 1990s, Swiss banks were accused of hiding money entrusted to them by European Jews who perished in the Holocaust (q.v.). The bad publicity was extended to other alleged wartime actions of the neutral country. Jolles answered the charges in a *Newsweek* article.

711. Recent news about Switzerland and the Nazi gold have brought a lot of long-forgotten history back into the public eye. Some of the allegations about Swiss banks may turn out to be true; clearly the banks were not diligent enough in tracking down wartime depositors, among them victims of the Nazis. But other allegations that Switzerland helped the Nazis and turned the war to our own profit strike me as completely unfair. . . .

In retrospect, Switzerland made some obvious mistakes, as did many countries. These included the restrictive immigration policies toward the Jews, and most of all, the failure to recognize the moral dimension of the Holocaust [q.v.]. . . .

In order to come to terms with this dire aspect of our past [dealing with victims' assets], Switzerland is now taking concrete action; more than $100 million has already been set aside to recompense depositors and their survivors. I appeal to those waging a campaign against Switzerland not to allow this issue to damage the friendly relations between our two countries. (From "My Turn," *Newsweek*, August 25, 1997.)

JOSEPH P. KENNEDY

(1888–1969)

Joseph Kennedy, the father of future President John F. Kennedy, was American ambassador to Britain from 1937 to 1940.

712. INDIRECT DISCOURSE: He [Kennedy] said Germany was hurting her own cause, not so much because we [Germans] want to get rid of the Jews but rather by the way we set out to accomplish this purpose with such a lot of noise. At home in Boston, for instance, Kennedy said there were clubs to which no Jews had been admitted in 50 years. . . . People simply avoided making a fuss about it. He himself understood our policy on Jews completely. (Telegram to Berlin from the German ambassador in London, June 15, 1938; cited in *A Man Called Intrepid*, by William Stevenson.)

713. [A toast to the Germans who] would badly thrash the British. (September 1939; from the "Kennediana" file of the British Foreign Office; Ibid.)

[Farewell party for his children who were returning home to America.]

714. England is fighting for her possessions. They are not fighting Hitler. They will spend every hour figuring how to get us in. (Message to Roosevelt, ca. 1940; Ibid.)

BRECKINRIDGE LONG
(1881–1958)

Long was the U.S. State Department official in charge of visas—and thus immigration—from 1940 to 1944. His delaying tactics trapped thousands of Jews trying to flee Nazi Europe.

715. We can delay and effectively stop for a temporary period of indefinite length the number of immigrants into the United States. We could do this by simply advising our consuls to put every obstacle in the way and to require additional evidence and to resort to various administrative advices which would postpone and postpone and postpone the granting of the visas. (Memo to State Department officials James Dunn and Adolf Berle, Jr., summer 1940; cited in *The Politics of Rescue*, by Henry L. Feingold.)

716. Discussed further restriction of immigration, including those who have visas. It is very apparent that the Germans are using visitor's visas to send agents and documents through the United States. (June 26, 1940; from *The War Diary of Breckinridge Long*, edited by Fred L. Israel.)

717. When I saw him [President Roosevelt] this morning, the whole subject of immigration, visas, safety of the United States, procedures to be followed, and all that sort of thing was on the table. I found that he was 100% in accord with my ideas. He said that when Myron Taylor [the president's representative to the Vatican] returned from Europe recently the only thing which they discussed outside of Vatican matters was the visa and refugee situation and the manner in which our Consulates were being deprived of a certain amount of discretion by the rulings of the Department. It was these very rulings which created the recent difficulty between [James G.] McDonald [chairman of the President's Advisory Committee on Refugees] and myself, because we had reinvested the Consuls with their legitimate authority after having noted from our experiences in the other and more lax administration that we were admitting persons who should not properly come into the United States. The President expressed himself as in entire accord with the policy which would exclude persons about whom there was any suspicion that they would be inimical to the welfare of the United States no matter who had vouchsafed for them and irrespective of their financial or other standing. . . . I specifically presented to him who had represented the Rabbi's organization but who professed to a long series of political activities in Europe and an intention to follow a course in the United States irrespective of the desires of the American Government but to take orders from the World

Jewish Congress. . . . The President agreed that those persons ought not be admitted to the United States in spite of the fact that Rabbi [Stephen] Wise in all sincerity desired them here. (October 3, 1940; Ibid.)

HUBERT MASARIK

(n.d.)

Masarik was with the Prague Foreign Office during the Munich crisis of October 1938. Neither he, nor any other Czech, was permitted to take part in any of the discussions by the four powers—Germany, Italy, France, and the United Kingdom. When the Munich Agreement (q.v.) was signed, giving up Czech territory to Germany, Masarik met with Prime Minister Neville Chamberlain (q.v.), Premier Edouard Daladier, and their associates. (Hitler and Mussolini [q.v.] had gone.)

718. I asked . . . whether they expected a declaration or answer of our Government to the Agreement. M. Daladier, noticeably nervous, M. Leger replied that the four statesmen had not much time. He added hurriedly and with superficial casualness that no answer was required from us, that they regarded the plan as accepted.. . . .They gave us a second slightly corrected map. Then they finished with us, and we could go. (Report to the Czech Foreign Office, 1938.)

YOSUKE MATSUOKA

(1880–1946)

Matsuoka was a Japanese diplomat.

719. Japan would take action in a decisive form [against Britain and America] if she had the feeling that otherwise she would lose a chance which could only occur once in a thousand years. (Conversation with Adolf Hitler, Berlin, March 27, 1941; cited in *The Second World War: The Grand Alliance*, by Winston Churchill.)

DOUGLAS MILLER

(n.d.)

Miller was an attaché at the U.S. embassy in Berlin in the early years of the Nazi regime.

720. The Nazis are not satisfied with the existing map of Europe. They are at heart belligerent and aggressive. True, they desire nothing more than a period of peace for several years in which they can gradually re-arm and discipline their people. This period may be 5 years, 10 years, or longer, but the more completely their experiments succeed the more certain is a large-scale war in Europe some day. (Report to State Department, April 17, 1934; cited in *Peace and War: United States Foreign Policy, 1931–1941.*)

721. In estimating the aims and purposes of the National Socialist movement, we must not make the mistake of putting too much reliance on public statements designed for consumption abroad which breathe the spirit of peace and assert the intention of the Government to promote the welfare of the German people and good relations with their neighbors. Nor should we imagine that the present Government leaders will feel and act as we would in their circumstances, namely think only of Germany's welfare. The real emotional drive behind the Nazi program is not so much love of their own country as dislike of other countries. The Nazis will never be content in merely promoting the welfare of the German people. They desire to be feared and envied by foreigners and to wipe out the memory of 1918 by inflicting humiliations in particular upon the French, the Poles, the Czechs and anybody else they can get their hands on.

A careful examination of Hitler's book and his public speeches reveals the fact that he cannot be considered as absolutely sane and normal on that subject. The same is true of many other Nazi leaders. They have capitalized on the wounded inferiority complex of the German people, and magnified their own bitter feelings into a cult of dislike against the foreign world which is past the bounds of ordinary good sense and reason. (Ibid.)

722. The control of this machine lies in the hands of narrow, ignorant and unscrupulous adventurers who have been slightly touched with madness from brooding over Germany's real or imagined wrongs, as well as the slights and indignities thrown in their own individual way as they attempt to organize the movement. Power of this kind concentrated in hands like these is dangerous. The Nazis are determined to secure more power and more territory in Europe. If this is voluntarily given to them by peaceful means, well and good; but if not, they will certainly use force. (Ibid.)

VYACHESLAV M. MOLOTOV

(1890–1986)

Stalin's Foreign Minister during the war, Molotov helped negotiate the Nazi-Soviet Pact (q.v.), represented the Soviet Union at major Allied meetings during the war, and personally read Russia's declaration of war against Japan to the Japanese ambassador.

723. It is war. Do you believe that we deserved that? (Comment to German Ambassador Friedrich von der Schulenburg [q.v.] upon receiving Germany's declaration of war, June 22, 1941.)

724. After the defeat and capitulation of Hitlerite Germany, Japan remained the only great power which still stands for the continuation of the war.

The demand of the three powers, the United States, Great Britain and China, of July 26 [1945] for the unconditional surrender of the Japanese armed forces was rejected by Japan. Thus the proposal made by the Japanese Government to the Soviet Union for mediation in the Far East has lost all foundation.

Taking into account the refusal of Japan to capitulate, the Allies approached the Soviet Government with a proposal to join the war against Japanese aggression and thus shorten the duration of the war, reduce the number of casualties, and contribute toward the most speedy restoration of peace. . . .

The Soviet Government considers that this policy is the only means able to bring peace nearer, to free the people from further sacrifice and suffering and to give the Japanese people the opportunity of avoiding the danger of destruction suffered by Germany after her refusal to accept unconditional surrender. (War declaration read to Japanese Ambassador Naotake Sato in Moscow, August 8, 1945.)

ROBERT D. MURPHY

(1894–1978)

An American career diplomat, Murphy served as chargé d'affaires in Vichy, France, following the French surrender. He is credited with negotiating the successful invasion of French North Africa in November 1942. He also helped to negotiate the Italian surrender in 1943 and ended the war as U.S. political adviser for Germany.

725. From the day when General Mark Clark [q.v.] flew into Algiers, bringing as an assistant, not a professional soldier but the motion picture producer Darryl Zanuck, my chief preoccupation in Africa concerned Americans. Being on duty in Algiers after November 8, 1942, seemed like the old days in Paris before the war, when both visiting and resident Americans expected our embassy to give them top priority over all other responsibilities. (From *Diplomat among Warriors*, by Robert D. Murphy.)

726. Just a word about the current trend. Apparently there is on the part of some of our officers no particular eagerness to occupy Berlin first. It is not at all impossible that our forces may linger along the Elbe "consolidating" their position. This will be true in the event there is substantial German resistance. One theory seems to be that what is left of Berlin may be tenaciously defended house by house and brick by brick. I have suggested the modest opinion that there should be a certain political advantage in the capture of Berlin even though the military advantage may be insignificant. (Memo to H. Freeman Matthews, director, Office of European Affairs, U.S. State Department, from London, April 16, 1945; cited in *On to Berlin*, by James M. Gavin.)

[Murphy was writing in his capacity as U.S. political adviser for Germany.]

KICHISABURO NOMURA
(1877–1964)

Nomura was Japanese ambassador to the United States from November 1940 until December 1941. He conducted peace negotiations in Washington while Japan was planning its surprise attack on Pearl Harbor. An admiral in the Japanese navy, he had been appointed Foreign Minister when the European war broke out in September 1939.

727. I am glad to inform you that I am now authorized by the Foreign Minister to assure you that there is no divergence of views in the Government regarding its fundamental policy of adjusting Japanese-American relations on a fair basis. (Letter to Secretary of State Cordell Hull [q.v.], July 4, 1941.)

SEMI PRAMOJ

(1905–1997)

Thailand's ambassador to the United States, Pramoj was ordered by the Japanese puppet government to deliver a Thai declaration of war against the United States. Instead, with the help of the Office of Strategic Services (q.v.), he organized a Thai guerrilla movement to fight the Japanese.

728. I'm keeping the declaration [of war] in my pocket because I am convinced it does not represent the will of the Thai people. With American help, I propose to prove it. (To Secretary of State Cordell Hull [q.v.], Washington, D.C., 1942; cited in the *New York Times*, July 29, 1997.)

JOACHIM VON RIBBENTROP

(1893–1946)

Initially the German ambassador in London, Ribbentrop later became Nazi Germany's Foreign Minister. His exploits included negotiating the Nazi-Soviet Nonaggression Pact and bringing Japan into what became the Rome-Berlin-Tokyo axis. He was hanged at Nuremberg as a war criminal.

729. After Molotov's [q.v.] visit [to Berlin], during which accession to the Three-Power Pact was offered, Russia had made conditions that were unacceptable. They involved the sacrifice of German interests in Finland, the granting of bases on the Dardanelles, and a strong [Soviet] influence on conditions in the Balkans. . . . The Fuehrer had not concurred because he had been of the opinion that Germany could not permanently subscribe to such a Russian policy. Germany needed the Balkan peninsula above all for her own economy, and had not been inclined to let it come under Russian domination. (Conversation with Yosuke Matsuoka [q.v.], Japanese envoy, Berlin, March 27, 1941.)

[As Matsuoka reported the conversation to Tokyo.]

730. Should Russia some day take a stand that could be interpreted as a threat to Germany, the Fuehrer would crush Russia. Germany was certain that a campaign against Russia would end in the absolute victory of German arms and the total crushing of the Russian Army and the Russian State. (Ibid.)

731. There was no doubt that the British would long since have abandoned that war if Roosevelt had not always given Churchill new hope. . . . The Fuehrer . . . believed that it would be advantageous if Japan would decide as soon as possible to take an active part in the war upon England. A quick attack upon Singapore, for instance, would be a decisive factor in the speedy overthrow of England. If . . . Japan were to succeed with one decisive stroke on Singapore Roosevelt would be in a very difficult position. If he declared war upon Japan he must expect that the Philippine question would be resolved in favor of Japan. (Ibid.)

732. Forgive them, for they know not what they do. (On the gallows, Nuremberg, October 16, 1946.)

JAMES W. RIDDLEBERGER
(1904–)

Riddleberger was a U.S. Foreign Service officer.

733. [John] Winant accused me of not having any faith in Soviet intentions and I replied that in this he was exactly right. In an effort to find some way out, I then suggested that the three zones [of occupied Germany] should converge upon Berlin as the center of a pie, but this idea got nowhere because Winant was very much opposed to it. (Spoken to Robert Murphy [q.v.], recalling events of fall 1944; quoted in *Diplomat among Warriors*, by Robert Murphy.)

[Winant, U.S. ambassador to Britain, served on the European Advisory Commission, which had drawn up plans for the coming occupation of Germany. Riddleberger had objected to having Berlin 100 miles inside the proposed Russian zone. In its initial stages, the plan called for three zones of occupation: American, British, and Russian. A French zone would be added later.]

FRIEDRICH VON DER SCHULENBURG

(n.d.)

Schulenburg was the German ambassador in Moscow. It was he who had to deliver the German declaration of war. Three years later, he was found guilty of conspiring to kill Hitler and was executed.

734. To sum up, the Government of the Reich declares, therefore, that the Soviet Government, contrary to the obligations it assumed,

1. has not only continued, but even intensified its attempts to undermine Germany and Europe,
2. has adopted a more and more anti-German foreign policy,
3. has concentrated all its forces in readiness at the German border. Thereby the Soviet Government has broken its treaties with Germany and is about to attack Germany from the rear in its struggle for life. The Fuehrer has therefore ordered the German Armed Forces to oppose this threat with all the means at their disposal. (Message from Berlin read personally to Soviet Foreign Minister Molotov [q.v.], Moscow, June 22, 1941.)

CONSUL-GENERAL SHEPHERD

(n.d.)

Consul-General Shepherd was the British consul in Danzig at the time of the Nazi threat to the Free City of Danzig and to Poland itself. Invasion would come on September 1, 1939.

735. Yesterday morning four German army officers in mufti arrived here by night express from Berlin to organize Danzig *Heinwehr* [home defense forces].

All approaches to hills and dismantled fort, which constitute a popular public promenade on western fringe of the city, have been closed with barbed wire and "verboten" notices.

The walls surrounding the shipyards bear placards: "Comrades keep your mouths shut lest you regret consequence." (Report to British Foreign Minister, July 1, 1939.)

[Introduced into evidence at Nuremberg.]

736. Master of British steamer "High Commissioner Wood" whilst he was roving Koenigsberg from 28th June to 30th June, observed considerable military activity, including extensive shipment of camouflaged covered lorries and similar material by small coasting vessels. On 28th June four medium-sized steamers, loaded with troops, lorries, field kitchens, etc., left Koenigsberg, ostensibly returning to Hamburg after maneuvers, but actually proceeding to Stettin. (Ibid.)

737. The same informant, whom I believe to be reliable, advises me that on 8th July he personally saw about 30 military lorries with East Prussian license numbers on the Bischofsberg, where numerous field kitchens had been placed along the hedges. There were also eight large anti-aircraft guns in position, which he estimated as being of over 3-inch caliber, and three six-barreled light anti-aircraft machine guns. There were about 500 men drilling with rifles, and the whole place is extensively fortified with barbed wire. (Ibid., July 10, 1939.)

PAUL-HENRI SPAAK
(1899–1972)

The Belgian Foreign Minister at the time of the Nazi invasion in 1940, Spaak became part of the government-in-exile. Before the war ended, he worked on the Benelux agreement for economic cooperation of Belgium, the Netherlands, and Luxembourg. He became Belgium's premier after liberation and went on to become head of the United Nations General Assembly and secretary general of the North Atlantic Treaty Organization.

738. Mr. Ambassador, the German Army has just attacked our country. This is the second time in 25 years that Germany has committed a criminal aggression against a neutral and loyal Belgium. What has just happened is perhaps even more odious than the aggression of 1914. No ultimatum, no note, no protest of any kind has ever been placed before the Belgian Government. It is through the attack itself that Belgium has learned that Germany has violated the undertakings given by her on October 13th, 1937, and renewed spontaneously at the beginning of the war [in a speech by Hitler on October 6, 1939]. The act of aggression committed by Germany, for which there is no justification whatever, will deeply shock the conscience of the world. The German Reich will be held responsible by history. Belgium is resolved to defend herself. Her cause, which is the cause of Right, cannot be vanquished. (Message from the Belgian government, read to the German ambassador, May 10, 1940.)

[The attack was already several hours old when the German ambassador presented himself to Spaak. The Belgian Foreign Minister insisted on reading his statement to the ambassador. He then listened to a German statement that the Nazis were really trying to ensure the neutrality of Belgium from British and French attack. Belgium was warned to cease resistance or face destruction.]

EDWARD R. STETTINIUS, JR.

(1900–1949)

Stettinius was U.S. Secretary of State, succeeding Cordell Hull (q.v.) in December 1944. His career included executive stints with General Motors and U.S. Steel. Early in the war, he served as Lend-Lease (q.v.) administrator and Under-Secretary of State.

739. I have been submitting regularly to Mr. Roosevelt a two-page daily report summarizing current secret developments in the field of foreign affairs. I shall of course continue this practice but in this my first report to you I felt it would be useful, rather than merely to transmit the developments of the last 24 hours, to present for your information a very brief summary of the background and present status of the principle [*sic*] problems now confronting this Government in its relations with other countries. [Excerpts follow.] (Memo to President Truman [q.v.], April 13, 1945.)

[Submitted to Truman the day after Roosevelt's death.]

740. UNITED KINGDOM: Mr. Churchill's policy is based fundamentally upon cooperation with the United States. It is based secondarily on maintaining the unity of the three great powers but the British Government has been showing increasing apprehension of Russia and her intentions. (Ibid.)

741. FRANCE: The best interests of the United States require that every effort be made by this Government to assist France, morally as well as physically, to regain her strength and her influence. It is recognized that the French Provisional Government and the French people are at present unduly preoccupied, as a result of the military defeat of 1940 and the subsequent occupation of their country by the enemy, with questions of national prestige. They have consequently from time to time put forward requests which are out of all proportion to their present strength and have in certain cases, notably in connection with Indochina, showed unreasonable suspicions of American aims and motives. (Ibid.)

742. SOVIET UNION: Since the Yalta Conference [q.v.] the Soviet Government has taken a firm and uncompromising position on nearly every major question that has arisen in our relations. The more important of these are the Polish question, the application of the Crimea agreements on liberated areas, the agreement on the exchange of liberated prisoners of war and civilians, and the San Francisco Conference [which would establish the United Nations as an international organization]. (Ibid.)

743. POLAND: The present situation relating to Poland is highly unsatisfactory with the Soviet authorities consistently sabotaging Ambassador Harriman's efforts in the Moscow Commission to hasten the implementation of the decisions at the Crimea Conference. Direct appeals to Marshal Stalin have not yet produced any worthwhile results. The Soviet Government likewise seeks to complicate the problem by initiating and supporting claims of the Warsaw Provisional Polish Government to represent and speak for Poland in international matters such as the San Francisco Conference, reparations and territorial questions. (Ibid.)

744. THE BALKAN AREA: The chief problem facing this Government in Rumania, Bulgaria and Hungary concerns the operation of the Allied Control Commissions [ACC] which were set up for the execution of the respective armistices. The essence is in the relations with the Soviet Government which, as the power in military control and as the predominant in the ACC's, uses its position for unilateral political interference in the respective countries. (Ibid.)

745. GERMANY: The policy of the United States toward Germany was outlined in a memorandum approved by President Roosevelt on March 23, 1945. The principal features of that policy are: destruction of National Socialist organizations and influence, punishment of war criminals, disbandment of the German military establishment, military government administered with a view to political decentralization, reparation from existing wealth and future production, prevention of the manufacture of arms and destruction of all specialized facilities for their production, and controls over the German economy to secure these objectives. (Ibid.)

746. AUSTRIA: The four principal Allies have declared their intention to liberate Austria from German domination and reestablish it as a free and independent country. (Ibid.)

747. ITALY: Our gravest problem at present, aside from the country's economic distress, is to forestall Yugoslav occupation of an important part of north-eastern Italy, prejudicing by unilateral action a final equitable settlement of this territorial dispute and precipitating serious trouble within Italy. (Ibid.)

HANS THOMSEN

(n.d.)

Hans Thomsen was the German chargé d'affaires in Washington prior to the entrance of the United States into the war.

748. As communicated to me by an absolutely reliable source, the [U.S.] State Department is in possession of the key to the Japanese coding system and is, therefore, also able to decipher information telegrams from Tokyo to Ambassador Nomura [q.v.] here regarding Ambassador Assume's reports from Berlin. (Telegram to Foreign Minister Joachim von Ribbentrop [q.v.], April 29, 1941; cited in *The Broken Seal*, by Ladislas Farago.)

[The source was quite roundabout. It apparently came to Thomsen from Constanatin Oumansky, Soviet ambassador to the United States. Oumansky had received coded information from Under-Secretary of State Sumner Welles that Hitler would soon attack the Soviet Union. Oumansky obviously did not believe the report but did believe that the Japanese security system had been compromised.]

SHIGENORI TOGO

(1882–1950)

Togo was the Foreign Minister of Japan during the 1941 peace negotiations with the United States.

749. There are reasons beyond your ability to guess why we want to settle Japanese-American relations by November 25, but if the signing could be completed by the 29th, we would be willing to wait until that date. This time we mean it that the deadline absolutely cannot be changed. After that things are automatically going to happen. (Message to Ambassador Nomura [q.v.], November 22, 1941.)

[At the time, Nomura was conducting negotiations with the United States. The dates specified by Togo were the points of no return for the Pearl Harbor attack.]

HUGH R. WILSON

(1885–1946)

Wilson was the last American ambassador to Nazi Germany. A career diplomat, Wilson served in minor posts in Berlin, Tokyo, and elsewhere before becoming Minister to Switzerland in 1927. He served there for ten years and then became U.S. ambassador in Berlin. He supported Hitler's takeover of Austria and the Munich Pact, which turned over part of Czechoslovakia to Nazi Germany. Recalled to Washington for "consultation" following the "Crystal Night" pogroms of November 1938, Wilson never returned to this post. U.S. interests were put in the hands of a chargé d'affaires until America entered the war. Wilson worked in the Office of Strategic Services (q.v.) during the war.

750. It was a moment of great interest to me to meet a man [Hitler] who had pulled his people from moral and economic despair into the state of pride and evident prosperity they now enjoyed. (Letter to Roosevelt, March 1938; cited in *Gentleman Spy: The Life of Allen Dulles*, by Peter Grose.)

751. If a spirit should develop in Europe which would permit a cessation of hostilities in the West to allow Germany to take care of the Russian encroachment, I, for one, should enthusiastically applaud and believe sincerely that the ends of civilization would be furthered thereby. (Prior to August 23, 1939, the date of the Nazi-Soviet Nonaggression Pact; Ibid.)

5

Warriors

BILL BAILEY

(n.d.)

Bailey went to sea at age fifteen and was an engineer during the war. He served in the Pacific.

752. We're on our way to Okinawa, when we got word that the atom bomb dropped. I thought it was Adam, A-D-A-M. Somebody dropped an Adam bomb. What kinda bomb is that? They said it wiped out a city. I said, "This son of a bitch of an Adam, who the hell is he?" At that particular moment I said, "Gee, that's great." But secretly you had these feelings that somethin' was wrong. You couldn't place your hands on it, but you had a feeling. And then bad things happened. That great camaraderie of savin' tinfoil, toothpaste tubes, or tin cans, all that stuff that made people part of somethin', that disappeared. Everybody was out for what they could get from then on. Everything changed. (From *The Good War*, by Studs Terkel.)

PAUL BOESCH

(n.d.)

Boesch was a lieutenant in the 121st Infantry, 8th Division. He fought in France, Belgium, Luxembourg, and Germany. His book on the Huertgen Forest engagement is a rare narrative on one of the bloodiest battles of the war. There were 28,000 American casualties, including killed, wounded, and missing.

753. [On their way to relieve another outfit in the Huertgen Forest, Boesch's company finds that its jeeps are stuck in the mud. In the pitch darkness and in a driving rain, machine guns and mortars must be transferred from the jeeps.] Reluctantly, I sent for my platoon and gave the unwelcome order . . . to carry the heavy weapons and equipment by hand. It would make the long trek through the wet and the dark even more arduous, but machine guns and mortars were vital and my platoon would be of no use in the attack without them. . . . We hoisted the weapons and ammunition to our shoulders. Holding fast to the man ahead, we slowly, painfully made our way to where the rest of the company had assembled. . . .

Down the narrow trail of a road between towering trees . . . we moved. The night seemed to get even blacker . . . and the rain came in great wind-driven sheets. . . .

It was not easy to hold onto the belt of the man in front while slipping and slithering forward and under the weight of a machine gun tripod or a mortar tube. . . .

The only light to pierce the blackness came from artillery. . . . After the sudden, brilliant burst of light, it was hard to adjust your vision again to the darkness. . . . Far on the horizon [came] answering reports from the enemy's big guns. . . .

The road was full of holes, and the holes were full of water and rocks, and it was almost impossible to keep your feet at times. . . .

For hours we fought for breath and struggled to maintain the exhausting pace. The knowledge that at the end of the march we faced the ticklish problem of relief in the face of the enemy, then attack, dragged at our feet at first; but as time passed we welcomed even this prospect as a way to end this nightmare walkathon.

Suddenly the line halted. . . . One man turned his head toward us. "This is as far as we go tonight. Pull off the road and get some sleep. Pass the word along." (Huertgen Forest, Germany, late fall 1944; from *Road to Huertgen: Forest in Hell*, by Paul Boesch.)

JOSEPH BRODER

(1923–)

Broder was a first lieutenant in the U.S. Air Force. During the war, he was a B-24 navigator, serving with the 8th Air Force in England. He was awarded the Distinguished Flying Cross.

754. Today there is much talk about abortions, both pro and con. I will not take sides.

In wartime flying, the only abortions I knew were when the Bomb Group had to turn back and the mission did not count towards the completion of a tour. They were usually called "recalls," when the aircraft were ordered home due to consistently bad British weather or pernicious continental weather systems.

Sometimes, of course, there were individual abortions due to mechanical failures; when the plane did not leave the ground, or when the aircraft and crew, for some reason, returned to base early. Malfunctions, mainly manifold pressure or fuel pump gauges or cylinder temperature or some pre-flight or in-flight check revealed problems. Abortions resulted.

Commanding officers did not take too kindly to most of these mishaps. . . . One abortion, a single one, was often regarded as habitual. ("Abortions," *The Beach Bell Echo*, December 15, 1995, 446th Bomb Group Association.)

755. World War II was won by mass production, by machines—not men.
Forget the Omaha Beaches and the Schweinfurts and the Okinawas.
Our soldiers and flyers and sailors had little to do with victory.
The revisionists are wrong. History answers. Battles are won by blood.

("The Revisionists," 1996.)

WILLIAM C. BROOKS

(n.d.)

Brooks, an ensign in the U.S. Navy, was flying antisubmarine patrol in the Philippines during the Leyte invasion. He was the first to spot a huge Japanese naval force heading toward San Bernardino

Strait—and toward the American invasion forces on the beaches of Leyte.

756. Enemy surface force of 4 battleships, 7 cruisers, and 11 destroyers sighted 20 miles northwest of your task group and closing in on you at 30 knots. (Message sent in the clear to Admiral C. A. F. Sprague [q.v.], October 25, 1944.)

757. Identification of enemy force confirmed. Ships have pagoda masts. (Ibid.)

[Believing that Brooks might have mistakenly sighted part of Halsey's [q.v.] fleet, Sprague requested confirmation.]

JOHN D. BULKELEY
(1911–1996)

Bulkeley was a U.S. naval hero of World War II. He commanded a patrol torpedo boat in the Philippines, where he carried out many exploits against the Japanese. He was responsible for evacuating General MacArthur from Bataan to Mindinao, from which the general escaped to Australia to head Allied forces in the South Pacific. In the European theater, Bulkeley led a fleet of mine sweepers and torpedo boats during the Normandy Invasion. He won many decorations for bravery, including the Congressional Medal of Honor and the Navy Cross.

758. As our [PT-]34 boat cleared the mine fields around Bataan, looking over toward Manila, I saw something very queer—shipping of all descriptions was pouring out of that Manila breakwater into the open harbor—destroyers, mine sweepers, Yangtze River gunboats, tramp steamers, all going hell for breakfast. And then I saw them—a big formation of about 27 bombers. By then I was beginning to learn that if we saw planes in the air, they would be Japs, not ours. (March 1942; quoted in *They Were Expendable*, by W. L. White.)

759. Invasion day itself is kind of blurred in my mind. I remember the black night in the bay of the Seine, so black I couldn't see a thing. All I could do was watch my radar. The beach was a single mass of flame. (Interview, describing D-Day [q.v.], the *New York Times*, October 1944.)

760. I don't know what a hero is. This business of the captain taking all the credit, ordering someone else and so forth—that's not it. The men who do the actual fighting, man the guns, they're the guys that really win the war. (Interview, CNN telecast, July 1995.)

HAROLD DIXON

(n.d.)

Dixon was a U.S. Navy bomber pilot. He was forced to ditch his plane in the Pacific Ocean early in 1942. He and his two companions spent thirty-four days in a rubber life raft. When they reached land, they were not sure if the island was in friendly or enemy hands. The trio decided to walk up the beach in some kind of military fashion.

761. If there are Japs on this island, they'll not see an American sailor crawl. We'll stand, and march, and make them shoot us down, like men-of-warsmen. (Quoted in *The Raft*, by Robert Trumbull.)

[The island turned out to be in friendly hands.]

JAMES H. DOOLITTLE

(1896–1994)

A little-known Army Air Corps colonel at the beginning of the war, Doolittle was to become a general and one of America's outstanding war heroes. Early in 1942, he planned the bombing of the Japanese mainland from an aircraft carrier and personally led the raid himself. Although his raiders reached their targets, Doolittle believed the mission had been a failure. The planes were forced to launch several hundred miles earlier than planned, because they had been spotted by Japanese ships. The American planes crash-landed before reaching their assigned landing fields in China. Actually, the raid forced the Japanese to pull back some of their warships to defend the home islands. Doolittle was awarded the Congressional Medal of Honor.

762. [If my plane is hit during the bomb run on Japan] I'm going to bail my crew out and then dive it, full throttle, into any target I can find where the crash will do the most good. I'm 46 years old and have lived a full life. (Aboard the USS *Hornet*, April 17, 1942.)

[Indicating that he would not allow himself to be taken prisoner by the Japanese. One of the American planes did crash-land in Japan, and several members of the crew were executed by the Japanese.]

ALEXANDER DRABIK

(n.d.)

Drabik, a U.S. Army sergeant, led his platoon over the Ludendorf Bridge at Remagen. It enabled American troops to cross the Rhine and secure the east bank before the bridge could be destroyed by the Germans.

763. We ran down the middle of the bridge, shouting as we went. I didn't stop because I knew that if I kept moving they couldn't hit me. My men were in squad column and not one of them was hit. We took cover in some bomb craters. Then we just sat and waited for others to come. That's the way it was. (Recollections of March 7, 1945, Remagen, Germany; cited in *Historical Guide to World War II*, by Louis L. Snyder.)

TEDDY DRAPER, SR.

(n.d.)

Draper was one of 400 U.S. Marine Navajo code talkers of the Pacific war. They used a combination of the Navajo language and code words for weapons and personnel that completely confounded enemy intelligence. For example, the Navajo word for "turtle" stood for "tank"; the Navajo word for "swallow" stood for "torpedo plane"; and the Navajo word for "buzzard" stood for "bomber." The enemy would first have to recognize the Navajo word, translate it into the

"We ran down the middle of the bridge, shouting as we went. I didn't stop because I knew that if I kept moving they couldn't hit me."

—SGT. ALEXANDER DRABIK, SEIZING THE RHINE BRIDGE AT REMAGEN

American troops pass through a railway tunnel on their way to the captured railroad bridge in the distance.

English word, and then determine what the English word stood for. The enemy never got past the first step. Talking, however, was only part of handling marine communications.

764. I participated in the bloody battle of Iwo Jima. . . . They told us to secure communications and telephone wire under combat conditions on the island within three days, but it took about a month. (Quoted in *Warriors: Navajo Code Talkers*, by Kenji Kawano.)

WILLIAM DYESS

(n.d.)

Dyess was a lieutenant colonel in the Army Air Corps. Captured by the Japanese on Bataan in April 1942, he was on the infamous Bataan Death March (q.v.). An estimated 10,000 American and Filipino prisoners of war died along the sixty-mile march, many murdered by sadistic guards. After the war, Japanese General Masaharu Homma would be held responsible for the actions of his troops and would be executed as a war criminal. Below, Dyess describes an incident at a compound during the march.

765. When it was observed that men were dying, Japanese noncommissioned officers entered the compound and ordered the Americans to drag out the bodies and bury them. We were told to put the delirious ones into a thatched shed a few hundred feet away. When this had been done the grave digging began.

We thought we had seen every atrocity the Japs could offer, but we were wrong. The shallow trenches had been completed. The dead were being rolled into them. Just then an American soldier and two Filipinos were carried out of the compound. They had been delirious. Now they were in a coma. A Jap noncom stopped the bearers and tipped the unconscious men into the trench.

The Japs then ordered the burial detail to fill it up. The Filipinos lay lifelessly in the hole. As the earth began falling about the American, he revived and tried to climb out. His fingers gripped the edge of the grave. He hoisted himself to a standing position.

Two Jap guards placed bayonets at the throat of a Filipino on the burial detail. They gave him an order. When he hesitated they pressed the bayonet points hard against his neck. The Filipino raised a stricken face to the sky. Then he brought his shovel down upon the head of his American comrade, who fell backward to the bottom of the grave. The burial detail filled it up. (From *The Dyess Story*, by William Dyess.)

JAMES M. GAVIN

(1907–)

A combat officer, Gavin led American forces in Sicily, Salerno, Arnhem, and the Battle of the Bulge (q.v.). He landed with his men in Normandy on D-Day (q.v.). Later, General Gavin was given command of the 82nd Airborne Division. He would serve as ambassador to France under President John Kennedy.

766. Airborne combat in Sicily and Italy had been invaluable in preparation for the Normandy operation. We learned what could be done by parachute troops and troop carrier pilots, but, more important, we learned what they could not do. The airborne troops had more than held their own against German infantry, but meeting German armor in good tank country could be disastrous. The airborne-troop carrier team had to be thoroughly trained and honed to a keen edge. Small mistakes could lead to disaster, with airborne troops badly scattered and heavy troop carrier losses. On the other hand, with hard work and thorough training, the team could be made into an extremely effective battle force, a force that could tip the scales to victory in any future combat operation. And although we had made a number of mistakes and learned costly lessons in Sicily, that had been a comparatively small operation. For OVERLORD [the Normandy Invasion] we would be three airborne divisions, more than 1,300 transports, and 3,300 gliders. It was to be a tremendous undertaking. (July 1943; from *On to Berlin*, by James M. Gavin.)

767. We were at about 600 feet, the green light went on, and I took one last precious look at the land below. We were about 30 seconds overtime. . . . Small-arms fire was increasing. About three seconds after the green light went on, I yelled, "Let's go," and went out the door, with everyone following. (Normandy, June 6, 1944; Ibid.)

768. In the third week of April [1945] First Lieutenant Arthur Hadley, who was a member of the Second Armored Division . . . went forward from his division bridgehead over the Elbe. He was in a tank, and he was followed by a jeep with several newspapermen. They moved in the direction of Berlin. They soon encountered a few Russian soldiers. They had neither heavy weapons nor radios. The newspapermen, after talking to the Russians, decided to go into Berlin and invited Hadley to come along. His orders forbade him to go any farther. The newspapermen drove directly into the city. They were Ernest Leiser of *Stars and Stripes* and Mack Morriss [q.v.] of *Yank*. (April 1945; Ibid.)

[The point being that the Americans could have beaten the Russians to Berlin.]

JACK GERRIE

(n.d.)

Jack Gerrie was captain and commanding officer of G Company, 11th Infantry, of the U.S. Third Army. His company was sent in to reinforce American troops trying to take Fort Driant in French Lorraine.

769. The situation is critical. A couple more barrages and another counterattack [by the Germans] and we are sunk. . . . We cannot advance. We may be able to hold till dark but if anything happens this afternoon I can make no predictions. The enemy artillery is butchering these troops. . . . We cannot get out to get our wounded and there is a hell of a lot of dead and missing. . . . There is only one answer. . . . First either to withdraw and saturate it with heavy bombers or reinforce with a hell of a strong force, but eventually they'll get it by artillery too. . . . This is just a suggestion but if we want this damned fort let's get the stuff required to take it and then go. (Report to his battalion commander, Fort Driant, Lorraine, October 5, 1944; from *The Lorraine Campaign*, by Hugh M. Cole.)

[The Americans held on for several more days and then withdrew. The fort was bypassed.]

HOWARD W. GILMORE
(1902–1943)

Gilmore commanded the submarine USS *Growler* during its Fourth War Patrol in the Southwest Pacific from January 10 to February 7, 1943. The Congressional Medal of Honor citation reads: "Boldly striking at the enemy in spite of continuous hostile air and antisubmarine patrols, Commander Gilmore sank one Japanese freighter and damaged another by torpedo fire, successfully evading severe depth charges following each attack. In the darkness of night on 7 February, an enemy gunboat closed range and prepared to ram the *Growler*. Commander Gilmore daringly maneuvered to avoid the crash and rammed the attacker instead, ripping into her port side and bursting wide her plates. In the terrific fire of the heavy machine guns, Commander Gilmore calmly gave the order to clear the bridge, and refusing safety for himself, remained on deck while his men preceded him below. Struck down by the fusillade of bullets and having done his utmost against the enemy, in his final moments, Commander Gilmore gave his last order to the officer of the deck. . . . The *Growler* dived, seriously damaged but under control. She was brought safely to port by her well-trained crew inspired by the courageous fighting spirit of their dead captain."

770. Take her down, Arnie. (Order to Arnie Schade, executive officer of the *Growler*, February 7, 1943; from *Medal of Honor Recipients*.)

[Gilmore's last order.]

HY HAAS

(1915–)

A U.S. Army sergeant, Haas was in charge of a self-propelled anti-aircraft artillery unit at Omaha beach on D-Day (q.v.). He later saw action at St. Lo, the Battle of the Bulge (q.v.), the Ludendorf Bridge at Remagen, and elsewhere.

771. Coming in on the landing craft approaching Omaha beach, it was very peaceful. When we landed it was pandemonium; it was complete terror. You didn't know if you would be alive the next minute. You saw nothing. But you heard artillery shells, mortar shells, machine gun fire. There were bodies everywhere. (Recollections of June 1944, interview, August 29, 1996.)

772. Our mission was to get up on the bluffs overlooking Omaha beach and set up an anti-aircraft unit. That became impossible. We faced a hill of little stones. You couldn't drive a half-track up there. So we were called on to do other things.

An officer came running up to us, pointing out a German bunker which stood in the way of anyone trying to get up those bluffs. He wanted us to take out that bunker.

I went into the surf first to check for mines in the water. Then we drove the half-track into the water, aiming it the best way to give us a clear field of fire. We got a clear shot and we knocked it out. That was during my first five or ten minutes on the beach.

This action opened a route up the hill because that bunker had been blocking the way. They called that Exit E-1. That was one of the three exits that opened up. Once that happened, vehicular traffic moved up.

When we were going up the exit road to the bluffs, we passed the bunker. And there were the Germans we had shot. They were in an awful state. And you could say, "Look, thousands of our guys were hit, and I don't know how many died." Yet when I saw what we had done, I didn't feel too good. Because I had never really hurt anybody before. Those Germans were our enemies, and yet to see those guys bleeding from the mouth. . . . They just lay out there on the bunker. I don't know if they lived or not.

Three days later, we moved out into the countryside. From that point, we were supporting infantry. (Ibid.)

773. When we got to the Ludendorf Bridge at Remagen [which the Nazis had failed to blow up], I set up on a hill overlooking the Rhine River and the bridge.

Suddenly, here comes a German jet. And right behind him were five P-38s [Army Air Force fighter planes].

The German was firing at the bridge and the P-38s were firing at the German. And we were in the way. I don't have to tell you about the firepower that went right past us.

The next morning we went over to the other side of the bridge. We were protecting the bridge and we were told to shoot at anything that floated along that looked like a mine. We thought the Germans might float a mine to crash into the bridge and bring it down. We also watched out for anybody who might try to get to the bridge to try to damage it. (Recollections of March 1945, ibid.)

EUNICE C. HATCHITT

(n.d.)

Eunice Hatchitt was a nurse on Bataan.

774. Days and nights [on Bataan] were an endless nightmare, until it seemed we couldn't stand it any longer. Patients came in by the hundreds, and the doctors and nurses worked continuously under the tents and the flies and heat and dust. We had our eight to nine hundred victims a day. (From "Bataan Nurse," in *Collier's*, August 1, 1942.)

ROGER HILSMAN

(1920–)

A West Point graduate in 1943, Hilsman became a guerrilla operating behind Japanese lines in Burma. This experience would later involve him in studying guerrilla warfare in Vietnam two decades later. He served in the Kennedy administration, later becoming professor of government at Columbia University.

775. In individual terms, I found being a guerrilla behind enemy lines considerably better than being a platoon leader in Merrill's Marauders . . . where I was told to lead my men straight into dug-in machine guns. Your only hope was that one or two men would still be on their feet when they got close enough to the pillbox to throw a grenade. In such circumstances, an infantry platoon leader could do almost nothing to influence the situation. His brains and skill were essentially irrelevant. The only thing that counted was his luck. (From *American Guerrilla*, by Roger Hilsman.)

[Merrill's Marauders was the name given to the guerrilla army led by Major General Frank Merrill in Burma.]

776. A guerrilla leader, on the other hand, could match his wits against the enemy's. If he was careful about gathering intelligence, perceptive in analyzing it, and knowledgeable about the tactics and strategy of guerrilla operations, he could do a great deal of damage to the enemy and at the same time minimize the risk to his own men. (Ibid.)

777. A guerrilla leader can be successful only in very special circumstances. For us, the circumstances had not been perfect, but they had certainly been good.

First and foremost is terrain. Guerrillas need cover to operate effectively—mountains, forest, or jungle. . . . On mountain and jungle trails, guerrillas on foot are as mobile as a motorized enemy. It was the terrain that made it possible for us to find safety in constant movement, rarely spending two nights in the same place. (Ibid.)

778. The second essential is the sympathy of the population. Mao Zedong used to say that guerrillas are fish swimming in the sea of the people. (Ibid.)

LEON W. JOHNSON
(1904–1997)

Johnson was one of five men to win the Congressional Medal of Honor for heroism during the Ploesti Raid (q.v.). This was an attack by the U.S. Air Force on important oil refineries in Romania on August 1, 1943. Johnson led the last bomber group over the heavily defended target. The Medal of Honor citation reads: "It was discovered that the target assigned to Col. Johnson's group had been attacked and damaged by a preceding element. Though having lost the element of surprise upon which the safety and success of such a daring . . . mission . . . depended, Col. Johnson elected to carry out his planned low-level attack despite the thoroughly alerted defenses, the destructive anti-aircraft fire, enemy fighter airplanes, the imminent danger of exploding delayed action bombs from the previous element. Col. Johnson so led his formation as to destroy totally the important refining plants and installations which were the object of his mission." Of the six planes in Johnson's formation, his was the only one to return to base. After the raid, Johnson tried to describe it.

779. It was more like an artist's conception of an air battle than anything I have ever experienced. We flew through sheets of flame, and airplanes were everywhere, some of them on fire and others exploding. It's indescribable to anyone who wasn't there. (From *The Brereton Diaries*, by Lewis H. Brereton.)

THOMAS KINKAID

(1888–1972)

Kincaid was an American admiral whose task forces saw action throughout the Pacific. Battles included Santa Cruz, Guadalcanal, the Aleutians, and—especially—Leyte Gulf. The last required a combination of courage and resourcefulness, as his outnumbered and outgunned units took on a superior Japanese force to prevent disaster on the Leyte beaches.

780. Urgently need fast battleships Leyte Gulf at once. (Dispatch to Admiral Halsey [q.v.] during battle of Leyte Gulf, October 1944.)

[Halsey had left the San Bernardino Straits unguarded, lured away by a decoy Japanese force.]

781. Our escort carriers being attacked by four battleships, eight cruisers plus others. Request Lee cover Leyte at top speed. Request fast carriers make immediate strike. (Follow-up dispatch to Halsey [q.v.], October 1944.)

[Vice Admiral Willis Lee, Jr., was commander of Task Force 34.]

782. Where is Lee? Send Lee. (Final dispatch to Halsey [q.v.], sent uncoded, October 1944.)

ROBERT LEWIS

(n.d.)

Lewis, an Army Air Force captain, was copilot of the *Enola Gay*, which dropped the atomic bomb on Hiroshima.

783. My God! (Log entry over Hiroshima, 8:15 A.M., August 6, 1945.)

ROSSI LOMANITZ

(n.d.)

Lomanitz was an American soldier stationed somewhere in the Pacific when the atomic bombs were dropped on Japan.

784. Hey, Oppie, you're about the best loved man in these parts. (Letter to J. Robert Oppenheimer [q.v.], August 1945; cited in *The Swift Years: The Robert Oppenheimer Story*, by Peter Michelmore.)

WILLIAM MANCHESTER

(1922–)

A U.S. Marine during the war, Manchester was wounded in action. He has written books of history, biography, and essays. Perhaps his most famous is *The Death of a President*, on the assassination of President John Kennedy.

785. One reason Americans at home had trouble following the war in the Pacific was that they were ignorant of its geography. . . . At the time of the Spanish-American War, Mr. Dooley had said that the average American didn't know whether the Philippines were "islands or canned goods," and to his grandsons, studying globes in the early 1940s, they still freckled the map like so many bewildering, unidentifiable Rorschach blots. (From *American Caesar*, by William Manchester.)

DONALD FRANCIS MASON

(1913–)

U.S. Navy pilot Mason transmitted to his base one of the shortest victory messages since Julius Caesar's "Veni, vidi, vici" (I came, I saw, I conquered).

786. Sighted sub, sank same. (Radio message, January 28, 1942.)

JIM MATTERA

(n.d.)

Mattera, a T/5 in the U.S. Army, was captured during the Battle of the Bulge (q.v.). Wounded in the Malmedy massacre, he lived to tell about it.

787. Here we are, hands up. They told us to line up. I had a wristwatch I got as a present while in high school. Little sawed-off officer took it off me. . . . There was a Lieutenant Goffman. When they got to him, he said, "The Geneva Convention don't allow you to take our belongings." Boom! Down he went. (From *A Blood-Dimmed Tide: The Battle of the Bulge by the Men Who Fought It*, by Gerald Astor.)

788. We were on the crossroads, not in the field. Then we were ordered down to the field. My recollection I seen them set up three tripods facing the field. There was an officer shouting to hurry up. Then I heard an officer command, "Machine alle kaput!" Kill them all. The machine gun bullets began. We all hit the ground, ten to thirteen minutes. I heard my buddies hollering. (Ibid.)

789. I heard the tanks and halftracks winding up, rrmmmm, rrmmmm. Down the road they come. Everyone who went by opened up with a machine gun [on the GIs lying in the field]. I heard one guy yell, "You will cross the Siegfried line, you American bastards!" Brrrp! Jesus Christ, I thought they'd never stop. Finally, no more hollering. I'm laying there, about ten degrees that afternoon. . . .

Finally I thought I heard somebody walking, there was maybe an inch or two of snow. Somebody's here, I thought. Thank God I didn't open my eyes to look. I was too scared to open them. I heard this mild voice say, "Hey, Joe, you hurt? I'm here to help you, Joe." Nobody answered.

Then it was, "Hey, John, you hurt?" Guy said, "Yeah, I'm hurt. I need help." Boom! Oh, I thought, you dirty sons of bitches. I don't know how many of them there were, maybe two or three Germans, sent them in there while they left one machine gun on the road. (Ibid.)

ANTHONY McAULIFFE
(1898–1975)

McAuliffe was a U.S. brigadier general who commanded the 101st Airborne at Bastogne during the Battle of the Bulge (q.v.). When the Germans ordered him to surrender, McAuliffe gave a one-word answer.

790. Nuts! (Bastogne, Belgium, December 21, 1944.)

[The German commander was puzzled by the response and asked what it meant. Colonel Joseph H. Harper, the American officer who delivered it, explained: "It means 'Go to hell!' "]

791. First of all let me emphasize that we all resent any indication that we were encircled [at Bastogne]. We were never encircled—we had placed ourselves in that position, and no one had the idea of being surrounded. (Press conference, Hotel Scribe, Paris, January 2, 1945; cited in *The Brereton Diaries*, by Lewis H. Brereton.)

792. When General [Maxwell] Taylor . . . said "How are things? How is the [101st] Division?" I said: "We are ready for offensive action." He said: "Well, I never should have doubted it, but there was so much gloom back at the rear areas I was beginning to get a bit worried." . . . We were in a camp in France. . . . We had several thousand replacements—had been training for about a week.

It amazes me to think that General Taylor and I had previously discussed this thing and figured it would not be possible for the 101st to go into combat before February first. It would take that long to get the replacements trained. (Ibid.)

793. Everybody was ready to leave the next afternoon, and we left in 500-odd trucks. Nobody slept except me. I took off for Bastogne the next day. . . . The situation was very confusing. Nobody knew the score, or where the enemy was, or much about our own troops. . . . They didn't know exactly what to do, or how the Division would be used. They told me to find a bivouac area. (Ibid.)

794. We got to this place [indicating on a map] and ran into all sorts of small-arms and tank fire. That was the beginning of a series of attacks from every direction. They attacked here two or three times, attacked back from Noville, and finally Christmas Day . . . with about 50 tanks from the west. (Ibid.)

795. The great tragedy for us was the loss of the hospital on the night of [December] 19–20. It was attacked here, and some time after midnight a German column came in here and started shooting. They found out it was a hospital and stopped firing, and a German officer gave them 30 minutes to get the patients and leave. Then the Germans left with all the surgical items and supplies. . . . The wounded started coming in and we had only the Detachment medics to take care of them. There was no surgeon in the place. (Ibid.)

796. On Wednesday the 20th, I was sent by Corps Headquarters to see General [Troy] Middleton. The Corps had moved on—they moved in a hurry, so fast that they left their liquor supplies behind. I reported to General Middleton and he gave me certain instructions and certain information and said that I would probably have to withdraw from Bastogne. There was a pretty good-looking piece of ground here, and he said he would like to keep these roads under fire as long as possible. All you have to do is look at a map to see how important Bastogne was. I asked him if he wanted me to withdraw and I told him: "I am sure I can hold it for another 48 hours, and if they don't throw a lot more stuff at me I don't believe they could ever get me out of here." He said another German Division was coming in and it might get pretty rugged, but he left it to my discretion to defend round the town or to withdraw, and the last caution he gave me was, "Don't get yourself surrounded." That was a laugh. (Ibid.)

DAVID McCAMPBELL

(1910–1996)

A U.S. naval air ace of the war, Commander McCampbell was credited with shooting down thirty-four Japanese planes. In one engagement, he shot down nine; in another, seven. For these and other exploits, he was awarded the Congressional Medal of Honor. After the war, he rose to the rank of captain and headed the plans division of the Joint Chiefs of Staff.

797. Well, it looked like a long fight, so I nursed my ammunition. I waited until I'd get right on a Jap's tail. And I'd fire only short bursts. (1944; cited in the *New York Times*, July 3, 1996.)

[Responding to the question of how he was able to shoot down nine Japanese planes in a single mission without running out of ammunition.]

MARCUS McDILDA

(n.d.)

McDilda, a first lieutenant in the U.S. Army Air Force, was shot down in his B-29 over Osaka, Japan, on August 8, 1945.

798. INDIRECT DISCOURSE: He [McDilda] told his captors that atomic bombs would fall on Kyoto and Tokyo "in the next few days." (Under Japanese interrogation, August 1945; cited in *Code-Name Downfall: The Secret Plan to Invade Japan—and Why Truman Dropped the Bomb*, by Thomas B. Allen and Norman Polmar.)

[McDilda knew nothing of possible targets. He was apparently being roughed up by his interrogators—and decided to say something to scare them.]

NODA MITSUHARU

(n.d.)

Mitsuharu was a sailor on the *Nagato*, Admiral Yamamoto's (q.v.) flagship.

799. After the successful attack on Pearl Harbor, we sailors talked about the opportunities we might get. My dream was to go to San Francisco, and there head up the accounting department in the garrison unit after the occupation. All of us in the navy dreamed of going to America. I don't think anybody wanted to go to China. (From *Japan at War*, edited by Haruko Taya Cook and Theodore F. Cook.)

ALFRED NAUJOCKS

(n.d.)

Naujocks was a young SS (Schutzstaffel) officer who carried out the provocative incident Hitler used as an excuse to invade Poland.

800. On or about August 10, 1939, the chief of the S.D. [Sicherheitsdienst], Heydrich [q.v.], personally ordered me to simulate an attack on the radio station near Glewitz, near the Polish border and to make it appear that the attacking force consisted of Poles. Heydrich said: "Practical proof is needed for these attacks of the Poles for the foreign press as well as for German propaganda." (Affidavit submitted at Nuremberg, November 1945.)

801. My instructions were to seize the radio station and to hold it long enough to permit a Polish-speaking German who would be put at my disposal to broadcast a speech in Polish. Heydrich [q.v.] told me that his speech should state that the time had come for conflict between Germans and Poles. (Ibid.)

802. Between the 25th and 31st of August, I went to see Heinrich Mueller, head of the Gestapo. . . . In my presence, Mueller discussed with a man named Mehlhoorn plans for another border incident, in which it should be made to appear that Polish soldiers were attacking German troops. Mueller stated that he had 12 to 13 condemned criminals who were to be dressed in Polish uniforms and left dead on the ground of the scene of the incident to show they had been killed while attacking. For this purpose they were to be given fatal injections . . . then . . . gunshot wounds. (Ibid.)

SAKAI SABURO

(n.d.)

Saburo was a Japanese air ace who flew a Zero. He was officially credited with downing sixty-four Allied planes.

803. When you've gotten used to combat, shot down one plane, two planes ten planes, then the moment you face an enemy plane you know instantly the skill of your opponent. You can pigeonhole him into Class A or Class B. Oh, this one's gutless. He's timid, you may think. But still you can't always hit him. So you shoot out a stream of bullets. . . . The only time you could be sure to shoot down a plane was when bullets hit the pilot, or the engine, causing it to malfunction, or the fuel tanks, causing a fire. You're not aiming at the pilot, that's impossible. But if you're lucky, you might get him. (From *Japan at War*, edited by Haruko Taya Cook and Theodore F. Cook.)

H. P. SAMWELL

(?–1945)

Samwell was an officer in the British Eighth Army. He was a lieutenant with the Argyll and Sutherland Highlanders in the fall of 1942 during the North African campaign. He later rose to the rank of major and died in the Ardennes. Below he describes what it was like to be a soldier in the desert.

804. We were beginning to get used to the sun, but the flies were appalling. One couldn't raise a piece of bread and jam from plate to mouth without being covered with flies. They buzzed around one's head, eyes, mouth and ears. Every precaution was taken with food, latrines, etc., but it was difficult to stop men from throwing rubbish away or even not using latrines during the night, when they had to go anything up to 15 times (from dysentery) and at night it was quite possible to get lost by moving just fifty yards from one's "bivy," so completely featureless was the desert. (From *An Infantry Officer with the Eighth Army*, by H. P. Samwell.)

BOB SLAUGHTER

(n.d.)

Slaughter, a U.S. Army sergeant, headed a machine gun squad in the 29th Division.

805. After the Omaha Beach massacre, I vowed never to take a German prisoner. During the fight for the beachhead, hatred intensified.

[Several weeks later, he spotted a young German paratrooper who was wounded.]

His right trouser leg was bloody and torn, the limb almost severed by shrapnel. Remembering my pledge taken back at the beach, my first reaction was to put him out of his misery. I believe he sensed what I was thinking. He said, tearfully, "Bitte [please]." He was an impressive-looking soldier and I just couldn't do it. Instead, I made sure he was unarmed and then I cut away his trouser leg and applied a pressure tourniquet. I gave him a shot of morphine and a drink from my canteen and then lit an American Lucky Strike cigarette for him.

As I departed, he smiled weakly, and said in guttural English, "Danke very much, may Gott bless you. Gut luck." That changed my mind. I still hated the German soldier but I couldn't kill one at close range if his hands were over his head. (From *June 6, 1944: The Voices of D-Day*, compiled by Gerald Astor.)

EDDIE SLOVIK

(1920–1945)

Slovik was a warrior who failed to do his duty. A private in the U.S. Army, Slovik was found guilty of desertion in the face of the enemy.

During World War II, some 2,864 men were court-martialed for desertion in combat with the enemy. Of these, 49 were sentenced to death. But only Slovik was shot by a firing squad, the only American soldier to be executed for such an offense since the Civil War.

806. I Pvt. Eddie D. Slovik #36896415 confess to the Desertion of the United States Army. At the time of my Desertion we were in Albuff [Elbeuf] in France. I came to Albuff as a Replacement. They were shelling the town and we were told to dig in for the night. The following morning they were shelling us again. I was so scared nerves and trembling that at the time the other Replacements moved out I couldn't move. I stayed their in my foxhole till it was quite and I was able to move. I then walked in town. Not seeing any of our troops so I stayed over night at the French hospital. The next morning I turned myself over to the Canadian Provost Corp. After being with them six weeks I was turned over to American M.P. They turned me lose. I told my commanding officer my story. I said that if I had to go out their again I'd run away. He said their was nothing he could do for me so I ran away again AND I'LL RUN AWAY AGAIN IF I HAVE TO GO OUT THEIR. (Confession, as written, October 9, 1944; cited in *The Execution of Private Slovik*, by William Bradford Huie.)

807. They're not shooting me for deserting the United States Army—thousands of guys have done that. They're shooting me for bread I stole when I was twelve years old. (Spoken to Sgt. Frank J. McKendrick at the execution site, St. Marie Aux Mines, France, January 31, 1945; Ibid.)

C. A. F. SPRAGUE

(n.d.)

Sprague, American admiral, led a small force against an oncoming Japanese armada during the battle of Leyte Gulf in 1944. Sprague's tactics so harassed and bewildered the Japanese force that it withdrew from the battle scene, securing the safety of American forces landing in the Philippines.

808. Nothing like this had happened in history. I didn't think we'd last 15 minutes. What chance could we have—6 slow, thin-skinned escort carriers, each armed with only one 5-inch peashooter, against the 16-, 14-, 8-, and 5-inch broadsides of the 22 warships bearing down on us at twice our top-speed? (From

"The Japs Had Us on the Ropes," by C. A. F. Sprague and Philip H. Gustafson, in *American Magazine*, April 1945.)

809. The failure of the enemy main body and encircling light forces to completely wipe out all vessels of this Task Unit can be attributed to our successful smoke screen, our torpedo counterattack, continuous harassment of the enemy by bomb, torpedo and strafing air attacks, timely maneuvers, and the definite partiality of Almighty God. (Statement following the battle of Leyte Gulf, ca. October 30, 1944.)

IRVING STROBING

(1920–1997)

Corporal Strobing was the U.S. Army radio operator who sent the last transmissions from Corregidor before its surrender. The following message from the doomed island fortress in Manila Bay appeared in newspapers throughout the United States several weeks later.

810. I feel sick at my stomach. I am really low down. They are around me now smashing rifles. They bring in the wounded every minute. . . . General [Jonathan] Wainwright [q.v.] is a right guy and we are willing to go on for him, but shells were dropping all night faster than hell. Damage terrible. Too much for guys to take. Enemy heavy cross-shelling and bombing. They have got us all around and from the skies. (Radio message, Corregidor, May 6, 1942.)

811. Corregidor used to be a nice place, but it's haunted now. Withstood a terrific pounding. . . . The jig is up. Everyone is bawling like a baby. They are piling dead and wounded in our tunnel. Arms weak from pounding key, long hours, no rest, short rations, tired. . . . I know how a mouse feels, caught in a trap waiting for guys to come along, and finish it up. (Ibid.)

812. My name is Irving Strobing. Get this to my mother, Mrs. Minnie Strobing, 605 Barbey Street, Brooklyn, N.Y. . . . Message: My love to Pa, Joe, Sue, Mac, Harry, Joy and Paul. Also to all family and friends. God bless 'em all. Hope they be there when I come home. Tell Joe, wherever he is, go give 'em hell for us. I love you all. God bless you and keep you. Love. Sign my name and tell my mother how you heard from me. (Ibid.)

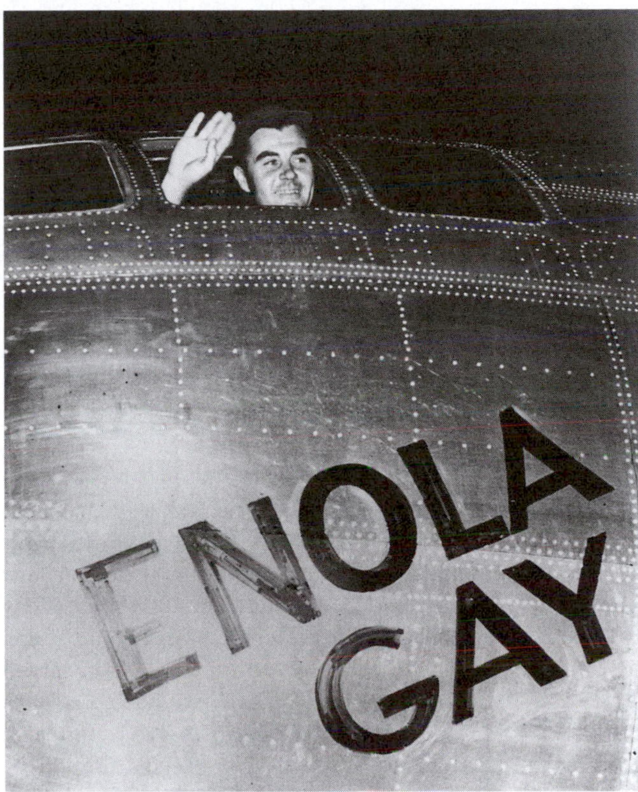

"Results clear cut, successful in all respects. Visible effects greater than Trinity [code name for the test bomb at Alamogordo]."
—PAUL W. TIBBETS, JR.

Tibbets in the *Enola Gay*, the plane that dropped the atomic bomb on Hiroshima.

PAUL W. TIBBETS, JR.

(1915–)

Tibbets, a colonel in the Army Air Force, piloted the *Enola Gay* on the mission to drop the atomic bomb on Hiroshima.

813. This is for history, so watch your language. We're carrying the first atomic bomb. (Spoken to the crew as the plane reached the Japanese coast August 6, 1945.)

[Tibbets was indicating that their conversation was being recorded.]

814. Put on your goggles and place them up on your forehead. When the countdown starts, pull the goggles over your eyes and leave them there until after the flash. (Ibid.)

815. Results clear cut, successful in all respects. Visible effects greater than Trinity [code name for the test bomb at Alamogordo]. (Radio message to base after bomb was dropped, Ibid.)

RUPERT TRIMMINGHAM

(n.d.)

Trimmingham was a corporal in the U.S. Army when he wrote this letter to the editors of *Yank*.

816. Here is a question that each Negro soldier is asking. What is the Negro soldier fighting for? On whose team are we playing? Myself and eight other soldiers were on our way from Camp Claiborne, La., to the hospital here at Fort Huachuca. We had to lay over until the next day for our train. On the next day we could not purchase a cup of coffee at any of the lunchrooms around there. As you know, Old Man Jim Crow rules. The only place where we could be served was at the lunchroom at the railroad station but, of course, we had to go into the kitchen. But that's not all; 11:30 A.M. about two dozen German prisoners of war, with two American guards, came to the station. They entered the lunchroom, sat at the tables, had their meals served, talked, smoked, in fact had quite a swell time. I stood on the outside looking on, and I could not help but ask myself these questions: Are these men sworn enemies of this country? Are they not taught to hate and destroy . . . all democratic governments? Are we not American soldiers, sworn to fight for and die if need be for this our country? Then why are they treated better than we are? Why are we pushed around like cattle? If we are fighting for the same thing, if we are to die for our country, then why does the Government allow such things to go on? Some of the boys are saying that you will not print this letter. I'm saying that you will. (From *The Best from Yank*.)

816a. Each day brings three, four or five letters to me in answer to my letter. I just returned from my furlough and found 25 letters awaiting me. To date I've received 287 letters, and, strange as it may seem, 183 are from white men and women in the armed service. Another strange feature about these letters is that most of these people are from the Deep South. They are all proud of the fact that they are of the South but ashamed to learn that there are so many of their own people who by their actions and manner toward the Negro are playing Hitler's game. Nevertheless, it gives me new hope to realize that there are doubtless thousands of whites who are willing to fight this Frankenstein that so many white people are keeping alive. All that the Negro is asking for is to be given half a chance and he will soon demonstrate his worth to his country. Should these white people who realize that the Negro is a man who is loyal—one who would gladly give his life for this our wonderful country—would stand up, join with us and help us to prove to their white friends that we are worthy, I'm sure that we would bury race hate and unfair treatment. (Ibid.)

[Follow-up letter.]

TERUICHI UKITA

(1925–)

A soldier in the Japanese army during the Sino-Japanese War, Ukita was a member of the Kenpeitai, the military police.

817. I saw lots of torture scenes, but I don't want to talk about it, or remember it. . . . Everybody was afraid of us. The word was that prisoners would enter the front gate but leave by the back gate—as corpses. . . .

If you look in a man's eyes as you torture him, then you understand him. When you ask him for information, you can tell from his eyes if he's telling the truth when he says, "I don't know, I don't know." The humane torturer would stop at that point, if they saw the man really didn't know. The cold ones would keep going. (Cited in "A Japanese Generation Haunted by Its Past," by Nicholas D. Kristof, in the *New York Times*, January 22, 1997.)

BUD WARNECKE

(n.d.)

Warnecke, a U.S. Army sergeant, was in charge of a mortar unit. He served in the 508th parachute regiment.

818. In the middle of the Channel we looked out the [airplane] door on a beautiful moonlit night at a sight no one will ever see again. Ships, so many ships it looked as if you could walk from England to France without getting your feet wet. (From *June 6, 1944: The Voices of D-Day*, compiled by Gerald Astor.)

SHOICHI YOKOI
(1915–1997)

Yokoi was the ultimate holdout of World War II. This Japanese soldier did not surrender until 1972—twenty-seven years after the official surrender in Tokyo Bay in 1945. During those years in hiding, he lived in a cave in the jungles of Guam. Although he had known that the war was over, he believed in the ancient Japanese tradition of fighting to the end and never giving up.

819. I am ashamed that I have returned alive. Your Majesties, I have returned home. I deeply regret that I could not serve you well. The world has certainly changed, but my determination to serve you will never change. (Address to Emperor Hirohito [q.v.] and the Empress, Imperial Palace, Tokyo, 1972; cited in the *New York Times*, September 26, 1997.)

6

Chaplains

WILLIAM CUMMINGS

(1903–1944)

Cummings was a U.S. Army chaplain who was captured by the Japanese on Bataan. Although there is no doubt about his famous quote, the sources appear to differ on the manner of his death. Cummings either died of dysentery on a Japanese prison ship or was killed when the unmarked ship was sunk by an American submarine.

820. There are no atheists in the foxholes. (Field service, Bataan, the Philippines, 1942; quoted in *I Saw the Fall of the Philippines*, by Carlos P. Romulo.)

HOWELL M. FORGY

(1908–1983)

Forgy was a U.S. Navy chaplain. Commander Forgy was on board ship at Pearl Harbor the morning of December 7, 1941. A chain of men passing shells inspired the most famous quotation of the war.

821. The big five-inch shells, weighing close to a hundred pounds, were being pulled up the powerless hoist by ropes attached to their long, tube-like metal cases.

A tiny Filipino messboy, who weighed little more than the shell, hoisted it to his shoulder, staggered a few steps, and grunted as he started the long, tortuous trip up two flights of ladders to the quarterdeck, where the guns thirsted for steel and powder.

A dozen eager men lined up at the hoist.

The parade of ammunition was endless, but the cry kept coming from topside for more, more, more. . . .

The boys were putting everything they had into the job, and it was beginning to tell on them. . . .

I wished I could boost one of the shells to my shoulder. The cool metal of the shell casing against my shoulder and neck would feel good. I would be busy, and feel better inside. But a chaplain cannot fire a gun or take material part in a battle.

Yet those devils—coming out of the sky without warning and sending to their death thousands of men of a nation at peace—were violating every rule of God and man.

There was little time for more reflection as I climbed the ladders to the quarterdeck above.

Minutes turned to hours. Physical exhaustion was coming to every man in the human endless-chain of that ammunition line. They struggled on.

They could keep going only by keeping faith in their hearts.

I slapped their wet, sticky backs and shouted, "Praise the Lord and pass the ammunition." (From " . . . *And Pass the Ammunition*," by Howell M. Forgy.)

JAMES H. O'NEILL

(n.d.)

O'Neill was chaplain of the American Third Army during the Battle of the Bulge (q.v.). General George Patton (q.v.) asked him to write a prayer for good weather so that Patton could get proper air support for his troops.

822. Almighty and most merciful Father, we humbly beseech Thee, of Thy great goodness, to restrain these immoderate rains with which we have had to contend. Grant us fair weather for battle. Graciously hearken to us as soldiers who call upon Thee that armed with Thy power, we may advance from victory to victory, and crush the oppression and wickedness of our enemies, and establish Thy justice among men and nations. Amen. (Prayer, Belgium, December 1944.)

JACOB P. RUDIN

(n.d.)

Jacob Rudin was an American chaplain who told of an incident at Dutch Harbor, Alaska. A USO (United Service Organizations; q.v.) camp show was presented at dockside for a loaded troop transport.

823. Every available inch of space aboard that ship was crowded with soldiers, each seeking a vantage point from which to see the show. They were lined several deep along the rail; they sat in the life boats and on the life rafts. I don't believe that any troupers ever played to a more appreciative audience than did those USO entertainers to the amusement-starved soldiers.

The show proceeded: songs, instrumental solos, dances, jokes, imitations. . . .

Then the USO man announced, "I have just been told that your ship is to shove off right now. But with your permission, we'll carry on the show just as long as you are within sight and hearing. Okay?" . . .

They sang funny verses to the tune of "Hinkey-Dinkey Parlez Vous," and the soldiers joined lustily in the chorus across the ever-widening gap of water. They finished their number and the girl with the accordion took the microphone. Tugs were bustling about the ship and were nudging her out into the stream. . . . Then she began, softly and warmly, to sing "Aloha." The voices of the men, joined with hers, drifted back across Dutch Harbor. . . . We could hear the men singing as they sailed for Attu. . . .

The wind nipped across the dock. (Letter to a friend, July 7, 1943; cited in *Home Away from Home: The Story of the USO*, by Julia M. H. Carson.)

7

Intelligence Officials and Spies

WILHELM CANARIS
(1887–1945)

Admiral Canaris was head of the Abwehr, the intelligence unit of the German General Staff. During the war, he clashed with Heinrich Himmler (q.v.), who wanted a unified intelligence service under himself. Himmler got it. Canaris was arrested following the unsuccessful attempt on Hitler's life. In April 1945, Canaris was executed. After the war, there was speculation that Canaris, a staunch anti-Nazi, might have been a British agent. If that had been so, he would undoubtedly have been more discreet about expressing his anti-Nazi sentiments.

824. I indicated to Keitel [q.v.] that I was informed of the plans for massive executions in Poland and that the nobility and clergy were to be exterminated. The world would hold the Wehrmacht responsible for these acts, since they would be committed in its presence. Keitel replied that the Fuehrer had taken the decision on this point. He had told the Commander-in-Chief of the army that if the army wished to have nothing to do with this business, it would have to accept the presence of its rivals, the SS [Schutzstaffel] and the Gestapo. Each military district would have beside its military commandant a civil commandant. The latter would be in charge of extermination. (Diary excerpt, September 12, 1939; cited in *Canaris*, by Andre Brissaud.)

[Recording a meeting in Silesia with Keitel and Ribbentrop (q.v.) shortly after the invasion of Poland.]

825. A war conducted in contempt of all ethics cannot be won. There is a divine justice even on earth. (Spoken to Vice-Admiral Leopold Burkner, chief of Abwehr's Foreign Branch, mid-September 1939, Ibid.)

826. The Fuehrer, who possesses an extraordinary knowledge of military detail, knows nothing of the problems of strategy. This ignorance is fundamental, because strategy and policy are closely interwoven. Hitler and certain generals of our High Command are foot-soldiers, provincials, mainlanders. They possess a superficial idea of the world and their ideas of other nations are like a gallery full of caricatures. Hitler lives among the images of *Mein Kampf* [q.v.]. (Spoken to General Hans Piekenbrock, head of Abwehr's Espionage Section, July 1940; cited in ibid.)

827. Hitler did not finish off the British army at Dunkirk when he could have done so, because he wishes for an Anglo-German settlement. . . . Hitler remains convinced that Britain will negotiate simply because he regards acceptance of the terms as a wise move. He is completely mistaken. Britain can only be moved to negotiate if she feels her Empire is in danger. We ought not to be making efforts to land in the British Isles, but in Gibraltar and Suez. (Ibid.)

828. I am dying for my country. I have a clear conscience. As an officer you will understand that I did no more than my patriotic duty in trying to oppose the criminal madness of Hitler, who was leading Germany to its ruin. It was in vain, as I know now that my country will go under, as I knew already in 1942. (Last message, tapped out in his cell, April 9, 1945; Ibid.)

EDDIE CHAPMAN

(1914–1997)

Chapman was a double agent who pretended to work for the Germans but spied for Britain. A safecracker before the war, Chapman was serving time on the island of Jersey in the English Channel. When the Nazis occupied the island, Chapman convinced them that he could be of service to them as a spy. The Nazis trained him in France for espionage work and then parachuted him into England to carry out acts of sabotage. On landing in Britain, Chapman contacted British intelligence and offered to work for them. By the end of the war, he was feeding disinformation to German intelligence. He was especially helpful in reporting false data on Nazi rocket targets.

829. The deal [with British intelligence] was that any money I made with the Germans I kept. (Cited in obituary in the *New York Times*, December 20, 1997.)

WILLIAM J. DONOVAN

(1883–1959)

America's first great spymaster, Donovan was first put in charge of the Office of Coordinator of Information, which became the Office of Strategic Services (q.v.) in mid-1942. He was in charge of espionage, sabotage, and evaluation of both bomb damage and enemy morale. This was carried out by sending American agents behind enemy lines to radio back information.

830. Our orientation has been wrong. We have been talking of aid to Britain as if Britain were a beggar at the gate, whereas, in point of fact, Britain has been our shield behind which we can pull up our socks, tie our shoelaces and get ready—and also our laboratory. (Speech, April 1941; cited in *The Secret Surrender*, by Allen Dulles.)

ALLEN DULLES

(1893–1966)

Allen Dulles was head of the Office of Strategic Services (q.v.) in Switzerland during the war. There he conducted American intelligence operations in Western Europe. He helped arrange the surrender of Italy in September 1943 and the surrender of German Armed Forces in northern Italy in May 1945.

831. Since the beginning of the present European conflict the American public have been advised to keep their emotions under control. . . . To recommend coolness is not to recommend indifference. . . . A cause to which we incline emotionally is not for that reason wrong any more than it is for that reason right. . . . The country should be slow to anger and should judge the acts of foreign governments in the light of our own national interests. This does not mean that Americans count the preservation of liberty here and the survival of human liberties in other countries as of only trifling importance in a world largely given over to *Machtpolitik* [power politics]. It would be a stupid foreign leader indeed who thought so. (1939; from *Can America Stay Neutral?* by Allen Dulles and Hamilton Fish Armstrong.)

832. The OSS [Office of Strategic Services; q.v.] was authorized, in addition to the collection and analysis functions of its predecessor, COI [Coordinator of Information] "to plan and operate such special services as may be directed by the United States Joint Chiefs of Staff." (Commenting on the charter of the Office of Strategic Services, created June 13, 1942; from *The Secret Surrender*, by Allen Dulles.)

833. "Special services" in intelligence terms meant unconventional warfare, commandos, support of partisans and guerrillas and the exploitation by covert means of all the weaknesses of Hitler's and Mussolini's [q.v.] empires. With the inclusion of this term "special services" in the OSS [q.v.] charter, an intelligence organization had been created for the first time in the United States which brought together under one roof the work of intelligence collection and counterespionage, with the support of underground resistance activities, sabotage and almost anything else in aid of our national effort that the regular armed forces were not equipped to do. (Ibid.)

834. The opposition group [in Nazi Germany] led by Tucky [General Ludwig Beck] and Lester [former Leipzig mayor Carl Gordeler] say that at this critical point they are now willing and prepared to try to start action to oust the Nazis and eliminate the Fuehrer. Theirs is the only group able to profit by a personal approach to Hitler and other Nazi chiefs, and with enough arms at hand to accomplish their ends. . . .

[The conspirators wanted to surrender to the Western allies but to continue their war against the Soviet Union.]

The principal motive for their action is the ardent desire to prevent Central Europe from coming ideologically and factually under the control of Russia. They are convinced that in such event Christian culture and democracy and all that goes with it would disappear in Europe and that the present dictatorship of the Nazis would be exchanged for a new dictatorship. (Message to Washington, April 7, 1944; cited in *Gentleman Spy: The Life of Allen Dulles*, by Peter Grose.)

[The offer was rejected. The conspiracy went forward, ending with the July 20, 1944, attempt on Hitler's life. Beck attempted suicide but failed to die. He called on a soldier to finish the job.]

835. Switzerland is the most incorruptible neutral nation in existence. (Cable to Washington, 1944; quoted in "My Turn," by Paul R. Jolles, *Newsweek*, August 25, 1997.)

REINHARD GEHLEN
(1902–1979)

Gehlen, a German general, was chief of military intelligence for Nazi Germany, spying on the Soviet Union. His espionage network was so extensive that he was brought to Washington after the war to transfer his files and contacts. He later became head of intelligence for what was then the West German government.

836. From the point of view of the general war situation, there is not one ground that could justify launching Operation Citadel [an attack on Kursk] at the present juncture. The prerequisite for victory in the offensive is two-fold . . . numerical superiority and the advantage of surprise. . . . But now . . . neither is met. For weeks the Russians have been just waiting for our attack in the very sector that we have picked for the offensive. And . . . they have done everything in their power—constructing line upon line of fortifications one behind the other, and moving up the necessary forces—to halt our offensive as soon as it begins. Thus there is little likelihood that the German offensive will achieve a strategic breakthrough.

Taking into account the total reserves available to the Russians, we are not even entitled to assume that Citadel will cost them so much in strength that they will later be incapable of carrying out their general plan at the time they choose. On the German side, our reserves, which will become desperately necessary as the war situation develops (particularly in the Mediterranean!), will be tied down and thrown away uselessly. I consider the operation that has been planned a particularly grave error, for which we shall suffer later. (Intelligence report, July 4, 1943; cited in *The Service: The Memoirs of General Reinhard Gehlen*, by Reinhard Gehlen.)

[The battle of Kursk led to the greatest tank battle in history. The Germans were decisively beaten. Some military historians believe Kursk to be as important as the Battle of Stalingrad (q.v.) in the eventual defeat of Adolf Hitler.]

837. It is in Hitler's failure to exploit the psychological potential of the Russian peoples, most of whom had shown the greatest warmth toward us in the opening phases of the campaign, that we can see the real mistake he made. We can see it again in the brutal way he imposed his satraps Koch, Sauckel, and Kube on the conquered Russian provinces and converted the people's frustrated hopes into blind hatred of the Germans. (Ibid.)

838. There is nobody less popular than a prophet of misfortune whose predictions have been proved true. (Ibid.)

TYLER KENT

(n.d.)

Kent was a cipher clerk at the U.S. embassy in London at the outbreak of the war. He arranged for transmission to the Germans of top secret coded messages between London and Washington. An American with diplomatic status, he was fired by the U.S. Foreign Service and then tried by British authorities.

839. [I wanted to thwart President Roosevelt's] secret and unconstitutional plot with Churchill to sneak the United States into the war. (To British investigators, May 1940; cited in *A Man Called Intrepid*, by William Stevenson.)

ALVIN D. KRAMER

(n.d.)

Kramer, a lieutenant commander, was chief of the Translation Section of the U.S. Office of Naval Intelligence. He was intimately involved in translating and interpreting the Japanese diplomatic and military messages obtained through a code-breaking process dubbed "Magic" (q.v.).

840. [Japan will] arm for all-out war against Britain and the United States to break the British-American encirclement. (Evaluation based on "Magic" intercepts, August 1941; cited in *The Broken Seal*, by Ladislas Farago.)

KANJI OGAWA

(n.d.)

Ogawa, a captain in the Japanese navy, was in charge of the Naval Intelligence Division's America Section. His special interest was the disposition of shipping at Pearl Harbor.

841. In gathering intelligence material, your office will pay particular attention to:

(1) Strengthening or supplementing of military preparations on the Pacific Coast and the Hawaiian area; amount and type of stores and military supplies, alterations to airports; also carefully observe the [Pan American] Clipper traffic;

(2) Ship and plane movements, including the flight of large bombers and seaplanes. (Telegram to Otojiro Okuda, vice consul of the Japanese consulate in Honolulu, February 15, 1941; cited in *The Broken Seal*, by Ladislas Farago.)

842. Henceforth please make your reports concerning the ships as follows as far as possible:

The waters are to be divided roughly into five subareas. . . . Area A: The waters between Ford Island and the Arsenal. Area B: Waters adjacent to but south and west of Ford Island. . . . Area C: East Loch. Area D: Middle Loch. Area E: West Loch and the Channel. (Telegram to Nagao Kita, at the Japanese consulate in Honolulu, September 24, 1941; Ibid.)

843. As relations between Japan and the United States are most critical, make your ships-in-harbor reports irregularly but at a rate of twice a week. Although you already are no doubt aware, please take extra care to observe secrecy. (Radiogram to Japanese consulate in Honolulu, November 15, 1941; Ibid.)

[Japanese messages decoded by American cryptographers.]

KIM PHILBY

(1912–1988)

Philby, a British intelligence agent, was a Soviet spy. This was not discovered until long after the war. He escaped to the Soviet Union and wrote his memoirs. During the war, he closely monitored the relationship between British and American intelligence agencies. William J. Donovan (q.v.) was creating the OSS, the Office of Strategic Services (q.v.), forerunner of the Central Intelligence Agency. He was doing it with the help of William Stephenson (q.v.), British intelligence official. Philby, in his book, assessed how this affected J. Edgar Hoover of the Federal Bureau of Investigation (FBI). Philby's job was to foster mistrust among the Western Allies. Although there is undoubtedly some truth in his analysis, it should probably be looked at within the context of who he was and what he was trying to do.

844. Stephenson's [q.v.] activity in the United States was regarded sourly enough by J. Edgar Hoover. The implication that the FBI was not capable of dealing with sabotage on American soil was wounding to a man of his raging vanity. He was incensed when Stephenson's strong boys beat up or intoxicated the crews of ships loading Axis supplies. But the real reason for his suspicious resentment, which he never lost, was that Stephenson was playing politics in his own yard, and playing them pretty well. Hoover foresaw that the creation of Bill Donovan's [q.v.] OSS [Office of Strategic Services (q.v.)] would involve him in endless jurisdictional disputes. The new office would compete with the FBI for Federal funds. It would destroy his monopoly of the investigative field. The creation and survival of the new OSS organization was to be the only serious defeat suffered by Hoover in his political career—and his career has been all politics. He never forgave Stephenson for the part he played as midwife and nurse to OSS. (Recalling events from mid-1940; from *My Silent War*, by Kim Philby.)

RICHARD SORGE

(1898–1944)

A master double agent, Sorge spied for both the Germans and the Soviets. Using his identity as a German journalist as a cover, he gained access to top Japanese diplomatic and military secrets. His real master was the Soviet Union. Among his exploits was uncovering the date of the German invasion of the Soviet Union and the forthcoming war between Japan and the United States. He was finally caught by the Japanese authorities and reportedly executed.

845. If no satisfactory reply is received from the U.S. to Japan's request for negotiations by the 15th or 16th of this month, there will either be a general resignation or drastic reorganization of the Japanese government. In either event . . . there will be war with the U.S. this month or next. (Report to Moscow, October 4, 1941.)

846. With respect to the Soviet Union, top-ranking elements are generally agreed that, if Germany wins, Japan can take over her gains in the Far East in the future and that therefore it is unnecessary for Japan to fight Russia. They feel that if Germany proves unable to destroy the Soviet government and force it out of Moscow, Japan should bide her time until next spring. In any event, the American issue and the question of the advance to the south [i.e., the Philippines, the Dutch East Indies, etc.] are far more important than the northern problem [i.e., the Soviet Union in the Pacific]. (Ibid.)

WILLIAM STEPHENSON
(1896–1967)

Stephenson was a British intelligence official who conducted espionage operations and oversaw guerrilla operations in Nazi-occupied Europe. Among his exploits, he discovered Nazi efforts to develop atomic weapons and he planned the assassination of Reinhard Heydrich (q.v.). He also helped William J. Donovan (q.v.) set up the Office of Strategic Services (q.v.). His story is recounted in *A Man Called Intrepid*, his code name.

847. The counter-offensive to mass raids by German Vengeance rockets saw the dawn of missile strategies in a world balanced on the edge of nuclear death. German work on "atomistics" and rockets was thwarted by us before it could mature—but it was thwarted through thousands of individuals, scattered from Poland where one secret army reassembled bits of German rockets to ship to London and New York, to Paris where Jewish scientists took terrible risks getting data on electronic brains to steer the new weapons onto London. (Quoted in *A Man Called Intrepid*, by William Stevenson.)

[Intrepid's secret army in Europe seemed to do the impossible—including the delivery to England of a V-1 rocket, fully intact.]

RICHARD WEIL, JR.

(n.d.)

Weil, an agent of the Office of Strategic Services (q.v.), parachuted into Yugoslavia in 1944 to meet with Tito, the Partisan leader.

848. In spite of his [Tito's] known affiliation with Russian Communism, most of the population seem to regard him first as a patriot and the liberator of his country and secondarily as a Communist. . . . For whatever it may be worth, my own guess is that if he is convinced that there is a clearcut choice between the two, on any issue, his country will come first. (Report to William J. Donovan [q.v.], April 4, 1944; cited in *Diplomat among Warriors*, by Robert Murphy.)

F. W. WINTERBOTHAM

(n.d.)

Winterbotham was a Royal Air Force (RAF) group captain in charge of security and dissemination of intelligence information from Ultra (q.v.). Ultra had broken the most secret of German codes, allowing British leaders to read German military and diplomatic messages. In September 1940, as Britain prepared for Sea Lion (q.v.)—the Nazi invasion—an important German military order was picked up by Ultra. Winterbotham describes what happened.

849. One of the main features of the German invasion plans had been the vast preparations that had been made in the Belgian and Dutch aerodromes for loading and quick turn-round of the supply and troop-carrying aircraft. . . .

On the morning of the 17th [of September 1940] the [German] officer-in-charge of these operations in Holland received a signal [picked up by Ultra (q.v.)] from the German General Staff to say that Hitler had authorized the dismantling of the air-loading equipment at the Dutch aerodromes. . . .

Winston arrived [for a meeting with his chiefs of staff]. I was struck by the extraordinary change that had come over these men in the last few hours. It was as if someone had suddenly cut all the strings of the violins in the middle of a dreary concerto. There were controlled smiles on the faces of these men.

Churchill read out the signal, his face beaming, then he rightly asked the Chief of the Air Staff Sir Cyril Newall to explain its significance. . . . He gave it as his considered opinion that this marked the end of Sea Lion [q.v.], at least for this year. . . .

[Churchill then asked the staff to step outside for some fresh air. There was an air raid in progress, and buildings were burning.]

It was a moment in history to remember, and above the noise came the angry voice of Winston Churchill: "By God, we will get the b——s for this." (From *The Ultra Secret*, by F. W. Winterbotham.)

8

Scientists and Engineers

KEN BAINBRIDGE

(n.d.)

Bainbridge was one of the physicists on the Manhattan Project.

850. Now we're all sons-of-bitches. (Spoken to J. Robert Oppenheimer [q.v.] following the explosion of the first atomic device, Alamogordo, New Mexico, July 16, 1945.)

WERNHER VON BRAUN

(1912–1977)

Braun was a German rocket engineer. His work at Peenemünde led to the development of the V-2 rocket missiles. They were fired during the war at England, France, and Belgium. As the war drew to a close, he and a large number of his staff surrendered to the American army. Braun and many of his colleagues came to the United States after the war and developed rocket programs for the American military. He played a major role in the National Aeronautics and Space Administration, became an American citizen, and was honored by the U.S. government for his work in rocketry and space exploration.

851. [My darkest hour] began in the fall of 1943 when [Heinrich] Himmler [q.v.] and his SS [Schutzstaffel] men wrenched control over the A-4 [rocket] program out of our hands in order to enforce mass production and military deployment of the rocket, long before its development and testing were completed. The most depressing fact was that I had absolutely no influence over this course of events. Even if I personally had withdrawn completely from the project, production and deployment would have continued, enforced by SS orders. The darkest hour came on 8 September 1944, when I learned that A-4 rockets named V-2 by Dr. [Joseph] Goebbels [q.v.], had been launched against Paris. We wanted our rockets to travel to the Moon, and Mars, but not to hit our own planet. (Quoted in *Wernher von Braun: Crusader for Space*, by Ernst Stuhlinger and Frederick Ordway III.)

EDWARD U. CONDON
(1902–1974)

Condon was one of the American scientists working on the atomic bomb project.

852. The thing which upsets me most is the extraordinarily close security policy. I do not feel qualified to question the wisdom of this since I am totally unaware of the extent of enemy espionage and sabotage activities. I only want to say that in my case I found that the extreme concern with security was morbidly depressing—especially the discussion about censoring mail and telephone calls, the possible militarization and complete isolation of the personnel from the outside world. I know that before long all such concerns would make me be so depressed as to be of little value. I think a great many of the other people are apt to be this way, otherwise I wouldn't mention it. (Letter to J. Robert Oppenheimer [q.v.], April 1945.)

[In this letter, Condon indicated his wish to return to the private sector—Westinghouse Research Laboratories.]

853. All aspects of this policy for which I am completely at a loss to find justification is the tendency to isolate this group intellectually from the key members of the other units of the whole project. While I had heard that there were to be some restrictions, I can say that I was so shocked that I could hardly believe my ears when General [Leslie] Groves [q.v.] undertook to reprove us, though he did so with exquisite tact and courtesy, for a discussion which you had concerning an important technical question with A[rthur] H. Compton. (Ibid.)

ALBERT EINSTEIN
(1879–1955)

Einstein, a distinguished physicist, fled his native Germany for safety in America.

854. In the course of the last four months it has been made probable through the work of Joliot, Fermi and Szilard in America that it may become possible to set up a nuclear chain reaction in a large mass of uranium, by which vast amounts of power and large quantities of new radium-like elements would be generated. Now it appears this could be achieved in the immediate future. This phenomenon would also lead to the construction of bombs, and it is conceivable, though much less certain—that extremely powerful bombs of a new type may thus be constructed. A single bomb of this type, carried by boat and exploded in a port, might well destroy the whole port, together with some of the surrounding territory. (Letter to President Roosevelt, August 2, 1939.)

J. ROBERT OPPENHEIMER
(1904–1967)

American physicist Oppenheimer headed the Manhattan Project's science group, the unit that developed the atomic bomb. He supervised thousands of scientists during the war at Los Alamos, New Mexico. Following the war, he was denied security clearance because of past associations with left-wingers plus his opposition to developing a hydrogen bomb.

855. But that would be treason. (Response to Haakon Chevalier, Berkeley, California, 1943; cited in *The Swift Years: The Robert Oppenheimer Story*, by Peter Michelmore.)

[Chevalier had proposed that Oppenheimer pass along to Russian agents details of the atomic bomb project.]

856. If the radiance of a thousand suns were to burst forth at once in the sky, that would be like the splendor of the Mighty One. (Quoting the *Bhagavad Gita*, Alamogordo, New Mexico, July 16, 1945.

[The ancient verse from the 2,000-year-old *Bhagavad Gita* of India flashed into Oppenheimer's mind at the instant the first atomic device exploded.]

857. I am become death, The Scatterer of Worlds. (Ibid.)

ARTHUR RUDOLPH

(n.d.)

Rudolph, a German engineer, was a member of the Peenemünde rocket center, where he worked with Wernher von Braun (q.v.). The V-2 rocket bombs developed there were produced in an underground factory called Mittelwerk. Located in the Harz mountains, the factory used concentration camp inmates to produce the weapons. The deplorable living and working conditions of the inmate-workers were described by Rudolph after the war.

858. When I first saw what was going on, I was totally shocked. I immediately tried to talk to one of the SS [Schutzstaffel] supervisors, but he cut me right off, saying: "That is none of your business. Shut up, or you will wear the same uniform!" A little later, I tried another approach with a higher SS guard. "Look," I said, pointing to some manufactured pieces, "this work is not good enough. It does not have the high accuracy we demand of these pieces. This is certainly not a result of ill will or sabotage, it simply reflects a state of extreme fatigue and emaciation on the part of the workers. Unless we keep them in a decent state of physical fitness, we'll not achieve acceptable products, and we cannot meet our production quotas." The result was some modest improvement, at least for the inmates in my A-4 directorate. (Quoted in *Wernher von Braun: Crusader for Space*, by Ernst Stuhlinger and Frederick Ordway III.)

ROBERT SERBER
(1909–1997)

A physicist who helped develop the atomic bomb, Serber had worked closely with J. Robert Oppenheimer (q.v.) even before the Manhattan Project.

859. I did not know much about planes, but I assured him that he and the *Enola Gay* would be safe. (Article, with Robert P. Crease, *The Sciences*, 1995; cited in the *New York Times*, June 2, 1997.)

[Referring to a conversation with Col. Paul Tibbets (q.v.), who would pilot the bombing of Hiroshima in August 1945.]

860. Oppie [Oppenheimer (q.v.)] had told me that the medical corps was prepared for half a million casualties [if the Japanese home islands were invaded], and I had no reason to doubt him. (Ibid.)

861. My thoughts about the wisdom of using the atomic bomb to bring a quick end to the war have not changed a bit since then. (Ibid.)

EDWARD TELLER
(1908–   )

Originally born in Hungary, Teller came to the United States in the 1930s. He worked on the atomic bomb and took part in the discussions with other scientists about whether and how the bomb should be used against Japan. After the war, he championed the development of a superbomb and became known as the father of the hydrogen bomb.

862. The things we are working on are so terrible that no amount of protesting or fiddling with politics will save our souls. (Letter to Leo Szilard, July 1945; cited in *The Swift Years: The Robert Oppenheimer Story*, by Peter Michelmore.)

863. The accident that we worked out this dreadful thing should not give us the responsibility of having a voice in how it is to be used. This responsibility must in the end be shifted to the people as a whole and that can be done only by making the facts known. This is the only cause for which I feel entitled in doing something: the necessity of lifting the secrecy at least as far as the broad issues of our work are concerned. (Ibid.)

9

Journalists and Cartoonists

JONAH BARRINGTON

(n.d.)

Barrington was an English journalist.

864. A gent I'd like to meet is moaning periodically from Zeesen. He speaks English of the haw-haw, damit-get-out-of-my-way variety, and his strong suit is gentlemanly indignation. (News article, *Daily Express*, London, September 14, 1939; cited in *Lord Haw-Haw: William Joyce, the Full Story*, by J. A. Cole.)

[This specific reference was to the voice of Norman Baillie-Stewart, an Englishman reading Nazi-slanted "news" via short-wave radio for the German Propaganda Ministry. The nickname "Lord Haw-Haw" would come to be identified with another English broadcaster, William Joyce (q.v.)].

MARGARET BOURKE-WHITE

(1904–1971)

A photographer for *Life* magazine, Bourke-White took memorable pictures of the war. She was also a gifted writer, authoring the book

They Called It Purple Heart Valley about the war in Italy. At one point, a ship she was on was torpedoed in the South Atlantic, and she wrote a vivid account for her magazine.

865. The torpedo did not make as loud a crash as I had expected, nor did the ship list as much as it does in the movies. But somehow everyone on the sleeping transport knew almost instantly that this was the end of her. ("Women in Lifeboats," *Life*, February 22, 1943, by Margaret Bourke-White.)

866. Instead of going to my boat station . . . I raced up to a spot under the bridge. In case of enemy action I had arranged with the commanding officer to stay on deck and take pictures. As I reached the top flight of steps I was hoping that dawn had come so I would be able to use a camera, but I came out under a night sky gleaming with moon and stars. (Ibid.)

867. In the lifeboat I was astonished to find myself in water up to my hips. . . . The sea, which from above had looked so calm, began beating us back against the ship. Our crew strained at the oars. There was so little space left in our crowded boat that we started singing, bending our bodies in rhythm to give the rowers room to move their arms. (Ibid.)

868. "Start bailing!" shouted the skipper, and those of us who were wearing helmets took them off and began to dip and pour. . . . In less than five minutes 40 nurses in that boat were as seasick as only human beings in a tossing lifeboat can be. (Ibid.)

869. When the last survivor had been transferred, the destroyer pulled away, leaving behind us the deserted lifeboats which swept down our wake like empty walnut shells. (Ibid.)

DAVID BREGER

1908–1970)

Breger was an American cartoonist. Shortly after entering the army, he sold his comic strip *Private Breger* to King Features Syndicate. It was based on his experiences in uniform and proved immensely popular. When the weekly army magazine *Yank* was launched, Breger was approached about doing a similar strip with a different title. Breger's name for his new strip would sweep the world and become the World War II equivalent of "Yankee Doodle," "Billy Yank,"

"Johnny Reb," and "Johnny Doughboy." Based on the army term *Government Issue*, Breger came up with the name:

870. G.I. Joe. (*The World Encyclopedia of Comics*, edited by Maurice Horn.)

WRIGHT BRYAN

(n.d.)

Bryan was a reporter for the *Atlanta Journal*. He described the first paratroop landings in Normandy on D-Day (q.v.).

871. "Are you all set?" asked the colonel. "Get this thing hooked for me," he said, as he took his own place closest to the door. They blinked as the pilot threw his switch and before I could look up they began jumping. I wanted to know how long it would take the 18 men to jump. I tried to count 101, 102, 103, to estimate the number of seconds. Before I had counted to ten seconds—it may have been 11 or 12, but no more—our passengers had left us, all but one of them. The paratroopers shoved each other so swiftly and heavily toward the open door that they jolted against the door frame. One man among the last half-dozen hit the rear of the door so heavily that he was thrown into the back of the cabin and dazed. The men behind shoved him aside and went on jumping. Before the unhappy soldier could get to his feet our plane was well past the drop zone and in a matter of minutes it was back over the water and setting a course for home. (In the sky over Normandy, June 6, 1944; cited in *The Brereton Diaries*, by Lewis H. Brereton.)

HOWARD COWAN

(n.d.)

Cowan, a correspondent for the Associated Press, was the first field reporter to cross the Rhine. He also rode on a glider with the 17th Airborne division into Germany. Cowan wrote about what it was like.

872. "Going down!" he shouts, and the nose pitches forward steeply. The speed slackens and the roar of the wind dies down and the battle noises suddenly are magnified into a terrifying din.

"Now," says the Sergeant, "is when you pray."

The right wing tilts sharply as the shadow of another glider flits past. It almost hits us.

Smoke is thick and acrid—almost like being inside a burning house. You can see half a dozen buildings aflame on the ground. Dozens of gliders are parked at crazy angles on every field. Everyone with a weapon has it cocked and across his lap.

Then, before you know it, the ground is racing underneath. You are in a pasture, crashing through a fence, bouncing across a gully, clipping a tree with a wingtip. You've made it—landed and nobody hurt.

You relax for a moment, but realize a split second later that that was a mistake. Bullets are ripping through the glider.

"Get outta here! Get outta here!" someone shouts, and prayers give way to curses as first one and then another kicks savagely at the door.

Men spill onto the grass haphazardly and begin crawling toward a ditch just beyond a barbed-wire fence. You're getting shot at from a house at the other end of the meadow.

Hot lead whines overhead. Bullets uproot little cupfuls of moist green turf around you until you are digging your toes in and clawing the earth with your fingers to move forward. . . . You check up and find that two men are hit—both medics. . . .

The firing slackens . . . more gliders come in. . . .

And you pray a prayer of thanksgiving and tell yourself—if you are a common, ordinary flat-footed reporter—that you've had your first and only glider ride. ("How It Feels to Ride a Glider into Germany," Associated Press, March 1945; cited in *The Brereton Diaries*, by Lewis H. Brereton.)

JOHN DALY

(1914–1991)

One of the radio war correspondents, Daly worked with Edward R. Murrow (q.v.) for the Columbia Broadcasting System. After the war, he became a television personality.

873. We interrupt this program to bring you a special news bulletin from CBS World News. A press association just announced that President Roosevelt is dead. All that has been received is that bare announcement. There are no further details as yet, but CBS World News will return in just a few moments with more information as it is received in our New York headquarters. We return you now to our regularly scheduled program. (Radio broadcast, 5:49 P.M. [Eastern War Time], April 12, 1945; cited in *Franklin Delano Roosevelt: A Memorial*, edited by Donald Porter Geddes.)

[The first press association to break the news was International News Service. Its news bulletin said simply: "F.D.R. DEAD." The program that was interrupted was *Wilderness Road*, a radio serial based on the life of Daniel Boone.]

WALTER DURANTY

(n.d.)

Duranty was a journalist with special interest in international affairs.

874. There remains a possibility—I do not say probability—which makes the present leaders of France and England sleep uneasily at night, namely, a Russo-German rapprochement, cooperation instead of war. (Dispatch from Paris, *New York Times*, October 10, 1938.)

JOHN GUNTHER

(1901–1970)

Journalist and author Gunther wrote a series of highly popular books on world affairs and world leaders: *Inside Europe* (1936), *Inside Asia* (1939), and *Inside Latin America* (1941). A firm believer in the influence of individuals on history, Gunther wrote about the major political personalities of the time. The judgments below appear in the 1940 revised edition of *Inside Europe*.

875. Adolf Hitler, irrational, contradictory, complex, is an unpredictable character; therein lies his power and his menace. To millions of honest Germans he is sublime; a figure of adoration; he fills them with love, fear, and nationalist ecstasy. To many other Germans he is meager and ridiculous—a charlatan, a lucky hysteric, and a lying demagogue. (From *Inside Europe*, by John Gunther.)

876. Benito Mussolini [q.v.], tempestuous and ornate, a blacksmith's son, the creator of modern Italy and the author of the Abyssinian war. . . . His career is that of the most formidable combination of turn-coat, ruffian, and man of genius in modern history. (Ibid.)

877. Prime Minister Neville Chamberlain [q.v.] is a business man. He personifies something very striking in the politics of England—the emergence of the middle trading class to a dominant note in government. . . . He is one of the comparatively few British statesmen of eminence who went neither to Eton nor Harrow, Cambridge nor Oxford. (Ibid.)

878. [Winston Churchill] is the most vital, pungent, and potentially powerful figure in British public life today. Chamberlain [q.v.] is prime minister. But warfare is a dynamic process, and just as Lloyd George replaced Asquith . . . so the ineluctable force may eventually push Churchill into Chamberlain's seat. (Ibid.)

879. Stalin is probably the nearest [of the European dictators] to a normal human being, but one should not forget that he was a criminal, viz., bomb thrower, in his youth. (Ibid.)

MARION HARGROVE

(1919–)

Hargrove was a North Carolina reporter who wrote about life as an army draftee for the *Charlotte News*. A collection of these articles appeared as the 1942 best-seller *See Here, Private Hargrove*. In those years of paper shortages, the book went through a dozen printings in its first six months. A favorite of both soldiers and civilians, it was later made into a motion picture.

880. Pay no attention to the advice that is being poured into your defenseless ears. . . . Form no idea of what Army life is going to be like. Leave your mind open.

Two weeks . . . [after induction], you will be thoroughly disgusted with your new job. You will have been herded from place to place, you will have wandered in nakedness and bewilderment through miles of physical examination, you will look upon privacy and individuality as things you left behind you in a golden civilian society.

Probably you will have developed a murderous hatred for at least one sergeant and two corporals. You will writhe and fume under what you consider brutality and sadism, and you will wonder how an enlightened nation can permit such atrocity in its army.

Take it easy, brother; take it easy. . . .

The first three weeks are the hardest. . . . You will bear the greatest part of the painful process of adjusting yourself to an altogether new routine. In those first three weeks you will get almost the full required dose of confusion and misery. . . . Unless you relax you can be very unhappy during those first three weeks.

You'll be inoculated against smallpox, typhoid, tetanus, yellow fever, pneumonia, and practically all the other ills that flesh is heir to. You'll be taught foot drill, the handling of a rifle, the use of the gas mask, the peculiarities of military vehicles, and the intricacies of military courtesy. . . . You'll be initiated into the mysteries of the kitchen police. . . . You'll haul coal and trash and ashes. You'll unpack rifles that are buried in heavy grease. . . .

All your persecution is deliberate, calculated, systematic. It is the collegiate practice of hazing, applied to the grim and highly important task of transforming a civilian into a soldier, a boy into a man. It is the Hardening Process. (From *See Here, Private Hargrove*, by Marion Hargrove.)

WILLIAM D. HASSETT

(1880–1965)

Former Washington correspondent for the Associated Press, Hassett became an aide to President Roosevelt during the war years.

881. A full and varied day's program was behind the president when he left for Hyde Park tonight. A delegation of several hundred Jewish rabbis sought to present him a petition to deliver the Jews from persecution in Europe, and to open Palestine and all the United Nations to them. The president told us in his bedroom this morning he would not see their delegation, told [Marvin] McIntyre to receive it. McIntyre said he would see four only—out of five hundred. Judge [Sam] Rosenman [q.v.], who with Pa [Edwin] Watson also was in the bedroom, said the group behind this petition was not representative of the most thoughtful elements in Jewry. Judge Rosenman said he had tried—admittedly without success—to keep the horde from storming Washington. Said the leading Jews of his acquaintance opposed this march on the Capitol.

The president and Sam spoke of the possibility of settling the Palestine question by letting the Jews in to the limit that the country will support them—with a barbed-wire fence around the Holy Land. Sam thought this would work if the fence was a two-way one to keep the Jews in and the Arabs out.

But the rabbis' hope of publicity out of their visit to the White House was dashed. Just as they came in from Pennsylvania Avenue, the newspaper correspondents left from the South Lawn to accompany the President to Bolling Field, where he dedicated four Liberator bombers. (Diary excerpt, October 6, 1943; from *Off the Record with F.D.R.*, by William D. Hassett.)

JOHN HERSEY

(1914–1993)

Hersey was a war correspondent for *Time* magazine. Although his early nonfiction books on the war achieved critical acclaim, he is probably best known for *Hiroshima*, the story of the atomic bombing told through the eyes of some of the people who lived through it. His war novels *A Bell for Adano*, *The Wall*, and *The War Lover* were also well received.

882. Three Japanese pursuits came up for a challenge, but [Colin] Kelly dropped them by climbing steeply to 20,000. There he found perfection—a dream of a target, a good clear day, a choice altitude, and three big babies [bombs] on the rack. . . . It was clearly a battleship. They told the bombardier, Corporal Meyer Levin, up in the nose, to get set.

Kelly brought her around for the run. He took her in tight and clean, steady as a locomotive on her tracks. . . . Corporal Levin, at the sight, deserves a lot of credit. He let the crossed hairs tickle into that beetle shape until they were right at the center. Then he let go.

It was perfect. The first of the stick hit the water close outboard to starboard; the third was a near miss to port. And the good second bomb hit her right in the midriff. . . . She started burning tremendously black. . . .

At 10,000 the Fortress shuddered and started, like a big animal wounded in its sleep. Three Japanese fighters had come up unobserved out of a cloud bank below and had given the Fortress a burst. . . .

Kelly made his decision and told the men to bail out.

The rear crew jumped first out of the after hatch. The bombardier and the radio operator left next from the frontal escape. Then the ship fell out of control and Kelly and [copilot] Robbins were thrown against the side of the cabin. Robbins remembers trying to claw his way to an overhead escape, but he doesn't remember exactly how he got out. He thinks perhaps an explosion threw him out.

Kelly got out somehow, too. One of the crew thinks that the tail surfaces may have struck him and stunned him. In any case, his parachute never opened. (December 1941; from *Men on Bataan*, by John Hersey.)

[The incident took place only a few days after Pearl Harbor, and Kelly became the first American hero of the war.]

883. Soon the word came whispering back along the line:

"Withdraw."

"Withdraw."

"Withdraw. . . ."

Then they started moving back, slowly at first, then running wildly, scrambling from place of cover to momentary cover. . . .

Despite snipers all around us, despite the machine guns and the mortars, he [Captain Charles Rigaud] stood right up on his feet and shouted out: "Who in Christ's name gave that order?"

This was enough to freeze the men in their tracks. They threw themselves on the ground, in attitudes of defense; they took cover behind trees from both the enemy and the anger of their captain.

Next, by a combination of blistering sarcasm, orders and cajolery, he not only got the men back into position; he got them in a mood to fight again.

"Where do you guys think you're going?" he shouted. And: "Get back in there. . . . Take cover, you. What do you guys do, just invent orders?. . . . Listen, it's going to get dark and we got a job to do. . . . You guys make me ashamed. . . ."

But the most telling thing he said was: "Gosh, and they call you marines." (October 1942; from *Into the Valley: A Skirmish of the Marines*, by John Hersey.)

[An incident that took place on Guadalcanal in October 1942.]

884. Army desk jobs are famous for dullness. And yet one of the most exciting things you can do in Sicily right now is to sit for a day by the desk of the Major who runs the town of Licata in the name of the Allies. . . .

After balancing his books he writes a couple of brief reports and then the process begins which makes his day both killing and fascinating—a stream of visitors bring their problems to him. . . . [Problems range from fishermen facing mines in the fishing waters to merchants refusing to sell food on credit to complaints of damage by American troops.]

Now a girl comes in who is quite pretty but very frightened-looking. She says her sweetheart is in the Army and she has heard that he was captured by the Americans. The Major asks his name. He calls up the prisoner-of-war enclosure and asks if the man is there. He is able then to tell the girl that her man is indeed a prisoner. Tears come into her eyes. "Mr. Major, thank you, I thank you and I kiss your hand," she says.

The Major says, "I think I'll go home. I like to end each day on a happy note if I can because there are so many unhappy ones." But before he leaves, if you ask him, he will tell you the ways in which the people of Licata are already, after only a handful of days, better off than they were under the Fascists whom they say with varying degrees of honesty that they hated. (*Life*, August 23, 1943.)

[This story became the basis for Hersey's *A Bell for Adano*.]

885. At exactly 15 minutes past eight in the morning, on August 6, 1945, Japanese time, at the moment when the atomic bomb flashed above Hiroshima, Miss Toshiko Sasaki, a clerk in the personnel department of the East Asia Tin Works, had just sat down at her place in the plant office and was turning her head to speak to the girl at the next desk. (August 1945; from *Hiroshima*, by John Hersey.)

[This is the first sentence of Hersey's stunning account of the first use of atomic warfare. It was originally prepared as a series of articles for *The New Yorker* magazine in 1946. Editor Harold Ross scrapped or postponed the rest of the editorial content of one issue so that the piece could run in full.]

886. It seems logical that he who supports total war in principle cannot complain of a war against civilians. The crux of the matter is whether total war in its present form is justifiable, even when it serves a just purpose. Does it not have material and spiritual evil as its consequences which far exceed whatever good might result? (Ibid.)

FRANK HEWLETT

(n.d.)

Hewlett was a correspondent who covered the war in the Pacific.

887.

We're the battling bastards of Bataan;
No mama, no papa, no Uncle Sam,
No aunts, no uncles, no cousins, no nieces,
No pills, no planes or artillery pieces,
And nobody gives a damn.

(February 1942; cited in *The Rising Sun*, by John Toland.)

[Although some books on the war have referred to "The Battling Bastards of Bataan," this is the first source I came across that specifically credited Hewlett.]

JAMES HILTON

(1900–1954)

This English novelist is most famous for novels such as *Lost Horizon* and *Goodbye, Mr. Chips*. In 1942 he interviewed Dr. Corydon Wassell, a U.S. Navy doctor who led wounded American sailors from a Java hospital to safety in Australia. The escape journey began with a ride to the railroad, where a train would take the wounded men to a hospital ship some sixty miles away.

888. When the men left in ambulances for the railway station the entire hospital staff stood round and waved. Before that there had been a few tearful farewells between the men and individual nurses, as if at such a moment many feelings were revealed that till then had been unsuspected by either party. Three Martini said good-bye to everyone, but lingered afterwards at the door of the ambulance where Renny was. She carried some flowers which she laid on his stretcher at the last moment, just before the doors were closed. She did not weep, or say anything but the one word she had learned especially for him—"good-bye."

Dr. Voorhuys also said good-bye to everyone, wishing them luck and *bon voyage*; whereupon the doctor from Arkansas [Dr. Wassell] replied that never, never would any of them forget the kindness of the Dutch and Javanese. The fact that he meant it so sincerely brought a tremor into his voice.

Thus the 41 men from the *Marblehead* and the *Houston* began the journey on that February day, and within 24 hours nine of them were back at the hospital. (Recalling events of February 1942; from *The Story of Dr. Wassell*, by James Hilton.)

[Eight of the men on stretchers—obviously unable to take care of themselves in an emergency—were not permitted to board the hospital ship. A ninth missed the boat. Wassell returned with the nine to the Dutch hospital. He would stay with them in their perilous trek to avoid Japanese captivity.]

GODFREY HODGSON

(n.d.)

Hodgson has written several books on American history and politics. He has worked for the London *Observer*, the London *Sunday Times*, and *The Independent* and has hosted news and discussion programs on British television.

889. The atomic bomb was in a significant sense a monument to the terror and hatred Hitler inspired. It was not until the last weeks of the war in Europe—not, in fact, until the War Department's secret Alsost teams found the last unaccounted-for tons of Belgian Congo uranium ore and a powerful American army corps shouldered its way across the front of the French army to seize the German nuclear physicists who had been evacuated to the little Black Forest town of Hechingen—that it became certain that there would be no German atomic bomb. Until then, everyone involved in building the atomic bomb in the West assumed that they were in a deadly race against a rival team working for Hitler, and that he would not hesitate to use an atomic weapon the moment he possessed one. (From *The Colonel: The Life and Ways of Henry Stimson*, by Godfrey Hodgson.)

RALPH INGERSOLL

(1900–1985)

A journalist who had worked for *Time* magazine and the *March of Time* film documentaries, Ingersoll founded his own newspaper, *PM*, in 1940. When the United States entered the war, he enlisted as a private in the army. By the end of the war he was a lieutenant colonel on the staff of General Omar Bradley (q.v.). In 1943 he wrote *The Battle Is the Pay-Off*. Shortly after the war, he wrote *Top Secret*, about what went on among the American and British army brass.

890. I chose to write about the battle because the battle is the pay-off. It is what training is for. (1943; from *The Battle Is the Pay-Off*, by Ralph Ingersoll.)

891. It [the battlefield] is . . . a place where men are tested in their ability to survive . . . to make and break camp, to know always where they are and to keep in touch with one another. It is a place where physical endurance counts. . . . It is a place where skill with weapons counts. For all these contingencies—and they are 90 per cent of any battle—any man can be well prepared. If he is well prepared, he will win and the odds on his being hurt or killed will go way, way down. (Ibid.)

892. Battles are like marriages. They have a certain fundamental experience they share in common; they differ infinitely but still they are all alike.

A battle seems to me a conflict of wills to the death in the same way that a marriage of love is the identification of two human beings to the end of the creation of life—as death is the reverse of life, and love of hate. Battles are commitments to death as marriages are commitments to create life. (Ibid.)

893. The fascist worship of battle is a suicidal drive, it is love of death instead of life.

In the same idiom, to triumph in battle over the forces which are fighting for death is—again literally—to triumph over death. It is a surgeon's triumph as he cuts a body and bloodies his hands in removing a cancer in order to triumph over the death that is in the body.

These are the thoughts that make it consistent for men who fight for life and hope and love to become hard and to inflict punishment and death on an enemy who stands for death, who is death itself. (Ibid.)

894. What Hitler did with the breathing spell which was given him in September [1944] can now be reconstructed. . . .

First he created the Volkssturm—a German version of the British Home Guard . . . giving it armbands for uniforms and whatever weapons could be found. . . . Into the bunkers of the West Wall went the home guard . . . [under] a handful of professional non-coms. . . .

Hitler emptied his convalescent hospitals and threw together a . . . force of what we would call 4-F's. . . .

Next he took . . . the boys who had just reached 17. . . . He ordered that . . . [the youngsters] be built into a brand new army. . . .

By this move, Hitler created a new force composed exclusively of able-bodied young men, fanatic in morale and magnificently equipped. . . . It was known as the Sixth SS [Schutzstaffel] Panzer Army—and it was this army which . . . was to spearhead the attack in the Ardennes. (1944; from *Top Secret*, by Ralph Ingersoll.)

895. The objective . . . was to blitz through . . . to the River Meuse, there to seize crossings. It was then to proceed through Liege . . . to Antwerp. . . . The drive would have split the American and British forces. With the loss of Antwerp, both Allied forces would be deprived of . . . virtually their sole source of supplies.

A second drive was to start from near the Channel coast to the north. This was to cut the cut-off British forces in two—and "force a second Dunkirk." From this second Dunkirk, the British were expected never to recover—and Hitler assured his commanders that after this campaign they would never have another British Army to face. So the Germans would be left with only the Americans. . . .

Hitler confidently expected the Americans to have to retreat to west of the Seine. . . . In the spring, when the whole Reich, invigorated by victory, would rise to throw the mongrels from the West back into the sea. (Ibid.)

JAMES JONES
(1921–1977)

An enlisted man in the U.S. Army, Jones served in the Pacific and later wrote of his experiences in the novels *From Here to Eternity* and *The Thin Red Line*. Both novels became highly successful motion pictures.

896. There was a lot of jealousy about [cartoonist Bill] Mauldin [q.v.] out in the Pacific because he only drew and worked for the European soldier. We wanted a share. Out there we didn't get *Stars and Stripes* (which was strictly a European paper) except only very occasionally, as when some air force planes fresh from Europe would put down near you. But since he drew and wrote of privilege by officers and noncoms and rear echelon types, we felt he was also drawing and writing about us as well. Mud was the same everywhere. So was the abuse of privilege. Our jungle rot was the equivalent of their trench foot. (From *WW II: A Chronicle of Soldiering*, by James Jones.)

897. We didn't have much in common in the way of female civilian populations, or wine cellars. But we did have "raisin jack," or what we guys from Honolulu called "swipe," which was a Hawaiian word for bootleg liquor. . . . Mauldin [q.v.] did a lot of cartoons about booze—cognac, Chianti, schnapps, vino, and wine—and, although later he made a sort of mild apologia for it in his book, in general he endorsed it. I am glad, because at least in my outfit we got blind asshole drunk every chance we got. . . .

We made our own "swipe" by stealing a five-gallon tin of canned peaches or plums or pineapple from the nearest ration dump, and putting a double handful of sugar in it to help it ferment, and then leaving it out in the sun in the jungle with a piece of cheesecloth or mosquito netting over it to keep out the bugs.

It was the most godawful stuff to drink, sickly sweet and smelling very raunchy, but if you could get enough of it down and keep it down, it carried a wonderful wallop. (Ibid.)

EDWARD KENNEDY

(n.d.)

Kennedy covered the war in Europe for the Associated Press (AP).

898. REIMS, France, May 7—Germany surrendered unconditionally to the Western Allies and the Soviet Union at 2:41 A.M. French time today.

The surrender took place at a little red schoolhouse that is the headquarters of Gen. Dwight D. Eisenhower.

The surrender, which brought the war in Europe to a formal end after five years, eight months and six days of bloodshed and destruction, was signed for Germany by Col. Gen. [Alfred] Gustav Jodl [q.v.]. General Jodl is the new Chief of Staff of the German Army.

The surrender was signed for the Supreme Allied Command by Lieut. Gen. Walter Bedell Smith [q.v.], Chief of Staff for General Eisenhower.

It was also signed by Gen. Ivan Susloparoff for the Soviet Union and by Gen. François Sevez for France. (Associated Press dispatch, May 7, 1945.)

[The AP story aroused a furor at Allied headquarters because Kennedy had broken the release date of May 8. That was when the victorious Allied leaders were scheduled to announce it publicly. Kennedy, however, had abided by the journalistic rule that if a release time is broken by anyone, the restriction no longer applies. Since the German radio had made the announcement, Kennedy had gone ahead and filed his story.]

HENRY KEYES

(n.d.)

Keyes, a correspondent for the London *Daily Express*, covered the war crimes trial of Japanese General Yamashita (q.v.) in the Philippines.

899. Yamashita [q.v.] trial continued today—but it isn't a trial. I doubt that it is even a hearing. Yesterday his name was mentioned once. Today it was not brought up at all. The Military Commission sitting in judgement continued to act as if it wasn't bound by any law or rules of evidence. I hold no brief for any Jap, but in no British court of law would accused have received such rough treatment as Yamashita. The Yamashita trial has been hailed as the most important of the Pacific, not because it is the first but because the present Commission is supposed to be setting precedents for all future war criminal trials. The trial is supposed to establish that a military commander is responsible for any acts of any of his troops. At the same time, under British law, anyway, he's supposed to have rights. The present Commission pleads saving of time and money, but the facts are so far that Yamashita's American counsel haven't had a hearing. (Dispatch to the London *Daily Express*, Manila, Philippines, October 1945; cited in *A Trial of Generals: Homma, Yamashita, MacArthur*, by Lawrence Taylor.)

ARTHUR KROCK

(1886–1974)

Krock headed the Washington bureau of the *New York Times*, for which he wrote a political column.

900. In my opinion, Hitler can throw at us both the dictionary and the facts when he says we "attacked" him. Why should the American Government ever have attempted to obscure it? If the Navy had not done what it did the United States would have been guilty of the most heart-breaking bluff ever made by a great nation. (Address, Columbia College alumni meeting, New York City, November 5, 1941; quoted in the *New York Times*, November 6, 1941.)

[Krock was referring to several military confrontations involving American destroyers and Nazi submarines. Although the administration had been insisting that the American ships were attacked without warning, there was growing belief that the destroyers were actually on convoy duty and may have taken an active part in locating enemy U-boats. The "bluff" that Krock alludes to was President Roosevelt's order to the U.S. Navy to shoot on sight any Axis warships it came upon in U.S-protected waters. That order came after the attack on the destroyer *Greer* (q.v.). Krock argues that the president's order was no bluff and that the navy was carrying out its duty.]

901. From that moment [that the Lend-Lease (q.v.) Act became law], whatever the political quibblers may say, we were committed to the military defeat of Germany. . . . Now American men are giving their lives that this armament reach its destination. To their memories, and to their brothers in arms who may die tomorrow, to the grown-up American nation they are defending, the Administration and Congress owe a solemn obligation: the truth. In wartime, for excellent reasons, it cannot always be the whole truth. But always it should be nothing but the truth. (Ibid.)

CHESLY MANLY

(n.d.)

Manly wrote for the *Chicago Tribune*.

902. F.D.R.'s WAR PLANS. (*Chicago Tribune*, December 4, 1941.)

903. July 1, 1943, is fixed as the date for the beginning of the final supreme effort by American land forces to defeat the mighty German army in Europe. (Ibid.)

[The article was based on contingency plans of the War Department. On December 5, 1941, Secretary of War Stimson (q.v.) commented, "What would you think of an American General Staff which in the present condition of the world did not investigate and study every type of emergency which may confront this country and every possible method of meeting that emergency?"]

BILL MAULDIN

(1921–)

A cartoonist for the U.S. Army newspaper *Stars and Stripes*, Mauldin depicted the war in Europe through the eyes of his characters Willie and Joe. Almost always haggard and unshaven, the foot soldiers displayed a grim humor about the war around them. In his book *Up Front*, Mauldin reprinted some of his cartoons and commented on different aspects of the war.

904. [Cartoon depicts a weary group of American soldiers trudging through a driving rain as they escort captured Germans.]

Caption: "Fresh, spirited American troops, flushed with victory, are bringing in thousands of hungry, ragged, battle-weary prisoners. . . ." (News Item) (From *Up Front*, by Bill Mauldin.)

905. [Cartoon depicts a soldier in a foxhole talking into a walkie-talkie radio. Directly above him is a huge German tank.]

Caption: Able Fox Five to Able Fox. I got a target but ya gotta be patient. (Ibid.)

906. [Depicts officer talking to infantryman.]

Caption: You have completed your fiftieth combat patrol. Congratulations. We'll put you on mortars awhile. (Ibid.)

907. I never once heard an infantry soldier who'd been in combat refer to Germans as Nazis. Or North Vietnamese or North Koreans as reds, or commie rats. . . . People who fight these wars could care less about ideology. (Quoted in *The Good War*, by Studs Terkel.)

MACK MORRISS

(n.d.)

Morriss was a U.S. Army sergeant during the war. The battle for Huertgen Forest, described below, has been compared with the battle for Argonne Forest during World War I. Huertgen, one of several forests on the Belgian-German border, was the site of bitter fighting in the fall of 1944.

908. The infantry . . . went on, but behind them they left their dead, and the forest will stink with deadness long after the last body is removed. The forest will bear the scars of our advance long after our scars have healed, and the Infantry has scars that will never heal.

For Huertgen was agony, and there was no glory in it except the glory of courageous men—the MP [military policeman] whose testicles were hit by shrapnel and who said, "Okay, doc, I can take it"; the man who walked forward, firing Tommy guns with both hands until an arm was blown off and then kept on firing the other Tommy gun until he disappeared in a mortar burst. (From *Yank—The GI Story of the War*, edited by Franklin S. Forsberg.)

IAN F. D. MORROW

(n.d.)

Morrow, a British reviewer, took part in the debate over the revisionist history *The Origins of the Second World War* by A. J. P. Taylor (q.v.).

909. When all [the criticisms of the book] have been taken into account it seems to the present reviewer that Mr. Taylor's learned critics have failed to comprehend or else have ignored the standpoint from which Mr. Taylor writes. It is certainly *not* an accepted traditional academic standpoint. On the contrary, Mr. Taylor expressly states . . . that he has "attempted to tell the story as it may appear to some future historian working from the records."

Mr. Taylor with disturbing originality has discovered or perhaps invented a new form of history—*imaginable* history. The judgments and opinions liberally scattered over these pages [of *The Origins of the Second World War*] are not necessarily Mr. Taylor's own *real* opinions and judgments. They are simply the opinions and judgments which Mr. Taylor rightly or wrongly imagines will be held and formed by an as yet unborn historian writing in 50 or 100 years' time. (Review, *International Affairs*, October 1961.)

EDWARD R. MURROW
(1908–1965)

Murrow was a radio news commentator for the Columbia Broadcasting System during the war. Murrow assembled a team of reporters—rather than announcers—to cover the war from the major European capitals: Berlin, Paris, Rome, and Moscow. He, himself, reported from London—and his reports on the London Blitz are considered classic radio journalism. After the war he became even more famous as the television journalist who brought down Senator Joseph McCarthy.

910. I have a feeling that Englishmen are a little proud of themselves tonight. They believe that their government's reply [to Hitler's s demands on Poland] was pretty tough, that the Lion has turned and that the retreat from Manchukuo, Abyssinia, Spain, and Czechoslovakia and Austria, has stopped. They are amazingly calm, they still employ understatement, and they are inclined to discuss the prospect of war with, oh, a casual "bad show," or "if this is peace, give me a good war." (Radio broadcast from London, August 26, 1939; cited in *Prime Time*, by Alexander Kendrick.)

911. I'm standing on a rooftop looking out over London. At the moment everything is quiet. . . . Off to my left, far away in the distance, I can see just that faint red angry snap of antiaircraft bursts against the steel-blue sky. (Radio broadcast from London, 1940; Ibid.)

912. Most of you [Americans] are probably preparing to welcome the new year. May you have a pleasant evening. You will have no dawn raid, as we shall

"I can see their chutes going down now. . . . [They are] hanging there, very gracefully, and seem to be completely relaxed, like nothing so much as khaki dolls hanging beneath green lampshades. . . . The whole sky is filled with parachutes."
—EDWARD R. MURROW

Paratroops float down into Holland in Operation Market-Garden—a daring attempt to outflank German defenses.

probably have if the weather is right. You may walk this night in the light. Your families are not scattered by the winds of war. . . . You have not been promised blood and toil and tears and sweat, and yet it is the opinion of nearly every informed observer over here that the decision you take will overshadow all else during this year that opened a few hours ago in London. (Radio broadcast, December 31, 1940; Ibid.)

913. A kind of orchestrated hell, a terrible symphony of light and flame. (Radio broadcast describing a bombing raid on Berlin, 1943; Ibid.)

914. Now every man is out. . . . I can see their chutes going down now. Every man clear . . . they're dropping beside the little windmill near a church, hanging there, very gracefully, and seem to be completely relaxed, like nothing so much as khaki dolls hanging beneath green lampshades. . . . The whole sky is filled with parachutes. (Radio broadcast from a troop carrier over Holland during Market-Garden [q.v.], September 17, 1944; cited in *The Brereton Diaries*, by Lewis H. Brereton.)

915. There surged around me an evil-smelling horde. Men and boys reached out to touch me; they were in rags and the remnants of uniforms. Death had already marked many of them, but they were smiling with their eyes. I looked out over that mass of men to the green fields beyond, where well-fed Germans were plowing. (Radio broadcast, Buchenwald concentration camp, April 1945; cited in *Prime Time*, by Alexander Kendrick.)

ERNIE PYLE
(1900–1945)

Pyle was an American war correspondent. He covered the war for Scripps-Howard newspapers, winning the Pulitzer Prize for his work. Pyle concentrated on the viewpoint of the GI in the foxhole, rather than the general back at headquarters. He covered the war in North Africa, Italy, France, and the Pacific. In April 1945, he was killed by a Japanese sniper on Ie Shima, a small island off Okinawa. He is buried at the military cemetery at Pearl Harbor, not because of his work as a correspondent of World War II but as a veteran of World War I.

916. War has its own peculiar sounds. . . .

The clank of a starting tank, the scream of a shell through the air, the ever-rising whine of fiendishness as a bomber dives—these sounds have their counterparts in normal life. . . .

Their nervous memories come back to you in a thousand ways—in the grind of a truck starting in low gear, in high wind around the eaves, in somebody merely whistling a tune. Even the sound of a shoe, dropped to the floor in a hotel room above you, becomes indistinguishable from the faint boom of a big gun far away. A mere rustling curtain can paralyze a man with memories. (March 3, 1943; from *Ernie's War*, edited by David Nichols.)

917. It was time for the planes to start coming back from their mission. . . .

Finally they were all in—all, that is, except one. . . . Returning pilots said it had lagged behind and lost altitude just after leaving the target. . . . Ten men were in that plane. . . .

We had already seen death that afternoon. . . . I had stood with others . . . as they hauled its dead pilot, head downward, through the escape hatch. . . .

Men talked in low tones about the dead pilot and the lost Fortress. . . .

And then . . . far off in the dusk a red flare shot into the sky. . . . The ten dead men were coming home! . . .

Then we saw the plane—just a tiny black speck. It seemed almost on the ground, it was so low. . . . Crippled and alone, two hours behind all the rest, it was dragging itself home. . . . And at that moment I felt something close to human love for that faithful, battered machine. . . .

With all our nerves we seemed to pull the plane toward us. I suspect a photograph would have shown us all leaning slightly to the left. Not one of us thought the plane would ever make the field, but on it came—so slowly that it was cruel to watch.

It reached the far end of the airdrome, still holding its pathetic little altitude. It skimmed over the tops of parked planes . . . reaching out—it seemed to us—for the runway.

A few hundred yards more now. . . .

They cleared the last plane, they were over the runway. They settled slowly. The wheels touched softly. And as the plane rolled on down the runway the thousands of men around that vast field suddenly realized that they were weak and that they could hear their hearts pounding. . . .

Our ten dead men were miraculously back from the grave. (Early 1943; from *Here Is Your War*, by Ernie Pyle.)

918. "This one is Captain Waskow," one of them said quietly. Two men unlashed his body from the mule and lifted it off and laid it in the shade beside the stone wall. . . .

The men . . . seemed reluctant to leave. They stood around, and gradually I could sense them moving, one by one, close to Captain Waskow. Not so much to look, I think, as to say something in finality to him and to themselves. . . .

One soldier came and looked down, and he said out loud, "God damn it!"

That's all he said, and then he walked away.

Another one came, and he said, "God damn it to hell anyway!" He looked down for a few last moments and then turned and left.

Another man came. I think he was an officer. It was hard to tell officers from men in the dim light, for everybody was bearded and grimy. The man looked down into the dead captain's face and then spoke directly to him, as though he were alive, "I'm sorry, old man."

Then a soldier came and stood beside the officer and bent over, and he too spoke to the dead captain, not in a whisper but awfully tenderly, and he said, "I sure am sorry, sir."

Then the first man squatted down, and took the captain's hand, and he sat there for a full five minutes holding the dead hand in his own and looking intently into the dead face. And he never uttered a sound all the time he sat there. . . .

He reached over and gently straightened the points of the captain's shirt collar, and then he sort of rearranged the tattered edges of the uniform around the wound, and then he got up and walked away down the road in the moonlight, all alone. (1944; from *Brave Men*, by Ernie Pyle.)

[Pyle's description of the death of Captain Henry Waskow was one of the most memorable accounts of the war. It was dramatized in the motion picture *The Story of G.I. Joe*.]

919. In the joyousness of high spirits it is easy for us to forget the dead. Those who are gone would not want themselves to be a millstone of gloom around our necks.

But there are many of the living who have had burned into their brains forever the unnatural sight of cold dead men scattered over the hillsides and in the ditches along the high rows of hedge throughout the world.

Dead men by mass production—in one country after another—month after month and year after year. Dead men in winter and dead men in summer.

Dead men in such familiar promiscuity that they become monotonous.

Dead men in such monstrous infinity that you come almost to hate them.

These are things that you at home need not even try to understand. To you at home they are columns of figures, or he is a near one who went away and just didn't come back. You didn't see him lying so grotesque and pasty beside the gravel road in France.

We saw him, saw him by the multiple thousands. That's the difference. (April 1945; from *Ernie's War*, edited by David Nichols.)

[This was part of a dispatch that Pyle planned to publish upon the surrender of Nazi Germany. It was found on his body three weeks before the end of the war in Europe.]

ANDY ROONEY

(1919–)

Rooney was a correspondent for the U.S. Army newspaper *Stars and Stripes* during the war. He is a syndicated columnist and commentator for the TV program *60 Minutes*.

920. What the R.A.F. did at night was called area bombing or saturation bombing. It was close-your-eyes-and-bombs-away bombing, although the R.A.F. didn't like to admit it. (From *My War*, by Andy Rooney.)

921. The French call D-Day [q.v.] "J-Jour" . . . but it was our day and I think they ought to call it by our name, D-Day. (Ibid.)

922. I landed on Utah Beach several days after the first assault waves went in on the morning of June 6. . . . When I came in, row on row of dead American soldiers were laid out on the sand just above the high-tide mark where the beach turned into weedy clumps of grass. They were covered with olive-drab blankets, just their feet sticking out at the bottom, their GI boots sticking out. . . .

No one can tell the whole story of D-Day [q.v.] because no one knows it. Each of the 60,000 men who waded ashore that day knew a little part of the story too well.

To them, the landing looked like a catastrophe. Each knew a friend shot through the throat, shot through the knee. Each knew the names of the hanging dead on the barbed wire in the water twenty yards offshore, three who lay unattended on the stony beach as the blood drained from holes in their bodies.

They saw whole tank crews drowned when the tanks rumbled off the ramps of their landing craft and dropped into twenty feet of water. . . .

Across the Channel in Allied headquarters in England, the war directors, remote from the details of tragedy, were exultant. They saw no blood, no dead, no dying. From the statisticians' point of view, the invasion was a great success. The statisticians were right. They always are—that's the damned thing about it. (Ibid.)

ROBERT SHERROD

(1909–)

Sherrod was a war correspondent. He went onto the beaches with the marines in the Gilbert Islands invasion of November 1943. This is about the assault on Betio, a small fortified island off Tarawa.

923. It was nearly nine o'clock when the fifth wave arrived at the boat rendezvous and began circling to wait for our turn to go in. . . . There were very few boats on the beach, and these were all amphibious tractors which the first wave used. There were no Higgins boats on the beach, as there should have been by now.

Almost before we could guess at what bad news was being foretold, the command boat came alongside. The naval officer shouted, "You'll have to go in right away, as soon as I can get an amphtrack for you. The shelf around the island is too shallow to take the Higgins boats." This was indeed chilling news. It meant something that had been dimly foreseen but hardly expected: the only way the Marines were going to land was in the amphtracks ("alligators") which could crawl over the shallow reef that surrounds Betio. It meant that the landings would be slow, because there were not enough amphtracks for everybody, and we would have to use the emergency shuttle system that had been worked out as a last resort. And suppose the amphtracks were knocked out before they could get enough men ashore to hold what the first wave had taken? And suppose the Marines already ashore were killed faster than they could be replaced under this slow shuttle system? . . .

An amphtrack bobbed alongside our Higgins boat. Said the Marine amphtrack boss, "Quick! Half you men get in here. They need help bad on the beach. A lot of Marines have already been killed and wounded." While the amphtrack was alongside, Jap shells from an automatic weapon began peppering the water around us. . . .

"An amphtrack bobbed alongside our Higgins boat. Said the Marine amphtrack boss, 'Quick! Half you men get in here. They need help bad on the beach. A lot of Marines have already been killed or wounded.' . . . Jap shells from an automatic weapon began peppering the water around us. . . . But the Marines did not hesitate."

—ROBERT SHERROD

Marines storm bloody Tarawa.

But the Marines did not hesitate. Hadn't they been told that other Marines "needed help bad"? (From *Tarawa*, by Robert Sherrod.)

MERRIMAN SMITH
(1913–1970)

Merriman Smith covered Washington politics for the United Press.

924. As the war continued, Mr. Roosevelt did virtually what he pleased, in public and in private, and in the secure knowledge it would not be on the radio or in the newspapers [in the interest of national security]. . . . That was all very fine, but the president began to put on and take off security like winter underwear. When he wanted it—as in the 1944 election campaign—off came all the wraps. . . . True the pressure of the presidency is heavy and seclusion a welcome antidote, but Mr. Roosevelt made a fetish of his privacy during the war. (Cited in *Off the Record with F.D.R.*, by William D. Hassett [q.v.].)

ROBERT ST. JOHN
(1902–)

St. John was a war correspondent for the Associated Press.

925. We [correspondents] sat in the open-faced dining room of the Srpski Kralj, in Belgrade, watching endless columns of cavalry and artillery parade past the windows on their way to the frontiers. We were full of admiration of the horses as well as the men. Sturdy men and husky little horses, their harnesses decorated with the first flowers or spring and with branches of trees that had just sprouted finger-sized leaves. The men all seemed eager for action, and even the animals looked happy about it. They were going off to battle. They were going to show Hitler. A pint-sized nation was going to speak up. Look out, Berlin, here we come!

"Listen," someone would suddenly lean across the table and say in dead earnest, "you can't throw horses and peasant carts and mountain guns like that assortment out there in the street against the steel and stuff the Nazis have got all oiled up and ready for this show!"

"But Serbia's a mountainous place," someone would pipe back. "This is no blitz country. These babies will lose the plains, but wait until they get the Nazis into the mountains. The Serbs know their mountains. Remember the last war? They can retire to the mountains of southern Serbia and fight there for a year."

"And if the Germans cut their transportation lines, how will they get food?"

Back came the answer: "Did you ever see what these peasants live on? Black bread and onions. They've got enough flour and onions back in those mountains to feed an entire army for at least a year. Besides they'll eat their shoe leather before they'll give in to the Germans." (*From the Land of Silent People*, by Robert St. John.)

[Tito's partisans tied up twenty German divisions in Yugoslavia for four years.]

I. F. STONE
(1907–1989)

A Washington journalist, Stone commented on national and international issues for *The Nation* and the newspaper *PM*. After the war, he launched the newsletter *I. F. Stone's Weekly*.

926. We may be on the eve of the greatest armed struggle of all time. . . . We are reaching out for imperial responsibilities and have become the focus of worldwide hopes and fears. ("A Time for Candor," *The Nation*, January 25, 1941; from *The War Years 1939–1945*, by I. F. Stone.)

[Written during the debate on Lend-Lease (q.v.).]

927. The second front is, of course, a military problem, but it is also, in many ways, a political problem. Here is one way, as explained by one of the most intelligent observers here. . . . He is in favor of a second front, and no doubt that colors his reasoning, but here it is: No general or admiral wants to advise an attack that may not be successful and may be fatal to that general's or that admiral's reputation and career. There are circumstances nevertheless in which it may be necessary, for political reasons, deliberately to take a risk that is unwise from a military point of view. This official feels that both the good-will of the Russian people and the morale of the Anglo-American peoples call for a second front. It may be a gamble but sometimes the greatest gamble in a war is not to gamble at all. He feels that the risk may be great but that not to take it is to resign ourselves to years of armed stalemate. ("Capital Thoughts on a Second Front," *The Nation*; October 3, 1942; Ibid.)

928. Were the principal events of the past week in Washington to be broadcast by the Axis radio, listeners in occupied Europe and Asia would be inclined to dismiss what they heard as typical Axis exaggerations, if not downright lies. They would have heard that in America race prejudice was still so strong that 16 Southern railroads preferred to suffer from a shortage of firemen rather than hire unemployed Negroes qualified by experience for such work. . . . The action of the railroads was largely due to pressure from one of the most advanced sections of the American labor movement, the Railroad Brotherhood. ("Grist for Goebbels," *The Nation*, December 25, 1943; Ibid.)

WALTER WINCHELL
(1891–1972)

Winchell was a newspaper columnist and radio commentator. Winchell invented the gossip column and—in the 1930s and early 1940s—he was one of the most influential journalists in America. He was an early foe of Hitler and an ardent supporter of Roosevelt. He invented words to express his displeasure, such as "Ratzis" for Nazis, "jackassolationists" for isolationists, and "Hitlerooters" for Americans who supported Nazi Germany. As early as September 1933, the German press had labeled him "the New Germany's American menace because he tells such unconscionable lies about the Fuehrer."

929. FDR motioned for me to sit down. He opened a desk drawer, picked out a letter, and read part of it.

"Dear Pop," it began, "I only hope one of us gets killed. Maybe then they will stop picking on the rest of the family."

I had seen and heard FDR laugh at jokes and stories, but I had never seen a president weep. His eyes filled. He tried to swallow a lump that stuck in his throat. He put the letter back in the drawer. (Early 1940s; from *Winchell Exclusive: Things That Happened to Me—and Me to Them*, by Walter Winchell.)

[Winchell told the president he wanted to do a story on the distinguished war records of the president's sons, to counter those in Congress who were attacking the president and members of his family. The president flatly refused. Later, Winchell decided to go ahead with an item on his radio show.]

930. I have some exclusive news for the few members of the Senate and Congress who keep picking on the excellent war records of the four Roosevelt boys. I also have unhappy news for Congressman [William] Lambertson, the most persistent attacker of FDR and his sons, all of whom performed heroic war duty without publicity.

Congressman Lambertson of Kansas! Your son was arrested last night for dodging the draft as a conscientious objector! (From radio broadcast, early 1940s; Ibid.)

[The president later thanked Winchell personally.]

931. And what happens [in a Nazi victory] to you—and you—and you? Well, this is what happens. A few of you who are American Quislings [q.v.] and Lavals [q.v.] will be in temporary power. Some of you—such as me—will be shot. Many of you will be put into concentration camps and the rest of you will be slaves. (Cited in *Let's Go to Press*, by Ed Weiner.)

932. In union there is stench. (Ibid.)

[Commenting on the formation of the isolationist America First Committee (q.v.).]

933. These bastards are vulnerable. They can't be the supermen they claim. They wouldn't squeal so loud if they were. (Ibid.)

[Commenting on Nazi responses to his attacks on them.]

10

Historians and Biographers

THOMAS B. ALLEN

(n.d.)

Allen and coauthor Norman Polmar have worked together on books on military and biographical subjects.

934. Had the invasion [of the Japanese home islands] occurred, there could be no doubt that it would have launched the bloodiest battles of the war. Thousands of young American men and perhaps millions of Japanese soldiers and civilians would have died. Terror weapons—poison gas, possibly germ warfare, and perhaps crop-destroying chemicals—could have scarred the land and made the end of the war an Armageddon even worse than the devastation caused by two atomic bombs. A third atomic bomb was ready before the end of August [1945]. It probably would have been dropped on another Japanese city. And from what is now known about [General George] Marshall's thinking on the tactical use of atomic bombs, the plans for Operation Downfall would have been modified to include their use in support of the landings. The devastation of Japan could have been total. (From *Code-Name Downfall: The Secret Plan to Invade Japan—and Why Truman Dropped the Bomb*, by Thomas B. Allen and Norman Polmar.)

STEPHEN E. AMBROSE

(1935–)

A historian and biographer, Ambrose has written extensively on World War II. His subjects include several books on Dwight D. Eisenhower, historical works on D-Day (q.v.) and on a company of the 101st Airborne, plus biographical works from Meriwether Lewis to Richard Nixon. One of his most notable works was *Citizen Soldiers*, accounts of GIs battling in Europe during World War II.

935. In general, in assessing the motivation of the GIs, there is agreement that patriotism or any other form of idealism had little if anything to do with it.

The GIs fought because they had to. What held them together was not country and flag, but unit cohesion. It has been my experience through four decades of interviewing ex-GIs, that such generalizations are true enough.

And yet there is something more. Although the GIs were and are embarrassed to talk or write about the cause they fought for, in marked contrast to their great-grandfathers who fought in the Civil War, they were the children of democracy and they did more to help spread democracy around the world than any other generation in history.

At the core, the American citizen soldiers knew the difference between right and wrong, and they didn't want to live in a world in which wrong prevailed. So they fought, and won, and we all of us, living and yet to be born, must be forever profoundly grateful. (From *Citizen Soldiers*, by Stephen E. Ambrose.)

MAURICE BAUMONT

(n.d.)

Baumont has been called the dean of French diplomatic historians. He served as chairman of the French Commission on the History of the Second World War.

936. In September 1939, Hitler's wish was to achieve his dream of hegemony without firing a shot, and, as he told Goering [q.v.], to renew the "Czech affair" with Poland, forcing her into vassalage without war. (From *The Origins of the*

Second World War, by Maurice Baumont, translated by Simone de Couvreur Ferguson.)

937. Since according to Tacitus "posterity gives each man his due," there are good reasons to believe that posterity will be guided by the judgment rendered on Hitler by one of his most intimate aides, Meissner, who was under-secretary for, successively, Ebert, Hindenburg, and Hitler—such dissimilar personalities that Meissner must have been "a monster of flexibility." Meissner denounces in Hitler a name soiled by blood and crime, a regime bound to the annihilation of millions of human lives, the destruction of German culture, and the debasement of Germany herself. Having grown into the most important figure of the 1930s, Hitler provoked the worst catastrophe in European history. He brought more calamities to the world than any other man of modern times. (Ibid.)

CHARLES A. BEARD
(1874–1948)

Beard was an American historian who achieved prominence with his *An Economic Interpretation of the Constitution*. He was an isolationist before the United States entered World War II. His final work, *President Roosevelt and the Coming of the War 1941*, was an attack on those political decisions to aid the Allies and involve America in the war against Hitler.

938. President Roosevelt entered the year 1941 carrying moral responsibility for his covenants with the American people to keep this nation out of war—so to conduct foreign affairs as to avoid war. Those covenants, made in the election campaign of 1940, were of two kinds. The first were the pledges of the Democratic party to which he publicly subscribed while he was bidding for the suffrages of the people. The second were his personal promises to the people, supplementing the obligations of his party's platform. (From *President Roosevelt and the Coming of the War 1941: A Study in Appearances and Realities*, by Charles A. Beard.)

939. Many reports of events in the press after the fall of the Konoye Cabinet [in Japan] on October 16 [1941] seemed to indicate that intransigent militarists were in power at Tokyo and that an explosion into war might happen at any time. From Manila, October 16, came a dispatch in which Francis Sayre, American commissioner in the Philippines, was reported as saying that the United States was moving close to the brink of war and that the Axis would be smashed.

From Tokyo, on the same day, Otto Tolischus reported to *The New York Times* that the Director of Japanese Naval Intelligence had declared that the relations of the United States and Japan were "now approaching the final parting of the ways." From Shanghai, October 16, came a dispatch stating that the Central China *Daily News*, organ of the Japanese-sponsored regime in Nanking, had asserted that war between Japan and the United States "is inevitable." (Ibid.)

ANTONY BEEVOR

(n.d.)

Beevor, a former British army officer, has written books on the British army, the Spanish Civil War, and the German invasion of Crete during World War II. The Greek island of Crete was the first ever to be conquered by air, involving paratroopers and glider troops.

940. While the action against the [German] glider troops was beginning on the top of the hill above the Creforce quarry, [Major General Bernard] Freyberg's staff officers observed the panoramic view over the coastal plain with a mixture of astonishment, dread, and professional fascination. The air fleet approached over the sea, and "the heavens shook with the roar of their engines." When they first saw the stream of black shapes coming out behind the troop-carriers, several observers thought for a moment that the aircraft were trailing smoke after being hit, but the shapes separated and sprouted canopies with a jerk, white for paratroopers and red, green or yellow for weapon canisters, equipment or supplies.

[Colonel] David Hunt, standing next to Group Captain [George] Beamish, heard him murmur, "What a remarkable sight! Looks like the end of the world." (From *Crete: The Battle and the Resistance*, by Antony Beevor.)

941. Within a matter of minutes, the outburst of firing up and down the coastal strip transformed the tranquil Mediterranean vista into a disturbingly ill-defined battlefield. Through their binoculars, Hunt and Beamish could see puffs of smoke rising above the olive groves and the odd patch of white where a parachute had caught in a tree or snagged on a telegraph pole.

While senior officers thought of H. G. Wells and feared the chaos of warfare without lines, younger officers and soldiers were much less awed. They recovered their aplomb and set to killing paratroopers as if it were a dangerous and exhilarating fairground sport.

New Zealand officers told their men to aim at the boots of the paratroopers since their descent was deceptively rapid. This seems to have worked well to judge by the number who jerked, dangled limply, then crumpled on hitting the ground. They were covered by their own parachutes as by instant shrouds. (Ibid.)

THOMAS B. BUELL

(n.d.)

Buell served twenty-five years in the U.S. Navy, spending part of that time commanding a destroyer. A naval historian, he has taught at both the Naval War College and the U.S. Military Academy. His works include biographies of Admiral Raymond A. Spruance and Fleet Admiral Ernest J. King (q.v.). Buell gives his own view of Admiral William F. Halsey (q.v.) and the Battle of Leyte Gulf.

942. The recriminations and second-guessing would persist for years and King [q.v.] must be held accountable for his own responsibility for events at Leyte Gulf. First, there is the matter of divided responsibilities. Halsey [q.v.] worked for Nimitz [q.v.], rather than MacArthur, because of King. Next, there is the question of Halsey's mission. King knew that Halsey's orders from Nimitz specified, "In case opportunity for destruction of major portion of the enemy fleet is offered or can be created, such destruction becomes the primary task." It is likely that King directed Nimitz (if not in writing, then at least orally) to give such an order to Halsey. The order also was exactly what Nimitz and Halsey wanted. In any event, King knew that Halsey would attack the Japanese fleet if it came near the Philippines. . . . Halsey was known for being headstrong and impetuous. Yet King by default gave Halsey carte blanche to abandon the beachhead in an operation that demanded the very closest cooperation between the amphibious forces and the covering forces. (From *Master of Sea Power: A Biography of Fleet Admiral Ernest J. King*, by Thomas B. Buell.)

IRIS CHANG

(1968–)

A journalist who became a full-time author, Chang first heard accounts of the Sino-Japanese War and the Rape of Nanking from her parents.

943. Americans think of World War II as beginning on December 7, 1941. . . . Europeans date it from September 1, 1939, and the blitzkrieg assault on Poland. . . . Africans see an even earlier beginning, the invasion of Abyssinia [Ethiopia] by Mussolini in 1935. Yet Asians must trace the war's beginning . . . to Japan's first steps toward the military domination of East Asia—the occupation of Manchuria in 1931. (From *The Rape of Nanking: The Forgotten Holocaust of World War II*, by Iris Chang.)

944. The broad details of the Rape are, except among the Japanese, not in dispute. In November 1937, after their successful invasion of Shanghai, the Japanese launched a massive attack on the newly established capital of the Republic of China. When the city fell on December 13, 1937, Japanese soldiers began an orgy of cruelty seldom if ever matched in world history. Tens of thousands of young men were rounded up and . . . mowed down by machine guns, used for bayonet practice, or soaked with gasoline and burned alive. For months the streets of the city were heaped with corpses and reeked with the stench of rotting human flesh. Years later, experts at the International Military Tribunal of the Far East estimated that more than 260,000 noncombatants died at the hands of Japanese soldiers at Nanking in late 1937 and early 1938, though some experts have placed the figure at well over 350,000. (Ibid.)

945. Estimates [on rapes of Chinese women by Japanese soldiers] range from as low as 20,000 to as high as 80,000. But what the Japanese did to the women of Nanking cannot be computed in a tally sheet of statistics. We will never know the full psychic toll, because many of the women who survived the ordeal found themselves pregnant, and the subject of Chinese women impregnated by Japanese rapists in Nanking is so sensitive that it has never been completely studied. . . . Numerous half-Japanese children were choked or drowned at birth. (Ibid.)

TERRY CHARMAN

(n.d.)

Charman has researched a number of historical projects at the Imperial War Museum, London. He has also been an adviser on feature films and television documentaries on the war.

946. Joseph C. Harsch of the *Christian Science Monitor* observed: "For a country which is supposed to be against sin, they seem to like their nudes rather hot and steamy," as he examined the display on a news-stand on the Unter den Linden. Such displays were, of course, part of a deliberate attempt to create an atmosphere of *gesunde Erotika* (healthy eroticism), designed to increase the birth rate, so important to future plans of expansion. The Nazis had loudly denounced the permissiveness of the Weimar Republic with its gay bars, nude cabarets and pornographic literature, but now as the war was getting underway, and the need to produce future soldiers for the Reich became a "patriotic duty," a flood of near-pornographic nudist and naturalist literature appeared on the news-stands. (From *The German Home Front, 1939–45*, by Terry Charman.)

WAYNE S. COLE

(n.d.)

Cole, a historian, has written major works on isolationism in America during the war. These include *Roosevelt & the Isolationists 1932–45, America First: The Battle against Intervention, 1940–1941*, as well as books on U.S. Senator Gerald P. Nye and Colonel Charles A. Lindbergh (q.v.).

947. A few isolationists continued to oppose the war even after Pearl Harbor—but they were the exceptions. Most prewar noninterventionists supported the war effort. Many did so on active duty in the armed forces and in combat. But they did so without abandoning their belief that they had been right before Pearl Harbor. And some were able to serve only over objections from the White House and the Roosevelt administration. (From *Roosevelt & the Isolationists: 1932–45*, by Wayne S. Cole.)

948. The Roosevelt administration not only blocked Lindbergh's [q.v.] efforts to serve as an air force officer during World War II, it also prevented him from serving as a civilian with various aviation businesses that had government contracts. . . . His failures and frustrations produced one of the rare instances when he allowed his spirits to flag and his discouragement to show. He wrote in his personal journal: "I have always believed in the past that every American citizen had the right and the duty to state his opinion in peace and to fight for his country in war. But the Roosevelt Administration seems to think otherwise." (Ibid.)

949. As long as they lived, old isolationists continued to believe that history would vindicate them and would demonstrate the wisdom of their guidance on foreign affairs and the accuracy of their charges against Roosevelt. Critics of American involvement in Vietnam 30 years later (many of them Democratic urban liberal internationalists) resurrected arguments that isolationists had used earlier. But the socio-economic bases for those older unilateralist and noninterventionist policies had eroded. A way of life and a mode of thinking were fading from the American scene. (Ibid.)

WILLIAM CRAIG

(n.d.)

Craig, an American historian, wrote *The Fall of Japan* and *Enemy at the Gates*, an account of the Battle of Stalingrad (q.v.).

950. Some Russians in Stalingrad never paused to reflect on the daily slaughter. They regarded the butchery as a punitive crusade, a purgative. Commando captain Ignacy Changar, a curly-haired, long-nosed 21-year-old, had come into the city to do the job he knew best, killing Germans. Changar was an expert guerrilla fighter and preferred to work with a knife—a technique he had perfected in the forests of the Ukraine where he spent months during the first year of the war. There he had seen the Germans at their worst and the experience affected him deeply.

Once, at the edge of a village, he watched from a tree line while two German soldiers accosted a woman, pushed her and demanded she give up her cow. When she said that other Germans had already taken it, they shoved her again. She continued to protest and the soldiers picked up her baby, grabbed a leg each and ripped the child apart.

In the woods, the stunned Changar had cursed and raised his rifle, but a companion knocked it down and warned him not to reveal their position. During the next months, as Changar retreated across Russia, the tormented cries of that bereaved woman followed him and, by October of 1942, he was killing Germans for the sheer pleasure of it. . . .

Ordered to occupy a half-demolished building [in Stalingrad] . . . he had led 50 men into it only to find a sizable German force entrenched in a large room across a ten-foot wide hallway. . . .

[After several days, he had his men dig a tunnel under the German position and then they dynamited it.]

. . . The next day . . . he went back to examine his handiwork. He counted 360 legs. (From *Enemy at the Gates*, by William Craig.)

EDWARD CRANKSHAW

(1909–)

A member of the British Military Mission to the Soviet Union, Crankshaw served there from 1941 to 1943. After the war, he wrote several books on various aspects of German and Russian history.

951. Certainly immense efforts were made to evacuate machinery factory by factory to the East, and [Nikita] Khrushchev [q.v.], among other, more urgent responsibilities concerned with trying to hold the line, was technically responsible for this. But his overseer was [Georgi] Malenkov, in charge of war production, and for every factory whose machinery was moved many were left intact. The workers, more often than not, were got away, but in the Urals they had to build new factories and new machines. At the height of the German threat to Moscow, when the city was all but surrounded, the train carrying the diplomatic corps and military missions away from danger took five days to cover the six hundred miles from Moscow to Kuibyshev. Most of that time was spent in sidings. And my most vivid memory is of the endless trains moving west from Siberia, carrying up fresh troops, fresh guns, fresh equipment, to fight under [Georgi] Zhukov [q.v.] in that last desperate battle for Moscow, quite blocking the lines to the east. While all along the line, in sidings, or tumbled into fields, were trainloads of machinery, rusting under the snow, machinery which had been wrenched from concrete beds, breaking the mountings which bolted it down, scattered uselessly and aimlessly all over that desolate landscape under the first early snow, and regiment after regiment of derelict and rusting locomotives, brought thus far from the west and left standing idle for want of men to drive them and to service them, for want of tracks to move them farther east. (Recalling events of late 1941; Soviet Union; from *Khrushchev: A Career*, by Edward Crankshaw.)

PETER FLEMING

(1907–)

An English author, Fleming wrote successful travel books before the war. During the war, he served in Norway, Greece, and Burma and was awarded the Order of the British Empire. He has written the authoritative account of the campaign that never was—*Operation Sea Lion* (q.v.), Hitler's plan to invade England.

952. Were there any circumstances in which, during the summer of 1940, Hitler could have successfully attempted the invasion of England?

There can be no doubt as to when a German invasion would have the best prospects of success. Had the Germans been able to put quite a small force—say three or four divisions—across the Channel early in June . . . might have done the trick. The reinforcement, and indeed the maintenance, of this force would have presented serious difficulties, but some of these could have been overcome by the capture of airfields in south-east England, which in those days would not have been a hard task.

At this time—immediately after Dunkirk, whence the last troops were taken off on the morning of 4 June—there simply did not exist in the islands the physical means of repelling, or even containing, a determined attack. The BEF [British Expeditionary Force], dead tired, disorganized, without artillery or transport, had temporarily ceased to cohere as a force. . . .

Almost more important, the nation, though outwardly defiant, had not really got its second wind. It was on its feet and still full of fight, but, like a man who has just been kicked sprawling in the gutter twice in rapid succession, it was dazed and off balance, and without a breathing-space might have gone down again to a blow which a little later it could have parried. (From *Operation Sea Lion*, by Peter Fleming.)

MARTIN GILBERT

(n.d.)

Gilbert, an English historian and biographer, has written extensively on the two world wars and on the Holocaust (q.v.). He has also produced atlases that shed light on various aspects of history.

953. Victory-in-Europe Day was proclaimed and celebrated in Britain, the United States and Western Europe on 8 May 1945. In the Soviet Union the celebrations were held on the following day. Newspaper photographs of VE-Day show dancing in the streets, fireworks, illuminations and scenes of jubilation. These moments of exhilaration remain fixed in the minds of all who took part in them, a high point of relief and rejoicing after the hardships, sorrows and privations of war. (From *The Day the War Ended: May 8, 1945—Victory in Europe*, by Martin Gilbert.)

954. VE-Day was the focal point of celebration and memory, but for many people, both soldiers and civilians, the war had ended earlier, for some much earlier. For the millions of military and civilian victims of combat, oppression and genocide, the war ended on the day of their death. Not a single day passed without the deaths of hundreds, in battle, in reprisal actions and in concentration camps. On average, more than 20,000 people, soldiers and civilians, were killed each day of the Second World War; the same number that were killed on the first day of the Battle of the Somme in 1916. For those who survived battle, aerial bombardment, execution and incarceration, the war ended with their liberation or repatriation from captivity. (Ibid.)

955. I myself remember the long wait for the return of my cousin Simmy Gordon, who had been captured by the Japanese at Singapore and had been held a prisoner-of-war for three and a half years. On his return we glimpsed, as thousands of families glimpsed, a hint of the ordeal through which those held captive by the Japanese had passed. In common with so many former prisoners-of-war, Simmy never fully recovered from his experiences, which were the subject of innumerable nightmares. In one sense, his war never ended. (Ibid.)

DORIS KEARNS GOODWIN

(1943–)

Historian and biographer, Goodwin is the author of *The Fitzgeralds and the Kennedys*, *Lyndon Johnson and the American Dream*, and *No Ordinary Time, Franklin and Eleanor Roosevelt: The Home Front in World War II*.

956. At the height of the Battle of the Bulge [q.v.], with the army desperate for replacements, a dramatic call went out for all Negro units in the European theater. Representing a major break with traditional army policy, which kept blacks segregated in . . . predominantly service divisions, the call invited Negro soldiers to volunteer as infantrymen and fight side by side with white troops. . . . Negro volunteers were promised a six-week training period and then, for the first time, assignment "without regard to color or race to the units where assistance is most needed." Those who answered the call would have "the opportunity of fighting shoulder to shoulder to bring about victory." . . .

Within a matter of weeks, more than four thousand Negro soldiers had volunteered. Currently serving as truck drivers, construction engineers, stevedores, and longshoremen, the Negro soldiers recognized they were being presented with an opportunity to affirm their competence and courage on the battlefield and to prove that whites and blacks could work together. (From *No Ordinary Time*, by Doris Kearns Goodwin.)

957. When the six weeks [of training] were up, officers arrived to take the soldiers to their new assignments. Only then did the Negro soldiers learn that . . . instead of being integrated on an individual basis, they were to be formed into platoons and then sent into white combat units. Though disappointed by the change, the Negro volunteers remained enthusiastic about their adventure. They were used to broken promises. (Ibid.)

958. Within the mixed divisions, blacks and whites ate, slept, and played ball together; they used the same bathrooms and the same showers; they were given a chance to know and respect each other. As they fought their way together across Germany, prejudices would break down.

When told about the plan for integrated platoons, 64 percent of the whites were skeptical. Three months later, 77 percent said their attitudes had become highly favorable. (Ibid.)

PETER GROSE

(n.d.)

Grose, the biographer of Allen Dulles (q.v.), was diplomatic correspondent for the *New York Times*. He has also worked as deputy director of the State Department's Policy Planning Staff.

959. For all the variety of philosophies and lifestyles revealed in the diaries and letters of the passionate German underground, the only Nazi crime that did not seem to generate their courage was the extermination of the Jews. None of the conspirators [against Hitler] seems actually to have defended the policy of anti-Semitism, to be sure, but its implementation did not rank high among the concerns of this circle. (From *Gentleman Spy: The Life of Allen Dulles*, by Peter Grose.)

NIGEL HAMILTON

(n.d.)

Hamilton, a British journalist, has written the authorized biography of Field Marshal Bernard Montgomery (q.v.). Hamilton had complete access to Montgomery's diaries, letters, and official papers.

960. Monty had his own opinions on those present [several days prior to D-Day (q.v.)]. Patton [q.v.] he regarded as a sabre-rattler, wilfully ignorant of battle in its administrative dimension, and of army/air co-operation, but still the most aggressive "thruster" in the Allied camp; Bradley [q.v.] he considered dull, conscientious, dependable and loyal . . . ; [Miles] Dempsey [who would lead the British Second Army on D-Day], though he lacked the Guardsman's ruthlessness and drive of [British Lieutenant-General Oliver] Leese, was cleverer, and he possessed a legendary eye for terrain, ran a high-calibre headquarters and was, behind his quiet manner, completely imperturbable. Only [Henry] Crerar [head of Canadian forces] really worried Monty. . . . Though undoubtedly an efficient headquarters manager, Monty felt grave doubts about Crerar as a battlefield leader, doubts which were to be unhappily confirmed in the months ahead.

It was not, therefore, the most spectacular team of Army Commanders to be leading the largest invasion in history. (From *Master of the Battlefield: Monty's War Years 1942–1944*, by Nigel Hamilton.)

GEORGE HICKS

(1936–)

An economist with special interest in Asia, Hicks has written a definitive account of the "Comfort Women" who were forced to serve as prostitutes for the Japanese military.

961. The plight of comfort women was not of major concern to the powers fighting World War II. Nor has it proved of interest to historians. There is no monument to the unknown comfort woman as there are monuments everywhere to the unknown soldier.

It has taken half a century for these women's ruined lives to become a human rights issue. (From *The Comfort Women*, by George Hicks.)

ANNETTE KAHN

(1941–)

A French journalist, Kahn was assigned to cover the trial of Klaus Barbie (q.v.), which took place more than forty years after the end of the war. Her father, a member of the French Resistance and a Jew, had been executed on Barbie's order. Kahn wrote a book describing not only what had happened during the trial but what the accused war criminal had done during the German occupation. She described how France had handled it all when the war ended.

962. French Jews have received little compensation for the suffering they endured in World War II. After the Nazi defeat and the liberation of the concentration camps by the Allies, France turned its entire attention to only one group of victims—those of the Resistance. To chant the praises of the shadow army that had fought for freedom was the easiest way for most French citizens to atone for a record tarnished by fear, cowardice, and collaboration. In the postwar years, the Resistance had far more acolytes and sympathizers than in the thick of battle. But whatever the case, in 1945 France was too busy dressing the wounds of its national ego to worry about the wounds of the Jews.

Military tribunals held one trial after another of French citizens accused of treason. Of the 150,000 people found guilty, 7,000 were sentenced to death and 800 were actually executed. . . . The collaborators tried in court were lucky; there were also many executions without trial, in woods and on street corners. (From *Why My Father Died*, by Annette Kahn.)

DAVID KAHN

(1930–)

Kahn's special field of interest is wartime intelligence and counter-intelligence. His books include *The Codebreakers* and *Hitler's Spies*.

963. Identity cards, pay books, distribution lists on orders or reports, all gave the [German] interrogator clues to the [Allied] prisoner's unit and its neighbors. He could then ask questions that merely required a confirmatory answer, and so get the prisoner talking, and he could often check the truthfulness of volunteered information. . . .

Letters gave a great deal of personal data about an airman, enabling the interrogator to seem to know all about him. The envelope often carried his complete address, including the name of his squadron. The service newspapers that airmen brought along to read during the long flight confirmed old units and revealed new ones. They gossiped about personnel, equipment, installations, and activities. Officers' identity cards showed where they had been commissioned and occasionally where they had been trained. A card issued at Langley Field, Virginia, or Boca Raton, Florida, indicated that its owner had probably taken blind bombing training. The diary of the leader of a flight of Marauders which strayed en route to England from America and lost three planes over France listed the names of all the crews in the entire group and reported the serviceability of every plane. Even nonverbal documents talked. Though all men in the European Theater of Operations had the same type of ration card, the post-exchange clerk at the 100th Bomb Group always cancelled them on a rough board counter with a heavy black pencil that picked up the wood grain. The Germans identified members of that unit with ease. The fake identity photographs given airmen to facilitate their escape via the underground sometimes helped the enemy more. The photographs of the 91st Bomber Group had a peculiar brown tint. The personnel of the 95th Bomb Group all wore the same checkered coat when they had their pictures taken. (From *Hitler's Spies: German Military Intelligence during World War II*, by David Kahn.)

WILLIAM L. LANGER
(1896–1959)

Langer, a Harvard University scholar, was invited by Secretary of State Cordell Hull (q.v.) to examine official government documents on U.S.-Vichy relations. Following the fall of France, Germany had initially occupied a large part of France, including Paris. A new French government, located in Vichy, was to run unoccupied France. There was great criticism of the U.S. relationship with Vichy. The Langer study resulted in the publication of *Our Vichy Gamble*, a painstaking study of American political, economic, diplomatic, and military policies with Vichy.

964. Almost all of the criticism of the Vichy policy was based on ideological considerations. In the eyes of the critics, the [Henri] Petain [q.v.] government was a fascist government . . . akin to the regimes of Mussolini [q.v.] and Hitler. . . .

As a matter of fact, this interpretation was substantially correct. Petain and his chief associates were fascist in their views and had long yearned for an authoritarian regime to put an end to what they considered democratic chaos and corruption.

But it should be remembered that in the beginning, when our decision to maintain relations was taken, the Vichy regime was in its infancy and had not yet revealed itself in its worst aspects. In any event, the United States government [q.v.] could hardly have based its policy toward France on considerations of the form of government. Throughout history our sympathies have naturally been on the side of the liberal, democratic states, but rarely before this had it been argued that we should not maintain relations with governments of which we disapproved. . . .

In the period after 1919 not only did we maintain relations with the Italy of Mussolini, but we ultimately accorded recognition to Bolshevik Russia which was at the other end of the ideological scale. We did not regard the victory of Hitlerism in Germany as a justification for breaking relations, and our connection with militaristic Japan was not ended until the bombs fell on Pearl Harbor. . . .

If our foreign policy in the modern world were to be based exclusively upon ideological affinity, we should probably find ourselves cut off from many of the most powerful and important nations . . .

The task of the Department of State is to protect American interests abroad, not to sit in judgment of other governments. (From *Our Vichy Gamble*, by William L. Langer.)

CALLUM MacDONALD

(n.d.)

MacDonald is a historian at the University of Warwick, England. He has written a vivid account of the assassination of Reinhard Heydrich (q.v.). Wounded just outside Prague, Czechoslovakia, on May 27, 1942, Heydrich died a week later. Nazi reprisals followed, including the destruction of the village of Lidice.

965. On 9 June [1942] a special train left Prague marked "AaH" . . . [initials which stood for] Assassination of Heydrich carrying 1,000 Czech Jews to their deaths in the SS [Schutzstaffel] extermination factories. It was followed by two more transports from the ghetto at Terezin. . . . In Poland the SS dedicated its ghastly work of mass murder to the memory of the lost hero, under the title . . . Operation Reinhard. (From *The Killing of Obergruppenfuehrer Reinhard Heydrich*, by Callum MacDonald).

966. For the Nazis, however, the murder of Jews was almost routine. Something more was required, a dramatic symbol which would show not only the Czechs but also all of Europe the consequences of defying German rule. . . .

Lidice was to be destroyed. The men were to be shot on the spot and the women sent to a concentration camp. Children worthy of Germanization were to be handed over to SS [Schutzstaffel] families. The village was to be burned to the ground and its remains levelled so that no trace remained. (Ibid.)

967. Males over 15 [were] herded together. A squad of security police under SS [Schutzstaffel] Hauptsturmfuehrer Max Rostock then began the ghastly work of execution, despatching its victims in groups of ten. . . . The Gestapo reported that 199 men were murdered in the operation and 195 women arrested. Of 95 children, 8 were ultimately considered worthy of Germanization. The majority simply vanished and only 16 could be traced after the war. (Ibid.)

968. In the Protectorate press, this act of mass murder was presented as justifiable retaliation for the assassination. . . . Emanuel Moravec, the Propaganda Minister, . . . predict[ed] death and destruction if the assassins were not found. In a speech at Brno on 12 June, he emphasized that there were only two alternatives. The Czechs could either work for the Reich and disregard Benes or "follow Benes and perish in the end . . . and . . . be wiped out as the Czech village of Lidice was wiped out." (Ibid.)

[Eduard Benes headed the Czech government-in-exile in London.]

ROBERT H. McNEAL

(n.d.)

McNeal is a professor of history at the University of Massachusetts at Amherst. He is the author of numerous books and articles on the leadership of the Soviet Union.

969. His [Stalin's] style of command in war was much as it had been in peace, reserving for himself not only the ultimate authority but also the prerogative of intervening at any level if it pleased him. According to [General Georgi] Zhukov [q.v.], Stalin mastered questions of the organization of front operations (there being about a dozen large sectors, or "fronts," at any given moment). (From *Stalin: Man and Ruler*, by Robert H. McNeal.)

970. Stalin knew not only all the commanders of the fronts and armies, and there were over a hundred of them, but also several commanders of corps and divisions, as well as the top officials of the People's Commissariat of Defense, not to speak of the top personnel of the central and regional party and state apparatus. (Ibid.)

971. His [Stalin's] vast knowledge of the war concerned the enemy, too. During daily reports if the briefing officer omitted reference to any particular German army, Stalin would prompt him to deal with it. Evidence of his intervention in details, especially in the first year or so of the war, abound and suggest excessive meddling. (Ibid.)

RICHARD OVERY

(n.d.)

Overy is a professor of modern history at King's College, London. He has written on World War II and on Nazi Germany.

972. The United States devoted only 15 percent of its war effort to the war with Japan. The other 85 percent was expended in the defeat of Germany. If the defeat of the German army was the central strategic task, the main theater for it was the conflict on the eastern front. The German army was first weakened there, and then driven back, before the main weight of Allied ground and air forces was brought to bear in 1944. Over four hundred German and Soviet divisions fought along a front of more than 1,000 miles.

Soviet forces destroyed or disabled an estimated 607 Axis divisions between 1941 and 1945. The scale and geographical extent of the eastern front dwarfed all earlier warfare. Losses on both sides far exceeded losses anywhere else in the military contest. The war in the east was fought with a ferocity almost unknown on the western fronts. The battles at Stalingrad [q.v.] and Kursk, which broke the back of the German army, drew from the soldiers of both sides the last ounces of physical and moral energy. Both sides knew the costs of losing—neither victors nor vanquished, Hitler announced in January 1943, only "survivors and annihilated." . . .

The German army fielded only 20–30 divisions at most in the Italian theater. . . . The war in France in 1944, where Germany could have employed over 50 divisions, mostly understrength and some indifferently armed, was fought in its decisive phase between 15 Allied divisions and 15 German. (From *Why the Allies Won*, by Richard Overy.)

EDVARD RADZINSKY

(n.d.)

Radzinsky is a Russian historian and playwright. His books include *The Last Tsar* and *Stalin*. He is also a popular television personality in Russia.

973. Stalin provided his fellow Muscovites with a new entertainment. I can still remember the cry heard in my childhood: "They're bringing them!" We war children would rush out to see German prisoners of war led along Gorky Street, ragged, dejected, unshaven, in filthy greatcoats. We were his pupils, and we happily threw stones at them. (From *Stalin*, by Edvard Radzinsky.)

974. After Hitler's attack on Russia, Churchill became Stalin's reluctant ally. The Boss [Stalin] understood his attitude very well: the ideal war for Churchill would be one in which the rival dictators bit through each other's throats. (Ibid.)

975. Stalin desperately wanted the Allies to open a second front in the terrible months of 1941–1942, but Churchill was in no hurry. He preferred to watch the Soviet armies bleed. The Boss understood this way of thinking very well. In his place, he would have done the same. (Ibid.)

976. His [Stalin's] intelligence service had told him that Churchill knew in advance about the Japanese attack on Pearl Harbor, but had kept it from his American friends to make sure of drawing them into the war. There, too, he would have done the same himself. (Ibid.)

TERENCE ROBERTSON

(n.d.)

Robertson is the author of a major work on the Dieppe raid. In August 1942, a commando raid in force was made at Dieppe on the coast of northern France. A test of Nazi defenses prior to the invasion of France, it was a disaster for the Allies. Particularly hard-hit were the Canadian forces, which suffered horrendous casualties. Robertson describes.

977. The Royals never achieved surprise, and if the beaches of Dieppe were the schoolrooms where the Allies learned the tactics and techniques of invasion, the one at Puits was the abattoir where the Germans learned how to dismember, dissect, and decimate the anatomy of invasion, how to rip out its heart with clawing fingers of fire. Of the 554 men from Toronto and surrounding areas who went to Blue Beach, 65 came back, only 32 of them unwounded. In slightly more than three hours of war the Regiment suffered 94.5 per cent casualties.

"The Royal Regiment of Canada," said the Military Plan, "must secure the East Headland (Bismarck) . . . with the minimum delay." (From *Dieppe: The Shame and the Glory*, by Terence Robertson.)

978. [Major General John Hamilton] Roberts [of Canada] had always believed that if Bismarck were not taken, its guns could lay down so murderous a fire over the main beaches that the battle might be lost. As long lines of assault forces stretched out for Fortress Europe he sat in his operations cabin waiting, hoping, knowing that the report he wanted more than any other must come from the Royals saying they had carried their objectives.

As the seconds flicked by, the minutes dragged into hours, and the sounds of battle reached a fierce crescendo ashore, he still sat—waiting, hoping, yet strangely frightened by a single unexpected development. The Royals were silent. There was no report, none of any kind. (Ibid.)

HANS ROTHFELS

(n.d.)

Rothfels, a German historian, taught at the University of Berlin and at Königsberg. Later he became emeritus professor of modern history at the University of Chicago. In 1947 he lectured at Chicago on the subject of German opposition to Hitler. A year later, the lecture was expanded into a book. It would be revised in a later edition.

979. The German Opposition to Hitler was not only numerically broader than has often been conceded, but was much more widespread than could have been expected under conditions of terror. It not only developed through various stages of non-conformity and non-agreement: from the hostility which was stifled behind prison walls and barbed wire, from the silence of a potential Opposition, from humanitarian protest and secret assistance rendered to victims of persecution . . . to underground activity, to a spiritual and religious attack on the basic ideas of all totalitarian systems and to active planning and political resistance. (From *The German Opposition to Hitler*, by Hans Rothfels.)

980. Beyond this it is a fact that the German Opposition was taking shape in various forms long before the war and reached its first climax in an attempt to prevent war. It was not the threat of defeat which spurred it to action; on the contrary, some of its leaders were convinced that the victory of Hitler would be the triumph of the Anti-Christ . . . and thus the greatest of all possible catastrophes. (Ibid.)

981. While the cutting edge, the "vanguard" of the Opposition, was military, as cannot be otherwise under a totalitarian system, its body and soul came from political and ethical considerations. Though the conspiracy was led by men prominent in limited social groups, the rank and file comprised all social elements, bourgeois and military, aristocratic and proletarian, spiritual and lay. . . . It maintained contact with foreign countries and did not fail to give warning as well as proof of its existence. While for obvious reasons the Opposition could never be a mass movement, it was equipped with a network of cells. . . . Moreover, it had a concrete program which, though not binding on all its elements, was accepted by a broad coalition of oppositional forces and extended far beyond merely negative aims. (Ibid.)

CORNELIUS RYAN

(1920–1974)

Ryan was a war correspondent. He flew missions with the U.S. Air Force in Britain and covered the D-Day (q.v.) landings and General Patton's (q.v.) sweep across northern France and Germany. After the war, he wrote the best-sellers *The Longest Day* and *A Bridge Too Far*.

982. Once more he [Major Werner Pluskat] swung the artillery glasses over to the left, picked up the dark mass of the Cherbourg peninsula and began another slow sweep of the horizon. The same low banks of mist came into view, the same patches of shimmering moonlight, the same restless, white-flecked sea. Nothing was changed. Everything seemed peaceful. . . .

He walked back to the aperture and stood looking out as the first streaks of light began to lighten the sky.

Wearily, he swung the glasses over to the left again. Slowly, he tracked across the horizon. He reached the dead center of the bay. The glasses stopped moving. Pluskat tensed, stared hard.

Through the scattering, thinning mist the horizon was magically filling with ships—ships of every size and description, ships that casually maneuvered back and forth as though they had been there for hours. There appeared to be thousands of them. It was a ghostly armada that somehow had appeared from nowhere. Pluskat stared in frozen disbelief, speechless, moved as he had never been before in his life. At that moment the world of the good soldier Pluskat began falling apart. He says in those first moments he knew, calmly and surely, that "this was the end for Germany."

"Block," said Pluskat [over the telephone], "it's the invasion. There must be ten thousand ships out there."

Block said, "What way are these ships heading?"

Pluskat, phone in hand, looked out the aperture of the bunker and reported, "Right for me." (From a German bunker, Omaha Beach, events of June 6, 1944; from *The Longest Day*, by Cornelius Ryan.)

ROBERT E. SHERWOOD
(1896–1955)

Sherwood was an American playwright and author. His plays included *Idiot's Delight*, *The Petrified Forest*, *Abe Lincoln in Illinois*, and *There Shall Be No Night*. During the war, he was a speech writer for the Roosevelt administration and served for a time as head of the Office of War Information overseas. His biographical work *Roosevelt and Hopkins* is regarded as a classic.

983. In those hours and days that followed Pearl Harbor the city of Washington was afflicted with jitters. Some people who knew the extent of the damage that the Japs had inflicted, were talking darkly of disaster. They were talking of the imminence of grave danger to our country—even of the possibility of Japanese invasion of our West Coast, or of Nazi raids on our East Coast.

I didn't know how real or how valid these fears might be.

But—when I went into the presence of the president himself—I heard no talk of "disaster," no jitters. I knew that I was back in America. The president loved those ships that were hit at Pearl Harbor. When they were hit, it was as if the Japs had hit his own family. But he knew—he knew with all the confidence of a loyal American—he knew that no Japs and no Nazis—nor all the Japs and all the Nazis put together—could ever deliver a knockout blow against this country. He knew—better, perhaps, than any man who ever lived—he knew what Americans are and what Americans can do.

And in those hours and days, after Pearl Harbor, the president would sit back and lean back in his chair, in his oval study up there on the second floor of the White House, and he stated very clearly and very simply what he thought our military strategy in this war ought to be. He completely rejected a defensive policy. He rejected the policy of withdrawing our Navy into our home waters, and of deploying our growing, magnificent Army in foxholes and trenches along our coasts.

What he said, immediately after Pearl Harbor, was this: "We must go out there, where our enemies are, and fight them on their own home grounds. We must go out and find them, and hit them—and hit them again."

And that has been the summary of our whole policy in fighting this war.

(Eulogy on the death of the president, April 13, 1945; cited in *Franklin Delano Roosevelt: A Memorial*, edited by Donald Porter Geddes.)

984. I do not know how it was arranged to give the Lend-Lease [q.v.] Bill the significant designation, "HR-1776," but it sounds like a Rooseveltian conception, for it was the veritable declaration of interdependence. (From *Roosevelt and Hopkins*, by Robert E. Sherwood.)

985. The very existence of any American-British joint [military] plans [early in 1941] had to be kept utterly secret. It is an ironic fact that in all probability no great damage would have been done had the details of these plans fallen into the hands of the Germans and the Japanese, whereas, had they fallen into the hands of the Congress and the press, American preparation for war might have been well nigh wrecked. (Ibid.)

WILLIAM L. SHIRER
(1904–1994)

Correspondent for the Columbia Broadcasting System, Shirer reported from Berlin until the end of 1940. After the war, he covered the Nuremberg trials and wrote the classic *The Rise and Fall of the Third Reich* and *The Collapse of the Third Republic*.

986. All the militarism in their blood surges to their heads. They spring, yelling and crying to their feet. . . . Their hands are raised in slavish salute, their faces now contorted with hysteria, their mouths wide open, shouting, shouting, their eyes, burning with fanaticism, glued on the new god, the Messiah. (Describing the Reichstag as Hitler announced the occupation of the Rhineland, March 1936; from *The Rise and Fall of the Third Reich*, by William L. Shirer.)

987. On the flaming, riotous night of November 9, 1938, the Third Reich had deliberately turned down a dark and savage road from which there was to be no return. (November 9, 1938; Ibid.)

[The reference is to the notorious "Night of Broken Glass," a government-ordered pogrom throughout Germany and Austria. Scores of Jews were murdered, hundreds beaten up, and thousands rounded up and put in concentration camps. Synagogues, Jewish-owned businesses, and private homes were looted, vandalized, and burned to the ground.]

988. On the exact spot in the little clearing in the forest of Compiegne where . . . on November 11, 1918, the Armistice which ended the World War was signed, Adolf Hitler today handed *his* armistice terms to France. To make German revenge complete, the meeting of the German and French plenipotentiaries took place in Marshal Foch's private car, in which Foch laid down the armistice terms to Germany 22 years ago. . . .

A warm June sun beat down on the great elm and pine trees, and cast pleasant shadows on the wooded avenues as Hitler . . . appeared. . . .

Through my glasses I saw the Fuehrer stop, glance at the monument, observe the Reich flags with their big swastikas in the centre. Then he strode slowly towards us, towards the little clearing in the woods. I observed his face. It was grave, solemn, yet brimming with revenge. There was also in it, as in his springy step, a note of the triumphant conqueror, the defier of the world. There was something else, difficult to describe, in his expression, a sort of scornful, inner joy at being present at this great reversal of fate—a reversal he himself had wrought. . . .

I looked for the expression on Hitler's face. . . . I have seen that face many times at the great moments of his life. But today it is afire with scorn, anger, hate, revenge, triumph. . . . Suddenly, as though his face were not giving quite complete expression to his feelings, he throws his whole body into harmony with his mood. He swiftly snaps his hands on his hips, arches his shoulders, plants his feet wide apart. It is a magnificent gesture of defiance, of burning contempt for this place now and all that it has stood for in the 22 years since it witnessed the humbling of the German Empire. (June 21, 1940; from *Berlin Diary*, by William L. Shirer.)

989. Dunkirk, it can be seen in retrospect, was the end of the beginning for the British, but for the French it was the beginning of the end. (1969; from *The Collapse of the Third Republic*, by William L. Shirer.)

990. I lived and worked in France for a good many years, beginning in 1925 when the country was not only the greatest power on the continent of Europe but, to me at least, the most civilized and enlightened. In the ensuing years I watched with increasing apprehension the Third Republic go downhill, its strength gradually sapped by dissension and division, by an incomprehensible blindness in foreign, domestic, and military policy, by the ineptness of its leaders, the corruption of its press, and by a feeling of hopelessness, and cynicism . . . in its people. (From ibid.)

991. In Leningrad, [in 1982] I went out to see the cemetery where a half a million people are buried. A half million! And I knew from reading about the Nazi siege of Leningrad, about how a million civilians were killed, or starved to death, or froze to death while the city was surrounded by the Germans from 1941 to 1944. Not to mention a quarter of a million troops who also died. . . . There was the museum showing pictures of corpses stacked up during the winter.

I suddenly thought of a day in June in 1940 when I came to Paris as an American correspondent with the German Army.

Paris I love. It has always been a sort of hometown for me. . . . When I came into Paris, I went to see some French friends. Paris had been declared an open city [by the French; that meant that the city was unarmed and would not be defended against the Germans]. I asked them, "What has happened to this country?" . . .

I asked them, "Why didn't you fight for Paris?"

And they looked at me like I was a nut. And they said, "Listen, you barbarian. This is a city unique in the world, and some day the Germans will be gone. And our beautiful city will be here. Intact."

The Russian people never thought that way for one second. It never crossed their minds. Leningrad was also a very beautiful city. . . . I was surprised how beautiful. They have rebuilt the city.

But they would never have stopped and let the Germans in. There's a difference in culture and a difference in the character of people. (From an interview with William L. Shirer by Howard Langer in *Social Education*, October 1983.)

991a. One of the mistakes that we all made with Hitler was to underestimate him. He was an extremely intelligent man, a very shrewd judge of character, and of events, and a very clear thinker about certain historical forces. (Ibid.)

WILLIAM STEVENSON

(n.d.)

William Stevenson was a journalist for both Canadian and British newspapers. He also wrote for television and authored a number of books. A flier during the war, he was given a special assignment with British intelligence, where he met William Stephenson (q.v.). The intelligence official would become better known as Intrepid. Many years after the war, Stephenson gave Stevenson complete access to his files, resulting in the biography *A Man Called Intrepid.*

992. After one conference with the U.S. War Plans Division, he [Stephenson] heard [General George C.] Marshall, the Army Chief of Staff, tell a Senate committee there was "absolutely no intention that America should enter the war." Nonetheless, that day's secret discussions centered on a projected American army of five million troops within two years. Marshall dared not disclose this. Nor could the president announce a "Germany first" policy. (From *A Man Called Intrepid*, by William Stevenson.)

[This was ABC-1—the first American-British Conference—held in Washington in January 1941. Top military leaders of both countries met in secret to discuss the future of the war.]

A. J. P. TAYLOR

(1906–1983)

A Fellow at the Magdalen College at Oxford, Taylor ignited a firestorm of controversy upon publication of his revisionist history *The Origins of the Second World War.*

993. Hitler did not make plans—for world conquest or for anything else. He assumed that others would provide opportunities and that he would seize them. (From *The Origins of the Second World War*, by A. J. P. Taylor.)

994. The state of German armament in 1939 gives the decisive proof that Hitler was not contemplating general war, and probably not intending war at all. (Ibid.)

995. [Munich is] a story without heroes and perhaps even without villains. . . . What was done at Munich mattered less than the way in which it was done, and what was said about it afterwards counted for still more. (Ibid.)

996. The blame for war can be put on Hitler's Nihilism instead of on the faults and failures of European statesmen—faults and failures which their public shared. Human blunders, however, usually do more to shape history than human wickedness. (Ibid.)

MARCEL THIRY

(n.d.)

Thiry wrote about modern Belgian history.

997. The thought of the King [Leopold of Belgium] was that even after the violation of our territory we had no *allies* but merely *guarantors* [i.e., governments that guaranteed Belgium's territorial integrity]. This was much more than a nuance; with allies, you make war to the end, cost what it may; guarantors, on the other hand, have the unilateral obligation to aid you by all their means without you assuming any obligations toward them. (From *La Belgique pendant la guerre*, by Marcel Thiry.)

[In 1940, King Leopold surrendered to the German invaders so quickly that French and British troops were overrun before they could form new defense lines. Eventually it would lead to Leopold's abdication.]

JOHN TOLAND

(1912–)

Toland has written major works on both the European and Pacific wars.

998. Now [German airman Gerhard] Cordes could see more shapes. The din of motors and clank of treads was tremendous. The earth trembled. He picked up a *Panzerfaust* [bazooka]. From behind came an abrupt, heavy-throated chorus; 88-mm shells screeched overhead and smashed into the first tanks. Flames shot up, parts of metal and shell fragments rained over the foxholes. At least six tanks were on fire, but others kept coming on and on. In the reddish glare they stood out with clarity and were helpless before the withering fire of the big guns. Red Army infantrymen began erupting from the middle of this massive conflagration. There must have been 800, and they scrambled up the hill shouting, Cordes thought, like madmen.

The airmen fired rifles and burp guns, and hundreds of Russians toppled over. The rest came on, still yelling. More fell and at last, like a great wave that has shattered its strength against a jetty, the attackers fell back. (Describing events of April 1945, Seelow Heights, Germany, on the road to Berlin; from *The Last 100 Days*, by John Toland.)

H. R. TREVOR-ROPER

(n.d.)

H. R. Trevor-Roper, Regius Professor of modern history at Oxford, wrote numerous historical works, including *The Last Days of Hitler*. He also attacked the revisionist theories of A. J. P. Taylor (q.v.) on the origins of World War II.

999. But is this [A. J. P. Taylor's (q.v.)] general philosophy true? Do statesmen really never make history? Are they, all of them, always "too absorbed by events to follow a preconceived plan"? Was this true of Richelieu, of Bismarck, of Lenin? In particular, was it true of Hitler? Was Hitler really just a more violent Mr. Micawber sitting in Berlin or Berchtesgaden and waiting for something to turn up; something which, thanks to historic necessity, he could then turn to advantage? (From "A. J. P. Taylor, Hitler, and the War," in *Encounter*, July 1961, by H. R. Trevor-Roper.)

1000. In the first world war, Hitler was a soldier; and when it failed, he blamed the politicians for betraying the soldiers. In those days he could not praise the German General Staff highly enough. . . . In the second world war he was a politician; when it failed, he blamed the soldiers for betraying the politicians, and all for betraying him. (From *The Last Days of Hitler*, by H. R. Trevor-Roper.)

1001. In these pages, which describe and illustrate so many varieties of human corruption and human lunacy, one figure stands out in extraordinary isolation. Whatever the errors of judgment, and neutrality of conscience, which enabled him to acquire and retain the personal friendship of the most bloodthirsty tyrant in modern history, it is quite clear that in Hitler's court Albert Speer [q.v.] was morally and intellectually alone. . . . As an administrator, he was undoubtedly a genius. He regarded the rest of the court with dignified contempt. . . . Nevertheless, in a political sense, Speer is the real criminal of Nazi Germany; for he, more than any other, represented their fatal philosophy which has made havoc of Germany and nearly shipwrecked the world. For ten years he sat at the very center of political power; his keen intelligence diagnosed the nature, and observed the mutations, of Nazi government and policy; he saw and despised the personalities around him; he heard their outrageous orders and understood their fantastic ambitions; but he did nothing. (Ibid.)

BARBARA W. TUCHMAN
(1912–1989)

Historian Tuchman won two Pulitzer Prizes for her historical works. The first was for *The Guns of August* (about World War I) and the second for *Stilwell and the American Experience in China: 1911–45*. She also wrote *The March of Folly*, an examination of official miscalculation—from the Trojan Horse to Vietnam.

1002. The United States Army . . . in September 1939 [when Hitler invaded Poland and set off World War II] ranked, with Reserves, 19th among the world's armed forces, after Portugal but ahead of Bulgaria. In percent of population under arms, it ranked 45th. The active Army numbered 174,000 men, less than two-thirds the peacetime strength authorized by Act of Congress in 1920. (Statistics cited in *Stilwell and the American Experience in China: 1911–45*, by Barbara W. Tuchman.)

1003. He [Roosevelt] was good-humored, intuitive, experimental, calculating, changeable, devious, compromising and given to leaps of thought without discernible coherence. He usually had several lines out and his motives were often mixed. The coherence that guided him, in a phrase used by his daughter, was "his sense of the future." . . . His dominant characteristic was confidence—over-confidence as some thought—perhaps the result of his own conquest of paralysis which may have left him with a sense that there was no problem that could not be solved. (Ibid.)

1004. The implication of his [Stilwell's (q.v.)] report [following the initial humiliating defeat in Burma] was that the British performance allowed only one interpretation: that they had never intended from the beginning to hold Burma and had deliberately scuttled it in order to weaken China. What is true in history is often less important than what people believe to be true. (Ibid.)

ALEXANDER WERTH

(1901–1969)

Werth has written the authoritative account of the Soviet Union during the war.

1005. The Russian command knew that by winning the battle of Kursk [in the summer of 1943] Russia had, in effect, won the war. (From *Russia at War*, by Alexander Werth.)

11

Influential Personalities

MADAME CHIANG KAI-SHEK

(1900–)

Madame Chiang Kai-shek was the wife of General Chiang Kai-shek (q.v.), leader of China during the war with Japan. Born Mei-Ling Soong, she was educated in the United States. She took an active part in running the affairs of China, along with her husband. Her sisters married other important Chinese political figures, including Sun Yat-sen.

1006. The prevailing opinion seems to consider the defeat of the Japanese as of relative unimportance and that Hitler is our first concern. This is not borne out by actual facts, nor is it to the interests of the United Nations as a whole to allow Japan to continue, not only as a vital potential threat but as a waiting sword of Damocles, ready to descend at a moment's notice. Let us not forget that Japan in her occupied areas today has greater resources at her command than Germany.

Let us not forget that the longer Japan is left in undisputed possession of these resources, the stronger she must become. Each passing day takes more toll in lives of both Americans and Chinese. (Address to Congress, February 18, 1943.)

JOHN FOSTER DULLES

(1888–1959)

Dulles was an international lawyer before the war, serving at the Paris Peace Conference of 1919, the Reparations Commission, and the Berlin Debt Conference. Dulles was a delegate to the San Francisco Conference of 1945, which created the United Nations. After the war, he became Secretary of State in the Eisenhower cabinet. His brother, Allen Dulles (q.v.), headed the Office of Strategic Services (q.v.) in Switzerland during the war.

1007. These dynamic peoples [the Germans, the Japanese, and the Italians] [were] determined to mold their states into a form which would permit them to take their destiny into their own hands and to attain that enlarged status which, under a liberal and peaceful form of government, had been denied them. (Early 1939; quoted in *Gentleman Spy: The Life of Allen Dulles*, by Peter Grose.)

1008. I see, neither in the underlying causes of the war, nor in its long-range objectives, any reason for the United States to become a participant. [If America entered the war it would be] as is the moth into the flame. (Speech, October 1939; cited in *John Foster Dulles: The Road to Power*, by Ronald W. Pruessen.)

1009. INDIRECT DISCOURSE: Dulles applauded the value of two government leaders [Roosevelt and Churchill] offering "their conception of a new world order," but was more than skeptical about the long-range value of this specific effort. He wondered if the [Atlantic] Charter [q.v.] was anything more than a string of airy words. No real actions had been proposed to vivify recommendations concerning equal trade privileges, equal access to raw materials or disarmament. "Unless we propose concrete measures," he insisted, "statements of good intentions . . . will be looked upon with grave and warranted skepticism. . . ." He believed that there ran through the Charter "a single, unifying conception, namely, that the post-war world should reproduce and stabilize the political organization of the pre-war world." (Statement on the Atlantic Charter, ca. August 1941; Ibid.)

QUEEN ELIZABETH

(1900–)

Queen Elizabeth was the wife of King George VI [q.v.] and mother of the then-Princess Elizabeth and Princess Margaret Rose. Princess Elizabeth would become Queen Elizabeth II upon the death of King George VI.

1010. The children will not leave unless I do. I shall not leave unless their father does, and the King will not leave the country in any circumstances whatsoever. (London, 1940.)

[Following a bombing attack on England that damaged Buckingham Palace, the queen was asked by a reporter if the princesses would be sent to Canada for their safety. This was her response.]

WILLIAM JOYCE

(1908–1946)

As Lord Haw-Haw, Joyce broadcast propaganda from Germany throughout the war. He had been a member of the British Union of Fascists before the war. Fearing internment on the impending outbreak of war, he fled Britain for Germany late in August 1939. He found work in Berlin with Goebbels's (q.v.) Propaganda Ministry. Through his broadcasts, Joyce tried to subvert the morale of British soldiers and civilians. He was tried for treason after the war, found guilty, and hanged.

1011. I, the undersigned, William Joyce, at present residing at 38a Eardley Crescent, S.W.5, London, hereby make application for the renewal of British passport No. 125943 issued me at London on the 6th July, 1933, for a further period of one year. I declare that I am a British subject by birth and I have not lost that national status, and that the whole of the particulars given by me in respect of this application are true. (Application for passport renewal, August 24, 1939; cited in *Lord Haw-Haw: William Joyce, the Full Story*, by J. A. Cole.)

[Brought to trial for treason after the war, Joyce argued that he had actually been born an American and that he had acquired German citizenship during the war. Therefore, he said, he could not be guilty of treason against the British crown. The court ruled that the above passport renewal application demonstrated his allegiance to the crown during its period of validity. It turned out to be Joyce's own death warrant.]

1012. How modest, how harmless does Germany's request for the return of Danzig seem in contrast to the immense acquisitions of the Soviet Union and the further ambitions of the Kremlin. Stalin is not content with Poland, Finland, the Baltic States, Rumania, Bulgaria, Hungary and Eastern Slovakia. He wants the whole of Central Europe, with Norway, Turkey and Persia thrown in. And if these territories fall to him, his lust for aggrandizement will only be stimulated still further. . . .

Britain's victories are barren. They leave her poor and they leave her people hungry. They leave her bereft of the markets and the wealth that she possessed six years ago. But above all, they leave her with an immensely greater problem than she had then. We are nearing the end of one phase in Europe's history, but the next will be no happier. It will be grimmer, harder and perhaps bloodier. And now I ask you earnestly, can Britain survive? I am profoundly convinced that without German help she cannot. . . .

Heil Hitler and farewell! (Final broadcast, April 30, 1945; Ibid.)

CHARLES A. LINDBERGH, JR.

(1902–1974)

An aviation hero of the 1920s, Lindbergh was the first pilot to fly solo across the Atlantic. In the 1930s, he made several trips to Nazi Germany to report on German air power. This was done at the specific request of the U.S. military attaché in Berlin. When war broke out in Europe, Lindbergh became a member of the America First Committee (q.v.), opposing U.S. involvement. After Pearl Harbor, he took part in Pacific missions as a civilian observer.

1013. It would be difficult to paint a more depressing picture. . . . [I do] not believe there will be a general European war in 1938, but war in 1939 seems probable. (Letter to Emory S. Land, later shared with President Roosevelt, September 12, 1938; cited in *Roosevelt & the Isolationists*, by Wayne S. Cole.)

1014. The German air fleet is more supreme in air than the British fleet at sea. (Ibid.)

1015. [Germany intends] to extend her influence still further to the east within the next year. . . . There would be nothing gained by a military attempt on the part of France and England to stop the German movement toward the east. The opportunity to do this was lost several years ago when German policies went unopposed. (Ibid.)

1016. This is no longer a question to be decided by our traditional ideas of what is legally right or wrong. It is now a question of the survival of European nations and races. (Ibid.)

JOE LOUIS
(1914–1981)

Joe Louis, the boxing champion, got first American licks at the Germans by knocking out Max Schmeling in the first round. Nazi propagandists had taken the position that an African American could not stand up against a German superman. Louis later served in the U.S. Army during the war.

1017. We are on God's side.

[In answer to a reporter's question, "Is God on our side?"]

MARGARET MEAD
(1901–1978)

American anthropologist Mead achieved fame by studying the cultures of Samoa and New Guinea in the years between the two world wars. In 1942, she examined the prospects of the future postwar world.

1018. If we are to draw upon the dynamics of American culture to fight the war on an all-out basis because we believe in the possibilities of a post-war world which is worth fighting for, what must we do? If that post-war world is to be built in accordance with the dictates of democracy, then we cannot make a finished blueprint into which we will force other people to fit. . . .

If the post-war world is to catch our American imaginations, then we must see it in American terms and must see our role in that building. And what are American terms? Briefly, we must see the emerging world as a world of plenty, of real expansion, of room for everybody to make a contribution and succeed. We must see a world in which every human being has a right to develop what he has in him—a right to succeed, a right to the rewards of success. We must see a world built with a moral purpose, built because we think that we are right in so building. Above all, we must see ourselves tackling a job which we believe can be done practically, like any other big job. We must be confident that if we put our minds to it, if we invoke every bit of science and every bit of inventiveness that is in us, we, the people of the world of 1942, can find the answers. We must believe that we can make war and tariff walls and passports, uneven distribution of the world's goods, and restriction of individuals to the special human inventions of his own society—to one language, one art style, one form of personal relations—as out of date as the cannibal feast, the barter market, the trial by fire, and the sign language of the Plains Indians. (From *And Keep Your Powder Dry: An Anthropologist Looks at America*, by Margaret Mead.)

EZRA POUND
(1885–1972)

An American poet, Pound broadcast Fascist propaganda during the war. When the war ended, he was brought up on charges of treason, but he was found to be insane. He spent a dozen years confined to St. Elizabeth's Hospital in Washington, D.C. In 1958 he was released, and he went back to Italy. Segments from some of his broadcasts follow.

1019. The kike and the unmitigated evil that has been centered in London since the British government set on the Red Indians to murder the American frontier settlers, has herded the Slavs, the Mongols, the Tartar openly against Germany and Poland and Finland. And secretly against all that is decent in America, against the total American heritage. This is my war all right. I've been in it for twenty years—my granddad was in it before me. (Radio broadcast, Rome, Italy, May 5, 1942; cited in *The Case of Ezra Pound*, by Charles Norman.)

1020. The next peace will not be based on international lending. Get that for one. The next peace will not be based on international lending, and England certainly will have nothing whatever to say about what its terms are. Neither, I think, will simple-hearted Joe Stalin, not wholly trusted by the kikery which is his master. (May 10, 1942; Ibid.)

1021. I am not arguing, I am just telling you, one of these days you will have to start thinking about the problem of race, breed, preservation. (July 2, 1942; Ibid.)

1022. What are you doing in the war at all? What are you doing in Africa? Who amongst you has the nerve or the sense to do something that would conduce to getting you out of it before you are mortgaged up to the neck and over it? Every day of war is a dead day as well as a death day. More death, more future servitude, less and less of American liberty of any variety. (May 4, 1943; Ibid.)

ELEANOR ROOSEVELT

(1884–1962)

Wife of the wartime president, Eleanor Roosevelt made goodwill visits to Britain, Australia, New Zealand, and the South Pacific, as well as to American military bases in the United States. After her husband's death, President Truman (q.v.) appointed her as a representative to the United Nations. There she helped draft the Universal Declaration of Human Rights.

1023. Tonight we saw the Joe Davies film "Mission to Moscow." It is propaganda but I'm sure Davies told the truth as he saw it but I can't quite believe the trials were so simple & above board. (Letter to Joseph P. Lash, May 1943; cited in *Love, Eleanor: Eleanor Roosevelt and Her Friends*, by Joseph P. Lash.)

1024. Just as the Marines were ready to leave Guadalcanal, an officer found a private looking very depressed, and he asked, "What's the matter with you?"

And the Marine said, "I can't go home yet. I haven't shot a Jap." And the officer said, "I'll tell you what to do. You go up on that ridge there, and you shout, 'To hell with Hirohito [q.v.]!' A Jap will jump out and you can shoot him."

A little while later, the Marine was still looking gloomy, and the officer said, "Did you do what I told you to do?"

And the private said, "Yes. I went up there, and I yelled 'To hell with Hirohito!' and a Jap jumped out, just as you said, and he yelled, 'To hell with Roosevelt!'—and I couldn't shoot a fellow Republican!" (Speech, New Zealand, August 1943.)

[Recounting a story she had heard in her travels in the South Pacific.]

1025. I went to a meeting last night of the Washington group (white & colored) that are trying to work out better race relations & heard Pauline Redmond explain how hard it was to reassure the young colored people about the future & keep them steady & I must say I worry about the future. . . . It really is discouraging because the Christian spirit seems so unChristlike! (Letter to Joseph P. Lash, January 16, 1944; cited in *Love, Eleanor: Eleanor Roosevelt and Her Friends*, by Joseph P. Lash.)

1026. The Dewey-Bricker [Republican presidential] ticket is not going to be a pushover. It is part of the fight of the future between power for big moneyed interests & govt. control & more interest on the part of the people in their govt. (Letter to Joseph P. Lash, July 9, 1944; Ibid.)

1027. The president slept away this afternoon. He did his job to the end as he would want you to do. Love, Mother. (Cable to their four sons on the death of the president, April 12, 1945.)

ALEXANDER P. de SEVERSKY
(1894–1974)

A bomber pilot for Imperial Russia in World War I, Seversky immigrated to the United States when the war ended. He became a test pilot for the Army Air Corps. Later he founded his own aircraft company, designing and producing bombsights and war planes, including the P-47 Thunderbolt. In 1942 he wrote *Victory through Air Power*, which he dedicated to the memory of his former boss Billy Mitchell, the air power pioneer.

1028. Here . . . are the most significant lessons of modern air power:

1. No land or sea operations are possible without first assuming control of the air above. . . .

2. Navies have lost their function of strategic offensive. . . . The days when battle fleets steamed boldly within striking distance of enemy shores and proceeded to pound them into submission are now relegated to history. Today these

fleets can approach only under the shield of a powerful umbrella of land-based air power. . . .

3. The blockade of an enemy nation has become a function of air power. . . .

4. Only air power can defeat air power. . . .

5. Land-based aviation is always superior to ship-borne aviation. . . .

6. The striking radius of air power must be equal to the maximum dimensions of the theater of operations. . . .

7. In aerial warfare the factor of quality is relatively more decisive than the factor of quantity. . . .

8. Aircraft types must be specialized to fit not only the general strategy but the tactical problems of a specific campaign. . . .

9. Destruction of enemy morale from the air can be accomplished only by precision bombing. . . . As a matter of plain fact, we have neither air power nor airmen, but only flying soldiers and flying sailors who do not even speak the same military language. . . .

10. The principle of unity of command, long recognized on land and on sea, applies with no less force to the air. . . .

11. Air power must have its own transport. (From *Victory through Air Power*, by Alexander P. de Seversky.)

NORMAN THOMAS
(1884–1968)

Head of the American Socialist Party, Thomas ran several times, unsuccessfully, for president.

1029. I insist that if once we let ourselves be plunged into this war, our liberties will be gone. The same oceans which are so mighty a barrier for our own defense will prove an insuperable obstacle to our conquest of distant continents by any price we can afford to pay. The probable cost of this war in the lives of our sons staggers the imagination. Its cost in money means bankruptcy, something close to a subsistence level of life during the war, and a post-war economic crisis besides which 1932 will be remembered as a year of prosperity. (Broadcast, New York City, June 29, 1941.)

WENDELL L. WILLKIE

(1892–1944)

The Republican candidate for president in 1940, Willkie ran against Franklin Roosevelt, who was trying for an unprecedented third term. After the election, Willkie was sent to England by Roosevelt to emphasize American support for that nation that was facing Hitler alone. In 1942, Willkie visited the Soviet Union, China, and the Middle East. His book about that trip, *One World*, emphasized the need for cooperation in the coming postwar world.

1030. It has been suggested that in order to present a united front to a threatening world, the minority should now surrender its convictions and join the majority. This would mean that in the United States of America there would be only one dominant party—only one economic philosophy—only one political philosophy of life. This is a totalitarian idea—it is a slave idea—it must be rejected utterly. (Radio address, November 11, 1940.)

[Delivered a week after the 1940 presidential election.]

1031. Our American unity cannot be made with words or with gestures. It must be forged between the ideas of the opposition and the practices and the policies of the administration. Ours is a government of principles and not one merely of men. Any member of the minority party, though willing to die for his country, still retains the right to criticize the policies of the government. This right is imbedded in our constitutional system. (Ibid.)

1032. We, who stand ready to serve our country behind our Commander in Chief, nevertheless retain the right, and I will say the duty, to debate the course of our government. Ours is a two-party system. Should we ever permit one party to dominate our lives entirely, democracy could collapse and we would have dictatorship. (Ibid.)

1033. Therefore, to you who have so sincerely given yourselves to this cause, which you chose me to lead, I say, "Your function during the next four years is that of the loyal opposition." (Ibid.)

1034. I have traveled through 15 countries. I have seen kingdoms, soviets, republics, mandated areas, colonies, and dependencies. I have seen an almost bewildering variety of ways of living and ways of ruling and of being ruled. But I have found certain things common to all the countries I have visited and to all the ordinary people in those countries with which I have talked:

They all want a chance at the end of the war to live in liberty and independence.

They all doubt, in varying degree, the readiness of the leading democracies of the world, to stand up and be counted for freedom for others after the war is over. This doubt kills their enthusiastic participation on our side.

Now, without the real support of these common people, the winning of the war will be enormously difficult. The winning of the peace will be nearly impossible. This war is not a simple, technical problem for task forces. It is also a war for men's minds. We must organize on our side not simply the sympathies but the active, aggressive, offensive spirit of nearly three-fourths of the people of the world who live in South America, Africa, eastern Europe, and Asia. We have not done this, and at present are not doing this. We have got to do it. (Statement to Chinese and Foreign Press, Chungking, China, October 7, 1942; cited in *One World*, by Wendell L. Willkie.)

1035. A war won without a purpose is a war won without victory. . . .

[Willkie then contrasted the American Revolution to the First World War.] The Revolution had been a great victory because our purpose was so clear, so lofty, and so well defined.

Unhappily this cannot be said of the war of 1914–18. . . . While we were engaged in it, we thought, or said, that we were fighting for a high purpose. . . . We were fighting to make the world safe for democracy—to make it safe, not just with a slogan, but by accepting a set of principles known as the Fourteen Points, and by setting up . . . the League of Nations. . . . But when the time came to execute it in a peace treaty, a fatal flaw was discovered. We found that . . . some of [our allies] . . . were more intent . . . upon pursuing traditional power diplomacy, than upon opening up the new vista that Mr. [Woodrow] Wilson had sought to define. . . . The net result was the abandonment of most of the purposes for which the war had supposedly been fought. Because those purposes were abandoned, that war was denounced by our generation as an enormous and futile slaughter. Millions had lost their lives. But no new idea, no new goal, rose from the ashes of their sacrifice. (From *One World*, by Wendell L. Willkie.)

1036. This is a war of liberation. . . . Are we yet agreed that . . . our common job of liberation includes giving to *all* peoples freedom to govern themselves as soon as they are able, and the economic freedom on which all lasting self-government inevitably rests?

It is these two aspects of freedom, I believe, which form the touchstone of our good faith in this war. I believe we must include them both in our idea of the freedom we are fighting for. Otherwise, I am certain we shall not win the peace, and I am not sure we can win the war. (Ibid.)

ROBERT E. WOOD

(n.d.)

Wood, president of Sears, Roebuck, founded the America First Committee (q.v.) in 1940 to keep the United States out of the war.

1037. [President Roosevelt is] not asking for a blank check, he wants a blank check book with the power to write away our man power, our laws and our liberties. (Response to Roosevelt's call for Lend-Lease [q.v.] aid to Britain, January 11, 1941.)

12

Civilians

JOHN BAKER

(n.d.)

Baker was seven years old when the war broke out in Europe.

1038. They issued gas masks [in England]. They were convinced the Germans would try gas attacks. Never happened. At school we all lined up in the playground with these rubber masks, like something you go snorkeling with. I don't think they would ever have worked. We make faces with 'em. When you breathed into 'em, they made funny noises, like a fart. We'd do that a lot, being small, laughing boys. (From *The Good War*, by Studs Terkel.)

EVA BRAUN

(1912–1945)

Braun was Hitler's mistress. She married him in his Berlin bunker in the last days of the war. There, as Russian soldiers closed in, they committed suicide. As Hitler had ordered, their bodies were cremated.

1039. Poor, poor Adolf, deserted by everyone, betrayed by all. Better that ten thousand others die than that he be lost to Germany. (April 29, 1945; from documents submitted at Nuremberg; cited in *The Rise and Fall of the Third Reich*, by William L. Shirer.)

[Following word that Goering (q.v.) had tried to take over leadership and that Himmler (q.v.) was trying to negotiate peace through Sweden.]

EMMA CALP

(n.d.)

Emma Calp was a teenager working as a secretary in the War Department when she met her sailor husband-to-be on a blind date.

1040. My Darling Jimmie,

They say that absence makes the heart grow fonder but not so in my case because, Jimmie, I couldn't possibly think any more of you than I do now. I never realized it was possible to love any one person so very much, but I know now. I do miss you more and more all of the time, but every day away from you just makes the day closer when we'll be able to be together again. That's what I keep telling myself. It is a little consolation but that still doesn't keep me from missing you. I read your letters over, eventually I think I'll know them by heart. . . .

For now, my sweet, I must say good-bye. . . .

Yours forever. (Letter to James Calp, Washington, D.C., August 24, 1943; cited in *Since You Went Away*, edited by Judy Barrett Litoff and David C. Smith.)

MRS. B. D. COOKSEY

(n.d.)

Mrs. B. D. Cooksey wrote a letter to a top American general after she was informed that her son had died in a Japanese prison camp.

1041. My Dear General MacArthur,

You are such a busy man and have so many perplexing problems, but I have arisen every morning, for three weeks, with such increasing desire to write you, that I am, at last, doing it.

My only son, Buford Cooksey, who with the 200th C.A. (A.A.) formerly of Ft. Stotsenburg and who was later taken prisoner, when Bataan fell—died in prison in Osaka, Japan on the 11th of June.

The questions I want to ask you—did those boys ever know it was impossible to get help to them—or did they harbor bitterness all of that seeming eternity—thinking their country figured the risk was too great—while Buford was drafted into the Army (he went in first draft) he was a very Patriotic boy.

Oh, this Bataan situation is almost more than we can stand. Please disregard this last—for we are still America's mothers.

Most Prayerfully

I wait an answer, if you ever have time. (Letter to General MacArthur, Seagraves, Texas, July 21, 1943; cited in *Since You Went Away*, edited by Judy Barrett Litoff and David C. Smith.)

HIROSAWA EI

(n.d.)

Hirosawa Ei, a prominent screenwriter, tells what it was like to make movies in Japan during the war.

1042. The content of movies was controlled by the government. Examining human character or entertaining audiences were secondary issues. The primary purpose of movies were the "theses" given by the state.

At the scenario stage, movies were censored—and the completed movies were censored again. The people who did this were high-ranking government officials. . . . They said whatever they thought, and what they said became orders. "Add this! Take out that!" . . . Even comedies had to include slogans supporting the war effort—things like "Be frugal to carry out the war properly." Movies thus became incoherent. (Cited in *Japan at War*, edited by Haruko Taya Cook and Theodore F. Cook.)

ANNE FRANK

(1929–1945)

The most famous diarist of the war, Anne Frank was born in Germany. Her Jewish family fled to Holland after Hitler came to power. When Hitler invaded Holland, the Frank family hid in the upper floor of a warehouse in Amsterdam. The Franks shared the space with other Jews. Anne kept a diary during the period of hiding. Betrayed by informers, those in hiding were sent to concentration camps. Anne died at Bergen-Belsen. Otto Frank, Anne's father, survived and found the diary after the war.

1043. It's an odd idea for someone like me to keep a diary; not only because I have never done so before, but because it seems to me that neither I—nor for that matter anyone else—will be interested in the unbosoming of a 13-year-old schoolgirl. Still, what does that matter? I want to write, but more than that, I want to bring out all kinds of things that lie buried deep in my heart. (Saturday, June 20, 1942; from *Anne Frank: The Diary of a Young Girl*, by Anne Frank.)

1044. It's really a wonder that I haven't dropped all my ideals, because they seem so absurd and impossible to carry out. Yet I keep them, because in spite of everything I still believe that people are really good at heart. (Saturday, July 15, 1944; Ibid.)

1045. I simply can't build up my hopes on a foundation consisting of confusion, misery, and death. I see the world gradually being turned into a wilderness, I hear the ever approaching thunder, which will destroy us too, I can feel the sufferings of millions and yet, I look up into the heavens, I think that it will all come right, that this cruelty too will end, and that peace and tranquility will return again. (Ibid.)

ARVID FREDBORG

(n.d.)

Fredborg was a Swedish civilian visiting Germany during the war.

1046. I was on my way to the police station . . . to report my departure [back to Sweden] when I noticed *die grune Minna*—the feared Black Maria, which is green in Berlin—standing outside. Suddenly a very old woman was brought out of the station into the carriage. Her face was numb with fright. As the car started an elderly German woman rushed up to it and tried to open the door, but was hustled off. All the while she was shouting hysterically, "But she is no Jewess—I've known her for 30 years, and I know that she is no Jewess." The car disappeared, and finally she went in to the officer I was on my way to see and beseeched him to save her friend, with whom she had been living for half a lifetime. . . . The policeman squirmed, embarrassed, and tried to calm her down by telling her that nothing would happen to her departed friend. But the woman cried, "I know what they do with the Jews." . . . When the policeman discovered me, whom he recognized as a foreigner, he took her by the arm and led her out, telling her that she was lucky to have been spared from accompanying her friend. We stood there silent, the policeman and I, while he noted down my departure. When I was about to leave he said half to himself: "We can't help it, you know." (Describing events of 1943, Berlin; from *Behind the Steel Wall*, by Arvid Fredborg.)

MAGDA GOEBBELS

(n.d.)

Magda Goebbels was the wife of Joseph Goebbels (q.v.), Nazi Minister of Propaganda. In Hitler's Berlin bunker the couple committed suicide and had their six children killed just before the fall of the city.

1047. The world which will succeed the Fuehrer and National-Socialism is not worth living in and for this reason I have brought the children here [to Hitler's bunker] too. They are too good for the life that will come after us and a gracious God will understand me if I myself give them release from it. You will go on living and I have one simple request to make of you: never forget that you are a German, never do anything dishonorable and ensure that by your life our death is not in vain. . . .

We have only one aim in life now—to remain loyal to the Fuehrer unto death; that we should be able to end our life together with him is a gift of fate for which we would never have dared hope.

Harald, my dear—I give you the best that life has taught me: be true—true to yourself, true to mankind, true to your country—in every respect whatsoever. (Letter to Harald Quandt, her son, April 28, 1945.)

MAX VON DER GRUN

(1926–)

Grun was thirteen years old when his family sat around the radio to hear Hitler's speech to the Reichstag. The Fuehrer was announcing the invasion of Poland.

1048. No one cheered at the end of his speech, not even my aunt who had always cheered for Hitler; no one cried "Heil!" or turned somersaults with joy. Perturbation was written on everyone's face. No one spoke, and even the neighbors who had come to listen with us said nothing. (Recalling events of September 1, 1939; from *Howl Like the Wolves: Growing Up in Nazi Germany*, by Max von der Grun.)

MARIA ROSA HENSON

(1928–1997)

As a fifteen-year-old Philippine girl during the war, Mrs. Henson was forced into a Japanese military brothel. She was one of the Japanese army's "Comfort Women." In 1996 she published *Comfort Woman: Slave of Destiny*, which told of her brutal treatment. She was deeply involved in a class action suit to force the Japanese government to take responsibility and pay damages to the victims. The Japanese government did issue an apology, and Mrs. Henson was compensated by a special fund created in Japan.

1049. My work began, and I lay down as one by one the soldiers raped me. Every day, anywhere from 12 to over 20 soldiers assaulted me. There were times when there were as many as 30. They came to the garrison in truckloads.

I lay on the bed with my knees up and my feet on the mat, as if I were giving birth. Whenever the soldiers did not feel satisfied they vented their anger on me. When the soldiers raped me, I felt like a pig. I was angry all the time. (From *Comfort Woman: Slave of Destiny*, by Maria Rosa Henson.)

1050. I learned to remember everything, to remember always, so that I will not go mad.

I am telling my story so that they [the Japanese] will feel humiliated. It is true: I am an avenger of the dead. (Interview with Japanese lawyers, November 1996; cited in the *New York Times*, August 27, 1997.)

JEANNE KAHN

(n.d.)

Jeanne Kahn was a French Christian married to a Jewish member of the French Resistance. During the war, she sought a baptismal certificate for herself from a Catholic priest.

1051. Please, Father, I promise when the war is over I'll take it as a sign of God. I'll come back. I'll take all the courses you want me to. But now there is no time. . . . My husband's been arrested. I must go back to Lyon to figure out what they've done with him. I'm in danger myself, Father, in great danger. If they arrest me, I will be as the wife of a Jew. They'll deport me, and I may never come back. I have two young daughters, Father. You're my only hope. (Spoken to the priest at St. Paul's parish, Paris, September 1943; quoted in *Why My Father Died*, by Annette Kahn.)

[The priest refused, saying that the Church could not be involved in a lie.]

URSULA VON KARDORFF

(n.d.)

Ursula von Kardorff was a young German journalist who worked in Berlin during the war. An anti-Nazi, she knew many of the conspirators who tried to kill Hitler and overthrow the Nazis in July 1944.

1052. Bussy, the compositor, told me that in his neighborhood, around the Rosenthalerplatz, working-class women had gathered and protested noisily against the deportation of the Jews. Armed SS [Schutzstaffel] men with fixed bayonets and steel helmets were dragging miserable figures out of the houses. Old women, children and terrified men were loaded into trucks and driven away. The crowd shouted, "Why don't you leave the old women alone? Why don't you go out to the front, where you belong?" In the end a fresh detachment of SS appeared and dispersed the crowd. (Diary excerpt, March 3, 1943; from *Diary of a Nightmare: Berlin 1942–1945*, by Ursula von Kardorff.)

1053. The newspapers give the first full report of the plot [to assassinate Hitler]. Miserable text and photographs which make one weep. Witzleben, his face haggard and terribly sad, without tie or braces [suspenders], in the ridiculous position of a man who has to hold up his trousers. Behind him Stieff. A new list of names has been published, including Fritzi Schulenburg and Peter York. . . . Fritzi facing the People's Court—the thought of it chokes me. What will happen to his wife? Who will explain to the children that their father was not a traitor? (Diary excerpt, August 12, 1944; Ibid.)

1054. Seven thousand aircraft over Germany today, evidently attacking the railway system. There is no railway traffic here. The line is said to have been wrecked all the way from here to Berlin. Is this the beginning of the end? (Diary excerpt, February 22, 1945; Ibid.)

1055. A dreadful scene of destruction, with beings from another world wandering along the ruins. Soldiers, homeward bound, in tattered, padded tunics, covered with sores, staggering along on home-made crutches. Just living corpses. We gave them the last of our bread. (Diary excerpt, September 17, 1945; Ibid.)

MADAM X

(1927–)

Madam X name is a pseudonym for a Chinese girl, then living in British Malaya, who was forced into prostitution by the Japanese military. Many years after the war, she described her life as a "Comfort Woman."

1056. I was forced to have sex with ten to twenty men a day. As a result I was continuously raw. Red raw. Sex was excruciating. Oh, you have no idea how painful it was! You couldn't imagine it! But I had to be gentle and serve every soldier well. If I didn't perform well, I would get beaten. Some of the men would be drunk and beat me anyway. One man, although drunk, stayed inside me his whole allotted hour. It was unbearable—but I had to bear it. (Quoted in *The Comfort Women*, by George Hicks.)

HADASSAH ROSENSAFT

(1912–1997)

A dental surgeon before the war, Rosensaft practiced in Poland. In 1943 she was sent to Auschwitz, where she worked in the infirmary. She survived the war and gave vivid testimony about her experiences in the concentration camps.

1057. [When a young woman inmate got out of the barracks late, Dr. Josef Mengele] ordered her to come forward. He knocked her down with his booted foot. [He placed his foot on her chest.] Humming an aria from *Madame Butterfly*, he kept his foot there until the woman was dead. (Recalling events of 1943, testifying before a U.S. Senate subcommittee, 1985; cited in the *New York Times*, October 8, 1997.)

EDUARD SCHULTE

(n.d.)

Schulte was a German businessman who was the source of the original report to the World Jewish Congress—who passed the information along to a U.S. consulate official in Switzerland—that Hitler was planning to kill all the Jews in Europe. At the request of Allen Dulles (q.v.), head of the Office of Strategic Services (q.v.) in Switzerland, Schulte submitted a plan for German economic recovery after the war.

1058. INDIRECT DISCOURSE: Schulte argued for the promotion of German agriculture to make the economy less dependent on industrial exports. Urban dwellers, he argued, should be encouraged to leave the crowded cities and live on independent farms. Small craft shops should be subsidized to preserve a middle class independent of big business. (Economic plan for postwar Germany, submitted to Allen Dulles [q.v.], 1943; cited in *Gentleman Spy: The Life of Allen Dulles*, by Peter Grose.)

KAY SUMMERSBY

(1908–1975)

Summersby was the civilian driver for General Eisenhower during the war. Summersby was born Kathleen McCarthy Morrogh in County Cork, Ireland. Before the war broke out, she went through a failed marriage and a modeling career. She joined Britain's Motor Transport Corps and drove an ambulance during the London blitz. When the United States entered the war, she became Eisenhower's driver and later his secretary. Summersby became an officer in the American Women's Army Corps. After the war there were reports that she had been Eisenhower's lover, that he had wanted to divorce his wife and marry her, and that General Marshall had threatened to relieve Eisenhower of his command if he did so.

1059. I saw nothing special or miraculous about the ticket. It merely noted that I, as a civilian [British] Army driver, was to pick up a passenger at Paddington Station. He was listed as a Major General Eisenhower.

I had never heard of the general. And, quite frankly, I was doubly disappointed in the assignment.

Half of the disappointment was natural. Five of us drivers had waited around American Army headquarters three days, to pick up a packet of Very Important Persons due in from the United States via Scotland. The first two mornings we staggered down to the motor pool at 5:30 A.M. And we stayed there until dark both times, only to be finally advised that the weather still held all London-bound planes at Prestwick Airport.

This morning it looked as though the Brass had abandoned their original plans. They were coming on down to London by train. Just when, no one knew. . . .

The other half of my disappointment came from snobbery. An army driver's prestige is based solely on the rank of the uniform in the back seat. So I had hoped to get General George Marshall or General "Hap" Arnold [q.v.]. Both were in this group, we knew. Both were known to all of us by name and reputation; either would be a bright feather in a driver's cap.

But Sheila and Betty had them. . . . As an American (married to an English officer from Sandhurst), she [Sheila] was my only hope.

"Eisenhower?" Sheila thought a moment. "Eisenhower? Never heard of him." (Recalling events of May 1942; from *Eisenhower Was My Boss*, by Kay Summersby.)

DR. TSUNO

(?–1945)

Dr. Tsuno was dean of the Nagasaki University Medical School.

1060. This new kind of bomb [dropped on Hiroshima] may be dropped on Nagasaki, and I feel sure it won't be enough just to take refuge in air raid shelters when you hear enemy planes approaching. (Emergency faculty meeting, Nagasaki University Medical School, Nagasaki, Japan, August 8, 1945; quoted in *Children of the Atomic Bomb*, by James N. Yamazaki with Louis B. Fleming.)

[The second atomic bomb would be dropped on Nagasaki the following day. Many faculty members would be killed, including Dr. Tsuno, who lived for thirteen days after the blast.]

1061. It's as if a huge thunderbolt struck the city [of Hiroshima] and ignited a firestorm that consumed the city. (Ibid.)

MARIE VASSILTCHIKOV

(1917–1978)

Born of Russian royalty in St. Petersburg, Vassiltchikov fled with her parents following the Russian Revolution. They lived, at various times, in Germany, France, and Lithuania. When the war broke out she was in Germany. She obtained a job as a translator in the Foreign Ministry Information Department.

1062. Mamma accompanied me by car to the station in Marienbad. It was snowing hard. The train was, as usual, late. We sat for an hour in the freezing station. Just as it was pulling in, the sirens sounded. I had hoped that by taking a late train I would avoid the now almost nightly raid and arrive in Berlin early in the morning. The lights were out and I climbed into the wrong carriage; it was full of sleeping soldiers returning from the Balkans in various states of disarray, most of them with beards several weeks old. They immediately started combing their hair and putting on bits of clothing. Later on, the female train controller told me to change carriages, but as planes were still flying overhead, I chose to remain under the protection of those Mamma calls in her letters ironically "the brave boys in blue" (she has probably picked this up in a corny novel). (January 2, 1944; from *Berlin Diaries, 1940–1945*, by Marie Vassiltchikov.)

1063. This afternoon Loremarie Schonburg and I sat chatting on the office stairs when Gottfried Bismarck burst in, bright red spots on his cheeks. I had never seen him in such a state of feverish excitement. He first drew Loremarie aside. . . .

I turned to Loremarie, who was standing at the window, and asked her why Gottfried was in such a state. Could it be the *Konspiration* [plot]? . . . She whispered: "Yes! That's it! It's done. This morning!" . . . I asked: "Dead?" She answered: "Yes, dead!" I . . . seized her by the shoulders and we went waltzing around the room. (July 20, 1944; Ibid.)

[This was a reference to the plot to kill Hitler. It failed. This part of her diary was originally stenographic notes that were reconstructed after the war.]

13

Institutional Quotations

ATLANTIC CHARTER

The Atlantic Charter was a statement of war aims by Franklin Roosevelt and Winston Churchill. The declaration was announced following a "meeting at sea" off the coast of Newfoundland in August 1941. The United States, not yet in the war, was providing Lend-Lease (q.v.) armaments to Britain. Text of the document:

1064. The President of the United States of America and the Prime Minister, Mr. Churchill, representing His Majesty's Government in the United Kingdom, being met together, deem it right to make known certain common principles in the national policies of their respective countries on which they base their hopes for a better future for the world.

First, their countries seek no aggrandizement, territorial or other;

Second, they desire to see no territorial changes that do not accord with the freely expressed wishes of the peoples concerned;

Third, they respect the right of all peoples to choose the form of government under which they will live; and they wish to see sovereign rights and self-government restored to those who have been forcibly deprived of them;

Fourth, they will endeavor, with due respect for their existing obligations, to further the enjoyment by all States, great or small, victor or vanquished, of access, on equal terms, to the trade and to the raw materials of the world which are needed for their economic prosperity;

Fifth, they desire to bring about the fullest collaboration between all nations in the economic field with the object of securing, for all, improved labor standards, economic adjustment and social security;

Sixth, after the final destruction of the Nazi tyranny, they hope to see established a peace which will afford to all nations the means of dwelling in safety within their own boundaries, and which will afford assurance that all the men in all the lands may live out their lives in freedom from fear and want;

Seventh, such a peace should enable all men to traverse the high seas and oceans without hinderance;

Eighth, they believe that all of the nations of the world, for realistic as well as spiritual reasons, must come to the abandonment of the use of force. Since no future peace can be maintained if land, sea or air armaments continue to be employed by nations which threaten, or may threaten, aggression outside of their frontiers, they believe, pending the establishment of a wider and permanent system of general security, that the disarmament of such nations is essential. They will likewise aid and encourage all other practicable measures which will lighten for peace-loving peoples the crushing burden of armaments.

BRITISH WAR CABINET

Following the French surrender to Nazi Germany, England feared that elements of the French fleet might fall into enemy hands. Early in July 1940, England moved to neutralize units of the French fleet in Oran, French North Africa. The French naval commanders were called upon to sail off with the British, scuttle their ships, or sail to French colonial ports in the Americas. The French refused. The British opened fire on the French force and sank or beached several warships. Some 1,300 French sailors lost their lives in the engagement. The final order of the British War Cabinet to Vice Admiral James F. Somerville, the British commander:

1065. French ships must comply with our terms or sink themselves or be sunk by you before dark.

CAIRO CONFERENCE

From November 22 to 26 of 1943 Roosevelt, Churchill, and Chiang Kai-shek (q.v.) conferred in Cairo on the war against Japan. On December 1, a statement was issued on conference decisions. Text of statement:

1066. The several military missions have agreed upon future military operations against Japan.

The three great Allies expressed their resolve to bring unrelenting pressure against their brutal enemies by sea, land and air. This pressure is already rising.

The three great Allies are fighting this war to restrain and punish the aggression of Japan.

They covet no gain for themselves and have no thought of territorial expansion.

It is their purpose that Japan shall be stripped of all the islands in the Pacific which she has seized or occupied since the beginning of the first World War in 1914, and that all the territories Japan has stolen from the Chinese, such as Manchuria, Formosa and the Pescadores, shall be restored to the Republic of China.

Japan will also be expelled from all other territories which she has taken by violence and greed.

The aforesaid three great powers, mindful of the enslavement of the people of Korea, are determined that in due course Korea shall become free and independent.

With these objectives in view, the three Allies, in harmony with those of the United Nations at war with Japan, will continue to persevere in the serious and prolonged operations necessary to procure the unconditional surrender of Japan.

CASABLANCA CONFERENCE

Roosevelt, Churchill, and top members of their military and diplomatic staffs met in Casablanca, North Africa, in January 1943. It was agreed to postpone the Second Front invasion until 1944, although the invasion of Sicily and the Italian mainland would take some pressure off the Russian front in 1943. The conference is best known for the terms of "unconditional surrender" for the Axis Powers—a phrase used by Roosevelt at a press conference at the conclusion of the meetings.

Text highlights of the January 24, 1943, Casablanca communiqué:

1067. For ten days the combined staffs have been in constant session, meeting two or three times a day, and recording progress at intervals to the President and the Prime Minister.

The entire field of the war was surveyed theater by theater throughout the world, and all resources were marshalled for a more intense prosecution of the war by sea, land, and air.

Nothing like this prolonged discussion between two allies has ever taken place before. Complete agreement was reached between the leaders of the two countries and their respective staffs upon war plans and enterprises to be undertaken during the campaigns of 1943 against Germany, Italy and Japan with a view to drawing the utmost advantage from the markedly favorable turn of events at the close of 1942.

Premier Stalin was cordially invited to meet the President and the Prime Minister, in which case the meeting would have been held very much farther to the east. He was unable to leave Russia at this time on account of the great offensive which he himself as Commander in Chief is directing.

The President and the Prime Minister realized up to the full the enormous weight of the war which Russia is successfully bearing along her whole land front, and their prime object has been to draw as much weight as possible off the Russian armies by engaging the enemy as heavily as possible at the best selected points.

DECLARATION OF UNION

The Declaration of Union was a proposal by the British government for joint British-French citizenship. In June 1940, France was being overrun by the German army. Britain hoped that France would remain in the war and use the French fleet and its armed forces in the French colonies to carry on the fight. Premier Paul Reynaud (q.v.) took the plan to his cabinet, which rejected it. The French chose surrender. Brief excerpts from the draft Declaration of Union follow:

1068. At this most fateful moment in the history of the modern world, the Governments of the United Kingdom and the French Republic make this declaration of indissoluble union and unyielding resolution in their common defense of justice and freedom against subjection to a system which reduces mankind to a life of robots and slaves.

The two Governments declare that France and Great Britain shall no longer be two nations, but one Franco-British Union. . . .

Every citizen of France will enjoy immediately citizenship of Great Britain; every British subject . . . a citizen of France. . . .

During the war there shall be a single War Cabinet, and all the forces of Britain and France, whether on land, sea, or in the air, will be placed under its direction. It will govern from wherever it best can. . . .

The union will concentrate its whole energy against the power of the enemy, no matter where the battle may be. And thus we shall conquer. (Cited in *Their Finest Hour*, by Winston Churchill.)

GERMAN ARMED FORCES

1069. I swear by God this sacred oath that I shall render unconditional obedience to Adolf Hitler, the Fuehrer of the German Reich, supreme commander of the armed forces, and that at all times I shall be prepared, as a brave soldier, to give my life for this oath. (Oath of the German Armed Forces, instituted August 2, 1934.)

GERMAN NAVY

1070. The Fuehrer has decided to wipe the City of Petersburg [Leningrad] from the face of the earth. After the defeat of Soviet Russia there will be no interest in the further existence of this large population center. . . . It is intended to blockade tightly the city and by artillery and uninterrupted bombings to raze it from the earth. If, as a result of the conditions created in the city, requests for surrender are made, they will be rejected. (Directive, German Naval Headquarters, September 22, 1941; cited in *Zhukov*, by Otto Preston Chaney, Jr.)

INTERNATIONAL MILITARY TRIBUNAL

This court was set up at the end of the war by the victorious Allies to try the top Nazi war criminals. The trial took place in Nuremberg, Germany, from November 1945 to October 1946.

The accused, the verdicts, and their sentences: Hermann Goering (q.v.; guilty on all four counts of the indictment below; sentenced to death but committed suicide); Rudolf Hess (q.v.; guilty on counts one and two; life imprisonment); Joachim von Ribbentrop (q.v.; guilty on all four counts; hanged); Wilhelm Keitel (q.v.; guilty on all four counts; hanged); Ernst Kaltenbrunner (guilty on counts three and four; hanged); Alfred Rosenberg (guilty on all four counts; hanged); Hans Frank (q.v.; guilty on counts three and four; hanged); Wilhelm Frick (guilty on counts two, three, and four; hanged); Julius Streicher (guilty on count four; hanged); Walther Funk (q.v.; guilty on counts two, three, and four; life imprisonment); Hjalmar Schacht (acquitted); Karl Doenitz (q.v.; guilty on counts two and three; ten years); Erich Raeder (q.v.; guilty on counts two, three, and four; life imprisonment); Baldur von Schirach (guilty on count four; twenty years); Fritz Sauckel (guilty on counts two and four; twenty years); Alfred Jodl (q.v.; guilty on all four counts; hanged); Franz von Papen (acquitted); Artur Seyss-Inquart (guilty on counts two, three, and four; hanged); Albert Speer (q.v.; guilty on counts three and four; twenty years); Constantin von Neurath (guilty on all four counts; fifteen years); Hans Fritzsche (q.v.; acquitted); Martin Bormann (tried in absentia; found guilty on counts three and four; sentenced to death; he had disappeared after the fall of Berlin and was never found).

These were the counts of the indictment:

1071. COUNT ONE—THE COMMON PLAN OR CONSPIRACY.

All the defendants, with diverse other persons, during a period of years preceding 8th May, 1945 [date of the German surrender], participated as leaders, organizers, instigators or accomplices in the formulation or execution of a common plan or conspiracy to commit, or which involved the commission of, Crimes against Humanity . . . [and] Crimes against Peace, in that the defendants planned, prepared, initiated and waged wars of aggression, which were also wars in violation of international treaties, agreements or assurances. In the development and course of the common plan or conspiracy it came to embrace the commission of War Crimes . . . and carried out ruthless wars against countries and populations, in violation of the rules and customs of war . . . [including] murder, ill-treatment, deportation for slave labor and . . . murder and ill-treatment of prisoners of war and of persons on the high seas, the taking and killing of hostages, the plunder of public and private property, the wanton destruction of cities, towns, and villages, and devastation not justified by military necessity. . . . The common plan of conspiracy contemplated and came to embrace as systematic means, and the defendants determined upon and committed, Crimes against Humanity, both within Germany and within occupied territories. (From *Nazi Conspiracy and Aggression.*)

1072. COUNT TWO—CRIMES AGAINST PEACE.

All the defendants and divers other persons . . . participated in the planning, preparation, initiation and waging of wars of aggression, which were also wars in violation of international treaties, agreements and assurances. (Ibid.)

1073. COUNT THREE—WAR CRIMES.

All the defendants committed War Crimes between 1st September, 1939, and 8th May, 1945, in Germany and in all those countries and territories occupied by the German armed forces since 1st September, 1939, and in Austria, Czechoslovakia, and Italy.

All the defendants, acting in concert with others, formulated and executed a common plan or conspiracy to commit War Crimes. . . . This plan involved, among other things, the practice of "total war" including methods of combat and of military occupation in direct conflict with the laws and customs of war, and the commission of crimes perpetrated on the field of battle during encounters with enemy armies, and against prisoners of war, and in occupied territories against the civilian population of such territories. (Ibid.)

1074. COUNT FOUR—CRIMES AGAINST HUMANITY.

All the defendants committed Crimes against Humanity . . . in Germany and in all those countries and territories occupied by the German armed forces since 1st September, 1939 and in Austria and Czechoslovakia and in Italy and on the High Seas.

All the defendants, acting in concert with others, formulated and executed a common plan or conspiracy to commit Crimes against Humanity. . . . This plan involved, among other things, the murder and persecution of all who were or who were suspected of being hostile to the Nazi Party and all who were or who were suspected of being opposed to the common plan alleged in Count One. . . . The said Crimes against Humanity were committed by the defendants and by other persons for whose acts the defendants are responsible. (Ibid.)

JAPANESE GOVERNMENT

The term *Comfort Women* was applied to tens of thousands—possibly 100,000—Asian women who were forced into prostitution for the Japanese military. The practice began in Shanghai in 1932 and continued until the end of the war. For nearly half a century, the Japanese government flatly denied the existence of "comfort stations" in the war zones. After lawsuits were filed in Korea by victims and their families, Japan launched an official investigation.

In 1993, Japan's Chief Cabinet Secretary issued a statement. An excerpt follows:

1075. The Government of Japan has been conducting a study on the issue of wartime "comfort women" since December 1991. I wish to announce the findings as a result of that study.

As a result of the study which indicates that comfort stations were operated in extensive areas for long periods, it is apparent that there existed a great number of comfort women. Comfort stations were operated in response to the request of the military authorities of the day. The then Japanese military was, directly or indirectly, involved in the establishment and management of the comfort stations and the transfer of comfort women. The recruitment of the comfort women was conducted mainly by private recruiters who acted in response to the request of the military. The Government study has revealed that in many cases they were recruited against their own will, through coaxing, coercion, etc., and that, at times, administrative/military personnel directly took part in the recruitment. They [the Comfort Women] lived in misery at comfort stations under a coercive atmosphere.

As to the origin of those comfort women who were transferred to the war areas, excluding those from Japan, those from the Korean Peninsula accounted for a large part. The Korean Peninsula was under Japanese rule in those days, and their recruitment, transfer, control, etc., were conducted generally against their will, through coaxing, coercions, etc.

Undeniably, this was an act, with the involvement of the military authorities of the day, that severely injured the honor and dignity of many women. The Government of Japan would like to take this opportunity once again to extend its sincere apologies and remorse to all those, irrespective of place of origin, who suffered immeasurable pain and incurable physical and psychological wounds as comfort women. It is incumbent upon us, the Government of Japan, to continue to consider seriously, while listening to the views of learned circles, how best we can express this sentiment.

We shall face squarely the historical facts as described above instead of evading them, and take them to heart as lessons of history. We hereby reiterate our firm determination never to repeat the same mistake by forever engraving such issues in our memories through the study and teaching of history. (Statement [unofficial translation], Chief Cabinet Secretary, August 4, 1993.)

[On July 18, 1995, Japanese Prime Minister Tomichi Murayama announced establishment of the Asian Women's Fund as an expression of atonement on the part of the Japanese people. He added that Japan would "collate historical documents concerning the former wartime comfort women, to serve as a lesson of history."]

MOSCOW DECLARATION ON ATROCITIES

On November 1, 1943, a statement was issued signed by Roosevelt, Churchill, and Stalin on atrocities and the prosecution of war criminals. The declaration was issued from Moscow, where the Foreign Ministers were concluding a series of conferences on war and postwar policies.

Complete text of the declaration:

1076. The United Kingdom, the United States, and the Soviet Union have received from many quarters evidence of atrocities, massacres, and cold-blooded mass executions which are being perpetrated by Hitlerite forces in many of the countries they have overrun and from which they are now being steadily expelled. The brutalities of Hitlerite domination are no new thing and all peoples of territories in their grip have suffered from the worst form of government by terror. What is new is that many of these territories are now being redeemed by the advancing armies of the liberating powers and that in their desperation, the recoiling Hitlerite Huns are redoubling their ruthless cruelties. This is now evidenced with particular clearness by monstrous crimes of the Hitlerites in the territory of the Soviet Union which is being liberated from Hitlerites, and on French and Italian territory.

Accordingly, the aforesaid three Allied Powers, speaking in the interests of the 33 United Nations, hereby solemnly declare and give full warning of their declaration as follows: At the time of granting of any armistice to any government which may be set up in Germany, those German officers and men and members of the Nazi Party who have been responsible for or have taken a consenting part in the above atrocities, massacres and executions will be sent back to the countries in which their abominable deeds were done in order that they may be judged and punished according to the laws of these liberated countries and of the free governments which will be erected thereon. Lists will be compiled in all possible detail from all these countries, having regard especially to invaded parts of the Soviet Union, to Poland and Czechoslovakia, to Yugoslavia and Greece including Crete and other islands, to Norway, Denmark, Netherlands, Belgium, Luxembourg, France and Italy.

Thus, Germans who take part in wholesale shooting of Polish officers or Cretan peasants, or who have shared in slaughters inflicted on the people of Poland or in territories of the Soviet Union which are now being swept clear of the enemy, will know they will be brought back to the scene of their crimes on the spot by the peoples whom they have outraged. Let those who have hitherto not imbrued their hands with innocent blood beware lest they join the ranks of the guilty, for most assuredly the three Allied Powers will pursue them to the uttermost ends of the earth and will deliver them to their accusers in order that justice may be done.

The above declaration is without prejudice to the case of German criminals, whose offenses have no particular geographical localization and who will be punished by joint decision of the governments of the Allies. (November 1, 1943.)

MUNICH AGREEMENT

On September 29, 1938, Neville Chamberlain (q.v.) of the United Kingdom, Edouard Daladier of France, Adolf Hitler of Germany, and Benito Mussolini (q.v.) of Italy agreed that Czechoslovakia would turn over its Sudeten area to Germany. Hitler had threatened war if he did not get it. Czechoslovakia had taken no part in the discussions, and the word "Munich" became a synonym for appeasement. Major parts of the agreement:

1077. Germany, the United Kingdom, France and Italy, taking into consideration the agreement, which has been already reached in principle for the cession to Germany of the Sudeten German territory, have agreed on the following terms and conditions governing the said cession. . . .

1. The evacuation will begin on the 1st October.

2. The United Kingdom, France and Italy agree that the evacuation of the territory shall be completed by the 10th October, without any existing installations having been destroyed and that the Czechoslovak Government will be held responsible for carrying out the evacuation without damage to the said installations.

3. The conditions governing the evacuation will be laid down in detail by an

international commission composed of representatives of Germany, the United Kingdom, France, Italy and Czechoslovakia.

4. The occupation by stages of the predominantly German territory by German troops will begin on the 1st October. The four territories marked on the attached map will be occupied by German troops in the following order [areas and dates are specified]. . . .

5. The international commission referred to in paragraph 3 will determine the territories in which a plebiscite to is to be held. These territories will be occupied by international bodies until the plebiscite has been completed. The same commission will fix the conditions in which the plebiscite is to be held, taking as a basis the conditions of the Saar plebiscite. The commission will also fix a date, not later than the end of November, on which the plebiscite will be held.

6. The final determination of the frontiers will be carried out by the international commission. This commission will also be entitled to recommend to the four Powers, Germany, the United Kingdom, France and Italy, in certain exceptional cases minor modifications in the strictly ethnographical determination of the zones which are to be transferred without plebiscite.

7. There will be a right of option into and out of the transferred territories, the option to be exercised within six months from the date of this agreement. A German-Czechoslovak commission shall determine the details of the option, consider ways of facilitating the transfer of population and settle questions of principle arising out of the said transfer.

8. The Czechoslovak government will within a period of four weeks from the date of this agreement release from their military and police forces any Sudeten Germans who may wish to be released, and the Czechoslovak Government will within the same period release Sudeten German prisoners who are serving terms of imprisonment for political offenses.

NAZI-SOVIET PACT

On August 23, 1939, German Foreign Minister Joachim von Ribbentrop (q.v.) and Soviet Foreign Minister Vyacheslav Molotov (q.v.) signed a nonaggression pact between Nazi Germany and the Soviet Union. Signed in Moscow, it was supposed to last for ten years. It would last less than two years, when Hitler invaded Russia.

The part of the treaty that was made public emphasized the desire of both parties to the cause of peace, promised not to war on one another, promised not to help a third party in a war against the other, and promised to settle any disputes in a friendly exchange of views or, if necessary, through arbitration.

The heart of the pact, however, was in the secret protocol that sealed the fate of Poland and the Baltic States.

Key parts of the secret protocol:

1078. On the occasion of the signature of the Nonaggression Treaty between Germany and the Soviet Union the undersigned plenipotentiaries discussed in strictly confidential conversations the question of the delineation of their respective spheres of interest in Eastern Europe.

1. In the event of a territorial and political transformation in the territories belonging to the Baltic States, the northern frontier of Lithuania shall represent the frontier of the spheres of interest both of Germany and the U.S.S.R.

2. In the event of a territorial and political transformation of the territories belonging to the Polish State, the spheres of interest of both Germany and the U.S.S.R. shall be bounded approximately by the line of the rivers Narew, Vistula and San.

The question whether the interests of both Parties make the maintenance of an independent Polish State appear desirable and how the frontiers of this State should be drawn can be definitely determined only in the course of further political developments.

In any case both Governments will resolve this question by means of a friendly understanding.

OFFICE OF STRATEGIC SERVICES/ SPECIAL OPERATIONS EXECUTIVE

Prior to Torch—the invasion of French North Africa in November 1942—the OSS and the SOE drew up a general rationale and initial plans for how their intelligence forces might be used on the ground. The American OSS was the forerunner of the Central Intelligence Agency, which would be created after the war. The British SOE had been created following the fall of France. It encouraged guerrilla activity in Nazi-held Europe.

1079. Plan envisages three simultaneous landings. . . . It is considered essential operation should be entirely American in first instance. Consequently all troops will be American, but will be assisted by Royal Navy and Royal Air Force [RAF]. Obviously impossible to disguise Royal Navy, but R.A.F. support will be disguised as American. (Cited in *Our Vichy Gamble*, by William L. Langer.)

1080. [Priority of tasks by intelligence forces inside North Africa:]

a). During assault: 1. light beaches; 2. neutralize batteries; 3. put out ultra-red detectors.

b). Safeguard dock installations from Arab destruction.

c). Safeguard wireless installations from Arab destruction.

d). Sabotage enemy air forces by any means.

e). Temporarily block roads and rails.

f). Damage French naval forces if they resist.

g). Provide guides for forces after landing. (Ibid.)

POTSDAM CONFERENCE

During the last two weeks in July 1945, the "Big Three" met at Potsdam, a suburb of Berlin, to discuss postwar policies in Europe. When the meetings began, the principals were Truman (q.v.), Stalin, and Churchill. The last was replaced by Clement Attlee following the British elections. The conference dealt with the zones of occupation for a defeated Germany, establishment of a Council of Foreign Ministers, boundary changes involving former Polish territory to the Soviet Union and former German territory to Poland, and a warning to Japan to get out of the war. On August 2, 1945, an official report was issued on the conference.

Segments of the report dealing with the German occupation follow:

1081. The purposes of the occupation of Germany by which the Control Council shall be guided are:

. . . Supreme authority in Germany is exercised on instructions from their respective governments, by the Commanders-in-Chief of the armed forces of the United States of America, the United Kingdom, the Union of Soviet Socialist Republics and the French Republic, each in its own zone of occupation, and also jointly, in matters affecting Germany as a whole, in their capacity as members of the Control Council. . . .

All German land, naval and air forces, the S.S., S.A., S.D., and Gestapo, with all their organizations, staffs and institutions, including the General Staff, the Officers Corps, Reserve Corps, military schools, war veterans' organizations and all other military and quasi-military organizations, together with all clubs and associations which serve to keep alive the military tradition in Germany, shall be completely and finally abolished in such manner as permanently to prevent the revival or reorganization of German militarism and Nazism.

All arms, ammunition and implements of war and all specialized facilities for their production shall be held at the disposal of the Allies or destroyed. The maintenance and production of all aircraft and all arms, ammunition and implements of war shall be prevented.

To convince the German people that they have suffered a total military defeat and that they cannot escape responsibility for what they have wrought upon themselves, since their own ruthless warfare and the fanatical Nazi resistance have destroyed the German economy and made chaos and suffering inevitable.

To destroy the National Socialist Party and . . . all Nazi institutions, to ensure that they are not revived in any form. . . .

To prepare for the eventual reconstruction of German political life on a democratic basis. . . .

All Nazi laws which provided the basis of the Hitler regime or established discrimination on grounds of race, creed, or political opinion shall be abolished. . . .

War criminals and those who have participated in planning or carrying out Nazi enterprises involving or resulting in atrocities or war crimes shall be arrested and brought to judgment.

RATION BOARD

A rationing system was used in many countries during the war for equitable distribution of limited resources. In the United States, the system was set up for the distribution of such items as meat, butter, sugar, shoes, tires, and gasoline. U.S. ration books contained stamps or coupons bearing the pictures of planes, tanks, and other war weapons. Rules for using American ration books included the following:

1082. Don't swap ration coupons.

Don't give your unused stamps to your dealer.

Don't try to buy rationed goods without coupons.

Don't pay over top legal prices.

Don't let any dealer let you buy something you don't want to get something you do want.

ROBERTS COMMISSION REPORT ON PEARL HARBOR

On December 7, 1941, Japanese planes from aircraft carriers launched a surprise attack on the American fleet at Pearl Harbor, Hawaii. There had been no declaration of war. The American Pacific fleet was crippled—but the country entered the war united against the Axis Powers. Isolationism was virtually dead.

President Roosevelt named a commission of five men to investigate and report on the Pearl Harbor disaster. The commission was headed by Owen J. Roberts, an associate justice of the United States Supreme Court. In its report dated January 23, 1942, the commission issued its findings.

The Roberts Commission report was the first of nine Pearl Harbor reports, including several congressional studies after the war. Some of the later reports tended to be political, depending on which party was in power and the nature of the political climate at the time.

One aspect of the Pearl Harbor controversy that could not be dealt with during the war was the fact that the United States had broken the Japanese code months prior to Pearl Harbor and that high officials in the Roosevelt administration might have known of the forthcoming attack in advance. It was revealed after the war that in the period from August 1 to December 6, 1941, fully twenty Japanese coded messages intercepted by American intelligence had dealt with what was happening at Pearl Harbor. But during the same time period, twenty-three intercepts had made queries about the Panama Canal Zone, and fifty-nine others had dealt with the Philippines.

The major conclusions of the Roberts commission:

1083. The Secretary of War [Henry L. Stimson (q.v.)] and the Secretary of the Navy [Frank Knox (q.v.)] fulfilled their obligations by conferring frequently with the Secretary of State [Cordell Hull (q.v.)] and with each other and by keeping the Chief of Staff [George C. Marshall] and the Chief of Naval Operations [Harold Stark (q.v.)] informed of the course of the negotiations with Japan and the significant implications thereof.

1084. The Chief of Staff and the Chief of Naval Operations fulfilled their obligations by consulting and cooperating with each other, and with their superiors, respecting the joint defense of the Hawaiian coastal frontier; and each knew of, and concurred in, the warnings and orders sent by the other to the responsible commanders with respect to such defense.

1085. The Chief of Staff of the Army fulfilled his command responsibility by issuing a direct order in connection with his warning of probable hostilities, in the following words: "Prior to hostile Japanese action you are directed to undertake such reconnaissance and other measures as you deem necessary."

1086. The Chief of Naval Operations fulfilled his command responsibility by issuing a warning and by giving a direct order to the commander in chief, Pacific Fleet, in the following words: "This dispatch is to be considered a war warning." and "Execute an appropriate defensive deployment preparatory to carrying out the tasks assigned."

1087. The responsible commanders in the Hawaiian area [General Walter Short and Admiral Husband Kimmel (q.v.)], in fulfillment of their obligations so to do, prepared plans which, if adapted to and used for the existing emergency, would have been adequate.

1088. In the circumstances the responsibility of these commanders was to confer upon the question of putting into effect and adapting their joint defense plans.

1089. These commanders failed to confer with respect to the warnings and orders issued on and after November 27 [1941], and to adapt and use existing plans to meet the emergency.

1090. The order for alert No. 1 for the Army command in Hawaii was not adequate to meet the emergency envisaged in the warning messages.

1091. The state of readiness of the naval forces on the morning of December 7 was not such as was required to meet the emergency envisaged in the warning messages.

1092. Had orders issued by the Chief of Staff and the Chief of Naval Operations November 27, 1941, been complied with, the aircraft warning system of the Army should have been operating; the distance reconnaissance of the Navy, and the inshore air patrol of the Army, should have been maintained; the aircraft batteries of the Army and similar shore batteries of the Navy, as well as additional aircraft artillery located on vessels of the fleet in Pearl Harbor, should have been manned and supplied with ammunition; and a high state of readiness of aircraft should have been in effect. None of these conditions was in fact inaugurated or maintained for the reason that the responsible commanders failed to consult and cooperate as to necessary action based upon the warnings and to adopt measures enjoined by the orders given them by the chiefs of the Army and Navy commands in Washington.

1093. There were deficiencies in personnel, weapons, equipment, and facilities to maintain all the defenses on a war footing for extended periods of time, but these deficiencies should not have affected the decision of the responsible commanders as to the state of readiness to be prescribed.

1094. The failure of the commanding general, Hawaii Department, and the commander in chief, Pacific Fleet, to confer and cooperate with respect to the meaning of the warnings received and the measures necessary to comply with the orders given and under date of November 27, 1941, resulted largely from a sense of security due to the opinion prevalent in diplomatic, military, and naval circles, and in the public press, that any immediate attack by Japan would be in the Far East. The existence of such a view, however prevalent, did not relieve the commanders of the responsibility for the security of the Pacific Fleet and our most important outpost.

1095. In the light of the warnings and directions to take appropriate action, transmitted to both commanders between November 27 and December 7, and the obligation under the system of coordination then in effect for some cooperative action on their part, it was a dereliction of duty on the part of each of them not to consult and confer with the other respecting the meaning and intent of the warnings, and the appropriate measures of defense required by the imminence of hostilities. The attitude of each, that he was not required to inform himself of, and his lack of interest in, the measures undertaken by the other to carry out the responsibility assigned to each other under the provisions of the plans then in effect, demonstrated on the part of each a lack of appreciation of the responsibilities vested in them and inherent in their positions as commander in chief, Pacific Fleet, and commanding general, Hawaiian Department.

1096. The Japanese attack was a complete surprise to the commanders, and they failed to make suitable dispositions to meet such an attack. Each failed properly to evaluate the seriousness of the situation. These errors of judgment were the effective causes for the success of the attack.

TEHERAN CONFERENCE

Roosevelt, Churchill, and Stalin met in Teheran, Iran, from November 27 to 30 in 1943. It was the first time that all three leaders had met face to face. The key issue was a Second Front to be launched by the Western Allies in the spring of 1944. Also discussed were such postwar issues as Russian boundaries and an international organization to keep the peace.

Partial text of communiqué signed by the three leaders, issued on December 1, 1943:

1097. We express our determination that our nations shall work together in the war and in the peace that will follow.

As to the war, our military staffs have joined in our roundtable discussions and we have concerted our plans for the destruction of the German forces, which will be undertaken from the east, west and south. The common understanding which we have here reached guarantees that victory will be ours.

And as to the peace, we are sure that our concord will make it an enduring peace. We recognize fully the supreme responsibility resting upon us and all the nations to make a peace which will command good will from the overwhelming masses of the peoples of the world and banish the scourge and terror of war for many generations.

With our diplomatic advisers we have surveyed the problems of the future. We shall seek the cooperation and active participation of all nations, large and small, whose peoples in heart and in mind are dedicated, as are our own peoples, to the elimination of tyranny and slavery, oppression and intolerance. We will welcome them as they may choose to come into the world family of democratic nations.

No power on earth can prevent our destroying the German armies by land, their U-boats by sea, and their war plants from the air. Our attacks will be relentless and increasing.

Emerging from these friendly conferences we look with confidence to the day when all the peoples of the world may live free lives untroubled by tyranny and according to their varying desires and their own consciences.

We came here with hope and determination. We leave here friends in fact, in spirit, and in purpose.

TIME MAGAZINE

1098. The link between the biggest military establishment in U.S. history and the U.S. people, George C. Marshall was at year's end the closest thing to "the indispensable man." (Announcing its "Man of the Year," *Time*, January 3, 1944.)

TRIPARTITE PACT

The Tripartite Pact was an agreement among Nazi Germany, Italy, and Japan, promulgated on September 27, 1940. It was also called the Rome-Berlin-Tokyo Axis and was to last for ten years. Major sections of the pact:

1099. The Governments of Germany, Italy and Japan consider it the prerequisite of a lasting peace that every nation in the world shall receive the space to which it is entitled. They have, therefore, decided to stand by and cooperate with one another in their efforts in Greater East Asia and the regions of Europe respectively. In doing this it is their prime purpose to establish and maintain a new order of things, calculated to promote the mutual prosperity and welfare of the peoples concerned.

It is, furthermore, the desire of the three Governments to extend cooperation to nations in other spheres of the world who are inclined to direct their efforts along lines similar to their own for the purpose of realizing their ultimate objective, world peace.

Accordingly, the Governments of Germany, Italy and Japan have agreed as follows:

Article 1. Japan recognizes and respects the leadership of Germany and Italy in the establishment of a new order in Europe.

Article 2. Germany and Italy recognize and respect the leadership of Japan in the establishment of a new order in Greater East Asia.

Article 3. Germany, Italy and Japan agree to cooperate in their efforts of the aforesaid lines. They further undertake to assist one another with all political, economic, and military means if one of the three Contracting Powers is attacked by a Power at present not involved in the European War or in the Sino-Japanese conflict.

UNITED NATIONS DECLARATION

On January 1, 1942, representatives of twenty-six nations fighting with one or more of the Axis Powers met in Washington to pledge full cooperation during the war and in the peace to follow. In the original draft of the declaration, the group was called the "Associated Powers." Roosevelt did not like the designation. He crossed it out, substituting the phrase "United Nations."

Major sections of the declaration:

1100. The Government signatory hereto,

Having subscribed to a common program of purposes and principles embodied in the . . . Atlantic Charter [q.v.].

Being convinced that complete victory over their enemies is essential to defend life, liberty, independence and religious freedom, and to preserve human rights and justice in their own lands as well as in other lands, and that they are now engaged in a common struggle against savage and brutal forces seeking to subjugate the world, DECLARE:

(1) Each Government pledges itself to employ its full resources, military or economic, against those members of the Tripartite Pact and its adherents with which such government is at war.

(2) Each Government pledges itself to cooperate with the Governments signatory hereto and not to make a separate armistice or peace with the enemies.

UNITED STATES GOVERNMENT

1101. Illumination is required to be extinguished before these premises are closed for business. (U.S. government sign posted at businesses to encourage energy conservation, 1942.)

[Translation: Turn out the lights.]

UNITED STATES NAVY

1102. WHAT TO DO IF TAKEN PRISONER. . . .

There is one rule to remember and only one. Give your name, rate and serial number—nothing else. (*The Bluejackets' Manual*, 1944.)

1103. If you know you are going to be captured, be sure that you get rid of any military information you may have with you. Hang on to your dog tag, your I.D. card and your money. Get rid of everything else, including pictures, letters and notes. (Ibid.)

1104. The enemy will try many ways to get information from you. He has clever men specially trained in the art of getting prisoners to talk. You can't outsmart them; don't try it. Don't try to lie or give false information, and don't try to decide what information is harmless. Remember that the enemy is questioning other prisoners and will put the parts of the puzzle together. (Ibid.)

1105. Many methods may be used to get you to talk. The enemy may act friendly and play on your feelings or be sympathetic about some minor personal grudge you may have. Fake prisoners may be planted among you; listening devices may be used. Special favors or rations may be offered to soften you up. Always keep in mind what the enemy is trying to do and don't be fooled. Remember that, once you have given information, the enemy will lose interest in you and will treat you no better than anyone else. (Ibid.)

1106. Occupy yourself by thinking about the possibility of escape and study the chances. Accumulate and remember any and all information about the enemy and try to learn his language. If you manage to escape anything you have learned will help the Navy. (Ibid.)

1107. Above all, be smart; don't talk smart. Keep your eyes and ears open and your mouth shut. Give your name, rate and serial number and then keep quiet. (Ibid.)

VOLKISHER BEOBACHTER

1108. Every German citizen now knows the fight has been bloody and bitter. We have recognized that we are dealing with the most difficult enemy we have met so far. (Editorial, *Volkisher Beobachter*, August 3, 1941.)

[Six weeks after the German invasion of the Soviet Union.]

YALTA CONFERENCE

Yalta was the last conference held by Roosevelt, Churchill, and Stalin. It took place from February 4 to 11 in 1945 in Yalta on the Crimean peninsula. With the war drawing to a close, the three leaders dealt with postwar Europe and the war with Japan. A statement was issued following the conference. Excerpts:

"We have agreed on common policies and plans for enforcing the unconditional surrender terms which we shall impose together on Nazi Germany after German armed resistance has been finally crushed. . . . Under the agreed plan, the forces of the three powers will each occupy a separate zone of Germany."
—YALTA CONFERENCE COMMUNIQUE

Churchill, Roosevelt, and Stalin at Yalta.

1109. We have agreed on common policies and plans for enforcing the unconditional surrender terms which we shall impose together on Nazi Germany after German armed resistance has been finally crushed. These terms will not be made known until the final defeat of Germany has been accomplished. Under the agreed plan, the forces of the three powers will each occupy a separate zone of Germany. . . .

We have agreed that a conference of United Nations should be called to meet at San Francisco in the United States on April 25, 1945, to prepare the charter of such an organization, along the lines proposed in the informal conversations at Dumbarton Oaks. . . .

The three heads of government consider that the Eastern frontier of Poland should follow the Curzon line. . . .

They recognize that Poland must receive substantial accessions of territory in the North and West.

[Secret agreements made at Yalta included the following: Russia agreed to enter the war against Japan three months after victory in Europe; Russia would get back from Japan what she had lost in the Russo-Japanese war; America and Britain would agree to support separate membership in the new United Nations organization for two Soviet states—the Ukraine and White Russia.]

14

Anonymous Quotations

1110. Today we own Germany, tomorrow the world! (Nazi slogan, ca. 1937.)

1111. Deduction on the report, German Embassy, London, regarding the future form of Anglo-German relations.

With the realization that Germany will not tie herself to a status quo in Central Europe, and that sooner or later a military conflict in Europe is possible, the hope of an agreement will slowly disappear among Germanophile British politicians, insofar as they are not merely playing a part that has been given to them. Thus the fateful question arises: Will Germany and England eventually be forced to drift into separate camps and will they march against each other one day? . . . Peace or war between England and Germany rests solely in the hands of France. . . . It follows therefore that war between Germany and England . . . can be prevented only if France knows from the start that England's forces would not be sufficient to guarantee their common victory. Such a situation might force England, and thereby France, to accept a lot of things that a strong Anglo-France coalition would never tolerate. (Memorandum to Hitler from an apparently high-placed source, January 2, 1938; cited in *Nazi Conspiracy and Aggression.*)

1112. This position would arise for instance if England, through insufficient armament or as a result of threats to her empire by a superior coalition of powers, e.g., Germany, Italy, Japan, thereby tying down her military forces in other places, would not be able to assure France her sufficient support in . . . Europe. (Ibid.)

1113. Therefore, conclusions to be drawn by us,

1. Outwardly, further understanding with England in regard to the protection of the interests of our friends. . . .

2. Formation under great secrecy, but with whole-hearted tenacity of a coalition against England, that is to say, tightening of our friendship with Italy and

Japan; also the winning over of all nations whose interests conform with ours directly or indirectly.

Close and confidential cooperation of the diplomats of the three great powers towards this purpose. Only in this way can we confront England be it in a settlement of or in war. England is going to be a hard, astute opponent in this game of diplomacy. (Ibid.)

1114. Winnie's back. (September 3, 1939.)

[Message radioed to the British navy on the appointment of Winston Churchill as First Lord of the Admiralty, a position he had held in World War I.]

1115. Why die for Danzig? (Antiwar slogan in Britain, 1939.)

[Hitler wanted the Free City of Danzig reunited with the Reich.]

1116. The Yanks are *not* coming! (Slogan of the American Communist Party during the Hitler-Stalin Non-Aggression Pact, 1939–1941.)

[The slogan ended abruptly on June 22, 1941, the date of the Nazi attack on the Soviet Union. After America entered the war, the Communist slogan changed to "Second Front Now!"]

1117. Columns marching westward. (Message to General Maurice Gamelin [q.v.] from a French agent in Germany, May 10, 1940.)

[Indicating that the German army was moving against France.]

1118. Never volunteer for anything. (U.S. Army saying, ca. 1940.)

> O.H.I.O.: In the summer of 1941, these letters appeared on barrack walls all over the United States. The draft law, passed in the fall of 1940, was due to expire in October 1941. There were doubts that the draft would be extended, and General George C. Marshall personally appealed to congressmen—particularly Republicans—on the grounds that America would be put in peril. The draft extension passed in the House of Representatives by a single vote.
>
> "O.H.I.O." stood for:

1119. "Over the Hill in October!" (1941.)

1120. It will be a piece of cake. (ca. late spring 1942.)

[This is one of the most controversial quotations of the war. It has been associated with one of the final planning sessions for the Dieppe raid of August 1942. Although it has been attributed to Major General John Hamilton Roberts, the chief of Canadian forces in the operation, this is hotly disputed by military historian Terence Robertson (q.v.), who feels that Roberts was made the scapegoat for the Dieppe disaster. The Canadian officer himself believes that the quote was actually made by Bernard Montgomery (q.v.), one of the top military planners of the Dieppe raid. Historian Robertson compares the remark to a similar sentiment Montgomery made to his troops prior to D-Day (q.v.).]

1121. They're over-paid, over-sexed, and over here. (Referring to American GIs stationed in England, ca. 1942.)

1122.

This [indicating] is my rifle.
This [indicating] is my gun.
This is for fighting.
This is for fun. (ca. 1942).

[Marine Corps learning experience. The idea was to ensure that a Marine refer to his weapon as a rifle or a piece. The "gun" was the male organ.]

1123. Kilroy was here. (ca. 1942.)

[This puzzling sentence is one of the great mysteries of World War II. It was scrawled on the walls of U.S. military bases and GI hangouts all over the world. Although there have been numerous theories about who inspired it, the mystery has never been authoritatively solved.]

1124. Letter to the "What's Your Problem?" column:

Dear *Yank*:

I have a problem. . . . But please don't use my name. Shortly after I was inducted, my wife and I agreed to separate, but we didn't get a divorce. Sometime later I started living with another woman. Of course, I'm not married to this woman, but not long ago she applied for and received, with my knowledge and approval, a family allowance as my wife. Now I've been worrying about this lately because I've got a good idea that my legal wife is going to apply for an allowance also. If that happens, what can they do to the girl friend?

[*Yank*'s advice: Brother, you'd better sit down in a hurry and write that girl friend a long letter. And the first thing you should tell her is to beg or borrow enough money pronto to pay back every cent. . . . Then she should send that dough together with a full and frank confession of her unenviable position to the Allowances Branch. . . . What can they do to the girl friend? . . . [She can] be punished by a fine of not more than $2,000 or imprisonment for not more than one year, or both. . . . [You can] be punished by a fine of not more than $5,000, imprisonment for not more than two years, or both. Come to think about it, mark that letter "Registered-Air Mail-Special Delivery."] (From *The Best from Yank.*)

1125. I wish to propose a toast to your future deliveries of Lend-Lease [q.v.] materiel which I am sure will arrive on time in the future, and will not be arriving late, as have shipments to date! (Russian official at dinner party, Teheran, November 1943; quoted in *As He Saw It* by Elliott Roosevelt.)

[During this part of the formal Russian dinner, all conversations were carried on through toasts.]

1126. To answer that question would make me a guesser, not a meteorologist. (Meteorologist at Allied Headquarters, June 5, 1944; cited in *My Three Years with Eisenhower*, by Harry C. Butcher.)

[In answer to Eisenhower's question, "What will the weather be on D-Day [q.v.] in the Channel and over the French coast?"]

1127. White sheets for Christmas! (A wounded U.S. infantryman, Huertgen Forest, Germany, fall 1944; quoted in *Road to Huertgen: Forest in Hell*, by Paul Boesch.)

1128. They got us surrounded—the poor bastards. (American medic to wounded soldier, Bastogne, Belgium, December 1944; cited in *Citizen Soldiers*, by Stephen E. Ambrose.)

1129. What are you looking for—fingerprints? (GI undergoing "short-arms inspection" after a year in Alaska, ca. 1944.)

1130. That's the mine in which the gold is buried. (German midwife to U.S. soldiers who had helped bring her to a woman about to give birth, Germany, April 1945.)

[The hiding place was a salt mine, with a cache of hundreds of millions in gold plus art treasures.]

1131. G.I. sure stands for General Ike. (American soldier freed from a German prison camp during a visit by Eisenhower, May 21, 1945; cited in *My Three Years with Eisenhower*, by Harry C. Butcher.)

1132. Thinking of atomic energy in terms of the atom bomb is like thinking of electricity in terms of the electric chair. (Late 1945.)

1133. The pessimists ended up in America. The optimists ended up in Auschwitz. (ca. 1945.)

[Referring to the Jews of Germany and Austria.]

1134. Anxious to rescue history from simple moral judgments, historians have been restoring the reputations of many a traditional villain. . . . But no one (outside Germany) seemed to have thought of scrubbing up Hitler—until now. In *The Origins of the Second World War*, Oxford historian A. J. P. Taylor [q.v.] finds excuses for Hitler and reasons to blame nearly everybody else. . . . Like other statesmen of his time, he [Hitler] was defending the national interest in a cleanly Machiavellian way. (Review, *Time*, January 12, 1962.)

15

War Movies

The title of every war movie is a quotation all its own. It may be the name of a famous battle or a slogan or a particular viewpoint. Maybe the title is a message of hope, defiance, or rage. Sometimes it is a tribute to some arm of the military—or just plain propaganda. Each movie title will speak for itself—and a brief description of the film will follow.

With some exceptions, as noted, the movies below represent American and British films made *during* the war *about* the war. Two Italian movies made shortly after the war are included because of their exceptional quality: *Shoeshine* and *Open City*. Several movies made during the war—ostensibly about earlier periods in history—contained less-than-subtle messages about the German and Japanese enemy. These include *Wilson*, *Fighting 69th*, and *Jack London*. The one postwar American movie included here is *Best Years of Our Lives*.

During the war, many successful films had absolutely nothing to do with the war. These included dramas, musicals, and sheer fantasies—for example, *Meet Me in St. Louis*, *Going My Way*, *Maltese Falcon*, *Double Indemnity*, *Lassie Come Home*, *Citizen Kane*, *Fantasia*, and *Dumbo*. Such films are not represented below.

1135. *Action in the North Atlantic*: Humphrey Bogart and Raymond Massey are merchant seamen fighting off Nazi submarines. (1943)

1136. *Aerial Gunner*: Richard Arlen and Chester Morris do basic training. (1943)

1137. *Air Force*: John Garfield, Harry Carey, and Gig Young in drama about a Flying Fortress battling the Japanese from Manila to the Coral Sea. (1943)

1138. *Air Raid Wardens*: Laurel and Hardy as Civil Defense wardens. (1943)

1139. *Back to Bataan*: John Wayne and Anthony Quinn organize Filipino guerrilla activity. (1945)

1140. *Bataan*: Robert Taylor, George Murphy, and Thomas Mitchell fight a lonely battle against Japanese invaders. (1943)

1141. *Battle of San Pietro*: Documentary of war in Italy, directed by John Huston. (1944)

1142. *Behind the Rising Sun*: Tom Neal, J. Carroll Naish, and Robert Ryan in a heavy-handed propaganda film. (1943)

1143. *Bell for Adano*: John Hodiak, William Bendix, and Gene Tierney in story of American occupation of an Italian town. Based on John Hersey (q.v.) novel. (1945)

1144. *Best Years of Our Lives*: Frederic March, Dana Andrews, and Harold Russell are returning GIs, and Myrna Loy, Teresa Wright, and Virginia Mayo are among the women they come home to. Classic film won top Academy Awards. Some years later, during the Korean War, cartoonist Milton Caniff invited readers of *Steve Canyon* to vote for the movie that they thought best portrayed American life. The idea was that, in the Caniff comic strip, Red Chinese soldiers would capture the film and get a chance to see what America was all about. Readers voted for *Best Years*. (1946)

1145. *Betrayal from the East*: Lee Tracy and Nancy Kelly in Japanese bad-guy film. (1945)

1146. *Blood on the Sun*: James Cagney is an American reporter in Tokyo who discovers Japanese plot prior to Pearl Harbor. (1945)

1147. *Bombardier*: Pat O'Brien, Randolph Scott, and Eddie Albert in drama about bombing crew and training. (1943)

1148. *Buck Privates*: Bud Abbott and Lou Costello in comedy about being in the army. Andrews Sisters provide the songs. (1941)

1149. *Casablanca*: Humphrey Bogart and Ingrid Bergman star in the great movie classic about love and sacrifice in French North Africa prior to Pearl Harbor. Rounding out the cast are Claude Rains, Paul Henreid, Conrad Veidt, Peter Lorre, and Sydney Greenstreet. A favorite with movie fans born decades after the film was made. Best known for the song "As Time Goes By" and for two lines of dialogue—one of which was never spoken in the film. Rains utters the line, "Round up the usual suspects." No one, however, ever said, "Play it again, Sam." Actual line by Bergman was: "Play it, Sam." Line by Bogart was: "You played it for her, you can play it for me. . . . Play it!" Took several Academy Awards. (1942)

1150. *Caught in the Draft*: Bob Hope, Dorothy Lamour, and Eddie Bracken in comedy about army life. (1941)

1151. *China*: Alan Ladd, William Bendix, and Loretta Young in drama about Japanese war in China. (1943)

1152. *China Sky*: Randolph Scott, Ruth Warrick, and Anthony Quinn in story about doctors in China. Loosely based on Pearl Buck story. (1945)

1153. *Commandos Strike at Dawn*: Paul Muni is a Norwegian working with the British commandos. (1942)

1154. *Confessions of a Nazi Spy*: Edward G. Robinson as a G-man tracking Nazi spies. Others in cast include George Sanders, Paul Lucas, and Francis Lederer. (1939)

1155. *Corvette K-225*: Randolph Scott in story of convoy crossing the Atlantic, bound for Russia. Much of the battle footage is real. (1943)

1156. *Crash Dive*: Tyrone Power and Dana Andrews are submarine officers; Anne Baxter, the love interest. (1943)

1157. *Cry Havoc*: Margaret Sullavan, Joan Blondell, Ann Southern, Fay Bainter, and Marsha Hunt play nurses on Bataan. (1943)

1158. *Days of Glory*: Gregory Peck leads a Russian guerrilla force against the Nazis. (1944)

1159. *December 7th*: Walter Huston plays a naive Uncle Sam in this John Ford "documentary." This heavy-handed propaganda film held Japanese-Americans in Hawaii up to scorn and contempt. It also pointed a finger at the American military for being asleep prior to the Pearl Harbor attack. The original eighty-two-minute version was suppressed by the U.S. government. A thirty-four-minute version was released during the war and won an Academy Award. (1943)

1160. *Der Fuehrer's Face*: Walt Disney cartoon, originally called *In Nutzy Land*. Donald Duck does not want to go to work in a defense plant. One night he has a nightmare in which he dreams about living in Nutzy Land. He awakes happily, ready to do his bit for the war effort. The name of the cartoon was changed to that of its featured song, which was to be popularized by Spike Jones. The cartoon won an Academy Award. (1942)

1161. *Desperate Journey*: Errol Flynn, Raymond Massey, and Ronald Reagan star in drama about Allied fliers downed in Poland. (1942)

1162. *Destination Tokyo*: Cary Grant is a submarine commander with crew members John Garfield and Alan Hale. They go into Japanese waters to carry the war to the enemy. (1943)

1163. *Dive Bomber*: Errol Flynn, Fred MacMurray, and Ralph Bellamy study physical problems in dive situations. (1941)

1164. *Dragon Seed*: Katharine Hepburn and Walter Huston in story about small village caught up in Sino-Japanese war. Based on Pearl Buck novel. (1944)

1165. *Eagle Squadron*: Eddie Albert, Robert Stack, and Nigel Bruce in story about American volunteers who join the Royal Air Force to fight Hitler. (1942)

1166. *Edge of Darkness*: Errol Flynn and Ann Sheridan as Norwegians fighting the Nazi occupiers. (1943)

1167. *Fallen Sparrow*: John Garfield, a veteran of the Spanish Civil War, is hunted by Nazis who are after a memento of that war. Other cast members include Walter Slezak and Maureen O'Hara. (1943)

1168. *Fighting Seabees*: John Wayne and Dennis O'Keefe are members of a Navy Construction Battalion (C.B.'s, later Seabees) in the Pacific. (1944)

1169. *Fighting 69th*: James Cagney, Pat O'Brien, and George Brent in story of the U.S. Army's 69th Division during World War I. The enemy was Germany. This had a subtle effect on American public opinion in the early years of World War II. (1940)

1170. *Fire over England*: see *That Hamilton Woman*.

1171. *First Yank into Tokyo*: Tom Neal, Keye Luke, and Barbara Hale in yarn about rescuing an American prisoner in Japan. (1945)

1172. *Five Graves to Cairo*: Franchot Tone and Erich von Stroheim in mystery thriller about how Nazis prepared for victory in Egypt. (1943)

1173. *Flight Command*: Robert Taylor, Walter Pidgeon, and Red Skelton in film about navy fliers. (1940)

1174. *Flight for Freedom*: Rosalind Russell and Fred MacMurray star in film that purports to tell what happened to flier Amelia Earhart, who disappeared over the Pacific in the late 1930s. The names have been chanaged, as well as the facts. (1943)

1175. *Flight Lieutenant*: Glenn Ford and Pat O'Brien in yarn about army pilots. (1942)

1176. *For Whom the Bell Tolls*: Gary Cooper, Ingrid Bergman, Akim Tamiroff, and Katina Paxinou in brutal, ugly story of Spanish Civil War. Truly extraordinary. Based on Ernest Hemingway novel. (1943)

1177. *Foreign Correspondent*: Joel McCrea, George Sanders, Herbert Marshall, Robert Benchley, Laraine Day, and Edmund Gwenn in spy thriller. Story of assassination, kidnapping, and a secret treaty protocol make for super Hitchcock. (1940)

1178. *49th Parallel*: Raymond Massey, Leslie Howard, and Laurence Olivier in British film about a manhunt for Nazis at large in Canada. (1941)

1179. *Four Jills in a Jeep*: Martha Raye, Carole Landis, Mitzi Mayfair, and Kay Francis on a USO (United Service Organizations) tour to entertain the troops. Features guest appearances by numerous stars. (1944)

1180. *God Is My Co-Pilot*: Dennis Morgan and Raymond Massey are American volunteers in the Flying Tigers in China. (1945)

1181. *Government Girl*: Olivia de Havilland helps Sonny Tufts cut through government red tape in Washington. (1943)

1182. *Great Dictator*: Charlie Chaplin's devastating satire of Adolf Hitler. Chaplin plays a dual role: the dictator and a lookalike barber. (1940)

1183. *Guadalcanal Diary*: William Bendix, Lloyd Nolan, Preston Foster, and Anthony Quinn in movie based on book by Richard Tregaskis. Battle for one of the Solomon Islands in the Pacific. (1943)

1184. *Gung Ho!*: Randolph Scott leads raid on Japanese-held island. (1943)

1185. *Guy Named Joe*: Spencer Tracy is a dead pilot who comes back to help a live pilot, Van Johnson. (1944)

1186. *Hail the Conquering Hero*: Eddie Bracken has been pretending to be a marine. When he has to go home, he is helped in the masquerade by real marines. (1944)

1187. *Hangmen Also Die*: Brian Donlevy in drama about atrocities in Czechoslovakia after the assassination of top Nazi Reinhard Heydrich (q.v.). (1943)

1188. *Happy Land*: Don Ameche and Frances Dee wonder if son's death in the war was worth it. (1943)

1189. *Hitler—Dead or Alive*: Ward Bond and a small group of bounty hunters are hired to kill Hitler. (1943)

1190. *Hitler Gang*: Robert Watson and Martin Kosleck in drama tracing the history of the top Nazi leaders. (1944)

1191. *Hitler's Children*: Bonita Granville, Tim Holt, and Otto Kruger in story of how Nazi education affects German youth. (1943)

1192. *Hollywood Canteen*: Bette Davis and John Garfield head a huge cast welcoming the canteen's opening for servicemen and -women. (1944)

1193. *Hotel Berlin*: Andrea King, Helmut Dantine, and Raymond Massey are hotel guests in the closing months of the war. (1945)

1194. *House on 92nd Street*: Signe Hasso, Lloyd Nolan, and William Eythe in story of German espionage in the United States. (1945)

1195. *Human Comedy*: Mickey Rooney is a Western Union messenger boy and Frank Morgan the telegraph operator in this poignant story of small-town life during the war. Other cast members include Marsha Hunt, Fay Bainter, and Van Johnson. Based on William Saroyan novel. (1943)

1196. *In Nutzy Land*: see *Der Fuehrer's Face.*

1197. *In the Navy*: Bud Abbott and Lou Costello in the navy with Dick Powell. Songs by the Andrews Sisters. (1941)

1198. *In Which We Serve*: Noel Coward and John Mills in stunning British drama of naval officers. Film ran into censorship problems in the United States because of what was then seen as strong language. (1942)

1199. *Jack London*: Michael O'Shea plays the title role in this story, which takes place early in the twentieth century. Film is included here because of strong anti-Japanese viewpoint shown during Russo-Japanese war sequences. (1943)

1200. *Joe Smith, American*: Robert Young is a defense worker set upon by Nazi spies. (1942)

1201. *Journey for Margaret*: Margaret O'Brien in her first starring role as survivor of London blitz. (1942)

1202. *Ladies Courageous*: Loretta Young, Diana Barrymore, Geraldine Fitzgerald in story of women taking active part in war effort through air transport. (1944)

1203. *Lifeboat*: Tallulah Bankhead, William Bendix, and Canada Lee are among ship surviors and Walter Slezak a U-boat survivor in a truly extraordinary war movie. Hitchcock scores as director. (1944)

1204. *Man Hunt*: Walter Pidgeon is a hunter who wants to see if it is possible to kill Hitler, while George Sanders is a Nazi on his trail. A thriller, taut with suspense. (1941)

1205. *Marine Raiders*: Pat O'Brien, Barton MacLane, and Robert Ryan invade Guadalcanal. (1944)

1206. *Master Race*: George Coulouris is an unreconstructed Nazi, even as defeat looms for the Third Reich. (1944)

1207. *Medal for Benny*: Arturo de Cordova, Dorothy Lamour, and J. Carroll Naish in simple story of a dead war hero and how his decoration affects his small town. (1945)

1208. *Mission to Moscow*: Walter Huston as U.S. ambassador to the Soviet Union, in movie based on book by Joseph E. Davies (q.v.). (1943)

1209. *Moon Is Down*: Cedric Hardwicke, Lee J. Cobb, and Henry Travers in powerful film version of John Steinbeck's novel about Norwegian resistance to the Nazis. (1943)

1210. *More the Merrier*: Jean Arthur, Charles Coburn, and Joel McCrea and how they solve the housing shortage in Washington during the war. Fun and innocence during a time of total war. (1943)

1211. *Mortal Storm*: James Stewart, Margaret Sullavan, and Frank Morgan as the good guys, and Robert Young and Dan Dailey as Nazis in the early years of the Third Reich. In deference to Neutrality Laws, specific reference to Jews as Nazi targets was avoided. Nevertheless, probably the toughest anti-Nazi film out of Hollywood prior to Pearl Harbor. (1940)

1212. *Mrs. Miniver*: Greer Garson, Walter Pidgeon, and Teresa Wright show stiff upper lip during English blitz. Academy Awards went to the picture, director, and stars Garson and Wright. At the awards ceremony, Garson delivered the longest acceptance speech in Academy history. (1942)

1213. *None Shall Escape*: Marsha Hunt and Alexander Knox in drama that foreshadowed Nuremberg. (1944)

1214. *North Star*: Anne Baxter, Walter Brennan, Dana Andrews, Walter Huston, and Erich von Stroheim in drama about Russians fighting Germans. (1943)

1215. *Objective Burma*: Errol Flynn takes on the Japanese almost single-handedly in action-packed drama. British were miffed at not being shown in this area of operations. (1945)

1216. *One of Our Aircraft Is Missing*: Godfrey Tearle and Eric Portman in British film about downed pilots trying to make their way back to freedom. (1941)

1217. *Open City*: Aldo Fabrizzi and Anna Magnani in Italian film about Italy at war. Frederico Fellini wrote and Roberto Rosselini directed this powerful, sensitive production. (1945)

1218. *Passage to Marseille*: Humphrey Bogart, Claude Rains, Peter Lorre, and Sydney Greenstreet in story of prison escapees fighting the Nazis. (1944)

1219. *Pied Piper*: Monty Woolley and Roddy McDowall in story of grumpy old man who reluctantly agrees to take children out of Nazi-held Europe. Heartwarming. (1942)

1220. *Pimpernel Smith*: Leslie Howard as the hero smuggling refugees out of Nazi Europe and Francis Sullivan as his pursuer in British thriller. Most memorable dialogue: As Howard escapes into the shadows, Sullivan cries out, "Come back! Come back!" Howard almost whispers his response: "I'll be back. We'll *all* be back." (1941)

1221. *Pride of the Marines*: John Garfield is Al Schmid. True story of marine hero blinded in battle and how he handles rehabilitation. (1945)

1222. *Purple Heart*: Dana Andrews, Sam Levene, and Farley Granger are captured American fliers put on trial in Japan. They can save their lives if they reveal the base from which they took off. (1944)

1223. *Sahara*: Humphrey Bogart and his tank crew, including Dan Duryea and Bruce Bennett, hold off a large German force in the North African desert. J. Carroll Naish shines as an Italian prisoner of war. (1943)

1224. *See Here, Private Hargrove*: Robert Walker plays draftee Marion Hargrove (q.v.) in film version of wartime best-seller. (1944)

1225. *Sergeant York*: Gary Cooper is World War I hero Alvin York, a role that won him an Academy Award. The need to take a stand against a deadly enemy influenced American moviegoers prior to Pearl Harbor. (1941)

1226. *Shoeshine*: Rinaldo Smerdoni, Franco Interlenghi, and Anielo Mele in Italian classic about life in Nazi-held Italy. Vittorio De Sica directed this—one of the finest movies made about the war. (1946)

1227. *Since You Went Away*: Claudette Colbert, Joseph Cotten, and Shirley Temple in film about a family left behind. (1944)

1228. *So Proudly We Hail*: Claudette Colbert, Paulette Goddard, and Veronica Lake as nurses on Bataan. (1943)

1229. *Somewhere I'll Find You*: Clark Gable and Lana Turner in film about war correspondents. (1942)

1230. *Song of Russia*: Robert Taylor and Susan Peters in a Russian-American love story. (1943)

1231. *Stage Door Canteen*: Katharine Hepburn, Harpo Marx, Edgar Bergen, and many others in star-studded film about canteen for GIs. (1943)

1232. *Stand By for Action*: Charles Laughton, Robert Taylor, and Brian Donlevy on U.S. destroyer. (1942)

1233. *Story of Dr. Wassell*: Gary Cooper as navy doctor serving in the Dutch East Indies during the war. Factual account based on book by James Hilton (q.v.). (1944)

1234. *Story of G.I. Joe*: Burgess Meredith as Ernie Pyle (q.v.), the war correspondent who wrote about the war from the GI's point of view. Although the movie is largely fictional, it does deal with Pyle's most memorable story—the death of an infantry captain in Italy. Robert Mitchum plays the captain. Superb. (1945)

1235. *The Sullivans*: Thomas Mitchell is the father of five sons who go down on the same ship. True story. (1944)

1236. *Tender Comrade*: Ginger Rogers lives with other wives of servicemen overseas. After the war, Leila Rogers, mother of the actress, told a congressional committee that she insisted that a line assigned to Ginger be spoken by someone else. The line: "We'll share and share alike. That's what I call democracy." Mrs. Rogers told the congressmen: "That's what *I* call Communism!" (1943)

1236a. *That Hamilton Woman*: Laurence Olivier as Lord Nelson and Vivien Leigh as Lady Hamilton. Although the movie dealt with the war against Napoleon, Winston Churchill felt it sent a strong message to an England then under siege by Hitler. (1941)

1237. *They Were Expendable*: Robert Montgomery commands torpedo boat squadron in the Pacific. Movie is based on book by W. L. White. (1945)

1238. *Thirty Seconds over Tokyo*: Spencer Tracy as Jimmy Doolittle and Van Johnson as Ted Lawson in story of the first bombing raid on Japan. Based on the Lawson book. (1944)

1239. *This Is the Army*: George Murphy, Ronald Reagan, and Irving Berlin appear in film version of GI stage show. (1943)

1240. *This Land Is Mine*: Charles Laughton, Maureen O'Hara, and George Sanders in tale of a Frenchman who takes on the Nazis. (1943)

1241. *Till We Meet Again*: Barbara Britton helps Ray Milland escape from the Nazis in occupied Europe. (1944)

1242. *To Be Or Not to Be*: Jack Benny and Carole Lombard in comedy about acting troupe trying to outwit Nazis in Poland. This was Lombard's last film before she was killed in a plane crash. (1942)

1243. *To the Shores of Tripoli*: John Payne in the marines. (1942)

1244. *Tomorrow the World*: Skippy Homeier and Frederic March in story of an American family adopting a young Nazi. Originally a successful Broadway play. (1944)

1245. *Two Girls and a Sailor*: Jimmy Durante, Gracie Allen, and Lena Horne provide some of the entertainment in canteen musical. Van Johnson is the sailor. (1944)

1246. *Uncertain Glory*: Errol Flynn is a French rogue who is given the opportunity to redeem himself and save Nazi hostages from death. (1944)

1247. *Underground*: Jeffrey Lynn and Philip Dorn as German brothers in conflict—one a Nazi and the other an anti-Nazi. (1941)

1248. *Up in Arms*: Danny Kaye in the army, his first starring role. (1944)

1249. *Vacation from Marriage*: Robert Donat and Deborah Kerr in British romantic comedy about stodgy married couple, separated by war, whose experiences change them. (1945)

1250. *Victory through Air Power*: Disney animation of the book by Alexander Seversky (q.v.), strong advocate of air power. (1943)

1251. *Wake Island*: Brian Donlevy, William Bendix, and Robert Preston are marines fighting off the Japanese invasion of tiny Pacific isle. (1942)

1252. *Watch on the Rhine*: Paul Lukas and Bette Davis in screen adapatation of Lilian Hellman play. German refugees on the run from Nazis in America. (1943)

1253. *Where Do We Go from Here?*: Fred MacMurray in musical fantasy about a man who finds a magic lamp during a scrap metal drive. He then goes back into history, sailing with Columbus and trying to warn Washington about Benedict Arnold. Music by Kurt Weill and Ira Gershwin. (1945)

1254. *Wilson*: Alexander Knox as President Woodrow Wilson during World War I and the later fight for the League of Nations. Incidents of unlimited submarine warfare and German promise to return Texas to Mexico strengthened American World War II resolve. (1944)

1255. *Wing and a Prayer*: Dana Andrews and Don Ameche on an aircraft carrier. (1944)

1256. *Yank in the R.A.F.*: Tyrone Power volunteers. (1941)

16

War Songs

1257. "Any Bonds Today?": Irving Berlin wrote this prior to Pearl Harbor to encourage savings in Defense Bonds.

1258. "Boogie Woogie Bugle Boy of Company B": Jazzy swing tune made popular by the Andrews Sisters.

1259. "Comin' in on a Wing and a Prayer": A letter from a pilot describing how he made it back to base inspired Jimmy McHugh and Harold Adamson to write this song.

1260. "Der Fuehrer's Face": Satirical look at the Third Reich was in a Disney cartoon called *In Nutzy Land.* Spike Jones version took off.

1261. "Don't Sit Under the Apple Tree": GI appeals to his girl to stay faithful to him.

1262. "G. I. Jive": A Johnny Mercer favorite both on the war front and the home front.

1263. "God Bless America": Kate Smith rendition of Irving Berlin patriotic song made it a favorite for all time.

1264. "Goodbye, Mamma, I'm Off to Yokohama": One of the less successful songs of the war.

1265. "I'll Be Seeing You": Originally presented in 1938, the song languished for awhile. It then became immensely popular during the war, a Bing Crosby hit.

1266. "It's Been a Long, Long Time": Sammy Cahn and Julie Styne wrote the favorite homecoming song of the war.

1267. "Johnny Zero": Novelty song about a kid who always got zeroes in school. He becomes a hero by shooting down Japanese Zero aircraft.

1268. "Last Time I Saw Paris": Sentimental ballad written after the fall of Paris to the Nazis.

1269. "Lili Marlene": German war song about a soldier and his girl. Originally a poem written in 1923, it was set to music in 1936. It was popular with both Allied and German soldiers.

1270. "Meadowlands": Red Army war song.

1271. "Oh, How I Hate to Get Up in the Morning": Originally written by Irving Berlin during World War I, it returned for the World War II show *This Is the Army*.

1272. "Praise the Lord and Pass the Ammunition": Frank Loesser wrote this song based on the incident of a navy chaplain at Pearl Harbor.

1273. "Remember Pearl Harbor": World War II battle cry became a popular war song.

1274. "Roger Young": Frank Loesser song about a real U.S. Army hero.

1275. "Rosie the Riveter": Honoring the women of America who went to work in the defense plants and shipyards.

1276. "There'll Always Be an England": British song of defiance during the Blitz.

1277. "They're Either Too Young or Too Old": Girl at home tells her serviceman why she stays faithful.

1278. "This Is the Army": Title song for Irving Berlin army show.

1279. "Three Little Sisters": Tongue-in-cheek ballad of fidelity at home.

1280. "We Did It Before": Early American patriotic song.

1281. "We're Gonna Hang Out the Washing on the Siegfried Line": Early British war song.

1282. "When the Lights Go on Again": Somber, reflective song that came out at a particularly low point in the war.

1283. "White Christmas": Irving Berlin's ballad of nostalgia and longing at Christmas time was probably the most moving song of the war.

1284. "White Cliffs of Dover": British song of hope and faith in the future.

17

War Lexicon

The lexicon of World War II could include thousands of military terms, slang expressions, nicknames, cover names, code names of conferences and battles, names of weapons, and so on. Here are some of the more famous.

1285. Ace: Fighter pilot who downed five enemy planes or more.

1286. Ack-ack: Antiaircraft fire.

1287. Admiral Q: President Franklin Roosevelt (British code name).

1288. Airacobra: P-39 fighter (U.S. Army Air Force).

1289. American Eagle: Mark Clark (q.v.) U.S. Army general.

1290. AMGOT: Allied Military Government of Occupied Territory. The abbreviation was later chanagd to AMG when it was discovered that AMGOT was an obscene word in a foreign language.

1291. Angel of Death: Joseph Mengele, Nazi doctor who made the "selections" at Auschwitz.

1292. Arcadia: U.S.-British conference in Washington (December 1941–January 1942).

1293. Argonaut: Roosevelt-Churchill-Stalin conference at Yalta (q.v., February 1945).

1294. Ash can: Depth charge.

1295. Atomic Bill: William L. Laurence, reporter for the *New York Times* who covered the race for the atomic bomb. (This was to distinguish him from William Lawrence, a foreign correspondent for the *Times*.)

1296. Avalanche: Code name for the Allied invasion of Salerno, Italy (September 1943).

1297. Avast!: Stop! (U.S. Navy).

1298. Avenger: TBF torpedo bomber (U.S. Navy).

1299. AWOL: Absent without official leave.

1300. Axis Sally: Mildred Gillars, an American who broadcast propaganda for the Nazis.

1301. Barbarossa: German plan for invasion of the Soviet Union (June 1941).

1302. Battle wagon: Battleship.

1303. Beast of Belsen: Josef Kramer, commandant of the Belsen concentration camp.

1304. Beaufort: British torpedo bomber.

1305. Beetle: Walter Bedell Smith (q.v.), who was Eisenhower's Chief of Staff at Supreme Allied Headquarters.

1306. Bigot: Code name for the secrets of the D-Day (q.v.) operation known as Overlord. An individual given access to this information was known as a Bigot, or was Bigotted.

1307. Binnacle list: Sick list (U.S. Navy).

1308. Bitch of Buchenwald: Ilse Koch, wife of the commandant at Buchenwald concentration camp.

1309. Blenheim: British bomber.

1310. Bodyguard: Allied code name for operations to fool the Germans about where the D-Day (q.v.) landings would take place.

1311. Bolero: Code name for the movement of American forces from the United States to Great Britain for the forthcoming invasion.

1312. Boot: Recruit.

1313. Braid: General George C. Marshall code name.

1314. Bride: Charles de Gaulle (q.v.) code name.

1315. Brig: Ship's prison.

1316. Buccaneer: SB2A dive bomber (U.S. Navy).

1317. Bull: William Halsey (q.v.), U.S. naval commander.

1318. Butcher of Lyon: Klaus Barbie (q.v.), Gestapo leader in occupied France.

1319. Buzz bomb: British name for Hitler's V-1 flying bomb, a jet-propelled plane. It was succeeded by the V-2, a rocket aircraft.

1320. Cargo: President Franklin D. Roosevelt code name.

1321. Catalina: PBY patrol bomber (U.S. Navy).

1322. Celestes: Chiang Kai-shek (q.v.) code name.

1323. Churchill: British tank.

1324. Cicero: Elias Basna, Albanian who spied for the Germans in the British embassy in Ankara, Turkey.

1325. Colonel Kent: Winston Churchill code name.

1326. Colonel Warren: Winston Churchill code name.

1327. Condition One: U.S. Navy designation aboard ship indicating that an enemy attack is imminent. Condition Two indicates a surprise attack may take place at any time. Condition Three indicates an attack is unlikely.

1328. Coronado: PB2Y patrol bomber (U.S. Navy).

1329. Coronet: Code name for the American plan to invade Japan.

1330. Corsair: F4U fighter (U.S. Navy).

1331. Cromwell: British signal that an invasion of England by Germany was imminent.

1332. Cut of his jib: Appearance (U.S. Navy).

1333. Dauntless: SBD dive bomber (U.S. Navy).

1334. Davey Jones' Locker: The bottom of the sea (U.S. Navy).

1335. Dear John: Letter from home to a GI breaking off a relationship.

1336. Desert Fox: Erwin Rommel (q.v.), leader of the German Afrika Korps.

1337. Dicker ("Fatty"): Field Marshal Hermann Goering (q.v.).

1338. Dogface: American infantryman.

1339. Dog tags: Identification tags worn around the neck of every member of the U.S. armed forces.

1340. Doughboy: Early in the war, name for the American soldier. Later replaced by GI Joe or just plain GI.

1341. Dragoon: Code name for the Allied invasion of southern France (September 1944).

1342. Duce ("leader"): Benito Mussolini (q.v.), dictator of Fascist Italy.

1343. Dugout Doug: Douglas MacArthur, commander of Allied forces in the Southwest Pacific.

1344. Egg in your beer: Expression used by an American soldier indicating too much of a good thing.

1345. English Parson (Hitler's reference): Prime Minister Neville Chamberlain (q.v.).

1346. Enigma: The German decoding machine whose secrets were uncovered by Ultra (q.v.).

1347. Eureka: Roosevelt-Churchill-Stalin conference at Teheran (November–December 1943).

1348. Fat Man: Atomic bomb dropped on Nagasaki (August 1945).

1349. Final Solution: Nazi plan to exterminate the Jews of Europe.

1350. Flattop: Aircraft carrier.

1351. Flying Fortress: B-17 bomber (U.S. Army Air Force).

1352. Focke-Wulf: Manufacturer of the German FW-190 fighter, the FW-200 bomber, and the FW-189 reconnaissance plane.

1353. Former Naval Person: Winston Churchill code name.

1354. Fuehrer ("leader"): Adolf Hitler, Nazi dictator.

1355. Fuehrer's Echo Chamber: Joachim von Ribbentrop (q.v.), German Foreign Minister.

1356. Geronimo!: Shouted by American parachute troops as they leaped from the airplane.

1357. GI Jill: Member of the Women's Army Corps.

1358. GI Joe: American soldier.

1359. Goldbricking: Goofing off. One who did so was a goldbrick.

1360. Gotha: Manufacturer of German gliders.

1361. Grand Inquisitor: Heinrich Himmler (q.v.), head of the Gestapo.

1362. Greetings: Draft notice.

1363. Griffin: German plan to dress some of their troops in American uniforms during Battle of the Bulge (q.v.; December 1944).

1364. Halifax: British bomber.

1365. Hangman: Reinhard Heydrich (q.v.), Nazi official initially assigned to carry out the "Final Solution of the Jewish Problem."

1366. Hap: Henry Arnold (q.v.), head of the U.S. Army Air Force.

1367. Head: Toilet (U.S. Navy).

1368. Heinkel: Manufacturer of German dive bomber He-111, the He-177 bomber, and He-115 reconnaissance plane.

1369. Hellcat: F6F fighter (U.S. Navy).

1370. Helldiver: SB2C dive bomber (U.S. Navy).

1371. Henry Farmer: Enrico Fermi, atomic scientist. Code name.

1372. Hurricane: British fighter plane.

1373. Husky: Code name for the Allied invasion of Sicily (July 1943).

1374. Iceberg: Code name for the American invasion of Okinawa (April 1945).

1375. Ike: Dwight D. Eisenhower.

1376. Intrepid: William Stephenson (q.v.), top British intelligence official.

1377. Jeep: Small U.S. Army automobile, named after an animal character in the comic strip *Popeye*.

1378. Jubilee: Code name for the raid in force on Dieppe, France, by mostly Canadian and British commandos (August 1942).

1379. Junkers: Manufacturer of German bombers, including the Stuka Ju-87 and 88, plus the transports Ju-52, 90, and 290.

1380. Kilroy Was Here: The most famous bit of graffiti of the war. It was scrawled on walls, barns, bunkers, and wherever else American troops fought or were stationed. Although there are a number of soldiers whose last name was Kilroy, the mystery of how and by whom it all started remains a mystery to this day.

1380a. Kingfisher: OS2O reconnaissance (U.S. Navy).

1380b. Kingpin: General Henri Giraud code name. He was a competitor of General de Gaulle (q.v.) for French leadership prior to the Normandy Invasion.

1381. Konstantinov: General Georgi Zhukov (q.v.), Russian officer. Code name.

1382. Lancaster: British bomber.

1383. Leatherneck: U.S. Marine.

1384. Liberator: B-24 bomber (U.S. Army Air Force).

1385. Lightning: P-38 Fighter (U.S. Army Air Force).

1386. Lightning Joe: Joseph Lawton Collins, U.S. Army general.

1387. Little Adolf: Adolf Eichmann, implementer of the "Final Solution."

1388. Little Boy: Atomic bomb dropped on Hiroshima (August 1945).

1389. Look: General Dwight D. Eisenhower code name.

1390. Lord Haw-Haw: William Joyce (q.v.), an Englishman who broadcast propaganda for the Nazis.

1391. Lord Root of the Matter: Harry L. Hopkins (q.v.), aide and confidante of President Roosevelt.

1392. Magic (q.v.): American intelligence program that broke the Japanese code. Messages obtained from this source were called "Magics."

1393. Majestic: U.S. code name for planned attack on Kyushu, Japan.

1394. Manhattan Project: Code name for America's top secret program to develop an atomic bomb.

1395. Marauder: B-26 bomber (U.S. Army Air Force).

1396. Market-Garden (q.v.): Code name for joint American-British air-ground assault in Holland (September 1944).

1397. Merchant of Venom: Joseph Goebbels (q.v.), German Minister of Propaganda.

1398. Messerschmitt: Manufacturer of German fighter planes, including the Me-109, 110, and 111.

1399. Mickey Mouse: U.S. armed forces training films dealing with venereal disease.

1400. Mitchell: B-25 bomber (U.S. Army Air Force).

1401. Mitsubishi: Manufacturer of Japanese fighter planes, including the Zero, and bombers.

1402. Monty: Bernard Montgomery (q.v.), field marshal of the British army.

1403. Mosquito: British fighter.

1404. Mulberries: Code name for the artificial harbors used by the Allies off the Normandy coast following the D-Day (q.v.) invasion (June 1944).

1405. Mustang: P-51 fighter (U.S. Army Air Force).

1406. Nakajima: Manufacturer of Japanese fighters, bombers, and reconnaissance planes.

1407. Ninety-Day Wonder: A brand-new second lieutenant in the U.S. Army, following three months in Officers Candidate School.

1408. Old Blood and Guts: George S. Patton, Jr. (q.v.), U.S. Army general.

1409. Old Whiskey Soak (Hitler's reference): Prime Minister Winston Churchill.

1410. Orange: Prewar code name for American military action against Japan in the event of future conflict.

1411. Overlord: Code name for the Allied invasion of northern France, D-Day (q.v.; June 6, 1944).

1412. Over the hill: Gone AWOL or deserted.

1413. Panther: German tank.

1414. Paper Clip: U.S. program to round up German scientists during the closing months of the war.

1415. Peanut: General Chiang Kai-shek (q.v.) of Nationalist China.

1416. Pecker checker: Doctor.

1417. Peter parade: *See* short arms inspection.

1418. Pigboat: American submarine.

1419. Pollywog: American sailor who has never crossed the equator.

1420. Priceless: American-British invasion of Italy (September 1943).

1421. Repple-depple: U.S. Army replacement depot for filling in the ranks.

1422. Rubber Lion: Werner von Blomberg (q.v.), German general.

1423. Ruptured duck: Discharge lapel pin in the form of an eagle.

1424. Sea Lion (q.v.): German plan to invade England.

1425. Scuttlebutt: Rumor. U.S. armed forces slang that became part of American standard English. Probable derivation: The scuttle butt on a U.S. naval vessel was a container of fresh water available for drinking. Thus, the scuttle butt was a rough equivalent of the office water cooler, where information was exchanged.

1426. Seabees: U.S. Navy Construction Battalion (C-Bs).

1427. Section 8: Army discharge for mental reasons. On the *M*A*S*H* television series, the character Klinger was seeking a Section 8 discharge.

1428. Semper Fi: Short for "Semper Fidelis" (Always Faithful), motto of the U.S. Marines. When one Marine said it to another, it was the rough equivalent of the British "I'm All Right, Jack."

1429. Sextant: Roosevelt–Churchill–Chiang Kai-shek (q.v.) conference at Cairo (q.v.; November 1943).

1430. Shangri-La: The mythical site of James Hilton's (q.v.) novel *Lost Horizon*. Roosevelt, in a jocular vein, told a press conference that the first U.S. air raid on Tokyo was launched from "Shangri-La."

1431. Sherman: American tank.

1432. Sho-Go: Japanese naval plan against American fleet in Leyte Gulf (October 1944).

1433. Short arms inspection: Medical examination for a sexually transmitted disease. (When inspection is done en masse, called a "peter parade.")

1434. Skinny: Jonathan Wainwright (q.v.), U.S. Army general.

1435. Skivvies: Underwear.

1436. Sky pilot: Chaplain (U.S. armed forces). Often addressed as Padre.

1437. Skymaster: C-54 transport (U.S. Army Air Force).

1438. Skytrain: C-47 glider tug (U.S. Army Air Force).

1439. Slim Jim: James M. Gavin (q.v.), U.S. Army general.

1440. SNAFU: Situation normal, all fouled up (bowdlerized).

1441. Spitfire: British fighter plane.

1442. Stirling: British bomber.

1443. Stormovik: Russian military aircraft, which the Germans called "Black Death."

1444. Stuffy: Hugh Dowding, chief marshal of the Royal Air Force.

1445. Superfortress: B-29 bomber (U.S. Army Air Force).

1446. Swabbie: American sailor.

1447. Terminal: Truman-Churchill-Stalin conference at Potsdam (July–August 1945). In midconference, following British elections, Churchill replaced by Clement Attlee.

1448. Thunderbolt: P-47 fighter (U.S. Army Air Force).

1449. Tiger: German tank.

1450. Tiger of Malaya: Tomoyuki Yamashita (q.v.), Japanese army general.

1451. Tin can: U.S. Navy destroyer.

1452. Tito: Josip Broz, leader of the Yugoslav Partisans.

1453. Tokyo Rose: Iva D'Aquino, an American who broadcast propaganda from Japan.

1454. Torch: Allied invasion of French North Africa (November 1942).

1455. Trinity: Site of the explosion of the first atomic device, Alamogordo, New Mexico (July 1945).

1456. TS: Tough shit. Derogatory response to a gripe or complaint. A constant complainer might get the advice, "Go see the chaplain and have him punch your TS card."

1457. Typhoon: British fighter plane.

1458. Ultra (q.v.): British intelligence operation that broke the German secret code of the Enigma machine.

1459. Uncle Joe: Joseph Stalin, dictator of the Soviet Union.

1460. Valkyrie: Plan by German generals to kill Hitler (July 1944).

1461. Vasilev: Joseph Stalin.

1462. V-E Day: Victory-in-Europe day, when Germany surrendered (May 8, 1945).

1463. Vinegar Joe: Joseph W. Stilwell (q.v.), U.S. Army general.

1464. V-J Day: Victory-over-Japan day, when Japan surrendered (September 2, 1945). Some observers believe that August 14, 1945, should be V-J Day, when the Japanese accepted Allied terms. The actual surrender, however, was signed on September 2 aboard the U.S.S. *Missouri*.

1465. Voice of Freedom: Carlos P. Romulo, aide to General MacArthur, who broadcast messages to the people of the Philippines.

1466. Warhawk: P-40 fighter (U.S. Army Air Force).

1467. Wellington: British bomber.

1468. White: German plan to invade Poland (September 1939).

1469. Wild Bill: William J. Donovan (q.v.), who set up the Office of Strategic Services (q.v.), a U.S. intelligence agency.

1470. Wildcat: F4F fighter (U.S. Navy).

1471. Zig-Zag: Code name for Eddie Chapman (q.v.), a British double agent who pretended to work for the Germans.

18

Miscellaneous Quotations

AMERICA FIRST COMMITTEE

The committee was founded by Sears, Roebuck president Robert E. Wood (q.v.) in September 1940. Its purpose was to keep the United States out of the war in Europe. The organization fought every effort by the Roosevelt administration to aid the Allies. The committee would fold following Pearl Harbor. It reached a peak of more than 800,000 members. Among the most prominent were General Hugh Johnson, Eddie Rickenbacker (q.v.), Chester Bowles, William Benton, William Randolph Hearst, Robert R. McCormick, Norman Thomas (q.v.), Alice Roosevelt Longworth, and U.S. Senators Henry Cabot Lodge, Gerald Nye, Burton K. Wheeler (q.v.), Robert M. LaFollette, Jr., and Arthur Vandenberg. Henry Ford was originally a member of the group, but he was dropped because of his reputation for promoting anti-Semitism. The commmittee's major spokesman was aviation hero Charles A. Lindbergh, Jr. (q.v.). His most well-known speech on behalf of the America First Committee was delivered at a rally in Des Moines, Iowa, in which he said:

1472. The three most important groups who have been pressing this country toward war are the British, the Jewish, and the Roosevelt administration.

APOCRYPHA

The personalities of World War II had their stories and legends.

It was rumored during the war that General George Patton (q.v.), on reaching the Rhine, had relieved himself in the river. After the war, it was learned that this was absolutely true.

It is said that when the British were ready to move Rudolf Hess (q.v.) from where he landed in Scotland to London, the trip was delayed so that he would be transported through an area of London where there was not a single bit of wreckage—not even a broken window. This was supposedly designed to shake him up. But that still remains a legend.

The following are regarded as apocryphal—though there may be more truth involved than historians can attest to.

1473. Eisenhower was the best filing clerk I ever had.

[Attributed to Douglas MacArthur, under whom Eisenhower had once served.]

1474. I studied dramatics under MacArthur.

[Attributed to Dwight D. Eisenhower, who had served under MacArthur.]

1475. That's only fair—*we* had them the last time.

[Attributed to Winston Churchill. This was allegedly in response to Joachim von Ribbentrop (q.v.) who boasted, "My dear Churchill, just remember that if a general war breaks out again, *this* time the Italians will be on *our* side."]

1476. As I have told you repeatedly, we British have absolutely nothing to hide.

[Supposedly said by Winston Churchill to President Roosevelt in the White House, when the president wheeled himself into the prime minister's bedroom to find him without any clothes on.]

1477. It was an honorary title—like being made a Kentucky Colonel.

[Attributed to Wernher von Braun (q.v.), explaining how he became a member of the SS.]

"Gallant foes and brave soldiers, the battling bastards had earned the right to be treated with consideration and decency, but their enemies had reserved for them even greater privations and deeper humiliation than any they had yet suffered on Bataan."

—LOUIS MORTON

Captured Japanese film shows Americans carrying their sick and wounded on litters during the Bataan Death March.

BATAAN DEATH MARCH

This sixty-five-mile march was made by American and Filipino prisoners of war who had surrendered on the Bataan peninsula. The six-day march from Mariveles to San Fernando lasted from April 15 to April 21 of 1942. It was a nightmare of Japanese brutality and murder. An estimated 10,000 prisoners lost their lives on the forced march. After the war, Japanese General Masaharu Homma (q.v.) was held responsible for the death march and was executed.

Details of the death march were not revealed to the American public until many months later, although photos of Bataan prisoners being led into captivity were widely published. On April 24, 1942, the *Japan Times & Advertiser* commented on the handling of Allied prisoners.

1478. To show them mercy is to prolong the war. (*Japan Times & Advertiser*, April 24, 1942.)

1479. Gallant foes and brave soldiers, the battling bastards had earned the right to be treated with consideration and decency, but their enemies had reserved for them even greater privations and deeper humiliation than any they had yet suffered on Bataan. (From *The Fall of the Philippines*, by Louis Morton.)

[After the war, historian Louis Morton wrote this about the Bataan prisoners on the death march.]

BULGE, BATTLE OF THE

On December 16, 1944, the German army launched its final offensive of the war. Two dozen Nazi divisions smashed into American positions in the Ardennes in southern Belgium. The German army, under Rundstedt (q.v.), planned to cut through the Ardennes, cross the Meuse River, and then head northwest to take Antwerp. This not only would have deprived the Allies of their supply port but would have allowed the Germans to seize Allied stores there. Eisenhower was determined that the Germans would not reach the Meuse.

The bad weather prevented Allied air attacks, and initially the German offensive was successful. The German assault was stalled at Bastogne, where surrounded American troops refused to surrender. It was during the Ardennes campaign that American prisoners of war were massacred by the Germans at Malmedy. Once the weather cleared, the Allies stabilized their lines and drove the Germans back. January 1945 saw a withdrawal of German forces from the Ardennes to the Eastern Front. Total German casualties in the Bulge: 120,000 killed, wounded, and missing. American casualties were over 75,000.

Military historian and Marshall biographer Forrest Pogue summarized the thinking behind Hitler's last gamble:

1480. As matters stood, he had two choices. If he could catch the Americans off balance in the Ardennes, perhaps he could sweep through to Antwerp, knocking out the timetable for the offensive and seizing and destroying vital stocks. At best a smashing success might slow Allied preparations until there might be a chance for a negotiated peace. At worst, time might be gained to develop some miracle weapon—the jet fighter, for example, against which the Allies . . . had no effective counter weapon. The gamble was extreme, but earlier risks had worked for Hitler. All in all it seemed better to hazard loss than to wait for certain disaster. (From *George C. Marshall: Organizer of Victory*, by Forrest Pogue.)

CLARK MISSION

On October 21, 1942, just sixteen days prior to the Allied landings in French North Africa, a group of American military and diplomatic officials assembled. They had a top secret mission: to land by submarine on the coast of North Africa and meet with French officials. The idea was to enable the landings to take place with a minimum of French resistance and to establish a working relationship with the emerging government of French North Africa. General Mark Clark (q.v.) and diplomat Robert Murphy (q.v.) headed the group. There were ticklish problems to be resolved. The military details proved far less sticky than the diplomatic ones. What part would Admiral Jean Darlan (q.v.) play in the new government—and what about General Henri Giraud? The secret meetings took place in a small farmhouse near Cherchell, seventy-five miles west of Algiers. When the mission returned to temporary headquarters at Gibraltar, a press briefing was held for the correspondents. Clark deemphasized the political and military problems and played up the adventurous aspects. Robert Murphy described Clark's performance:

1481. Since wartime security made it advisable to conceal the serious complications which had arisen at Cherchell, Clark diverted attention from the political aspects by describing some comical aspects of the venture. At one point the local police had burst in upon us, forcing the American visitors to hide in a wine cellar, while I posed as a somewhat inebriated member of a raucous social gathering. Fortunately the police were not looking for military conspirators but for smugglers. They had been tipped off by our host's Arab servants, who suspected that smugglers were involved in the unusual activities around the remote farmhouse, and hoped to collect the generous rewards for information leading to seizure of smuggled goods. This incident made lively newspaper copy, a welcome diversion from the war's somber happenings, and Clark further embellished his tale by relating how he lost his pants while getting back into the submarine. But the amusing manner in which Clark described the dangerous French-American meetings added unintentionally to the British-American publics' downgrading of the importance—actually the vital necessity—of French assistance to our precarious expedition. Few Britons or Americans appreciated at the time of the invasion, or in the months which followed, how serious prolonged French resistance would have been to the Allied operations. Support from the French military and political administrations in Africa was even more essential to the campaign's success during the months following the invasion than it was on African D-Day. (From *Diplomat among Warriors*, by Robert Murphy.)

COAL STRIKE

In June 1943, following months of negotiations with the War Labor Board, John L. Lewis of the United Mine Workers struck the coal mines. He had been trying to get a $2-a-day increase for the miners. The country was in an uproar, as coal was essential to the war effort. President Roosevelt took over the coal mines and urged miners to return to work. Meanwhile, Congress passed the Smith-Connally Bill, making it illegal to strike government plants. Lewis gave in after six days, and the miners went back to work. The president later vetoed the bill, but his veto was overridden by Congress.

There are numerous quotations of outrage by citizens, soldiers, editorial writers, and members of Congress. But the two most memorable are probably by Lewis and by one of his union members:

1482. You can't dig coal with bayonets. (John L. Lewis, shortly after the U.S. government seized the mines.)

1483. I ain't a traitor, damn 'em I ain't a traitor. I'll stay out until hell freezes over. Dickie was fighting for one thing, I'm fighting for another and they ain't so far apart. (Anonymous coal miner who received word during the strike that his son had been killed in action in the Pacific.)

COMMITTEE TO DEFEND AMERICA BY AIDING THE ALLIES

This organization was founded in 1940 to counter the work of the isolationist America First Committee (q.v.). William Allen White, the editor of the *Emporia Gazette* of Kansas, was chairman of the group. Its executive director was Clark Eichelberger. Other distinguished members included columnist Walter Lippman, Professor Paul Douglas of the University of Chicago, and retired General of the Army John J. Pershing, America's top military hero of World War I. The organization backed Roosevelt administration policies on Lend-

Lease (q.v.), conscription, and increased aid to Great Britain. Its basic message was for America to mobilize to stop Hitler.

Eichelberger put it this way:

1484. We must point out with all possible vigor that the United States will have a right to participate in the building of the future world peace if it will make its full contribution to the defeat of the aggressors. Consequently our participation in the conflict should be speeded up.

D-DAY

On June 6, 1944, the Allies invaded Normandy. The invasion's code name was Overlord. American, British, and Canadian troops were landed on code-named beaches called Utah, Omaha, Juno, Gold, and Sword. More than a 100,000 Allied troops came ashore in the first forty-eight hours. In less than two weeks, that number had swollen to nearly half a million.

The most crucial decision of Overlord was the timing of the operation. Not only the weather but also the tides, the presence of moonlight the night before, and the coming of daylight on the morning of the invasion all had to be taken into account. Originally set for June 5, D-Day had to be postponed because of the bad weather. Eisenhower had to decide whether to postpone for a few days or a few weeks—the longer the delay, the worse the opportunity for surprise. When the weatherman reported a window of opportunity opening up on the morning of June 6, the Supreme Commander made his decision. June 6 it would be:

1485. I'm quite positive we must give the order. I don't like it, but there it is. I don't see how we can possibly do anything else. (Eisenhower, statement to key staff, June 4, 1944.)

DRESDEN FIREBOMBING

On February 13–14, 1945, British and American planes firebombed the German city of Dresden on the Elbe River. Known over the centuries for its magnificent architecture, Dresden had become a major industrial and transportation center. German supplies to the Russian front ran through Dresden. At the time of the bombing, the city held close to 900,000 people, including refugees from other cities and Allied prisoners of war.

The massive use of incendiary bombs created a firestorm in the city, resulting in the destruction of the city and enormous loss of life. Initially, the Germans put the number of dead at 60,000. Later estimates ran much higher.

In her book *Berlin Underground*, Ruth Andreas-Friedrich described the human horror:

1486. All the splendor of a centuries-old civilization had gone up in smoke. Thousands of people met their deaths; they ran like burning torches through the streets, stuck fast in the red-hot asphalt, flung themselves into the waters of the Elbe. They screamed for coolness; they screamed for mercy. Death is mercy. Death is good when you are burning like a torch. Dresden was a glorious city, and it is a little hard getting used to the idea that Dresden, too, no longer exists. (From *Berlin Underground*, by Ruth Andreas-Friedrich.)

DUNKIRK EVACUATION

The Dunkirk Evacuation involved the withdrawal of more than 300,000 British, French, and Belgian soldiers from northern France from May 26 to June 3, 1940. The armies had been trapped by German forces that had smashed through Belgium into the French countryside. About 900 ships of all types and sizes—from private yachts to fishing boats to navy destroyers—took part in the cross-Channel ferrying operation.

The numbers of men and ships in the evacuation are impressive, but the individual stories are even more so. This is the account of retired naval commander Lightoller who took his sixty-foot yacht *Sundowner* across the Channel to the Dunkirk beaches.

1487. Half-way across we avoided a floating mine by a narrow margin. . . . A few miles later we had our first introduction to enemy aircraft. . . .

We made the fairway buoy to the Roads shortly after the sinking of a French transport with severe loss of life. Steaming slowly through the wreckage we entered the Roads. . . .

By now dive-bombers seemed to be eternally dropping out of the cloud of enemy aircraft overhead. . . .

[On the Dunkirk pier, I said] I could take about a hundred (though the most I had ever had on board was 21). . . . My son . . . was to pack the men in and use every available inch of space. . . . At 50 [troops taken on and sent below deck] I called below, "How are you getting on?" getting the cheery reply, "Oh, plenty of room yet." At 75 my son admitted they were getting pretty tight. . . .

I now started to pack them on deck. . . . By the time we had 50 on deck, I could feel her getting distinctly tender, so took no more. Actually we had exactly 130 on board. . . .

Casting off and backing out we entered the Roads again, there it was continuous and unmitigated hell. The troops were just splendid and of their own initiative detailed look-outs ahead, astern, and abeam for inquisitive planes as my attention was pretty wholly occupied watching the steering and passing orders to Roger at the wheel. . . . One bomber that had been particularly offensive, itself came under the notice of one of our fighters and suddenly plunged vertically into the sea. . . .

The impression ashore [upon arrival in England] was that the 50-odd lying on deck plus the mass of equipment was my full load. . . . I gave the order "Come up from below," and the look on the official's face was amusing to behold. . . . As a stoker . . . said, "God's truth, mate! Where did you put them?" (From *Dunkirk*, by A. D. Divine.)

EDITORIAL CARTOONS

During 2,000 days of war, tens of thousands of editorial cartoons appeared in newspapers and magazines throughout the world. Caricatures of Hitler, Mussolini (q.v.), Roosevelt, Churchill, Stalin, and Tojo (q.v.) became more familiar than characters in comic strips. Other figures depicted were far less familiar. Cartoonists supported friends and denounced enemies—though labels could change overnight. Many of the foreign cartoons described below appeared in *The World War 1939–1945: The Cartoonists' Vision*, by Roy Douglas.

1488. [Uncle Sam is selling armaments to the Allies, with a list of weapons clearly shown. He tells purchasers not to hurt anybody. A sign reads, "Credit spoils relationships." This cartoon appeared four months after the Nazi-Soviet Pact (q.v.) was signed and a year and a half before Hitler attacked the Soviet Union.]

Caption: Uncle's benevolence. (*Krokodil*, Moscow, December 1939.)

1489. [World War I Belgian King Albert is standing up to the enemy, while his son, King Leopold, shrinks from the battle. The reference is to a too-quick surrender by Leopold, allowing a Nazi sweep into France.]

Caption: The father and the son. (*Marianne*, Paris, June 5, 1940.)

1490. [The scene is a wedding ceremony. The bride, representing France, is bound and gagged. The groom is "Hitlerini." The father of the bride, Marshal Petain (q.v.), speaks for her. This appeared shortly after the French signed an armistice with Hitler.]

Caption: *Petain*: She says, "I do." (*Daily Herald*, London, June 25, 1940.)

1491. [J. Edgar Hoover is guarding eight German prisoners who had landed in the United States by submarine. Attorney General Francis J. Biddle is searching through a stack of law books.]

Caption: "You hold on to them, Edgar, and I'll find something here that we can punish them under." (Clifford Berryman, *Washington Evening Star*, June 1942.)

EL ALAMEIN

El Alamein is the North African site of one of the most important battles of the war. The principal figures were British General Bernard Montgomery (q.v.) and German General Erwin Rommel (q.v.) of the Afrika Korps. The battle took place from late October to early November of 1942. It was fought sixty miles from Alexandria, Egypt. The British Eighth Army decisively defeated a force of Germans and Italians, sending them into full retreat across the North African desert.

In *Master of the Battlefield: Monty's War Years*, Nigel Hamilton (q.v.) summed up the significance of the victory:

1492. The battle was decisive in a more profound respect than any other Allied engagement in the West during the war, save perhaps D-Day [q.v.] and the Battle of Normandy. Not only did it herald a new era in Allied offensive operations in the West, but it rocked Axis morale to an incalculable extent. The legendary Rommel had been beaten, and a demonstration of the relentless Allied intention to prosecute the war until final victory had at last been given. (From *Master of the Battlefield: Monty's War Years*, by Nigel Hamilton.)

FIFTH COLUMN

This was an expression used by Allied war leaders to describe Nazi sympathizers working against the interests of their own country. Although there is no doubt that the phrase was first used in the Spanish Civil War, there is disagreement about who used it first. Historian Louis L. Snyder said it was Nationalist General Queipo de Llano. *Bartlett's* credits General Emilio Mola. It is often attributed to the man who defeated the Spanish Loyalists, Generalissimo Francisco Franco (q.v.). The quotation generally appears along the following lines:

1493. For every four columns of troops I lead against Madrid, I have a fifth column inside the city.

FLYING TIGERS

The Flying Tigers is the nickname of the American volunteer group of pilots and mechanics who volunteered to fight the Japanese for Free China prior to Pearl Harbor. Originally conceived by Claire L. Chennault, the group had the active support of America's highest government officials. The group was supplied by an organization called China Defense Supplies Inc., which arranged for lend-leasing war materials to the government of China. American pilots were recruited from the Army and Navy Air Corps. Organized in the spring and summer of 1941, the Flying Tigers arrived in China in

November of that year and became part of the U.S. Army Air Corps in 1942.

Any aid to China—particularly aircraft—meant less not only for Great Britain but for America's own defense buildup. Barbara W. Tuchman (q.v.), in her *Stilwell and the American Experience in China: 1911–45*, summed up the American rationale this way:

1494. Yet everyone—the president, [Treasury Secretary Henry] Morgenthau [q.v.], [Secretary of War Henry] Stimson [q.v.], [Secretary of State Cordell] Hull [q.v.] and the Joint Board of the armed services—favored planes for China, less for China's sake than to buy time for America to arm. (From *Stilwell and the American Experience in China, 1911–45*, by Barbara W. Tuchman.)

GREER ENCOUNTER

A confrontation between the American destroyer *Greer* and Nazi submarine U-652 occurred on September 4, 1941. It took place southeast of Greenland more than three months before Germany declared war on the United States. The historians agree that depth charges were dropped near the U-boat and that torpedoes were fired at the destroyer. The controversy is over who did what to whom first. The U-boat commander stated that the *Greer* had dropped depth charges and that the sub fired torpedoes in response. The captain of the *Greer* reported that it had been attacked without warning by the U-boat and that its torpedoes had missed the mark. Historian Louis L. Snyder has written that the incident began when a British plane dropped depth charges on the sub. Here is how the two sides responded to the confrontation:

1495. In the waters which we deem necessary for our defense, American naval vessels and American planes will no longer wait until Axis submarines lurking under water, or Axis raiders on the surface of the sea, strike their deadly blow—first. . . . Let this warning be clear. From now on, if German or Italian vessels of war enter the waters, the protection of which is necessary for American defense, they do so at their own peril. The orders which I have given as Commander in Chief of the Army and Navy are to carry out that policy—at once. (President Roosevelt, radio address, September 11, 1941.)

1496. Roosevelt . . . is endeavoring with all the means at his disposal to provoke incidents for the purpose of baiting the American people into the war. (Official German response, September 1941.)

HESS FLIGHT TO SCOTLAND

On May 10, 1941, Rudolf Hess (q.v.), Deputy Fuehrer and closest confidante of Adolf Hitler, flew a German plane over Great Britain. He bailed out over Scotland and asked to see the Duke of Hamilton. Hess told the duke that he had come on his own to bring about peace between England and Nazi Germany. Hitler was six weeks away from invading the Soviet Union, and this was an attempt to get England out of the war so that Hitler would have only the Russian front to consider.

England never considered the proposal seriously. Hitler would call the flight the work of a madman.

In a statement appearing in the *New York Times* in 1943, British Foreign Affairs Secretary Anthony Eden reported the following six-point peace terms that had been offered by Hess in the 1941 flight:

1497. 1. That Germany should be given a free hand in Europe.

2. That England should have a free hand in the British Empire, except that former German colonies should return to Germany.

3. That Russia should be included in Asia, but that Germany had certain demands to make of Russia which would have to be satisfied either by negotiation or as a result of war. There was, however, no truth in rumors that the Fuehrer contemplated an early attack on Russia.

4. That the British should evacuate Iraq.

5. The peace agreement would have to contain a provision for reciprocal indemnification of British and German nationals whose property had been expropriated as a result of the war.

6. The proposal could only be considered on the understanding that it was negotiated by Germany with an English Government other than the present British Government. Mr. Churchill, who had planned the war since 1936, and his colleagues who had lent themselves to his war policy were not persons with whom the Fuehrer would negotiate. (*New York Times*, September 22, 1943.)

HOLOCAUST

The term *Holocaust* is applied to the deliberate destruction of 6 million European Jews by the Nazi government and its allies. Hitler's

Mein Kampf (q.v.) was filled with anti-Semitic statements. When the Nazis came to power in Germany, they instituted a program designed to deprive Jews of their civil rights and their livelihoods, to pauperize them, terrorize them, lock them up in concentration camps, and expel them from Germany.

Once World War II began, the Nazis turned to murder, starvation, and disease to solve what they called "the Jewish Problem." Jews who could work were put into slave labor camps. Others were killed by a variety of methods—from mass shootings to gassing.

Hans Frank, as governor general of Poland, was in charge of carrying out Hitler's policies in his part of the Nazi world. Frank, who would later be hanged at Nuremberg, summarized the overall Nazi goal in a speech delivered in Berlin in August 1940:

1498. It is clear that herewith, a serious warning must be given—the Jews must vanish from the face of the earth.

HOSSBACH MEMORANDUM

Friedrich Hossbach, a colonel in the German army, was Hitler's adjutant. A virtual unknown during the war, he achieved fame—or notoriety—by having his name attached to the minutes of a secret meeting of Germany's top military leaders on November 5, 1937, in Berlin. The memorandum cites Hitler's view of Germany's future place in Europe and the world. What appears below are *not* Hossbach's ideas but his summary of what Hitler said at the meeting.

Some historians have labeled the document "the Hossbach Protocol." It was introduced into evidence at Nuremberg. Only brief excerpts appear here. Although Hitler dealt with possible scenarios over different periods of time, the quotations here have been carefully selected to show his general attitudes toward specific European nations.

Hossbach, summarizing in indirect discourse, used the past tense to indicate what was said at the time and place of the secret meeting.

1499. The aim of German policy was to make secure and to preserve the racial community [in Germany] and to enlarge it. It was therefore a question of space. The German racial community comprised over 85 million people and, because of their number and the narrow limits of habitable space in Europe, constituted a tightly packed racial core such as was not to be met in any other country and such as implied the right to a greater living space than in the case of other peoples. (From *Documents on German Foreign Policy*, Series D.)

1500. Germany's future was therefore wholly conditional upon the solving of the need for space, and such a solution could be sought, of course, only for a foreseeable period of one to three generations. (Ibid.)

1501. If, then, we accept the security of our food situation as the principal question, the space necessary to insure it can only be sought in Europe, not, as in the liberal-capitalist view, the exploitation of colonies. It is not a matter of acquiring population but of gaining space for agricultural use. Moreover, areas producing raw materials can be more usefully sought in Europe in immediate proximity to the Reich, than overseas. (Ibid.)

[Following an analysis of natural resources and food production in Germany.]

1502. The history of all ages—the Roman Empire and the British Empire—had proved that expansion could only be carried out by breaking down resistance and taking risks; setbacks were inevitable. There had never in former times been spaces without a master, and there were none today; the attacker always comes up against a possessor. The question for Germany ran, where could she achieve the greatest gain at the lowest cost? (Ibid.)

1503. German policy had to reckon with two hate-inspired antagonists, Britain and France, to whom a German colossus in the center of Europe was a thorn in the flesh, and both were opposed to any further strengthening of Germany's position either in Europe or overseas; in support of this opposition they were able to count on the agreement of their political parties. Both countries saw the establishment of German military bases overseas as a threat to their own communications, a safeguarding of German commerce, and, as a consequence, a strengthening of Germany's position in Europe. (Ibid.)

1504. Germany's problem could only be solved by means of force and this was never without attendant risk. The campaigns of Frederick the Great for Silesia and Bismarck's wars against Austria and France had involved unheard-of risk, and the swiftness of the Prussian action in 1870 had kept Austria from entering the war. (Ibid.)

1505. For the improvement of our politico-military position our first objective, in the event of our being embroiled in war, must be to overthrow Czechoslovakia and Austria simultaneously in order to remove the threat to our flank in any possible operation against the west. (Ibid.)

1506. The Fuehrer believed that most certainly Britain, and probably France as well, had already tacitly written off the Czechs and were reconciled to the fact that this question would be cleared up in due course by Germany. (Ibid.)

1507. Difficulties connected with the Empire, and the prospect of being once more entangled in a protracted European war, were decisive considerations for Britain against participation in a war against Germany. Britain's attitude would certainly not be without influence on that of France. (Ibid.)

1508. It had to be remembered that the defense measures of the Czechs were growing in strength from year to year, and that the actual worth of the Austrian Army also was increasing in the course of time. Even though the populations concerned, especially of Czechoslovakia, were not sparse, the annexation of Czechoslovakia and Austria would mean an acquisition of foodstuffs for 5 to 6 million people, on the assumption that the compulsory emigration of 2 million people from Czechoslovakia and 1 million people from Austria was practicable. The incorporation of these two States with Germany meant, from the politico-military point of view, a substantial advantage because it would mean shorter and better frontiers, the freeing of forces for other purposes, and the possibility of creating new units up to a level of about 12 divisions, that is, 1 new division per million inhabitants. (Ibid.)

INDIANAPOLIS DISASTER

The *Indianapolis* was the heavy cruiser that had transported the atomic bomb to Tinian Island for eventual use on Japan. On the evening of July 29, 1945, it was torpedoed by a Japanese submarine, sinking in less than fifteen minutes. Of the 1,200 men on board, only 316 survived. A number of the dead went down with the ship, but others died of wounds, burns, and attacks by sharks and other carnivorous predators. Some sailors drank seawater. Others went mad and attacked their comrades in the water.

On August 2, survivors were spotted by a navy plane. The following day, a ship picked up those who were still alive.

Indianapolis Captain Charles B. McVay, who survived, was court-martialed and found guilty of culpable inefficiency in the performance of his duty and negligently endangering the lives of others.

Naval historian Samuel Eliot Morison, in his *Victory in the Pacific*, cited the command decisions that may have had a bearing on the tragedy:

1509. Without an escort possessing sound gear, the cruiser was dependent on radar and eyesight to detect a submarine. And she was not zigzagging when she encountered the underwater enemy. It was an overcast night and standing fleet instructions required ships to zigzag only in good visibility. Captain McVay's routing instructions directed him to zigzag "at discretion," which he did by day, but not at night. He did not appear to be disturbed that in his briefing there was a report of a submarine near his estimated position of 0800 next day, and of another 105 miles from his ship's track on 25 July. Nor was the ship "buttoned up" above the second deck. Since these old heavy cruisers had no air conditioning, the Captain, to make sleep possible for his men in tropical waters, allowed all ventilation ducts and most of the bulkheads to remain open. The entire main deck was open, as well as all doors on the second deck, and all hatches to living spaces below. (From *Victory in the Pacific*, by Samuel Eliot Morison.)

JAPANESE RELOCATION

In April 1942, the United States government ordered the evacuation and relocation of more than 100,000 persons of Japanese ancestry from the West Coast of the United States. The majority were American citizens. They had to leave homes and businesses behind and move to relocation camps away from the coast. Decades after the end of the war, some compensation was voted by Congress to those who had been evacuated. One such evacuation order:

1510. TO ALL PERSONS OF JAPANESE ANCESTRY LIVING IN THE FOLLOWING AREA: [Geographic boundaries in northern California are specified.]

Pursuant to the provisions of Civilian Exclusion Order No. 27, this Headquarters, dated April 30, 1942, all persons of Japanese ancestry both alien and non-alien, will be evacuated from the above area by 12 o'clock noon P.W.T. [Pacific War Time], Thursday, May 7, 1942.

No Japanese person living in the above area will be permitted to change residence after 2 o'clock noon, P.W.T., Thursday, April 30, 1942, without obtaining special permission from the representative of the Commanding General, Northern California Sector, at the Civil Control Station located at: 530 Eighteenth Street, Oakland, California.

Such permission will only be granted for the purpose of uniting members of family, or in cases of grave emergency.

The Civil Control Station is equipped to assist the Japanese population affected by this evacuation in the following ways:

1. Give advice and instructions on the evacuation.
2. Provide services with respect to the management, leasing, sale, storage or

other disposition of most kinds of property, such as real estate, business and professional equipment, household goods, automobiles and livestock.

3. Provide temporary residence elsewhere for all Japanese in family groups.

4. Transport persons and a limited amount of clothing and equipment to that new residence.

THE FOLLOWING INSTRUCTIONS MUST BE OBSERVED:

1. A responsible member of each family, preferably the head of the family, or the person in whose name most of the property is held, and each individual living alone, will report to the Civil Control Station to receive further instructions. This must be done between 8:00 A.M. and 5:00 P.M. on Friday, May 1, 1942, or between 8:00 A.M. and 5:00 P.M. on Saturday, May 2, 1942.

2. Evacuees must carry with them on departure for the Assembly Center the following property:

(a) Bedding and linens (no mattress) for each member of the family;

(b) Toilet articles . . . ;

(c) Extra clothing . . . ;

(d) Sufficient knives, forks, spoons, plates, bowls and cups . . . ;

(e) Essential personal effects . . . ;

All items carried will be securely packaged, tied and plainly marked with the name of the owner and numbered in accordance with instructions obtained at the Civil Control Station. The size and number of packages is limited to that which can be carried by the individual or family group.

3. No pets of any kind will be permitted.

4. No personal items and no household goods will be shipped to the Assembly Center.

5. The United States Government through its agencies will provide for the storage at the sole risk of the owner of the more substantial household items, such as iceboxes, washing machines, pianos, and other heavy furniture. Cooking utensils and other small items will be accepted for storage if crated, packed and plainly marked with the name and address of the owner. Only one name and address will be used by a given family.

6. Each family, and individual living alone, will be furnished transportation to the Assembly Center or will be authorized to travel by private automobile in a supervised group. All instructions pertaining to the movement will be obtained at the Civil Control Station.

Go to the Civil Control Station between the hours of 8:00 A.M. and 5:00 P.M. Friday, May 1, 1942, or between the hours of 8:00 A.M. and 5:00 P.M., Saturday, May 2, 1942, to receive further instructions. (J. L. DeWitt, Lieutenant General, U.S. Army, Commanding, April 30, 1942.)

"All persons of Japanese ancestry both alien and non-alien, will be evacuated from the above area [of California] by 12 o'clock noon . . . Thursday, May 7, 1942."

—JAPANESE RELOCATION ORDER

Japanese Americans assemble at the Santa Anita racetrack prior to being evacuated to relocation camps.

KAMIKAZE

Japanese for "divine wind," *Kamikaze* is the name given to suicide attacks on American ships. The plan was developed following the virtual destruction of what remained of the Imperial Fleet in the Battle of Leyte Gulf. Japanese planes were loaded with explosives, and their pilot volunteers were directed to crash into American ships. These kamikaze attacks began off the Philippines and continued off Okinawa. Scores of American ships were sunk, and more than 160 were damaged in the attacks. Japanese pilot losses have been estimated at between 2,000 and 4,000. The attacks began to drop off toward the end of the war when the Japanese ran out of pilots—and volunteers.

The following is from the official "First Order to the Kamikazes."

1511. It is absolutely out of the question for you to return alive. Your mission involves certain death. Your bodies will be dead, but not your spirits. The death of a single one of you will be the birth of a million others. Neglect nothing that may affect your training or your health. You must not leave behind you any use for regret, which would follow you into eternity. And, lastly: If you cannot find your target, turn back, next time you may find a more favorable opportunity. Choose a death which brings about a maximum result. (From *The Divine Wind*, by Captain Rikihei Inoguchi and Commander Tadashi Nakajima.)

KATYN FOREST MASSACRE

This massacre represented the slaughter of some 4,400 Polish army officers by the Soviet Union. The officers had been prisoners of war since the Russian invasion of Poland in mid-September 1939. After Hitler invaded the Soviet Union in June 1941, the Polish government-in-exile had recommended that a new Polish army be formed to help fight Hitler, with former prisoners of war used as the nucleus of the new army. The Poles were surprised to learn that Polish officers located in a prison camp near Smolensk had mysteriously vanished. Various Soviet explanations of the disappearance did not satisfy the Poles, who kept pressing for an explanation.

In April 1943, Berlin reported that the bodies of thousands of Polish officers had been found in mass graves in a forest just outside the town of Katyn. The Germans said that each officer had been shot in the back of the neck, killed by the Soviets. Moscow hotly denied the charge, saying that the Nazis had killed the officers. The debate raged for many decades after the war.

It was not until April 1995 that the Russians admitted that the massacre at Katyn was indeed the work of the KGB—the Soviet security force. At a press conference in Smolensk, A. Krayushkin, a Russian security official, stated flatly that more than 20,000 Polish prisoners of war had been killed in Soviet camps, including the 4,400 at Katyn. It was also revealed that Premier Khrushchev (q.v.) had ordered the documentation of the massacres destroyed in 1959. The official rationale for destruction of documents:

1512. [They have] neither operational nor historical importance.

LEND-LEASE

In March 1941, Congress overwhelmingly approved the Lend-Lease Act. (In the House of Representatives, it had received the bill number H.R. 1776, which was used effectively by its supporters.) This law allowed President Roosevelt to sell, lease, lend, or transfer war materials to those countries he "deems vital for the defense of the United States." The problem had been that Britain was broke and did not have the money to pay for the guns, ships, tanks, and planes it needed to carry on the war. Lend-Lease would later be used to provide aid to the Soviet Union and other countries at war with the Axis Powers.

The American people's acceptance of Lend-Lease was largely due to a brilliant analogy voiced by Roosevelt at a press conference on December 17, 1940.

1513. There was no doubt in the minds of "a very overwhelming number of Americans that the best immediate defense of the United States is the success of Great Britain in defending itself; and that, therefore, quite aside from our historic and current interest in the survival of democracy in the world as a whole, it is equally important from a selfish point of view of American defense, that we should do everything to help the British Empire to defend itself." The Axis was waging war without money, he went on. The democracies had to find nontraditional methods of their own. There was no need to repeal the Neutrality Act or Johnson Act; nor was there need for an outright gift to the British. Rather the United States could "lease or sell" to Great Britain that portion of its production of munitions that events demanded. He was trying, Roosevelt said, to get rid of the "silly, foolish, old dollar sign." His analogy was to a man whose neighbor's house was on fire; in such a case that man would not say: "Neighbor, my garden hose cost me fifteen dollars; you have to pay me fifteen dollars for it." No, he would connect the hose, help put out the fire and get the hose back later. (From *From the Morgenthau Diaries*, by John Morton Blum.)

MacARTHUR CANDIDACY

In 1944—as the war reached its ferocious peak—Franklin Roosevelt was clearly heading for an unprecedented fourth-term nomination by the Democrats. Some Republican Party leaders felt that Douglas MacArthur could be a strong candidate against Roosevelt. Trial balloons were floated on behalf of the general's possible candidacy. The boomlet collapsed, wrote biographer William Manchester (q.v.), because "[h]e had been writing too many letters."

1514. One of his correspondents was a . . . Nebraska congressman named A. L. Miller. . . . Miller had written him that "unless this New Deal can be stopped, our American way of life is forever doomed." MacArthur had replied, "I do unreservedly agree with the complete wisdom and statesmanship of your comments," adding that he was deeply troubled by "the sinister drama of our present chaos and confusion." In another exchange, the congressman had bitterly attacked F. D. R., predicting that four more years of "this monarchy" would "destroy the rights of the common people." The general had associated himself with that view, too, and when Miller wrote him that he was needed to "destroy this monstrosity . . . which is engulfing the nation and destroying free enterprise and every right of the individual," MacArthur had thanked him for his "scholarly letter," adding that "your description of conditions in the United States is a sober one indeed and is calculated to arouse the thoughtful consideration of every true patriot." Finally the General had injected into this highly partisan dialogue an issue which, in a nation at war, should have transcended both parties. "Out here we are doing what we can with what we have," he wrote. "I will be glad, however, when more substantial forces are placed at my disposition."

On April 14 [1944] Congressman Miller, without consulting MacArthur, or anyone else, turned all the letters over to the press, apparently in the belief that they would help him. That pricked the General's bubble. (From *American Caesar*, by William Manchester.)

1514a. I have had brought to my attention a number of newspaper articles professing in strongest terms a widespread public opinion that it is detrimental to our war effort to have an officer in high position, on active service at the front, considered for nomination for the office of President. I have on several occasions announced I was not a candidate for the position. Nevertheless, in view of these circumstances, in order to make my position entirely unequivocal, I request that no action be taken that would link my name in any way with the nomination. I do not covet it nor would I accept it. (Douglas MacArthur, Statement, April 30, 1944.)

MAGIC

Magic was the name given to the U.S. Army's breaking of the Japanese secret code in September 1940. It enabled the United States to read many Japanese military and diplomatic messages throughout the war, proving critical in the Battle of Midway. Because a number of "Magics" dealt with requests for information about American naval forces at Pearl Harbor, there has always been speculation over whether the U.S. government knew in advance that an expected Japanese surprise attack had specifically targeted Pearl Harbor. The sensitive nature of "Magic" may be gleaned from the following message that was addressed to the Japanese ambassador in Berlin on November 30, 1941—a week before Pearl Harbor.

1515. Say very secretly to them [Hitler and Ribbentrop (q.v.)] that there is extreme danger that war may suddenly break out between the Anglo-Saxon nations and Japan through some clash of arms, and add that the time of the breaking out of this war may come quicker than anyone dreams.

MARKET-GARDEN

Market-Garden was the code name of a failed Allied operation in Holland in September 1944. The plan was to have Allied airborne troops seize five Dutch bridges intact and then to hold them until relieved by armored units. The key failure was at Arnhem, where British and Polish troops took heavy casualties waiting for relief that never came. Among the reasons for the failure were unexpected bad weather and the presence of an SS (Schutzstaffel) Panzer Corps at Arnhem. Many years after the war, there were reports that a Dutch resistance leader had betrayed the operation to the Germans.

The most quoted reason for the defeat was the observation by Lieutenant General Frederick Browning, who had questioned General Montgomery (q.v.) about the Arnhem bridge, which was fully sixty miles behind the German lines. Told that the airborne troops would be reached in two days, Browning told Montgomery:

1516. We can hold it for four. But, sir, I think we might be going a bridge too far. (Cited in *A Bridge Too Far*, by Cornelius Ryan.)

MEIN KAMPF

Subtitled *Four-and-a-Half Years of Struggle against Lies, Stupidity, and Cowardice*, *Mein Kampf* (My Struggle) was Hitler's autobiography. Much of it was written in prison between 1923 and 1924 when Hitler served nine months for attempting to overthrow the German government. The book was published in two parts, the first in 1925 and the second in 1927.

Mein Kampf became the bible of the Nazi Party and the blueprint of the Third Reich. It was introduced into evidence at the Nuremberg war crimes trial in 1946. The prosecution cited specific quotations from the book as evidence of "aggression as a basic Nazi idea." The International Military Tribunal (q.v.) pointed out both general and specific expressions by Hitler showing his belief in using force in carrying out national policy, the need for slave labor (q.v.) by "inferiors," and the need for expanding into foreign territory, specifically Austria and Russia. The following are some of the quotations cited from *Mein Kampf*.

1517. The soil on which we now live was not a gift bestowed by Heaven on our forefathers. But they had to conquer it by risking their lives. So also in the future our people will not obtain territory, and therewith the means of existence, as a favor from any other people, but will have to win it by the power of a triumphant sword. (Cited in *Nazi Conspiracy and Aggression*, Vol. 1.)

1518. In regard to the part played by humane feeling, Moltke stated that in time of war the essential thing is to get a decision as quickly as possible and that the most ruthless methods of fighting are at the same time the most humane. When people attempt to answer this reasoning by highfaluting talk about aesthetics, etc., etc., only one answer can be given. It is that the vital questions involved in the struggle of the nation for its existence must not be subordinated to any nation for aesthetic considerations. (Ibid.)

1519. Had it not been possible for them to employ members of the inferior race which they conquered, the Aryans would never have been in a position to take the first steps on the road which led them to a later type of culture; just as without the help of certain suitable animals which they were able to tame, they would never have come to the invention of mechanical power, which has subsequently enabled them to do without these beasts. For the establishment of superior types of civilization the members of inferior races formed one of the most essential prerequisites. (Ibid.)

1520. If in its historical development the German people had possessed the unity of herd instinct by which other people have so much benefited, then the German Reich would probably be mistress of the globe today. World history would have taken another course, and in this case no man can tell if what many blinded pacifists hope to attain by petitioning, whining and crying may not have been reached in this way; namely, a peace which would not be based upon the waving of olive branches and tearful misery-mongering of pacifist old women, but a peace that would be guaranteed by the triumphant sword of a people endowed with the power to master the world and administer it in the service of a higher civilization. (Ibid.)

1521. German-Austria must be restored to the great German Motherland. And not, indeed on any grounds of economic calculation whatsoever. No, no. Even if the union were a matter of economic indifference, and even if it were to be disadvantageous from the economic standpoint, still it ought to take place. People of the same blood should be in the same Reich. The German people will have no right to engage in a common policy until they shall have brought all their children together in one State. When the territory of the Reich embraces all the Germans and finds itself unable to assure them a livelihood, only then can the moral right arise, from the need of the people, to acquire foreign territory. The plough is then the sword; and the tears of war will produce the daily bread for the generations to come. (Ibid.)

1522. In regard to this point [restoring Germany's 1914 boundaries] I should like to make the following statement: To demand that the 1914 frontiers should be restored is a glaring political absurdity that is fraught with such consequences as to make the claim itself appear criminal. The confines of the Reich as they existed in 1914 were thoroughly illogical; because they were not really complete in the sense of including all the members of the German nation. Nor were they reasonable, in view of the geographical exigencies of military defense. They were not the consequence of a political plan which had been well considered and carried out, but they were temporary frontiers established in virtue of a political struggle that had not been brought to a finish; and indeed, they were partly the chance result of circumstances. (Ibid.)

1523. We National Socialists must stick firmly to the aim that we have set for our foreign policy, namely, that the German people must be assured the territorial area which is necessary for it to exist on this earth. And only for such action as is undertaken to secure those ends can it be lawful in the eyes of God and our German posterity to allow the blood of our people to be shed once again. Before God, because we are sent into this world with the commission to struggle for our daily bread, as creatures to whom nothing is donated and who must be able to win and hold their position as lord of the earth only through their own intelligence and courage. And this justification must be established also before our German posterity, on the grounds that for each one who has shed his blood the life of a thousand others will be guaranteed to posterity. The territory on which one day our German peasants will be able to bring forth and nourish their sturdy sons will justify the blood of the sons of the peasants that has to be shed today. And the statesmen who will have decreed this sacrifice may be persecuted by their contemporaries, but posterity will absolve them from all guilt for having demanded this offering from their people. (Ibid.)

1524. Germany will either become a world power or will not continue to exist at all. But in order to become a world power, it needs that territorial magnitude which gives it the necessary importance today and assures the existence of its citizens. (Ibid.)

1525. From the past we can learn only one lesson, and that is that the aim which is to be pursued in our political conduct must be two-fold, namely: (1) the acquisition of territory as the objective of our foreign policy and (2) the establishment of a new and uniform foundation as the objective of our political activities at home, in accordance with our doctrine of nationhood. (Ibid.)

1526. Therefore we National Socialists have purposely drawn a line through the line of conduct followed by pre-war Germany in foreign policy. We put an end to the perpetual Germanic march towards the South and West of Europe and turn our eyes towards the lands of the East. We finally put a stop to the colonial and trade policy of pre-war times and pass over to the territorial policy of the future. But when we speak of new territory in Europe today we must principally think of Russia and the border states subject to her. (Ibid.)

1527. As long as the eternal conflict between France and Germany is waged only in the form of a German defense against the French attack, that conflict can never be decided, and from century to century Germany will lose one position after another. If we study the changes that have taken place, from the 12th century up to our day, in the frontiers within which the German language is spoken, we can hardly hope for a successful issue to result from the acceptance and development of a line of conduct which has thereto been so detrimental for us. Only when the Germans have taken all this fully into account will they cease from allowing the national will-to-live to wear itself out in merely passive defense; but they will rally together for a last decisive contest with France. And in this contest the essential objective of the German nation will be fought for. Only then will it be possible to put an end to the eternal Franco-German conflict which has hitherto proved so sterile. (Ibid.)

1528. Of course it is here presumed that Germany sees in the suppression of France nothing more than a means which will make it possible for our people finally to expand in another quarter. Today there are 80 million Germans in Europe. And our foreign policy will be recognized as rightly conducted only when, after barely a hundred years, there will be 250 million Germans living on this Continent, not packed together as the coolies in the factories of another Continent but as tillers of the soil and workers whose labor will be a mutual assurance for their existence. (Ibid.)

NAZI SABOTEURS

On the evening of June 12, 1942, four Germans were landed by U-boat on the shore of Long Island, New York. Several days later, four more were landed by a second U-boat on the coast of Florida. The eight were equipped with enough explosives, incendiary devices, and fuses to cause considerable damage to American defense plants and military installations. A Coast Guardsman spotted the Long Island four, pretended to take a bribe, and reported the incident to the proper authorities. Within a few weeks, all eight had been rounded up. They were tried in a secret military trial. Six were executed. Two, who cooperated, were given prison sentences and were deported back to Germany after the war.

The military trial was made possible by a proclamation of President Roosevelt:

1529. I, . . . do hereby proclaim that all persons who are subjects, citizens or residents of any nation at war with the United States or who give obedience to or act under the direction of any such nation, and who during time of war enter or attempt to enter the United States or any territory or possession thereof, through coastal or boundary defenses, and are charged with committing or attempting or preparing to commit sabotage, espionage, hostile or warlike acts, or violations of the law of war, shall be subject to the law of war and to the jurisdiction of military tribunals; and that such persons shall not be privileged to seek any remedy or maintain any proceeding, directly or indirectly, or to have any such remedy or proceeding sought on their behalf, in the courts of the United States. (Proclamation, July 2, 1942, cited in *They Came to Kill*, by Eugene Rachlis.)

OPEN CITY

Under international law, a belligerent nation, facing possible attack, may declare the target an "open city." That means that the city will be unarmed and will not be defended.

Theoretically, that designation should mean that the city will not be attacked, thus safe from assault. That did not always work. During World War II, the "open city" of Rotterdam was devastated by Nazi bombers. The two most prominent open cities were Rome and Paris.

On June 10, 1940, General Maxime Weygand (q.v.) informed Premier Paul Reynaud (q.v.) that Paris would be declared an open city. Weygand explained why and how:

1530. In order that Paris shall preserve its character as an Open City it is my intention to avoid any defensive organization around the city on the belt of the old fortifications or on that of the ancient forts.

PHONY WAR

"Phony war" was the name given by American correspondents to the period from late September 1939 to early April 1940—between the fall of Poland to the invasion of Norway and Denmark. During this six-month period, nothing happened on the battlefield. One American correspondent, Robert J. Casey, actually took a taxicab across the French lines all the way to the German Siegfried Line. The Germans had another name for the phony war, a play on the word "blitzkrieg" (lightning war).

1531. Sitzkrieg (sit-down war).

PLOESTI RAID

Operation Tidal Wave began on the morning of August 1, 1943. Some 177 B-24 Liberator bombers took off from an airfield in Benghazi, North Africa. Of these, 164 reached their targets: the Ploesti oil fields of Rumania. The mission was a 2,500-mile round-trip, requiring the storage of additional fuel. On reaching the target, the bombers had to drop their payloads at tree-top level, over one of the most heavily defended areas in Europe. The Ploesti oil refineries were set on fire, putting them out of commission for the Nazis—at least temporarily. The cost was roughly 50 Liberators shot down and 55 more damaged. More than 440 American airmen lost their lives in the attack. Another 100 became prisoners of war.

Historian Louis L. Snyder summarized the differing opinions on the operation's effectiveness:

1532. Allied war leaders professed satisfaction. General Dwight D. Eisenhower pronounced the Ploesti attack "reasonably successful." An official U.S. Strategic Survey later declared that the raid was effective. "It was the Nazis' lack of gasoline, not the loss of plane production, that gave us air superiority." German sources, on the other hand, claimed that little damage was done, that full production started soon, and that their problem was not production of oil but its distribution. Neutral opinion had it that although carefully planned and courageously carried out, Operation Tidal Wave was a costly failure. (From *Historical Guide to World War II*, by Louis L. Synder.)

QUISLING

Quisling was a traitor. Vidkun Quisling (1887–1945) was a Norwegian official who transmitted military secrets to Nazi Germany, encouraging a Nazi invasion. Hitler put him in charge of the puppet regime, and Quisling was held responsible for the deaths of many Norwegian patriots. After the war, he was tried as a traitor and executed.

On June 12, 1941, Churchill gave the Norwegian's name definition:

1533. Quisling . . . the new word which will carry the scorn of mankind down the centuries.

ROSENBERG CASE

One of the most sensational stories of espionage to emerge from the war was the Rosenberg Case. According to the Federal Bureau of Investigation, Julius and Ethel Rosenberg were part of a spy ring that turned over atomic secrets to the Soviet Union between 1944 and 1946. It was not until March 1951 that the Rosenbergs were put on trial. They were charged with conspiracy to commit espionage in time of war. Based largely on the testimony of David Greenglass, who was Ethel's brother, the Rosenbergs were convicted. Greenglass confessed to being a member of the spy ring. He had worked at an atomic installation in Los Alamos during the war. Greenglass would receive a fifteen-year sentence for his cooperation. The Rosenbergs would die in the electric chair on June 19, 1953.

Although there was little doubt that the Rosenbergs had transmitted information to the Russians, there was substantial dispute over how valuable that data was in allowing the Soviets to acquire the atomic bomb as soon as they did. Klaus Fuchs, a top British scientist in the atomic bomb project, had confessed that he had turned over atomic secrets to the Russians. There was also controversy over the suitability of the death penalty for providing secret information to a wartime ally of the United States at the time of the transmission. Differing opinions on the punishment issue follow:

1534. I say to the Court that we have had situations in the United States within the last few years, where people like Tokyo Rose and Axis Sally, who were convicted of treason and who were aiding our enemy, Germany, during our war against Germany. I find that these people received terms of 10 to 15 years. (Emanuel Bloch, defense attorney, 1951; cited in *Ethel Rosenberg: Beyond the Myths*, by Ilene Philipson.)

1535. [Addressing the defendants:] I consider your crime worse than murder. Plain deliberate contemplated murder is dwarfed in magnitude by comparison with the crime you have committed. In committing the act of murder, the criminal kills only his victim. The immediate family is brought to grief and when justice is meted out the chapter is closed. But in your case, I believe your conduct in putting into the hands of the Russians the A-bomb years before our best scientists predicted Russia would perfect the bomb has already caused, in my opinion, the Communist aggression in Korea, with the resultant casualties exceeding 50,000 and who knows but that millions more of innocent people may pay the price of your treason. Indeed, by your betrayal you undoubtedly affected the course of history to the disadvantage of our country. . . .

We have evidence of your treachery all around us every day—for the civilian defense activities throughout the nation are aimed at preparing us for an atom bomb attack. . . .

The sentence of the Court upon Julius and Ethel Rosenberg is, for the crime for which you have been convicted, you are hereby sentenced to the punishment of death. (Judge Irving Kaufman, 1951; Ibid.)

1536. It is too bad that drawing and quartering has been abolished. (William H. Rehnquist, memo to Justice Robert H. Jackson [q.v.], 1953; Ibid.)

SEA LION

Sea Lion was the German code name for the invasion and occupation of Britain. Following the fall of France in June 1940, Britain braced itself for the expected attack. The Germans began bombing British airfields and assembling landing barges and troop-carrier aircraft. Three things stopped Hitler: One was Ultra (q.v.), which broke the German code. The second was the Royal Air Force. The third was the Fuehrer's own evil miscalculation. Military historian Hanson Baldwin tells how Hitler went wrong:

1537. On September 7 [1940], with potential victory in sight, Hitler vented his fury and London replaced Fighter Command as the principal target. This decision, in retrospect, put the seal on British victory. It was one of the great miscalculations of history. The bombing of London gave Fighter Command a chance to recuperate, and it forced the Luftwaffe to a deeper penetration and thus exposed the bombers and short-legged fighters to greater loss. It antagonized world public opinion, mobilized global sentiment in support of Britain, stiffened English resolution and helped to lead to Germany's loss of the war. (From *Battles Lost and Won: The Great Campaigns of World War II*, by Hanson Baldwin.)

SLAVE LABOR

In the slave labor system of Nazi Germany, millions of men and women were forced to work on farms, in factories, and on military installations for the Third Reich. Beginning with Poland, foreign workers of conquered territories were enslaved for the Nazi war effort.

On December 11, 1945, Deputy Prosecutor Thomas J. Dodd told the International Military Tribunal (q.v.) at Nuremberg of the responsibility for the slave labor system:

1538. We shall show that the defendants [Fritz] Sauckel and [Albert] Speer [q.v.] are principally responsible for the formation of the policy and for its execution. . . . [We will also show] that the defendant Speer, as Reichsminister of the Central Planning Board, bears responsibility for the determination of the numbers of foreign slaves required by the German war machine, was responsible for the decision to recruit by force, and for the use under brutal, inhumane and degrading conditions of foreign civilians and prisoners of war in the manufacture of armaments and munitions, the construction of fortifications, and in active military operations. . . . We say this system of hatred, savagery and denial of individual rights, which the conspirators erected into a philosophy of government within Germany . . . followed the Nazi armies as they swept over Europe—the Jews of the occupied countries suffered the same fate as the Jews of Germany, and foreign laborers became the serfs of the "master race" and they were deported and enslaved by the million. Many of the deported and enslaved laborers joined the victims of the concentration camps, where they were literally worked to death in the course of the Nazi program of extermination through work. (Deputy Prosecutor Thomas J. Dodd, addressing the International Military Tribune, Nuremberg, December 11, 1945; cited in *Albert Speer: His Battle with Truth*, by Gitta Sereny.)

STALINGRAD, BATTLE OF

Located on the Volga River, Stalingrad was the site of one of the major battles of the war. It represented Hitler's furthest penetration into the Soviet Union. In the summer of 1942, German troops were sent smashing deeper and deeper into the Russian heartland. The German Sixth Army, under General Friedrich von Paulus (q.v.), was ordered to take Stalingrad, a major industrial city. Stalingrad produced machinery needed by Russia to carry on the war against Hitler.

The Germans entered the city, with fierce fighting not only house to house but room to room. As winter approached, Paulus wanted to withdraw to regroup and resupply his army. Hitler refused, ordering that there would be no retreat. As the winter wore on, the German situation became desperate. With efforts to withdraw forbidden by Hitler, the Germans and their allies were soon trapped. In January 1943, they surrendered. The name Stalingrad no longer appears on the map. The city is now called Volgograd. The statue of a woman holding the Stalingrad victory sword in her upraised hand now towers over the city. It is taller than the Statue of Liberty.

Before the surrender, a German plane brought to Berlin letters from German soldiers trapped at Stalingrad. After examining the letters for possible propaganda use, Goebbels (q.v.) ordered them suppressed because they were so negative. Identification of the writers and intended recipients was removed. Well after the war, some of the letters were published. One example:

1539. You are the wife of a German officer, so you will take what I have to tell you, upright and unflinching, as upright as you stood on the station platform the day I left for the East. . . .

I am no letter writer and my letters have never been longer than a page. Today there would be a great deal to say, but I will save it for later, i.e., six weeks if all goes well and a hundred years if it doesn't. . . .

You know how I feel about you, Augusta. We have never talked much about our feelings. I love you very much and you love me, so you shall know the truth. It is in this letter. The truth is the knowledge that this is the grimmest of struggles in a hopeless situation. Misery, hunger, cold, renunciation, doubt, despair and horrible death. I will say no more about it.

. . . We were man and wife, and the war, however necessary, was an ugly accompaniment to our lives. . . .

I tell myself that, by giving my life, I have paid my debt. One cannot argue about questions of honor. Augusta, in the hour in which you must be strong, you will feel this also. Don't be bitter and do not suffer from my absence. I am not cowardly, only sad that I cannot give greater proof of my courage than to die for this useless, not to say criminal, cause. You know the motto of the von H—s: "Guilt recognized is guilt expiated." (From *Last Letters from Stalingrad*, edited and translated by Franz Schneider and Charles Gullans.)

SYNTHETIC RUBBER SCANDAL

Early in 1942, Assistant U.S. Attorney Thurman Arnold accused Standard Oil of New Jersey of "stifling" production of synthetic rubber because of an agreement with I. G. Farbenindustrie, a German company. The cartel arrangement, made before the outbreak of the war, was that Standard would control the market for synthetic gasoline while Farben would control the market for synthetic rubber for a specified period.

The result was that Standard, three of the company's officers, and six subsidiary companies were fined $5,000 each.

At hearings held before a Senate committee, Standard Oil had argued that the cartel agreement it had made was with a private company and not the Nazi government.

Outspoken Senator Harry S Truman (q.v.) of Missouri had another opinion:

1540. I still think it's treason.

ULTRA

Ultra was the name given to the cracking of the top secret German code by British intelligence. Ultra led to the unlocking of German military and diplomatic correspondence throughout the war.

The key to Ultra was a cipher machine that was called Enigma. In 1938, the machine had been worked on in Germany by a Polish mechanic, who notified British agents in Warsaw. The British worked with the Polish Secret Service and got hold of an Enigma machine. From that point on, it was a question of figuring out how the machine worked and then decoding the secret messages.

A month before the outbreak of the war, a group of British mathematicians and cryptographers assigned to the project were set up at Bletchley Park.

In his book *The Ultra Secret*, F. W. Winterbotham (q.v.) wrote about what it was like to be in charge of security and dissemination of the secrets of the Enigma machine. The Royal Air Force group captain told of his own initiation into the mysteries of the machine:

1541. It is no longer a secret that the backroom boys of Bletchley used the new science of electronics to help them solve the puzzle of Enigma. I am not of the computer age nor do I attempt to understand them, but early in 1940 I was ushered with great solemnity into the shrine where stood a bronze-colored column surmounted by a larger circular bronze-colored face, like some Eastern Goddess who was destined to become the oracle of Bletchley, at least when she felt like it.

USO

The initials stand for United Service Organizations, founded in February 1941. To American servicemen and -women, it stood for recreation and entertainment. The service organizations involved were the YMCA, the YWCA, the National Catholic Community Service, the National Jewish Welfare Board, the Salvation Army, and the Travelers Aid Association. The USO came about when Army Chief of Staff George C. Marshall visited a training camp and discovered that soldiers on a day or weekend pass had nowhere to go to spend their time. Funded by voluntary contributions, the USO was provided with hundreds of buildings by the federal government to carry out USO activities. The official purposes of the USO:

1542. To aid in the war and defense program of the United States and its Allies by serving the religious, spiritual, welfare, and educational needs of the men and women in the armed forces and the war and defense industries of the United States and its Allies in the United States and throughout the world, and in general, to contribute to the maintenance of morale in American communities and elsewhere. (USO Constitution, cited in *Home Away from Home*, by Julia M. H. Carson.)

V FOR VICTORY

One of the most striking images of the war was that of Winston Churchill holding up his fingers to make the V (for victory) sign. It was a well-conceived and-executed propaganda campaign of the British government, launched on July 20, 1941. Churchill explained it this way:

1543. The V sign is the symbol of the unconquerable will of the occupied territories, and a portent of the fate awaiting the Nazi tyranny.

WAR HUMOR

As with every war in American history, humor has played many a role. It could raise morale, poke fun at the enemy, deal with hardship, defy authority, fight boredom, or allow the luxury of wishful thinking. Humor shows up in some war movies (q.v.), some war songs (q.v.), and some items in the war lexicon (q.v.). It also showed up in books, on the radio, in newspapers, and along the assembly line. Jokes were passed along in barracks, in bars, on board ship, and in foxholes. Considering the number of countries involved, the assortment of allies as well as enemies, the variety of frustrations, heroes, and villains, the numbers of jokes must have run in the scores of thousands.

Some samples:

1544. Heard in London: "Ever hear of the new utility knickers? One Yank and they're off." (From *The Wits of War*, edited by Edwin J. Swineford.)

1545. Italy under Mussolini [q.v.] had a good appetite, but poor teeth. (Ibid.)

1546. [Addressing Hitler:] "Chief, being your double, up to now, was no problem. But, here in the bunker, staying on while you escape to South America . . . that's something we hadn't agreed upon when I took the assignment." (Ibid.)

1547. [Sailor, at home, picks up a megaphone, rolls it up, and yells:] "Now hear this! Now hear this!" [Wife to children:] "Sometimes I wish Henry had served in the army instead of the navy." (Ibid.)

1548. [Tojo (q.v.) calls Hitler on the phone:] "Hello, Adolf? How do you declare war?" (Ibid.)

In addition to jokes, cartoons were extremely popular sources of war humor, both in service and back home. David Breger (q.v.), Bill Mauldin (q.v.), George Baker, and Milton Caniff were among the popular cartoonists.

Bill Mauldin's humor was grim, touching on GI gripes, fears, and frustrations. But sometimes it was just plain funny, based on army tradition. His work appeared in *Stars and Stripes*, but one cartoon he did for *Yank*:

1549. [Captionless cartoon:] A cavalry sergeant, with one hand over his eyes, aims his revolver at the engine of a jeep with a broken axle.

George Baker's *Sad Sack* in *Yank* was pure pantomime. Conversation never appeared in balloons over the characters' heads—but Baker always made his point abundantly clear. The Sad Sack was often the little guy who got the dirty end of the stick. He would wind up carrying the broom and dustpan behind the movie starlet on a horse; if he did a wonderful job cleaning the garbage pails, that became his duty. Sometimes, however, he would fool the reader until the last panel of the strip:

1550. [Captionless] First panel shows a voluptuous lady, with slit skirt, standing under a street lamp at night. The *Sad Sack* approaches her and whispers in her ear. She holds out her hand and he gives her some money. The two walk together to her apartment. The *Sad Sack* sits on her bed while she pulls off his pants. Last panel shows her ironing his trousers.

Milton Caniff, whose *Terry and the Pirates* and *Steve Canyon* were adventure favorites, did a strip during the war called *Male Call*. Appearing in post newspapers, it featured a shapely young lady whose name was Lace. Today *Male Call* would probably be looked upon as sexist, as her body was often the butt of the joke. (No pun intended.) Example:

1551. Panel shows Lace crouching over a pool table to make a shot as G.I.'s crouch around and ogle. She is wearing a low-cut dress—and no bra.

WARSAW UPRISINGS

There were two uprisings in Warsaw during the war. The first was the uprising of the Warsaw Ghetto in April 1943. In that uprising, Polish Jews fought their forced evacuation to death camps. The ghetto was obliterated by the Germans while life went on in Warsaw outside the ghetto walls.

Sixteen months later—in August 1944—Warsaw Poles rose up against the Nazi occupiers. The Soviets withheld its attack on Warsaw, refused to supply the Polish fighters from the air, and would not grant permission for American or British supply planes to land on Russian airfields following a proposed airlift. This second uprising was also crushed by the Germans.

In the midst of the 1944 uprising, a message was sent to Pope Pius XII.

1552. Most Holy Father, we Polish women in Warsaw are inspired with sentiments of profound patriotism and devotion for our country. For three weeks, while defending our fortress, we have lacked food and medicine. Warsaw is in ruins. The Germans are killing the wounded in hospitals. They are making women and children march in front of them in order to protect their tanks. There is no exaggeration in reports of children who are fighting and destroying tanks with bottles of petrol. We mothers see our sons dying for freedom and the Fatherland. Our husbands, our sons, and our brothers are not considered by the enemy to be combatants. Holy Father, no one is helping us. The Russian armies which have been for three weeks at the gates of Warsaw have not advanced a step. The aid coming to us from Great Britain is insufficient. The world is ignorant of our fight. God alone is with us. Holy Father, Vicar of Christ, if you can hear us, bless us Polish women who are fighting for the Church and for freedom. (Cited in *The Second World War: Triumph and Tragedy*, by Winston Churchill.)

WINDS MESSAGE

The Winds Message was a Japanese code indicating that war was about to break out between Japan and a potential adversary. The code was sent out to Japanese diplomatic officials on November 28, 1941. The message indicated that a "weather report" would be broadcast by radio as follows:

1553. EAST WIND RAIN to mean that relations with America are not according to expectations.

NORTH WIND CLOUDY to mean the same concerning Japanese-Russian relations.

WEST WIND CLEAR to mean the same concerning relations with England . . .

When you hear any or all these phrases repeated twice in the newscasts destroy your codes and confidential papers.

WOMEN IN UNIFORM

In May 1942, Congress authorized the formation of the Women's Army Auxiliary Corps (WAAC) to free soldiers for combat duty. The word "auxiliary" would later be dropped from the title and units of women added to the navy (WAVES), marines (Women Appointed for Voluntary Emergency Services Marines), and Coast Guard (SPARS). By the end of the war, well over 100,000 women would serve brilliantly in these four uniformed services. But the program was not without its bumpy starts.

In the beginning, there were misconceptions over what the women's role would be. Some individuals saw their role as pure morale building for men in service.

In *American Women and World War II*, Doris Weatherford wrote:

1554. "Keeping up morale" was traditionally associated in their minds [i.e., those of the public] with quite another role for women in cheering men. Indeed, one of the first difficulties the WAAC faced was overcoming public misperceptions that WAAC's would be used as "hostesses" and would entertain in "soldier shows." Both terms were commonly used in speculative news articles and lent credence to a widely held historical view of women's role in war being largely that of "camp followers."

Emphasis on models and showgirls in recruiting drives did nothing to discourage this grossly erroneous image, and the Army took far too long to fire the ad agency responsible. By early 1943 when WAAC's were arriving in North Africa, leadership acknowledged the harm being done by this false image; among the actions taken was to close down an Algiers show entitled, "Swing, Sister Wac, Swing." (From *American Women and World War II*, by Doris Weatherford.)

Appendix: Quotations by Category

THE WAR LEADERS

Winston Churchill
Adolf Hitler
Franklin D. Roosevelt
Joseph Stalin

MILITARY OFFICERS

Harold Alexander
Seizo Arisue
Henry H. Arnold
Claude Auchinleck
Patrick Bellinger
Werner von Blomberg
Guenther Blumentritt
Tadeusz Bor-Komorowski
Omar N. Bradley
Walther von Brauchitsch
Lewis H. Brereton
Mark W. Clark
Belton Cooper
Andrew B. Cunningham
W. Scott Cunningham
Charles de Gaulle
Karl Dittmar
Karl Doenitz
Ernest Dupuy
Dwight D. Eisenhower
John Eisenhower
Thomas F. Farrell
Erich Fellgieber
Maurice Gamelin
Hermann Goering
Leslie R. Groves
Heinz Guderian
Franz Halder
William F. Halsey, Jr.
Gotthard Heinrici
Adolf Heusinger
Courtney Hodges
Masaharu Homma
Hastings Ismay
Alfred Jodl
Wilhelm Keitel
Husband E. Kimmel
Edward P. King, Jr.
Ernest J. King
William D. Leahy

Raymond E. Lee
Douglas MacArthur
Hasso von Manteuffel
George C. Marshall
Lesley McNair
F. W. von Mellenthin
Walther Model
Bernard Montgomery
Chester W. Nimitz
Edmund North
George S. Patton, Jr.
Friedrich von Paulus
William N. Porter
Erich Raeder
General Rohricht
Erwin Rommel
Elliott Roosevelt
Gerd von Rundstedt
Frank A. Schofield
Gordon S. Seagrave
Walter Bedell Smith
Brehon B. Somervell
Harold R. Stark
Claus von Stauffenberg
Joseph W. Stilwell
Charles Tench
Matoi Ugaki
Jonathan Wainwright
Walter Warlimont
Paul M. Wenneker
Maxime Weygand
I. E. Yakir
Isoruku Yamamoto
Tomoyuki Yamashita
Harry E. Yarnell
Georgi K. Zhukov

GOVERNMENT OFFICIALS

Pietro Badoglio
Klaus Barbie
William Beaverbrook
Alexander Cadogan
Neville Chamberlain
Chiang Kai-shek
Jean Darlan
Elmer Davis
Francisco Franco
Hans Frank
Hans Fritzsche
Walther Funk
George VI
Joseph Goebbels
Haile Selassie
Paul Hennicke
Rudolf Hess
Reinhard Heydrich
Heinrich Himmler
Hirohito
Harry L. Hopkins
John Houseman
Robert H. Jackson
Nikita S. Khrushchev
Frank Knox
Pierre Laval
Louis L. Ludlow
Henry L. Morgenthau, Jr.
Frank Murphy
Benito Mussolini
Henri Philippe Petain
Nelson Poynter
Paul Reynaud
Robert R. Reynolds
Edward V. Rickenbacker
Samuel I. Rosenman

Hans Rumpf
Albert Speer
Henry L. Stimson
Harlan F. Stone
Hans-Georg von Studnitz
Hideki Tojo
Harry S Truman
Andrei Y. Vishinsky
Henry A. Wallace
Burton K. Wheeler
Andrei Zhdanov

DIPLOMATS

William C. Bullitt
Galeazzo Ciano
Joseph E. Davies
Joseph C. Grew
Cordell Hull
Paul R. Jolles
Joseph P. Kennedy
Breckinridge Long
Hubert Masarik
Yosuke Matsuoka
Douglas Miller
Vyacheslav M. Molotov
Robert D. Murphy
Kichisaburo Nomura
Semi Pramoj
Joachim von Ribbentrop
James W. Riddleberger
Friedrich von der Schulenburg
Consul-General Shepherd
Paul-Henri Spaak
Edward R. Stettinius, Jr.
Hans Thomsen
Shigenori Togo
Hugh R. Wilson

WARRIORS

Bill Bailey
Paul Boesch
Joseph Broder
William C. Brooks
John D. Bulkeley
Harold Dixon
James H. Doolittle
Alexander Drabik
Teddy Draper, Sr.
William Dyess
James M. Gavin
Jack Gerrie
Howard W. Gilmore
Hy Haas
Eunice C. Hatchitt
Roger Hilsman
Leon W. Johnson
Thomas Kinkaid
Robert Lewis
Rossi Lomanitz
William Manchester
Donald Francis Mason
Jim Mattera
Anthony McAuliffe
David McCampbell
Marcus McDilda
Noda Mitsuharu
Alfred Naujocks
Sakai Saburo
H. P. Samwell
Bob Slaughter
Eddie Slovik
C. A. F. Sprague
Irving Strobing
Paul W. Tibbets, Jr.
Rupert Trimmingham

Teruichi Ukita
Bud Warnecke
Shoichi Yokoi

CHAPLAINS

William Cummings
Howell M. Forgy
James H. O'Neill
Jacob P. Rudin

INTELLIGENCE OFFICIALS AND SPIES

Wilhelm Canaris
Eddie Chapman
William J. Donovan
Allen Dulles
Reinhard Gehlen
Tyler Kent
Alvin D. Kramer
Kanji Ogawa
Kim Philby
Richard Sorge
William Stephenson
Richard Weil, Jr.
F. W. Winterbotham

SCIENTISTS AND ENGINEERS

Ken Bainbridge
Wernher von Braun
Edward U. Condon
Albert Einstein
J. Robert Oppenheimer
Arthur Rudolph
Robert Serber
Edward Teller

JOURNALISTS AND CARTOONISTS

Jonah Barrington
Margaret Bourke-White
David Breger
Wright Bryan
Howard Cowan
John Daly
Walter Duranty
John Gunther
Marion Hargrove
William D. Hassett
John Hersey
Frank Hewlett
James Hilton
Godfrey Hodgson
Ralph Ingersoll
James Jones
Edward Kennedy
Henry Keyes
Arthur Krock
Chesly Manly
Bill Mauldin
Mack Morriss
Ian F. D. Morrow
Edward R. Murrow
Ernie Pyle
Andy Rooney
Robert Sherrod
Merriman Smith
Robert St. John
I. F. Stone
Walter Winchell

HISTORIANS AND BIOGRAPHERS

Thomas B. Allen
Stephen E. Ambrose

Maurice Baumont
Charles A. Beard
Antony Beevor
Thomas B. Buell
Iris Chang
Terry Charman
Wayne S. Cole
William Craig
Edward Crankshaw
Peter Fleming
Martin Gilbert
Doris Kearns Goodwin
Peter Grose
Nigel Hamilton
George Hicks
Annette Kahn
David Kahn
William L. Langer
Callum MacDonald
Robert H. McNeal
Richard Overy
Edvard Radzinsky
Terence Robertson
Hans Rothfels
Cornelius Ryan
Robert E. Sherwood
William L. Shirer
William Stevenson
A. J. P. Taylor
Marcel Thiry
John Toland
H. R. Trevor-Roper
Barbara W. Tuchman
Alexander Werth

INFLUENTIAL PERSONALITIES

Madame Chiang Kai-shek
John Foster Dulles
Queen Elizabeth
William Joyce
Charles A. Lindbergh, Jr.
Joe Louis
Margaret Mead
Ezra Pound
Eleanor Roosevelt
Alexander P. de Seversky
Norman Thomas
Wendell L. Willkie
Robert E. Wood

CIVILIANS

John Baker
Eva Braun
Emma Calp
Mrs. B. D. Cooksey
Hirosawa Ei
Anne Frank
Arvid Fredborg
Magda Goebbels
Max von der Grun
Maria Rosa Henson
Jeanne Kahn
Ursula von Kardorff
Madam X
Hadassah Rosensaft
Eduard Schulte
Kay Summersby
Dr. Tsuno
Marie Vassiltchikov

INSTITUTIONAL QUOTATIONS

Atlantic Charter
British War Cabinet
Cairo Conference
Casablanca Conference
Declaration of Union

German Armed Forces

German Navy

International Military Tribunal

Japanese Government

Moscow Declaration on Atrocities

Munich Agreement

Nazi-Soviet Pact

Office of Strategic Services/Special Operations Executive

Potsdam Conference

Ration Board

Roberts Commission Report on Pearl Harbor

Teheran Conference

Time Magazine

Tripartite Pact

United Nations Declaration

United States Government

United States Navy

Volkisher Beobachter

Yalta Conference

ANONYMOUS QUOTATIONS

WAR MOVIES

WAR SONGS

WAR LEXICON

MISCELLANEOUS QUOTATIONS

America First Committee

Apocrypha

Bataan Death March

Bulge, Battle of the

Clark Mission

Coal Strike

Committee to Defend America by Aiding the Allies

D-Day

Dresden Firebombing

Dunkirk Evacuation

Editorial Cartoons

El Alamein

Fifth Column

Flying Tigers

Greer Encounter

Hess Flight to Scotland

Holocaust

Hossbach Memorandum

Indianapolis Disaster

Japanese Relocation

Kamikaze

Katyn Forest Massacre

Lend-Lease

MacArthur Candidacy

Magic

Market-Garden

Mein Kampf

Nazi Saboteurs

Open City

Phony War

Ploesti Raid

Quisling

Rosenberg Case

Sea Lion

Slave Labor

Stalingrad, Battle of

Synthetic Rubber Scandal

Ultra

USO

V for Victory

War Humor

Warsaw Uprisings

Winds Message

Women in Uniform

Bibliography

Allen, Thomas B., and Norman Polmar. *Code-Name Downfall: The Secret Plan to Invade Japan—and Why Truman Dropped the Bomb*. New York: Simon & Schuster, 1995.

Ambrose, Stephen E. *Citizen Soldiers*. New York: Simon & Schuster, 1997.

Andreas-Friedrich, Ruth. *Berlin Underground*. New York: Henry Holt, 1947.

Astor, Gerald. *A Blood-Dimmed Tide: The Battle of the Bulge by the Men Who Fought It*. New York: Donald I. Fine, Inc., 1992.

Astor, Gerald. *June 6, 1944: The Voices of D-Day*. New York: St. Martin's Press, 1994.

Baldwin, Hanson. *Battles Lost and Won: Great Campaigns of World War II*. New York: Konecky & Konecky, 1966.

Baumont, Maurice. *The Origins of the Second World War*. Translated by Simone de Couvreur Ferguson. New Haven, CT: Yale University Press, 1978.

Beard, Charles A. *President Roosevelt and the Coming of the War 1941: A Study in Appearances and Realities*. New Haven, CT: Yale University Press, 1948.

Beevor, Antony. *Crete: The Battle and the Resistance*. Boulder, CO: Westview Press, 1994.

Benet, William Rose, orig. ed. *Benet's Reader's Encyclopedia*. 3rd ed. New York: Harper & Row, 1987. (Edition was revised after Benet's death.)

The Best from Yank: The Army Weekly. Selected by the editors of *Yank*. New York: E. P. Dutton & Co., Inc., 1945.

The Bluejackets' Manual. 12th ed. Annapolis, MD: United States Naval Institute, 1944.

Blum, John Morton. *From the Morgenthau Diaries: Years of Urgency, 1938–1941*. Boston: Houghton Mifflin, 1965.

Blum, John Morton. *Roosevelt and Morgenthau: A Revision and Condensation of From the Morgenthau Diaries*. Boston: Houghton Mifflin, 1970.

Boca, Angelo Del. *The Ethiopian War, 1935–1941*. Translated from the Italian by P. D. Cummins. Chicago: University of Chicago Press, 1969.

Boelcke, Willi A., ed. *The Secret Conferences of Dr. Goebbels: The Nazi Propaganda War 1939–43*. Translated from the German by Ewald Osers. New York: E. P. Dutton, 1970.

Boesch, Paul. *Road to Huertgen: Forest in Hell*. Houston, TX: Gulf Publishing Co., 1962.

Bower, Tom. *Klaus Barbie: The Butcher of Lyons*. New York: Pantheon Books, 1984.

Bradley, Omar N. *A Soldier's Story*. New York: Henry Holt & Co., 1951.

Brereton, Lewis H. *The Brereton Diaries*. New York: William Morrow & Co., 1946.

Brissaud, Andre. *Canaris: The Biography of Admiral Canaris, Chief of German Military Intelligence in the Second World War*. Translated and edited by Ian Colvin. New York: Grosset & Dunlap, 1974.

Buell, Thomas B. *Master of Sea Power: A Biography of Fleet Admiral Ernest J. King*. Boston: Little, Brown & Co., 1980.

Butcher, Harry C. *My Three Years with Eisenhower*. New York: Simon & Schuster, 1946.

Carson, Julia M. H. *Home Away from Home: The Story of the USO*. New York: Harper & Brothers, 1946.

Casten, Ron, ed. *The Blockbuster Guide to Movies and Videos*. New York: Dell Publishing, 1995.

Chaney, Otto Preston, Jr. *Zhukov*. Norman: University of Oklahoma Press, 1971.

Chang, Iris. *The Rape of Nanking: The Forgotten Holocaust of World War II*. New York: Basic Books, 1997.

Charman, Terry. *The German Home Front, 1939–45*. New York: Philosophical Library, 1989.

Churchill, Winston S. *While England Slept: A Survey of World Affairs 1932–1938*. New York: Putnam, 1938.

Churchill, Winston S. *The Second World War: The Gathering Storm*. Boston: Houghton Mifflin, 1948.

Churchill, Winston S. *The Second World War: Their Finest Hour*. Boston: Houghton Mifflin, 1949.

Churchill, Winston S. *The Second World War: The Grand Alliance*. Boston: Houghton Mifflin, 1950.

Churchill, Winston S. *The Second World War: Triumph and Tragedy*. Boston: Houghton Mifflin, 1953.

Churchill, Winston S. *Great Destiny*. New York: Putnam, 1962.

Ciano, Count Galeazzo. *Ciano's Hidden Diary, 1937–1938*. Garden City, NY: Doubleday, 1945.

Ciano, Edda Mussolini, as told to Albert T. Zarca. *My Truth*. Translated from the French by Eileen Finletter. New York: William Morrow & Co., 1976.

Clark, Mark. *Calculated Risk*. London: George G. Harrap & Co., Ltd., 1951.

Cole, Hugh M. *The Lorraine Campaign: The European Theater of Operations Series*. Washington, D.C.: Department of the Army, 1950.

Cole, J. A. *Lord Haw-Haw: William Joyce, the Full Story*. New York: Farrar, Straus & Giroux, 1964.

Cole, Wayne S. *Roosevelt & the Isolationists 1932–45*. Lincoln: University of Nebraska Press, 1983.

Collins, Larry, and Dominique Lapierre. *Is Paris Burning?* New York: Simon & Schuster, 1965.

Cook, Haruko Taya, and Theodore F. Cook, eds. *Japan at War: An Oral History*. New York: New Press, 1992.

Costello, John. *Days of Infamy*. New York: Pocket Books, 1994.

Craig, William. *Enemy at the Gates: The Battle for Stalingrad*. New York: Reader's Digest Press/E. P. Dutton, 1973.

Crankshaw, Edward. *Khrushchev: A Career*. New York: Viking Press, 1966.

Cunningham, W. Scott, with Lydel Sims. *Wake Island Command.* Boston: Little, Brown, 1961.

de Gaulle, Charles. *Memoires de Guerre.* 3 vols. Paris, 1954.

Dilks, David, ed. *The Diaries of Sir Alexander Cadogan, O.M., 1938–1945.* New York: Putnam, 1972.

Divine, A. D. *Dunkirk.* A. Watkins, Inc., 1948.

Documents on German Foreign Policy. Series D. Washington, D.C.: U.S. Government Printing Office, 1949.

Doherty, Thomas. *Projections of War: Hollywood, American Culture, and World War II.* New York: Columbia University Press, 1993.

Douglas, Roy. *The World War 1939–1945: The Cartoonists' Vision.* London: Routledge, 1990.

Doyle, Jerry. *According to Doyle.* With text by Charles Fisher. New York: G. P. Putnam's Sons, 1943.

Dulles, Allen. *The Secret Surrender.* New York: Harper & Row, 1966.

Dulles, Allen, and Hamilton Fish Armstrong. *Can America Stay Neutral?* New York: Harper & Brothers, 1939.

Dyess, William. *The Dyess Story.* New York: G. P. Putnam's Sons, 1944.

Eisenhower, Dwight D. *Crusade in Europe.* Garden City, NY: Doubleday & Co., 1948.

Farago, Ladislas. *The Broken Seal: The Story of "Operation Magic" and the Pearl Harbor Disaster.* New York: Random House, 1967.

Feingold, Henry L. *The Politics of Rescue: The Roosevelt Administration and the Holocaust, 1938–1945.* New Brunswick, NJ: Rutgers University Press, 1970.

Field, James A., Jr. "Admiral Yamamoto." In *U.S. Naval Institute Proceedings.* Annapolis, MD: Naval Institute Press, October 1949.

Findling, John E. *Dictionary of American Diplomatic History.* Westport, CT: Greenwood Press, 1980.

Fleming, Peter. *Operation Sea Lion: The Projected Invasion of England in 1940—An Account of the German Preparations and the British Countermeasures.* New York: Simon & Schuster, 1957.

Foreign Relations of the United States, 1940. Vol. I. Washington, D.C.: U.S. Government Printing Office.

Forgy, Howell M. *". . . And Pass the Ammunition."* New York: Appleton-Century, 1944.

Forsberg, Franklin S., ed. *Yank—The GI Story of the War.* New York: Duell, Sloan & Pearce, 1947.

Frank, Anne. *The Diary of a Young Girl.* Garden City, NY: Doubleday & Co., 1952.

Fredborg, Arvid. *Behind the Steel Wall.* London: Harrap, 1944.

Freiden, Seymour, and William Richardson, eds. *The Fatal Decisions.* New York: William Sloane Associates, 1956.

Galante, Pierre, with Eugene Silianoff. *Operation Valkyrie: The German Generals' Plot against Hitler.* Translated from the French by Mark Howson and Cary Ryan. New York: Harper & Row, 1981.

Gamelin, Maurice. *Servir.* 3 vols. Paris, 1947.

Gavin, James M. *On to Berlin: Battles of an Airborne Commander, 1943–1946.* New York: Viking Press, 1978.

Geddes, Donald Porter, ed. *Franklin Delano Roosevelt: A Memorial.* New York: Pocket Books, 1945.

Gehlen, Reinhard. *The Service: The Memoirs of General Reinhard Gehlen*. Translated by David Irving. New York: World Publishing, 1972.

Gilbert, Martin. *The Second World War: A Complete History*. New York: Henry Holt & Co., 1989.

Gilbert, Martin. *The Day the War Ended: May 8, 1945—Victory in Europe*. New York: Henry Holt & Co., 1995.

Goerlitz, W., and D. Irving, eds. *The Memoirs of Field Marshal Keitel*. 1961.

Goodwin, Doris Kearns. *No Ordinary Time, Franklin and Eleanor Roosevelt: The Home Front in World War II*. New York: Simon & Schuster, 1994.

Grew, Joseph C. *Ten Years in Japan*. Boston: Houghton Mifflin, 1944.

Grew, Joseph C. *Turbulent Era*. 2 vols. Boston: Houghton, Mifflin, 1952.

Grose, Peter. *Gentleman Spy: The Life of Allen Dulles*. Boston: Houghton Mifflin, 1994.

Groves, Leslie R. *Now It Can Be Told: The Story of the Manhattan Project*. New York: Harper & Row, 1962.

Grun, Max von der. *Howl Like the Wolves: Growing Up in Nazi Germany*. New York: William Morrow, 1980.

Guderian, Heinz. *Panzer Leader*. Translated by Constantine Fitzgibbon. New York: E. P. Dutton, 1952.

Gunther, John. *Inside Europe*. New York: Harper & Brothers, 1940.

Halsey, William F., Jr., and J. Bryan, III. *Admiral Halsey's Story*. New York: Whittlesey/McGraw-Hill, 1947.

Hamilton, Nigel. *Master of the Battlefield: Monty's War Years: 1942–1944*. New York: McGraw-Hill Book Co., 1983.

Hargrove, Marion. *See Here, Private Hargrove*. New York: Henry Holt, 1942.

Hart, B. H. Liddell. *The German Generals Talk*. New York: William Morrow & Co., 1948.

Hassett, William D. *Off the Record with F.D.R.: 1942–1945*. New Brunswick, NJ: Rutgers University Press, 1958. Reprint, Westport, CT: Greenwood Press.

Henson, Maria Rosa. *Comfort Woman: Slave of Destiny*. Philippines: Philippine Center for Investigative Journalism, 1996.

Hering, Pierre. *La Vie Exemplaire de Philippe Petain*.

Hersey, John. *Men on Bataan*. New York: Knopf, 1942.

Hersey, John. *Into the Valley: A Skirmish of the Marines*. New York: Knopf, 1943. Reprint, with a new introduction by Hersey. New York: Schocken Books, 1989.

Hersey, John. *Hiroshima: A New Edition with a Final Chapter Written 40 Years after the Explosion*. New York: Vintage Books, 1989.

Hicks, George. *The Comfort Women: Japan's Brutal Regime of Enforced Prostitution in the Second World War*. New York: W. W. Norton, 1994.

Hilsman, Roger. *American Guerrilla: My War behind Japanese Lines*. Washington, D.C.: Brassey's (U.S.), Inc., 1990.

Hilton, James. *The Story of Dr. Wassell*. Boston: Little, Brown & Co., 1943.

Hodgson, Godfrey. *The Colonel: The Life and Ways of Henry Stimson*. New York: Alfred A. Knopf, 1990.

Horn, Maurice. *The World Encyclopedia of Comics*. New York: Chelsea House, 1976.

Huie, William Bradford. *The Execution of Private Slovik*. New York: Delacorte Press, 1970.

Hurd, Charles. *A Treasury of Great American Speeches*. New York: Hawthorn Books, 1959.

Ingersoll, Ralph. *The Battle Is the Pay-Off*. New York: Harcourt, Brace & Co., 1943.

Ingersoll, Ralph. *Top Secret*. New York: Harcourt, Brace & Co., 1946.

Inoguchi, Rikihei, and Tadashi Nakajima. *The Divine Wind*. Annapolis, MD: U.S. Naval Institute, 1958.

Ismay, Hastings. *The Memoirs of General Lord Ismay*. New York: Viking Press, 1960.

Israel, Fred L., ed. *The War Diary of Breckinridge Long: Selections from the Years 1939–1944*. Lincoln: University of Nebraska Press, 1966.

Jones, James. *WW II: A Chronicle of Soldiering*. New York: Ballantine Books, 1976.

Kahn, Annette. *Why My Father Died: A Daughter Confronts Her Family's Past at the Trial of Klaus Barbie*. Translated by Anna Cancogni. New York: Summit Books, 1991.

Kahn, David. *Hitler's Spies: German Military Intelligence during World War II*. New York: Macmillan, 1978.

Kardorff, Ursula von. *Diary of a Nightmare: Berlin 1942–1945*. Translated by Ewan Butler. New York: John Day Co., 1966.

Kawano, Kenji. *Warriors: Navajo Code Talkers*. Flagstaff, AZ: Northland, 1990.

Kendrick, Alexander. *Prime Time: The Life of Edward R. Murrow*. Boston: Little, Brown & Co., 1969.

Kersaudy, François. *Churchill and de Gaulle*. New York: Atheneum, 1982.

Khrushchev, Nikita S. *Khrushchev Remembers*. Translated and edited by Strobe Talbott. Boston: Little, Brown & Co., 1970.

Kimball, Warren F., ed. *Churchill & Roosevelt: The Complete Correspondence, Volume III, February 1944–April 1945*. Princeton, NJ: Princeton University Press, 1984.

Kimmel, Husband E. *Admiral Kimmel's Story*. Chicago: Henry Regnery Co., 1955.

Landstrom, Russell, ed. *The Associated Press News Annual, 1945*. New York: Rinehart & Co., 1946.

Langer, Howard J. "The Impact of Personality on History: An Interview with William L. Shirer." In *Social Education*. Washington, D.C.: National Council for the Social Studies, October 1983.

Langer, Howard J. *The History of the Holocaust: A Chronology of Quotations*. Northvale, NJ: Jason Aronson, Inc., 1997.

Langer, William L. *Our Vichy Gamble*. New York: Alfred A. Knopf, 1947.

Lash, Joseph P. *Love, Eleanor: Eleanor Roosevelt and Her Friends*. Garden City, NY: Doubleday & Co., 1984.

Litoff, Judy Barrett, and David C. Smith, eds. *Since You Went Away: World War II Letters from American Women on the Home Front*. New York: Oxford University Press, 1991.

MacArthur, Douglas. *Reminiscences*. New York: McGraw-Hill, 1964.

MacDonald, Callum. *The Killing of SS Obergruppenfuehrer Reinhard Heydrich*. New York: Free Press, a division of Macmillan, 1989.

Macdonald, Dwight. *Memoirs of a Revolutionist: Essays in Political Criticism*. New York: Farrar, Straus and Cudahy, 1957.

Manchester, William. *American Caesar: Douglas MacArthur, 1880–1964*. Boston: Little, Brown & Co., 1978.

Mauldin, Bill. *Up Front*. New York: Henry Holt & Co., 1945.

McNeal, Robert H. *Stalin: Man and Ruler*. New York: New York University Press, 1988.

Mead, Margaret. *And Keep Your Powder Dry: An Anthropologist Looks at America*. New York: William Morrow and Co., 1943.

Medal of Honor Recipients 1863–1978. Prepared by the Committee on Veterans Affairs, U.S. Senate. Washington, D.C.: U.S. Government Printing Office, 1979.

Mellenthin, F. W. von. *Panzer Battles: A Study of the Employment of Armor in the Second*

World War. Translated by H. Betzler. Norman: University of Oklahoma Press, 1956.

Michelmore, Peter. *The Swift Years: The Robert Oppenheimer Story*. New York: Dodd, Mead & Co., 1969.

Morison, Samuel Eliot. *Victory in the Pacific*. Boston: Little, Brown, 1960.

Morton, Louis. *The Fall of the Philippines*. Office of the Chief of Military History, Department of the Army. Washington, D.C.: Superintendent of Documents, U.S. Government Printing Office, 1953.

Murphy, Robert. *Diplomat among Warriors*. Garden City, NY: Doubleday & Co., Inc., 1964.

Nichols, David, ed. *Ernie's War: The Best of Ernie Pyle's World War II Dispatches*. New York: Random House, 1986.

Norman, Charles. *The Case of Ezra Pound*. New York: Funk & Wagnalls, 1968.

Office of United States Chief of Counsel for Prosecution of Axis Criminality. *Nazi Conspiracy and Aggression*. Washington, D.C.: U.S. Government Printing Office, 1946.

Overy, Richard. *Why the Allies Won*. New York: W. W. Norton & Co., 1995.

Patton, George S. *War as I Knew It*. Boston: Houghton Mifflin, 1947.

Peace and War: United States Foreign Policy, 1931–1941. Washington, D.C.: U.S. Government Printing Office, 1943.

Philby, Kim. *My Silent War*. New York: Grove Press, 1968.

Philipson, Ilene. *Ethel Rosenberg: Beyond the Myths*. New York: Franklin Watts, 1988.

Pogue, Forrest C. *George C. Marshall: Ordeal and Hope, 1939–1942*. New York: Viking, 1966.

Pogue, Forrest C. *George C. Marshall: Organizer of Victory, 1943–1945*. New York: Viking, 1973.

Preston, Paul. *Franco: A Biography*. New York: Basic Books, 1994.

Pruessen, Ronald W. *John Foster Dulles: The Road to Power*. New York: Macmillan Publishing Co., Inc., 1982.

Pyle, Ernie. *Here Is Your War*. New York: Henry Holt, 1943.

Pyle, Ernie. *Brave Men*. New York: Henry Holt, 1944.

Rachlis, Eugene. *They Came to Kill: The Story of Eight Nazi Saboteurs in America*. New York: Random House, 1961.

Radzinsky, Edvard. *Stalin*. Translated by H. T. Willetts. New York: Doubleday, 1996.

Reid, Warren R., ed. *Public Papers of the Presidents of the United States: Harry S Truman, 1945*. Washington, D.C.: U.S. Government Printing Office, 1961.

Rickenbacker, Edward V. *Seven Came Through: Rickenbacker's Full Story*. Garden City, NY: Doubleday, Doran & Co., 1943.

Robertson, Terence. *Dieppe: The Shame and the Glory*. Boston: Atlantic Monthly Press/Little, Brown & Company, 1962.

Romanus, Charles, and Sunderland, Riley. *Stilwell's Mission to China*. Washington, D.C.: Department of the Army, Historical Division, 1953.

Romulo, Carlos P. *I Saw the Fall of the Philippines*. Garden City, NY: Doubleday, Doran, and Co., 1940.

Rooney, Andy. *My War*. New York: Random House, 1995.

Roosevelt, Elliott. *As He Saw It*. New York: Duell, Sloan and Pearce, 1946.

Rosenman, Samuel I. *Working with Roosevelt*. New York: Harper, 1952.

Rothfels, Hans. *The German Opposition to Hitler*. Translated by Lawrence Wilson. Rev. ed. Chicago: Henry Regnery Company, 1962.

Rumpf, Hans. *The Bombing of Germany*. Translated by Edward Fitzgerald. New York: Holt, Rinehart & Winston, 1962.

Ryan, Cornelius. *The Longest Day: June 6, 1944*. New York: Simon & Schuster, 1959.

Ryan, Cornelius. *The Last Battle*. New York: Simon & Schuster, 1966.

Ryan, Cornelius. *A Bridge Too Far*. New York: Simon & Schuster, 1974.

Samwell, H. P. *An Infantry Officer with the Eighth Army*. London: Blackwood & Sons, 1945.

Schapsmeier, Edward L., and Frederick H. Schapsmeier. *Political Parties and Civic Action Groups*. Westport, CT: Greenwood Press, 1981.

Schmidt, Paul. *Hitler's Interpreter*. New York: Macmillan, 1951.

Schneider, Franz, and Charles Gullans, eds. and trans. *Last Letters from Stalingrad*. New York: William Morrow, 1962.

Seagrave, Gordon S. *Burma Surgeon*. New York: Norton & Norton, 1943.

Sereny, Gitta. *Albert Speer: His Battle with Truth*. New York: Alfred A. Knopf, 1995.

Seversky, Alexander P. de. *Victory through Air Power*. New York: Simon & Schuster, 1942.

Sherrod, Robert. *Tarawa*. New York: Duell, Sloan and Pearce, 1944.

Sherwood, Robert E. *Roosevelt and Hopkins*. New York: Harper & Brothers, 1948.

Shirer, William L. *Berlin Diary*. New York: Alfred A. Knopf, 1941.

Shirer, William L. *The Rise and Fall of the Third Reich*. New York: Simon & Schuster, 1960.

Shirer, William L. *The Collapse of the Third Republic: An Inquiry into the Fall of France in 1940*. New York: Simon & Schuster, 1969.

Snyder, Louis L. *Historical Guide to World War II*. Westport, CT: Greenwood Press, 1982.

Speer, Albert. *Infiltration*. Translated by Joachim Neugroschel. New York: Macmillan, 1981.

Stevenson, William. *A Man Called Intrepid: The Secret War*. New York: Harcourt Brace Jovanovich, 1976.

Stimson, Henry L., and McGeorge Bundy. *On Active Service in Peace and War*. New York: Harper & Brothers, 1948.

St. John, Robert. *From the Land of Silent People*. Garden City, NY: Doubleday, Doran, 1942.

Stone, I. F. *The War Years 1939–1945*. Boston: Little, Brown & Co., 1988.

Studnitz, Hans-Georg von. *While Berlin Burns*. London: Weidenfeld & Nicholson, 1963.

Stuhlinger, Ernst, and Frederick Ordway III. *Wernher von Braun: Crusader for Space*. Malabar, FL: Krieger Publishing Co., 1994.

Summersby, Kay. *Eisenhower Was My Boss*. Edited by Michael Kearns. New York: Prentice-Hall, 1948.

Swineford, Edwin J. *The Wits of War: Unofficial GI Humor—History of World War II*. Fresno, CA: Kilroy Was There Press, 1989.

Taylor, A. J. P. *The Origins of the Second World War*. New York: Fawcett, 1961.

Taylor, Lawrence. *A Trial of Generals: Homma, Yamashita, MacArthur*. South Bend, IN: Icarus Press, 1981.

Terkel, Studs. *The Good War*. New York: Pantheon Books, 1984.

Thiry, Marcel. *La Belgique pendant la guerre*.

Toland, John. *The Last 100 Days*. New York: Random House, 1966.

Toland, John. *The Rising Sun*. New York: Random House, 1970.

Trevor-Roper, H. R. *The Last Days of Hitler*. New York: Macmillan, 1947.

Trevor-Roper, H. R. *Final Entries 1945: The Diaries of Joseph Goebbels*. Translated by Richard Barry. New York: G. P. Putnam's Sons, 1978.

Trumbull, Robert. *The Raft*. New York: Henry Holt & Co., Inc., 1942.

Tuchman, Barbara W. *Stilwell and the American Experience in China: 1911–45*. New York: Macmillan, 1970.

Vassiltchikov, Marie. *Berlin Diaries, 1940–1945*. New York: Alfred A. Knopf, 1987.

Walter, Claire, ed. *Winners: The Blue Ribbon Encyclopedia of Awards*. New York: Facts on File, Inc., 1978.

Warlimont, Walter. *Inside Hitler's Headquarters, 1939–45*. Translated from the German by R. H. Barry. Novato, CA: Presidio Press, 1964.

Watts, Franklin, ed. *Voices of History 1943*. New York: Gramercy Publishing Co., 1944.

Weatherford, Doris. *American Women and World War II*. New York: Facts on File, 1990.

Weiner, Ed. *Let's Go to Press: A Biography of Walter Winchell*. New York: G. P. Putnam's Sons, 1955.

Werth, Alexander. *Russia at War: 1941–1945*. New York: E. P. Dutton & Co., 1964.

Weygand, Maxime. *Rappele au Service*. Paris, 1950.

White, W. L. *They Were Expendable*. New York: Harcourt, Brace & World, 1942.

Willkie, Wendell L. *One World*. New York: Simon & Schuster, 1943.

Wilson, Hugh, ed. *The Ciano Diaries: 1939–1943*. New York: Doubleday, 1946.

Winchell, Walter. *Winchell Exclusive: Things That Happened to Me—and Me to Them*. Englewood Cliffs, NJ: Prentice-Hall, Inc., 1975.

Winterbotham, F. W. *The Ultra Secret*. New York: Harper & Row, 1974.

Yamazaki, James N., with Louis B. Fleming. *Children of the Atomic Bomb: An American Physician's Memoir of Nagasaki, Hiroshima, and the Marshall Islands*. Durham, NC: Duke University Press, 1995.

Yank: The Story of World War II Written by the Soldiers. New York: Greenwich House, a division of Arlington House, 1984.

Young, Desmond. *Rommel: The Desert Fox*. New York: Harper, 1950. Reprint, 1987. New York: William Morrow Quill.

Young, Peter, ed. *The World Almanac Book of World War II*. New York: World Almanac Publications, 1981.

Name Index

All numbers refer to quotation numbers and not pages. Numbers *in italics* refer to a specific entry for the individual. Numbers in roman type may indicate that the individual is mentioned in the quote, or in the introductory material that precedes the quote, or in explanatory material that follows it.

Subject Index

All numbers refer to quotation numbers and not pages. Numbers *in italics* refer to a specific entry for the subject matter. Numbers in roman type may indicate that the subject is dealt with in that quotation, or in the introductory material that precedes it, or in the explanatory material that follows it.

About the Author

HOWARD J. LANGER is an author and freelance writer. Before becoming a full-time writer, he worked as a newspaper reporter, magazine editor, textbook editor, marketing director, and director of publications. His most recent books are *American Indian Quotations* (Greenwood, 1996) and *The History of the Holocaust: A Chronology of Quotations* (1997).